Touring the Middle Tennessee Backroads

ALSO BY ROBERT BRANDT

Tennessee Hiking Guide (University of Tennessee Press)

OTHER TITLES IN JOHN F. BLAIR'S *TOURING THE BACKROADS* SERIES

Touring the Western North Carolina Backroads by Carolyn Sakowski
Touring the East Tennessee Backroads by Carolyn Sakowski
Touring the Coastal South Carolina Backroads by Nancy Rhyne
Touring the Coastal Georgia Backroads by Nancy Rhyne
Touring the Backroads of North Carolina's Upper Coast by Daniel W. Barefoot
Touring the Backroads of North Carolina's Lower Coast by Daniel W. Barefoot

Touring the Middle Tennessee Backroads

Robert Brandt

John F. Blair
Publisher
Winston-Salem,
North Carolina

BOOK DESIGN BY DEBRA LONG HAMPTON
COMPOSITION AND MAPS BY LIZA LANGRALL
PRINTED AND BOUND BY R. R. DONNELLEY & SONS

*The paper in this book meets the guidelines
for permanence and durability of the
Committee on Production Guidelines for Book Longevity
of the Council on Library Resources.*

Photographs on front cover, clockwise from top left—
Savage Gulf State Natural Area, from The Caney Fork Tour
Burgess Falls, from The Caney Fork Tour (Courtesy of Tennessee Tourist Development)
Carnton, from The Franklin Tour (Courtesy of Tennessee Tourist Development)
Falls Mill, from The Elk River Tour
Fort Donelson National Battlefield, from The Lower Cumberland Tour
Bethlehem United Methodist Church, from The Lower Cumberland Tour

Library of Congress Cataloging-in-Publication Data
Brandt, Robert S., 1941–
Touring the middle Tennessee backroads / Robert Brandt.
    p.   cm. — (Touring the backroads series)
Includes bibliographical references (p.   ) and index.
        ISBN 0-89587-129-7 (alk. paper)
1. Tennessee, Middle—Tours. 2. Automobile travel—Tennessee, Middle—
    Guidebooks. I. Title. II. Series.
            F442.2.B73 1995
    917.68'50453—dc20   95–15101

To my father, Sandy Brandt,
from whom I learned that there is
probably something interesting over the next hill

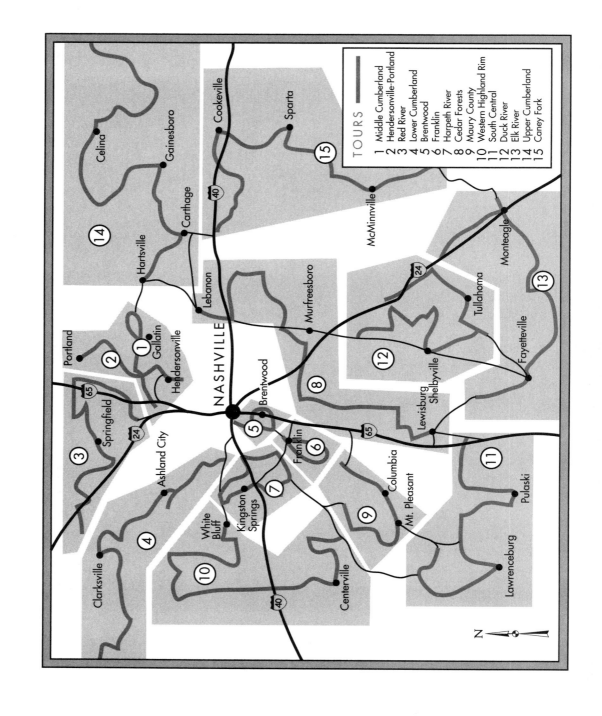

Table of Contents

Preface

Converts are the most fervent zealots. I am a convert to Middle Tennessee. And I confess to being a zealot. I love the place.

I first lived here during college when I had a summer job on Old Hickory Lake between the quintessential Middle Tennessee towns of Gallatin and Lebanon. After three more summers on the lake and three years at law school in Nashville, Middle Tennessee felt more like home than my native East Tennessee. I have lived here ever since.

I love to explore, and I enjoy learning about places and people. I like to write, too. So when I first saw Carolyn Sakowski's *Touring the East Tennessee Backroads*, I thought I could write a book like that about Middle Tennessee.

Except for the East Coast, I cannot think of any place that has more of America's history woven through its story. The expanding frontier, the age of Jackson, the Civil War, the Great Depression, the New Deal, two world wars, the struggle for civil rights—Middle Tennessee played key roles in all of them.

The Middle Tennessee landscape offers much to write about, too. The scenery may not inspire awe, but it is beautiful. It is intimate. It can be taken in and loved. And it is much more diverse than many people realize, ranging from the mountains of the Cumberland Plateau to the swampy bottoms along the Tennessee River. In between are dense forests, rolling bluegrass pastures, and some of America's most lovely rivers.

When I began this project, two questions had to be addressed. What boundaries define Middle Tennessee? And what is a backroad?

The boundaries on the north, south, and west are easy—Kentucky, Alabama, and the Tennessee River. But the eastern boundary is not so easy, for Tennesseans who care about geography argue about where on the Cumberland Plateau East Tennessee ends and Middle Tennessee begins. For this book, I have left out the Cumberland Plateau entirely, except for a few places on the western escarpment. The plateau is covered by other excellent books, including *Touring the East Tennessee Backroads.*

Some of the tours in this book follow heavily traveled highways that cannot honestly be called backroads. They began as buffalo paths, then were used by Indians, explorers, and pioneers, then evolved into the main roads. Much of the story of Middle Tennessee unfolds along these highways. They cannot be bypassed just because they are busy.

Urban sprawl has consumed land that was until quite recently rural countryside. Of the 1.6 million people who live in the thirty-five counties included in this book, over two-thirds of them live in the ten counties in and around Nashville. Some of Middle Tennessee's most important sites are in congested areas near Nashville. They cannot be bypassed either.

Nashville is not included in this book to any great extent. Neither are Clarksville and Murfreesboro. They, too, are now cities. But the three of them possess some of Middle Tennessee's most valued treasures, so do not overlook them.

Most books about Tennessee places start in the east and work west. I have not done that. Instead, I have roughly followed the sequence of the settlement of Middle Tennessee. It started at the site of today's Nashville and spread out from there, and that is how the story of this region unfolds. The first four tours cover areas generally north of Nashville settled between 1779 and the end of the Indian wars about 1795. The next five tours describe areas settled between Tennessee's statehood in 1796 and about 1804. The remaining tours cover parts of the midstate settled after an 1805 Indian treaty made it legal. Of course, it isn't quite that neat, but that's the general idea.

I do not mean to slight Native Americans in this book. It's just that none of them lived in Middle Tennessee during historic times. Information about prehistoric cultures that flourished in the region is included, but the story of Indian tribes during historic times is not part of Middle Tennessee's legacy.

The scenery along the way played an important role in planning the tours. A tour may follow a certain route just because it is a pretty drive. I have tried to avoid the cluttered commercial areas that seem to line at least one main road leading into every town in America. They are all the same. You could be anywhere.

In obtaining the information for the book, I relied upon secondary sources almost exclusively. I checked my information against other sources when I could, but that was not always possible. Some of the stories included here may be exaggerations. Some may even be made up. But the basic historical facts are true.

It was not possible to include every interesting and beautiful area of Middle Tennessee, nor was it possible to include every interesting place along the routes. Curious people will enjoy exploring areas and sites not on the tours.

Be careful as you travel. Middle Tennesseans have done a magnificent job preserving much of their heritage, but they often do not seem to have much patience with people who want to slow down to see it. Pull off if possible. If you can, plan trips to the congested areas when traffic is light. Weekend and holiday mornings are good times. Weekday afternoons seem to be the worst.

Get out of your car. In the towns particularly, walking is the best way to see the sights. The parks included in this book have hiking trails, and most are not demanding. Get out and enjoy them.

If you pay attention to the directions in this book, you should not have difficulty in finding your way. Odometers vary from vehicle to vehicle and measure only down to the tenth of a mile, so distances may be slightly off. The mileages to most houses and other buildings were measured from the drives leading to them, even though they may be seen better from other locations. Distances to and from bridges were measured from their midpoints.

State highways are designated *TN* and federal highways *U.S.* Some of Middle Tennessee's roads are clearly marked. Others are not. Also note

---

that road designations on signs may differ from those on maps. If both are known, both are given initially in the text. Keep in mind that roads sometimes change names, usually at intersections.

This book has maps, but using supplementary maps will help you find your way. A good source is the *Tennessee Atlas and Gazetteer*, a book containing topographic maps of the entire state. Because most of the tours begin on numbered highways, using the free Tennessee Department of Transportation state highway map will be useful. County road maps are available from the TDOT for a small charge.

Middle Tennessee enjoys a pleasant four-season climate. For touring and outdoor activities in general, each season has its advantages. Most people find the weeks around the beginning of April and November ideal. At those times, there is enough foliage for some color but not enough to obstruct views. Tours that emphasize houses—The Brentwood Tour, The Franklin Tour, and The Maury County Tour, for example—can probably be enjoyed most when there is little or no foliage. On the other hand, tours that emphasize the natural environment—The Lower Cumberland Tour, The Upper Cumberland Tour, and The Caney Fork Tour—are most pleasant when there is some foliage.

Take time to enjoy the great places to stay, eat, and shop. Slow down and participate in the many festivals, fairs, celebrations, and tours. Details about these topics are beyond the scope of this book. A good source is *Travel Tennessee*, the official guide of the Tennessee Department of Tourism. Another good source is *Day Trips from Nashville*, by Susan Chappell. Middle Tennessee offers an abundance of opportunities for outdoor recreation. Some guides that will help you plan outings are listed in the bibliography.

Finally, watch out for the coming of Interstate 840. The superhighway that is to loop around Nashville will pass through many areas described in these tours. Roads may be closed and places described in the text may be destroyed.

There is much to see and learn in this beautiful part of the country. And whether you are one of the millions of tourists who come to Middle Tennessee each year, one of the many new residents, or a native, you are sure to find something new and interesting. I know I did.

Acknowledgments

Many people helped me write this book, and I would like to mention some of them.

Eve Saal, with whom I have worked for many years, helped me through the mysteries of word processing. Elizabeth Murray, my niece, an excellent writer, edited the text. John Chastain, who teaches at Nashville Tech, took the picture of me on the back cover, and the folks at Durys on West End in Nashville processed my photos.

Gathering the information for the book required the help of many people. Claudette Stager and the staff at the Tennessee Historical Commission helped me with the national register files and kept me on good terms with their copying machine. Bob McGaw allowed me to raid his complete set of *Tennessee Historical Quarterly*.

It is fortunate that I love libraries, for I spent a good deal of time in them—twenty-seven in all. I was always greeted courteously and given all the assistance I needed. The staff at the Nashville Room in Nashville's main library deserves special mention. They have assembled a remarkable collection of literature about Middle Tennessee and could not have been more helpful in helping me find what I needed.

The people who really make a book like this possible are the countless local historians and storytellers who have recorded their knowledge of their own special parts of Middle Tennessee. Some have written scholarly books, but many more have just written down what they knew or heard. These are the sources for most of the stories repeated in this book. The works of Walter Durham and Jim Crutchfield, two historical writers who have done much to preserve the story of early Middle Tennessee, were particularly helpful.

I cannot say enough about Carolyn Sakowski and the other people at John F. Blair, Publisher. Not only did they give me the chance to write this book, they were always ready to answer any questions, including the dumb ones. And they didn't make me feel dumb for asking.

To Anne, my wife, and Marshall, my son, the rest of my family, and my many friends and associates, thank you for your interest, patience, and encouragement.

Touring the Middle Tennessee Backroads

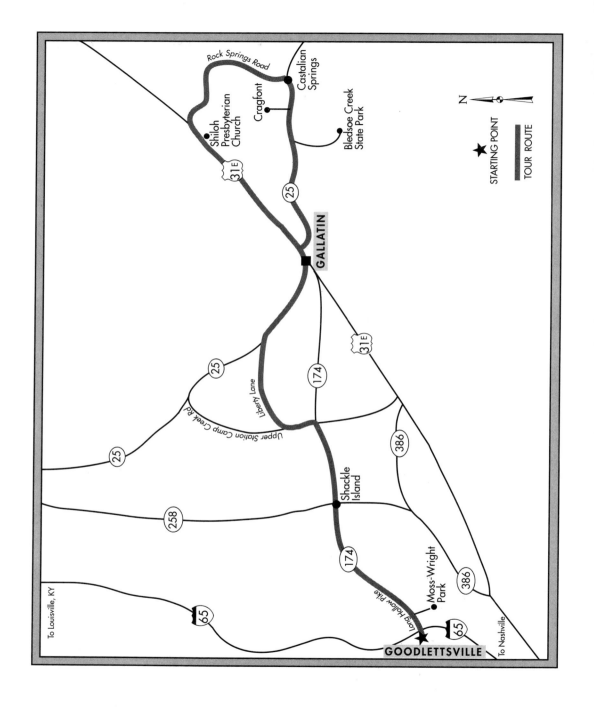

The Middle Cumberland Tour

This tour through the prosperous Sumner County bluegrass includes sites associated with the exploration and early settlement of Middle Tennessee. In Goodlettsville, the tour stops at the reconstructed fort at Mansker's Station and the region's oldest brick house, built in 1787. Cragfont, General James Winchester's splendid home near Castalian Springs, is on the tour, as is nearby Wynnewood, an early inn that is Tennessee's largest log structure. The tour takes in the Shackle Island Historic District before ending in Gallatin.

Total length: approximately 41 miles

This tour begins at the grave of Kasper Mansker in Goodlettsville. Mansker's grave is on Memorial Drive off Dickerson Road (U.S. 31W/ U.S. 41) just south of the intersection of Dickerson Road and Long Hollow Pike (TN 174).

It was on an ancient buffalo path near here on a cold December day in 1779 that James Robertson led his group of weary settlers on the last leg of their long overland journey from the Watauga settlements in today's East Tennessee. Soon, they would reach the Cumberland River—frozen solid by the coldest weather in memory—cross on the ice, climb to The Bluff, and start the permanent settlement of Middle Tennessee.

The birth of Middle Tennessee had its genesis in the Transylvania Purchase, a deal masterminded by land speculator Richard Henderson. In a treaty signed at Sycamore Shoals on the Watauga River in 1775, the Cherokees sold the vast wilderness beyond the Cumberland Plateau. The Cumberland country was not really the Cherokees' to sell. For fifty years, it had been uninhabited hunting ground claimed by several tribes—Cherokees, Chickasaws, Creeks, and Shawnees. Nor was Henderson authorized by the colonial governments of North Carolina and Virginia to buy it. It was soon evident to Henderson that to make the claim take hold, the land would have to be settled. He chose James Robertson and John Donelson to lead the way.

Robertson would lead an overland party, and Donelson would lead another group by water. Robertson came to explore the Cumberland country in the spring of 1779 with eight other men, seven white and one black. Near the great salt lick—the French Lick—they cleared some land and planted a corn crop. When the settlers arrived, there would be something to eat. And planting the corn stood as a symbol of their intent to stake out a claim.

Back on the Watauga, planning for the treks to the Cumberland continued. The first group, about two hundred men led by Robertson, left the Watauga settlements in early November 1779. It followed a circuitous overland route that took it through the Cumberland Gap and into what is now central Kentucky. Some families joined along the way, so that by the time the settlers reached the Middle Cumberland, the group included women and children.

Tradition has it that on Christmas Day 1779, James Robertson led his party across the frozen Cumberland River to the French Lick and The Bluff just upstream. Thus was Nashville born. (For details of the Donelson party's voyage to the Middle Cumberland, see The Lower Cumberland Tour, pages 71–72.)

James Robertson is rightly honored as the Father of Tennessee, for he was not only the leader of the first settlement of Middle Tennessee, but the leader of the settlement of East Tennessee as well. And it was Robertson who dealt with the Chickasaws who occupied West Tennessee.

Born in Virginia in 1742, he married Charlotte Reeves in 1768, and the two of them lived in Wake County, North Carolina. Robertson led settlers over the Appalachians into the Watauga country in 1770 before reaching the Cumberland in 1779. From then until his death in 1814, Robertson played a prominent role in every aspect of life in Middle Tennessee. He was a surveyor, a soldier, a political leader, a land speculator, a manufacturer, a farmer, and an Indian agent to the Chickasaws.

The settlers who arrived with Robertson on Christmas Day 1779 had been preceded in the Cumberland country by explorers and hunters. But as historian James A. Crutchfield points out in *Early Times in the Cumberland Valley*, the line between exploration and settlement was a thin one. The same can be said for the line between hunting and exploration. Kasper Mansker, whose remains lie hidden beneath the rocks here at Goodlettsville, was a hunter. He was also an explorer. And he was one of the first settlers. As much as anyone, Kasper Mansker was the ultimate Middle Tennessee pioneer.

Born to German parents in 1750 on the ship that brought them to the New World, Mansker ended up in Virginia. When Elizabeth White's parents would not approve of her marriage to the frontiersman, she and Kasper eloped and settled along the Holston River in southwestern Virginia not too far from today's Bristol. This was an area that would produce many of Middle Tennessee's pioneers.

Kasper Mansker was a long hunter, one of the men who came into the Middle Cumberland wilderness from the fringe of colonial America between 1760 and 1779. They stayed for long periods at a time—hence the name long hunter. Mansker made his first trip into the Cumberland country as part of a twenty-man expedition that started in June 1769. Several of the men returned home in April 1770, but Mansker and some others built boats and floated their furs and bear meat down the Cumberland and eventually all the way to the Spanish outpost of Natchez on the Mississippi River.

In 1771, Mansker, Joseph Drake, Isaac Bledsoe, John Montgomery, and others made a return trip to the Cumberland wilderness. The following year, most of them came back to the Middle Cumberland and camped along a tributary north of the Cumberland River. Exploring west of their camp, Kasper Mansker discovered two sulphur springs, or licks, along a creek that came to be called Mansker Creek. Here, he reportedly killed nineteen deer in one day. Mansker returned to the Cumberland in 1775 and again in 1779.

Then he came back for good. In 1780, he and other pioneers built a fort on Mansker Creek. But under pressure from Indian attacks, they abandoned it and moved to the security of Fort Nashborough on The Bluff—today's Nashville—in the fall of that year. Mansker returned to his creek in 1782, and with the help of such pioneers as Hugh Rogan and Isaac

Replica of 1782 Mansker's Station at Goodlettsville

Grave of Kasper Mansker, long hunter and pioneer settler

Bledsoe, he built his second fort. There, at Mansker's Station, as it was called, he and Elizabeth presided over one of the most important outposts in the early Cumberland settlements. Kasper Mansker lived until 1828.

The town that grew up around Mansker's Station came to be called Goodlettsville, after A. G. Goodlett, the respected pastor of the Cumberland Presbyterian Church from 1848 to 1853. The congregation dates to 1843. The picturesque church, located just south of Memorial Drive on Dickerson Road, was constructed in 1902.

Once a small country village, Goodlettsville is now a busy Nashville suburb. It was one of six incorporated towns allowed some measure of autonomy when Nashville and Davidson County combined in 1963 to form the first significant consolidated city-county government in the United States.

After visiting Kasper Mansker's grave, follow Memorial Drive to Dickerson Road, then head north on Dickerson to the intersection with Long Hollow Pike (TN 174). Drive east on Long Hollow Pike. You will soon enter Sumner County. After 1 mile on Long Hollow Pike, turn right onto

Caldwell Drive. Go 0.8 mile to Moss-Wright Park, on the right. Enter the beautiful park along Mansker Creek to see the reconstruction of Mansker's Station—the Mansker's Station Frontier Life Center.

The early Middle Cumberland settlers apparently believed that the treaty Richard Henderson negotiated with the Cherokees on the Watauga in 1775 would guarantee their safety from Indian attacks. They were wrong—dead wrong. When John Donelson's party floated by the Cherokee Lower Towns on the Tennessee River at present-day Chattanooga, they were attacked by the Indians, and the violence inflicted on Donelson's thirty-boat flotilla was a preview of the dark days to come. For fifteen full years, life in the Cumberland country was marked by one Indian attack after another. These attacks claimed many lives. And they almost claimed the settlements themselves. It was not until 1795 that the settlers could lead anything approaching normal lives.

For protection, the settlers established a series of forts they called stations, over thirty of them in all before 1795. Some of the better-known ones were Freeland's in North Nashville; Dunham's, where Belle Meade Plantation was later established; Buchanan's, where present-day Elm Hill Pike crosses Mill Creek; and Bledsoe's, near what is now Castalian Springs. Two stations—Mansker's here in Goodlettsville and Fort Nashborough on Nashville's river front—have been reconstructed.

The stations varied in appearance. Some were just a collection of cabins. The more secure ones were rectangular stockades, some with blockhouses—two-story structures that offered clear shots at attackers. The stations not only afforded protection to those living inside them; they were places of refuge for settlers living on the outside as well.

At the reconstructed Mansker's Station, visitors can observe demonstrations of frontier life from March to December. Occasional reenactments showcase the variety of skills needed to survive on the Middle Cumberland frontier.

Continue around the park loop to the Bowen-Campbell House.

William Bowen's house is reported to be the first brick house built in Middle Tennessee. But so is James and Charlotte Robertson's house west of Nashville. Both were built around 1787. The Robertsons' house is gone, so the Bowen-Campbell House can certainly claim to be the oldest brick house still standing.

The 1787 Bowen-Campbell House, Middle Tennessee's oldest brick home

It may not seem too imposing today, but consider the circumstances under which this and other early houses were built. "The great leap westward" is how historian Walter T. Durham describes the Middle Cumberland settlement in his book of the same title. And indeed, it was a leap. James Robertson, John Donelson, Kasper Mansker—they all passed 200 miles of mountainous wilderness to get to the Middle Cumberland. And once here, they were separated from civilization as they knew it. It was a remarkable accomplishment to assemble the workers, the material, and the know-how to build this and the other seemingly indestructible houses in such an isolated land.

Captain William Bowen came from Virginia in 1781, then brought his wife, Mary Henley Russell, and the rest of his family to the Middle Cumberland in 1784. A flood in the spring of 1786 forced the Bowens to abandon their two-story log house closer to Mansker Creek, after which they moved to higher ground and built this brick one.

The Bowens' grandson, William Bowen Campbell, was one of Middle Tennessee's most prominent citizens before the Civil War. Trained as an attorney, Campbell served in several military capacities in both the Seminole and Mexican wars and held a number of political offices. In 1851, he defeated Sumner County's William Trousdale, the incumbent, to become the last Whig governor of the Volunteer State.

The Campbell-Trousdale race was fought largely on the issue of sectionalism, a preview of the carnage of the next decade. Trousdale accused Campbell and the Whigs of being too favorable to Northern views. Campbell was indeed a firm Unionist. He opposed secession, and when war came, he briefly held the rank of brigadier general in the Union army. He served in Congress as a Democrat when Tennessee was readmitted to the Union, then died in 1867. Fort Campbell, the sprawling army post near Clarksville, is named for William Bowen Campbell.

The Bowen-Campbell House has been restored and is open to the public.

From Moss-Wright Park, return to Long Hollow Pike. Turn right (E) toward Gallatin. After about 4 miles, you will crest a hill before descending into the Shackle Island Historic District.

The district contains five beautifully preserved buildings—four houses and a church—that date to the early 1800s. The two men most responsible for the buildings are William Montgomery and Robert Taylor. Montgomery was a wealthy landowner and merchant. Taylor was a builder.

Like thousands of others, Montgomery settled in the Middle Cumberland on a grant made to him by the state of North Carolina, which, until 1790, included today's Tennessee. In 1783, with no money in its treasury to pay its Revolutionary War soldiers, the infant state voided Richard Henderson's questionable 1775 Transylvania Purchase and enacted a law that provided for payment to the veterans with a currency it now had in abundance— land in the Cumberland country.

A vast military reservation—all of the northern part of today's Tennessee midstate—was set aside for grants to the veterans. North Carolina granted 640 acres to privates and more for men of higher rank—up to 12,000 acres. A special grant of 25,000 acres outside the reservation was made to General Nathanael Greene. (For more information about Greene's grant and what became of it, see The Maury County Tour, page 212.) To protect settlers who were already living in the Cumberland country by 1783, the state made preemption grants to them. And the state also made grants as payment for services such as surveying.

William Montgomery received his surveyor's pay in land and eventually came to own six thousand acres along Drake's Creek, where he settled in 1786. Under his leadership, Shackle Island became a thriving, prosperous community. Montgomery contracted with Robert Taylor to complete construction of the Pennsylvania-style brick house he began around 1804. Taylor, a cabinetmaker, had come to Middle Tennessee from North Carolina in 1800 and found plenty of work from the second generation of settlers, who were arriving after the Indian threat finally ended.

The first Shackle Island historic building you will reach is the Taylor-Montgomery House, located on the right 5.2 miles from the Long Hollow–Caldwell intersection. The date in the cornerstone—1824—reflects when Robert Taylor completed the house for his brother, Benjamin.

The Kirkpatrick House is on the left 0.1 mile east of the Taylor-Montgomery House.

This house is an example of the transition in styles so often seen in the earliest Middle Tennessee homes. First, it was a two-story log house, probably built before 1800. In the style common on the frontier, two log structures, or

House built by Robert Taylor for his brother in 1824

pens, were built side by side and covered by a common roof, creating a passage known as a "dogtrot." Later, the dogtrot was enclosed to make a central hallway, and the structure was covered with weatherboard. That, too, is typical. Many of the region's older houses that show frame exteriors are log homes underneath. Still later, a Greek Revival–influenced portico was added to the Kirkpatrick House. This is not uncommon either. So what looks like a Greek Revival house from the 1840s is actually a log house from the 1700s that was twice remodeled.

Continue 0.2 mile to Beech Cumberland Presbyterian Church, on the left.

This Presbyterian congregation was organized in 1798. In 1810, it affiliated with the new Cumberland Presbyterian movement that grew out of the Great Revival of 1800. When Robert Taylor built the church between 1828 and 1830, it was of such quality that the three-foot-thick stone walls survived devastating fires in 1940 and 1951. (For information on the Cumberland Presbyterians and the Great Revival, see The Western Highland Rim Tour, pages 229–30.)

Past the church, Long Hollow Pike intersects TN 258, called Shackle Island Road on the south and Tyree Springs Road on the north. Turn left (N) onto Tyree Springs Road. It is 0.4 mile to the drives leading to two more historic structures, Old Brick on the left and Greystone on the right.

Old Brick is William Montgomery's house, completed by Taylor in 1808. Montgomery was this area's leading citizen until his death in 1838, serving in the Tennessee General Assembly from statehood in 1796 until 1819. His business activities at Shackle Island included a fulling mill, a sawmill, a distillery, a gristmill, a general store, and a blacksmith shop. In *Old Sumner*, Walter T. Durham quotes an advertisement from an 1814 Nashville newspaper that gives some insight into Montgomery's business: "I have now got sheers at my Fulling Mill and other necessary apparatus which cloth will be dressed, etc., in good country style with dispatch." He also advertised that he had grafted apple trees "now of right size to set out of the most approved choice fruit."

Daniel Montgomery, William's son and business partner, hired Robert Taylor to build a house across Drake's Creek. Greystone was completed in 1830. Daniel did well as a planter and merchant. He also bred, raised, and traded mules throughout the region.

There are several theories about how Shackle Island got its name. One is that a tavern keeper named Shackle had his business between the creek and a branch at a place called "the island." Another is that someone sold illegal whiskey from a shack at the island. Whatever the origin of the name, Shackle Island remained an important commercial center well into the twentieth century. The E. A. Dorris Milling Company operated a large flour mill here and sold its product under the brand name "Bell of Sumner Flour."

After viewing Old Brick and Greystone, return to Long Hollow Pike. Turn left (E) toward Gallatin and cross Drake's Creek, named for early settler Joseph Drake and a member of the 1772 long-hunter expedition; the next turn is to the left after 3.6 miles.

It is 1.3 miles on Long Hollow Pike from Shackle Island to Robert Taylor's house, which stands on a hill to the right, barely visible only when there is no foliage. One of his seven children, Alexander K. Taylor, is credited with the "A. K. T. 1822" inscription on the stone house. Taylor meant for this house to last. The walls measure four feet thick on the gable ends and two feet thick on the sides. It is built on solid bedrock.

Long Hollow Pike intersects Upper Station Camp Creek Road after another 2.3 miles; turn left (N).

This is the creek along which Kasper Mansker, Isaac Bledsoe, and the other long hunters camped from May to August 1772. It has been known ever since as Station Camp Creek.

After driving 0.5 mile along Station Camp Creek, turn right (E) onto Liberty Lane. Stay on Liberty Lane through splendid bluegrass country past several fine old homes and the 1891 Liberty Church. You will reach TN 25 after 4.4 miles. Turn right (SE) toward Gallatin.

Traveling between ancient stone fences through the lush Middle Cumberland countryside, this stretch of TN 25 is lined with beautiful, interesting homes, some historic and some nearly new.

When you reach the junction with U.S. 31E, stay on TN 25 through the congested intersection; the road becomes Gallatin's Main Street. After 0.2 mile, you will arrive at Trousdale Place, on the right. This is a convenient place to park if you care to enjoy a short walking tour of Gallatin.

When North Carolina created Davidson County in 1783, it took in all of the Tennessee midstate as it exists today. Sumner County was Middle Tennessee's second county, established by the North Carolina legislature in 1786 and named for Revolutionary War general Jethro Sumner. Though the county existed for a decade before Tennessee became a state, it had no permanent seat of government. In 1796, one of the first acts of the new state's legislature called for the appointment of commissioners to locate a county seat.

Political squabbling between different sections of the county frustrated the effort. The year 1796 came and went with no county seat. The legislature passed a similar act again in 1797. There was more squabbling. No county seat was selected. Gallatin was chosen as the name for a county seat in 1801, but there was still no agreement on where it should be located. Finally, in 1802, a site a few miles north of the Cumberland River was selected. The town is named for Albert Gallatin, the Swiss-born Pennsylvania congressman who advocated statehood for Tennessee and who later served as secretary of the treasury under Presidents Thomas Jefferson and James Madison.

This home became known as Trousdale Place in 1822, when William Trousdale bought it from John H. Bowen, uncle of William Bowen Campbell, the man who defeated Trousdale in the 1851 election. Before he was governor, Trousdale served in several important positions in government and the military. After his 1851 defeat, President Franklin Pierce named him minister to Brazil, a position he held for four years. Trousdale died in 1872.

The house passed to Julius Trousdale, William's son, whose widow, Annie, deeded the property to the local chapter of the United Daughters of the Confederacy in 1900. The Civil War monument on the grounds was erected in 1903. During World War II, Trousdale Place was a USO canteen.

The house is furnished with Trousdale family antiques and is open to the public. The Sumner County Museum is located behind the main house.

The original part of Gallatin Presbyterian Church, located next door to Trousdale Place, is a fine example of Greek Revival architecture. The congregation organized in 1828 and built this church in 1836. During the

Gallatin Presbyterian Church

Civil War, this church and more than thirty other buildings around Gallatin were used as hospitals by the Union army.

Walk one block east of the church to the town square, a remarkably well-preserved mix of commercial buildings dating from the second decade of the nineteenth century to the 1930s. The 1939 courthouse is a Depression-era public work that includes Art Deco and classical influences.

It was not far from the square that Eliza Allen Douglass, the wife of Dr. Elmore Douglass, was near death on the night of March 3, 1861. As she lay in her house, she instructed her family to burn her letters in the bedroom fireplace. She was determined to carry the secret of her failed marriage to Sam Houston to her grave. And she did.

It had been over a quarter-century since the twenty-year-old daughter of a prosperous Sumner County planter married the thirty-five-year-old Tennessee governor. The wedding took place in January 1829, just a few weeks before Houston's good friend Andrew Jackson was to take the oath as the seventh president of the United States.

By the time Sam Houston came to Middle Tennessee in 1818, the East Tennessean had seen and done more than a dozen men would in a lifetime. He had lived with the Cherokees. He had founded and taught in his own school. He had fought alongside Jackson against the Creeks. A giant of a man at six feet, five inches, Houston had a body scarred from war wounds. He also suffered from malaria.

Along with his friend Jackson, Houston was a frequent visitor at Allendale Plantation, where he witnessed Eliza's growth to womanhood. Eliza's father was pleased to see his daughter, barely out of her teens, marry the sitting governor. Whether it was an arranged marriage is disputed, but whatever produced it, the marriage went bad from the start. The day after their wedding, the Houstons set out for Nashville, but bad weather forced them to stop for the night at the home of Thomas Martin. The following morning, while watching Sam in a snowball fight with the Martin children, Eliza was heard to remark, "I wish they would kill him." Her astonished hostess looked at the bride of less than forty-eight hours. "Yes, I wish from the bottom of my heart that they would kill him," Eliza said. What was it that Eliza had seen in Houston that first night?

The newlyweds took up residence at the Nashville Inn. But in early

April, Eliza left Houston and returned to her parents' Sumner County home. Houston was stricken and went into a decline. Public sentiment turned against him, too. On April 16, 1829, the only person ever to serve as governor of two states resigned as Tennessee's chief executive. And on April 23, three months and a day after his celebrated marriage, Sam Houston boarded a steamboat and sailed out of the pages of Tennessee history and into the pages of Texas history. In Texas, he divorced Eliza. They both remarried.

The cause of their breakup remained the subject of intense speculation for generations. Then, in 1962, Louise Davis, a feature writer for *The Tennessean*, the Nashville newspaper, uncovered a document that seemed to provide an answer. Davis describes it in her book *Frontier Tales of Tennessee*.

Balie Peyton was one of Eliza's close friends. Eliza confided in Peyton, a future diplomat and congressman. Peyton kept her secret, but years later, he repeated it to his daughter Emily. Emily Peyton recorded her father's account in a seven-page document but never made it public. It was not until 1962 that it was discovered by one of Emily's nieces.

Eliza believed that Houston was demented. "I believe him to be crazy," she confided to Peyton. Houston was insanely jealous, according to Eliza, and even went so far as to lock her in their rooms at the Nashville Inn "until late at night, without food, debarred from the society of my relatives, and as a prey to chagrin, mortification and hunger." As further evidence of Houston's unsound mind, Eliza related his fear of the dark and his communication with the "spirit world."

Louise Davis uncovered a more personal reason for the breakup. It had to do with Sam Houston's body. It seems that Eliza also confided in her son-in-law, Nashville physician William D. Haggard. As it turns out, Haggard was also Houston's doctor. Haggard's descendants related to Davis that an abdominal wound from a barbed arrow had never completely healed, creating a "running sore," as Eliza described it. Eliza discovered Houston's wound and its intestinal discharge on her wedding night.

Not all of the town's history falls in the 1800s. In the 1950s, the name Gallatin was well known to millions of radio listeners all over the eastern United States, who listened as WLAC in Nashville broadcast blues, rhythm-and-blues, and gospel music sponsored by several mail-order record shops.

One of the shops was Randy's in Gallatin, founded by Randy Wood. Night after night, disc jockey Gene Nobel reminded listeners to send their C.O.D. orders to Randy's in Gallatin—"That's G-A-L-L-A-T-I-N, Tennessee." Randy Wood was a recording-industry pioneer who started Dot Records in Gallatin. Dot Records was an important label in early rock-'n'-roll and pop music. Wood moved the business to Hollywood in 1956 and sold out to Paramount Pictures the next year.

Walk back to your car at Trousdale Place, then continue driving east on Main Street (TN 25). The building on the right 0.2 mile past the square once housed students of the Howard Female Institute, which began enrolling young women in 1856. Joseph Smith Fowler was hired to head the school. Until the outbreak of the Civil War, Howard Female Institute thrived, though not without controversy.

Most teachers in those days were also ministers, and local Presbyterian minister William A. Harrison reportedly wanted the job that went to Fowler. Harrison began a campaign attacking Fowler's religious beliefs. "I was shocked at the thought of having a confirmed and inveterate infidel at the head of a female school," Harrison declared. The school's board conducted a hearing, satisfied itself of Fowler's fitness, and dropped the matter. But Harrison would not let go. He published a pamphlet, *Conclusive Proof that Mr. Jo. Smith Fowler is an Infidel*. Fowler then published his own pamphlet, which he described as an examination of Harrison's "scurrilous pamphlet." The public, tired of the dispute, sided with Fowler, and he remained at the school until the war.

Fowler was a Union man, so when Tennessee seceded in 1861, he moved to Springfield, Illinois. A year later, he returned to Tennessee, where he served as state comptroller under Military Governor Andrew Johnson. After Tennessee was readmitted to the Union, Fowler served in the United States Senate from 1866 to 1871. Johnson was then president, and Fowler married Johnson's widowed daughter, Mary Louise Embry. Fowler remained in Washington and practiced law following his Senate service. He died in 1902.

The school in Gallatin reopened after the Civil War under the name Howard College, using funds raised in the North by its new president, Hugh Blair Todd. It remained open until 1922.

Shiloh Presbyterian Church

Continue east on Main Street for 0.5 mile to the Y intersection of East Main and Hartsville Pike (TN 25). Take the left fork—East Main Street—for 1.6 miles to U.S. 31E. Turn right (NE) on U.S. 31E and follow it through the rolling bluegrass for 4.2 miles to Sideview Road. Turn right onto Sideview Road at Shiloh Presbyterian Church.

The Presbyterians were the first denomination to send ministers to the Cumberland frontier. Princeton graduate Thomas B. Craighead was the first to arrive. He established a meeting house in Davidson County in 1785. The congregation that meets here was organized in 1793, the second Presbyterian congregation to be formed in Middle Tennessee. The current building was completed in 1869.

Return to U.S. 31E. Turn right (NW). After 0.9 mile, turn right onto Rogana Road (Dry Creek Road).

Hugh Rogan came from County Donegal, Ireland, where he was born in 1747. This "raw-boned Irishman," as he has been called, first visited the Middle Cumberland as part of a 1779 surveying party, then came for good as part of John Donelson's expedition in 1780. He was an important man on the Cumberland frontier, known for his bravery, kindness, and generosity. For his surveying, he received a grant of land where Vanderbilt University is now located in Nashville.

To raise money to return to Ireland to get his wife and son, he traded his Davidson County grant for land here in Sumner County. Then he set out, stopping first in North Carolina. He discovered that a brother-in-law, Daniel Carlin—who had left a wife in Ireland, too—had married someone in America. Apparently fearing that he would be exposed as a bigamist if Rogan went to Ireland, Carlin made up a story. He said that Nancy Rogan, back in Ireland, had concluded that her husband was dead. She had married another man, Carlin said. Rogan returned to the Cumberland a brokenhearted man.

In 1796, the year of Tennessee's statehood, a nephew of Rogan's came to Sumner County from Ireland. He was carrying a letter from Nancy bearing the words, "Deliver to your uncle if alive and on the continent of America." She was still waiting for him, she told Rogan in the letter. Off to Ireland Hugh Rogan went. When Nancy heard he was in an Irish port, she dispatched their son, Bernard, to find him.

"What does he look like?" she asked Bernard upon his return.

"He is an old man," the son replied, "wearing a tall hat."

"That's not my Hughie. My Hughie is a young man."

The couple was rejoined, and with Bernard, twenty-two years old, they set out to start a new life on Hugh Rogan's land here along Bledsoe Creek. Their house was a traditional Irish stone cottage, complete with a thatched roof. It still stands today. Their second son, Francis, was born here.

There were not many Catholics in the Middle Cumberland in those early days. What few there were met at the houses of Hugh and Frances Rogan until a church was formed in Gallatin in 1837. The community of Rogana, named for Hugh Rogan, grew up here, but nothing much is left of it today.

After 1.2 miles on Rogana Road, you will cross Bledsoe Creek. The house on the hill off to the right is the one built by Frances Rogan in 1825. Hugh Rogan's cottage is nearby.

Continue on Rogana Road for 0.9 mile to Greenfield Road. Go straight on Greenfield to where it ends at Rock Springs Road. Turn right (S) onto Rock Springs and head toward Castalian Springs.

It is safe to say that no place outside Nashville holds as much of Middle Tennessee's history as the area within 10 to 15 miles of Castalian Springs. As Jay Guy Cisco says in his 1909 book, *Historic Sumner County, Tennessee*, it would be difficult to find a territory "more beautiful, more fertile, or one richer in historical associations. And, too, it would be hard to find a territory of the same extent in which more men known to fame have had their homes."

From the time it was first inhabited around 15,000 B.C. right up until it was selected as the site for the world's largest nuclear power plant in the 1970s, this rich land on the Cumberland's north bank has felt most of the currents of history that have flowed through the region.

As Kasper Mansker explored and hunted west of Station Camp Creek in 1772, Isaac Bledsoe followed a well-worn buffalo path to the east. He came upon a lick where the buffalo were so thick that he would not dismount for fear of being trampled. The lick became known as Bledsoe's Lick and the nearby creek as Bledsoe Creek. Water, rich land, and salt were the most important factors in determining the location of settlements. Isaac

Bledsoe found all three here, and he returned years later to establish his station. By 1784, it was a full-fledged fort.

The years 1783 and 1784 saw an influx of new settlers in the Cumberland country, as Revolutionary War veterans, surveyors, and others came to claim their grants. Anthony Bledsoe followed his younger brother Isaac to the Cumberland country and established his own station, Greenfield, in 1784. The Indians stepped up their attacks about that time, too.

No one was more important to the early settlement of this part of the Middle Cumberland than the Bledsoe brothers. Born two years apart in the mid-1730s in what is now Culpeper County, Virginia, they and their brother Abraham moved to the southwestern Virginia frontier along the Holston River to escape an abusive stepmother. Both Isaac and Anthony were experienced Indian fighters by the time they migrated to the Cumberland country. Isaac was married to Katherine Montgomery, sister of John Montgomery, the member of the 1780 Donelson expedition for whom Montgomery County is named. Anthony was married to Mary Ramsey of Augusta County, Virginia, daughter of noted Indian fighter Thomas Ramsey.

For extra security, Anthony Bledsoe moved his household 2 miles south from his station to his brother Isaac's fort in 1788. In the bright moonlight of July 20 of that year, Anthony Bledsoe momentarily abandoned his customary caution. It cost him his life.

In 1850, the United States Supreme Court decided a case that arose out of a dispute over Bledsoe's will, which he had drawn up in the predawn hours of the morning of his death. The Court summarized the testimony of a witness this way:

> Upon the night of the 20th of July, 1788, about the hour of midnight, the Indians approached the house of Isaac Bledsoe, and lay in ambuscade about forty yards in front of the passage dividing the house, and, with a view of drawing out those in the house, caused a portion of the Indians to ride through a lane rapidly by the house; upon which Anthony Bledsoe and his servant man, Campbell, arose and walked into the passage, when A. Bledsoe and Campbell were both shot down. Colonel A. Bledsoe was shot with a large ball, which struck within a half inch of his naval, and passed straight

through his body, coming out at his back; and from the great pain and rack of misery he suffered from the time he was shot till his death, he was satisfied his intestines were torn to pieces. He died at sunrise the next morning.

The death of Anthony Bledsoe deprived the fledgling Middle Cumberland settlements of a valued leader, a man second in stature only to James Robertson. Bledsoe served on the first Davidson County and Sumner County courts, was one of the commissioners who set the boundary for the military grants reservation, represented Davidson County and then Sumner County in the North Carolina Senate, and became, in 1785, one of the founders of Davidson Academy, along with pioneer minister-teacher Thomas Craighead. That early school eventually became Peabody College, now part of Vanderbilt University. When the Tennessee General Assembly created a new county in the Sequatchie Valley in 1805, it was named in honor of Anthony Bledsoe.

Then it was Isaac Bledsoe who fell prey to the attackers. On the morning of April 9, 1793, while on his way to a clearing, Isaac Bledsoe was murdered by Indians. Like Anthony, Isaac was a valued leader among the stations. He was buried next to his brother.

Little remains today of Greenfield, Anthony Bledsoe's station. The entrance to Greenfield is on Rock Springs Road 1.1 miles south of the intersection with Greenfield Road. A marker erected in 1987 highlights the site, but it is not visible from the road.

David Chenault bought the Greenfield property from Anthony Bledsoe's son in 1836 and engaged architect-builder John Fonville to construct a house. This was the first of several brick Federal-style houses that Fonville built in Sumner County, most of which are still standing and owned by Gallatin attorney and historian Nathan Harsh. Greenfield, as Chenault called his house, is still occupied.

Continue south on Rock Springs Road through this rich countryside. At 1.2 miles from Greenfield, you will reach the Bate House, located on the left.

Born here in 1826, William Brimage Bate was destined to play important roles in the military and political affairs of Tennessee for two generations. Though he had no formal military training, this Mexican War veteran was an able leader for the Confederacy in the West and achieved the rank of major general. Before the Civil War, Bate edited a weekly newspaper, practiced law, and became the district attorney for Nashville at the age of twenty-eight.

In the spring of 1863, with most of Middle Tennessee under Union control, a convention of Confederate Tennesseans met at Winchester to nominate a candidate for governor. When Bate, stationed with the Army of Tennessee near Wartrace, learned that he was being considered, he declined. He wired the convention, "As a son of Tennessee and a Southern soldier, I would feel dishonored in this hour of trial to quit the field. No sir, while an armed foe treads our soil, and I can fire a shot or draw a blade, I will take no civic honor." Bate did end up serving as Tennessee's governor, though. He was elected in 1882 and again in 1884, then served in the United States Senate until his death in 1905.

In the late 1950s, evidence was uncovered that identified Bate as a poet. A volume of writings entitled *American Rhymes* was published anonymously in 1855 by "a Southern poet." Why had Bate insisted upon anonymity? It is only speculation, but it is believed that the politically ambitious Bate felt that the Middle Tennessee culture of the time was decidedly against literary people.

Though William B. Bate is not as widely remembered as other leaders in Tennessee, this citizen, soldier, and statesman is remembered elsewhere. On Memorial Day weekend in 1994, officials from the Cherokee nation in Oklahoma traveled to Nashville to honor Bate. In a ceremony at Mount Olivet Cemetery, the Cherokees laid a wreath on his grave as a memorial to his opposition in Congress to the passage of the Curtis Act of 1898, a federal law that took away Cherokee land.

After driving 1.1 miles from the Bate House, you will reach TN 25. The site of Isaac Bledsoe's station is at the northwest corner of this intersection. The Bledsoes' descendants erected a handsome monument at the graves of the brothers in 1908. Plans call for the creation of a historical park on the site as part of Tennessee's 1996 bicentennial.

Turn left (E) on TN 25 and drive 0.2 mile to Lackey Road. A historical marker is located just beyond this intersection where Governor Hall Road leads off to the left.

William Hall was not Tennessee's governor for long. As speaker of the state senate when Sam Houston resigned, the Sumner Countian succeeded Houston and served out the remainder of his term. Hall also served in many political capacities besides governor, including that of congressman.

Hall came to the Cumberland country in 1785 as a ten-year-old boy, accompanying his parents, Major William and Thankful Doak Hall. He was witness to eleven years of the bloody Indian war. It was his testimony that the United States Supreme Court summarized in the case arising out of Anthony Bledsoe's will. In 1852, a Nashville periodical, *The South-Western Monthly*, published Governor Hall's two-part narrative, "Early History of the South-West." Hall's firsthand account of the Indian wars is the source for many of the histories of the region.

His account is vivid. On June 3, 1787, Hall and his brother James were ambushed by Indians while on the way to a neighbor's house. Somehow, Hall managed to get away. James was not so fortunate. Hall wrote, "Two of them struck my brother as he turned around, each sinking their tomahawks into his brain one on each side of his forehead." And that was just the beginning. In the Indian war, Hall lost his father, two brothers, two brothers-in-law, a sister, and her child. "I have suffered as it seems to me, as much as any one could have suffered in the early settlement of this country," Hall noted.

Turn right off TN 25 onto Lackey Road to reach the village of Castalian Springs. Drive 0.2 mile to old TN 25 in the village. Turn right. You will arrive at the site of Bledsoe's Lick after 0.1 mile.

A marker indicates that it was here Thomas Spencer spent the winter of 1778–79 living in a large, hollow sycamore tree. Spencer has taken on a larger-than-life image. As historian Walter T. Durham notes, the story of "Big Foot" Spencer's life "was long ago snatched away from the serious student of history by the yarn-spinners and tellers of tall tales." But it cannot be denied that Spencer was a huge man who ranked with Daniel Boone as one of the most accomplished woodsmen on the Kentucky-Tennessee frontier. In *The Great Leap Westward*, Durham describes Spencer as a Paul Bunyan of the Cumberland country. One early historian describes Spencer as "a Hercules—stronger than two common men."

Thomas Spencer came from the same southwest corner of Virginia that sent Kasper Mansker, Isaac Bledsoe, and the other long hunters into the Cumberland country. Of Spencer, Governor Hall wrote, "He appeared to have no fear of the Indians. . . . He would hardly ever allow anyone to go into the woods with him not being sure that others would not talk. . . . He seemed to delight in solitude, and with his extraordinary strength and courage there was no bluster about him, but he was one of the most kindly disposed men I ever knew."

But he finally did fall at the hands of the Indians. And he fell while engaged in an act of kindness. Spencer was leading a group of settlers to the Middle Cumberland in 1794 when he was ambushed crossing the Cumberland Plateau.

When the plateau county of Van Buren was created in 1840, the county seat was named for Thomas Spencer.

Just past the Spencer marker is Wynnewood, a remarkably well-preserved 1828 inn. This is not only the largest surviving log building in Tennessee, but is speculated to be the largest log structure ever built in the state.

During the first several decades of permanent settlement in Middle Tennessee, the main route between Nashville and Knoxville ran north of the Cumberland River as far as Carthage, rather than south of the river as it does today. In 1828, three men—William Cage, Stephen Roberts, and A. R. Wynne—selected this site for their stagecoach inn and named it Castalian Springs. According to Greek mythology, Castalia was a spring at the foot of Mount Parnassus at Delphi.

When traffic between Nashville and Knoxville shifted south of the river, business dropped off. In 1834, Wynne bought out his partners and began using Wynnewood as a family residence. For a time, an effort was made to develop a mineral-springs resort here, but it never achieved much success.

Wynnewood remained in the Wynne family until 1971, when it was donated to the state of Tennessee. It is open to the public.

In *Historic Sumner County*, Jay Guy Cisco remarks about "men known to fame" who have had their homes around Castalian Springs. Women from here knew fame, too. One knew it in a most unusual way—as an Italian countess.

Born at Castalian Springs in 1826, Eugenia Bate had a life of fame and

fortune, tragedy and trouble. Her marriage to a Mississippi planter ended with his death in 1855. She went on to survive her second husband and each of her four children as well. Much of her later life was tied up managing debts left by her husbands.

After her first husband's death, Eugenia Bate Bass left her considerable Mississippi holdings in the care of others and moved with her children to Washington, D.C. There, according to Cisco, "she reigned as a belle and was famous for her beauty and mental accomplishments." When the nation split, she returned to Mississippi. Though many of her family members—including her cousin William B. Bate, the general—were active in the cause of the Confederacy, she stayed loyal to the Union cause, at least when it suited her needs.

Eugenia Bate Bass was not shy. When she wanted to protect her plantation from confiscation by Federal troops, she went directly to the Union commander in the region. General Ulysses S. Grant "was most kind and unassuming in manner," according to Eugenia. After she took the oath of allegiance to the United States, Grant issued orders that her property was not to be disturbed. Before the war ended, she was back in Washington. When she learned that Grant's orders had not been followed, she went to see someone else who could help her. In a letter dated January 15, 1864, President Abraham Lincoln instructed the military authorities to restore the property.

In Washington, she met and then married Count Giuseppe Bertinatti, Italy's ranking diplomat in Washington—the Italian Envoy Extraordinary and Minister Plenipotentiary to the United States. From then until her death in 1906, she spent most of her time either with her husband at his posts in Turkey and the Netherlands or shuttling back and forth between Europe and the United States looking after her varied interests, including her Mississippi plantation. Her visits to America brought her back to Castalian Springs.

Upon her death and burial in Washington, one Nashville paper noted that the countess "had the friendship and confidence of many of the great people of Europe." Another paper referred to her as "without doubt one of the most remarkable women of her day."

Not all the Bates of Castalian Springs achieved fame in politics or the military. When the Grand Ole Opry first went on the air in the 1920s, one of the regular bands was a Castalian Springs group known as Dr. Humphrey Bate and the Possum Hunters. Thirteen-year-old Alcyone Bate, the doctor's daughter—he really was a medical doctor—became the first female to sing on America's longest-running radio show.

From Wynnewood, continue 0.2 mile to TN 25. Turn left (W). After 1.2 miles, turn right onto Cragfont Road. You will reach Cragfont, one of the most impressive homes in Middle Tennessee, after 0.6 mile.

General James Winchester began building the house in 1798 and completed it in 1802. Few men or women contributed as much as Winchester to the development of Tennessee. From his arrival in the Middle Cumberland in 1785 until his death in 1826, the Maryland native was a major force in just about every phase of life in Middle Tennessee—the military, politics, commerce, and education. He was a member of the 1788 North Carolina convention that voted to ratify the United States Constitution; he served as Tennessee's first speaker of the senate in 1796; and he held countless other public offices. He was also a successful miller, merchant, and planter.

The British captured Winchester three times in two wars.

Cragfont

The first time was in 1777 on Staten Island, New York, while he was serving as a lieutenant in the Maryland infantry in General George Washington's army. Following his exchange, he was sent south. He was captured again at Charleston in 1780. Released, he was on hand to witness the British surrender at Yorktown in 1781.

His military career continued during the struggle against the Indians. When Tennessee became a state in 1796, Governor John Sevier named Winchester brigadier general in charge of the Mero District, as Middle Tennessee was then known. War with the mother country broke out again in 1812, and Winchester accepted an appointment as brigadier general in the regular army. He commanded troops in the Northwest—now Ohio, Indiana, and Illinois—and suffered a bitter defeat there in January 1813. He was captured for the third time, imprisoned in Canada, released in April 1814, and sent to command the Mobile area.

General Winchester was attracted by ancient names. He was a founder of the nearby town of Cairo. It was he who selected the name Castalian Springs for Bledsoe's Lick. When he served as a commissioner to fix the boundary between Tennessee and Mississippi in 1819, he gave the name Memphis to the new town he, Andrew Jackson, and John Overton started on the Mississippi River. Winchester and his wife, Susan Black, had fourteen children. Among them were Lucilius, Valerius Publicola, and Marcus Brutus. Marcus served as the first mayor of Memphis.

Winchester was an educated man who obviously knew what he wanted when he built Cragfont, for the house duplicates many features of houses in the Virginia and Maryland Tidewater, houses with which the general was no doubt familiar. It is believed that Winchester hired craftsmen from Baltimore to make the difficult trek to the Middle Cumberland to work on Cragfont and perhaps other Sumner County houses as well.

The general chose the name Cragfont because the home stands on a rocky bluff above a big spring. Cragfont is a state historic site and is open to the public from mid-April through mid-October. A magnificent garden was once located east of the house.

From Cragfont, return to TN 25 and turn right (W). After recrossing Bledsoe Creek, you will reach the James B. Jameson House, located on the right at 0.6 mile from Cragfont Road. John Fonville, the noted builder, constructed this house for Jameson around 1844.

Continue on TN 25 past the James B. Jameson House and past Ziegler's Fort Road, which leads to Bledsoe Creek State Park. The park is a rather small one, but it has an abundance of wildflowers in the spring and is a popular place for wildlife viewing, particularly in the winter, when Canadian geese and mallards visit the area.

The unmarked site of Ziegler's Fort, or Ziegler's Station, is south of TN 25. This station was one of several established in 1791, a year relatively free from Indian attacks. But it was a short-lived peace, for in June 1792,

James B. Jameson House

the station was attacked and burned to the ground. Several settlers were killed, including Jacob Ziegler and two blacks. Two of Ziegler's children were captured, as were several other children and the wife of Joseph Wilson. The settlers were later able to purchase the freedom of most of the captives from the Cherokees and Creeks. The fate of the other captives is unknown. The death of five settlers, the wounding of fourteen, and the capture of eighteen more made the Ziegler's Station raid one of the costliest on the Cumberland frontier.

Continue on TN 25 to where another John Fonville–built house, Oakland, stands back from the highway on the right 0.9 mile from the James B. Jameson House. By 1848, Dr. Daniel Wade Mentlo had acquired 650 acres east of Gallatin, where he built Oakland. The small white frame building near the house served as his doctor's office.

Continue on TN 25 as it enters Gallatin. Just before you reach the Y intersection of Hartsville Pike and East Main Street, you will pass the Edward Ward Carmack Library.

Edward Ward Carmack was another of the Castalian Springs "men known to fame." The imposing statue of Carmack in front of the state capitol in Nashville stands as a reminder of his death near that spot in 1908. Robin Cooper's slaying of Edward Ward Carmack is arguably the most sensational event in the history of Tennessee politics.

Cooper and Carmack had once been allies. Duncan Brown Cooper, Robin's father, hired Carmack as editor of his newspaper, the *Nashville American*. Before that, Carmack had practiced law in Columbia, served in the Tennessee House of Representatives, and edited newspapers in Columbia and Nashville. In 1892, Carmack moved to Memphis, where he edited the *Memphis Commercial* before running for Congress in 1896. Carmack won his congressional election against Josiah Patterson, but just barely; the contested election was eventually decided by the United States House of Representatives. Carmack was elected to the United States Senate in 1900, and served with William B. Bate. Thus, for a time, both of Tennessee's United States senators were Castalian Springs natives.

By the time of the next Senate election six years later, the issue of prohibition of alcoholic beverages had risen to the top of the political agenda. Carmack was a stout prohibitionist. Duncan Cooper of the *Nashville Ameri-*

can was firmly in the opposite camp. Cooper supported former governor Bob Taylor, who defeated Carmack in the 1906 primary. Then Cooper backed Malcolm Patterson—the son of the man Carmack defeated for Congress in 1892—in his successful race for governor in 1908.

Carmack was especially vitriolic in his comments about Governor Patterson. Following Patterson's reelection, Carmack became editor of Luke Lea's *Nashville Tennessean*. (For more information about Luke Lea, see The Harpeth River Tour, page 143–44.) Carmack stepped up his attacks on Cooper, his former employer. The hostility between the two men escalated. They both armed themselves.

On November 9, 1908, Duncan Cooper and his son Robin were heading to a meeting with Governor Patterson when they encountered Carmack walking up the street. There is no agreement on what happened next. Every witness had a different story. But there is no dispute that Robin Cooper fired three bullets into Carmack, killing him instantly.

On March 19, 1909, after a sensational trial, a jury found the Coopers—father and son—guilty of second-degree murder. The case was appealed to the Tennessee Supreme Court, which reversed Duncan Cooper's conviction but upheld Robin's. Governor Patterson pardoned Robin Cooper the day the supreme court decided the case.

This tour ends here, at Gallatin.

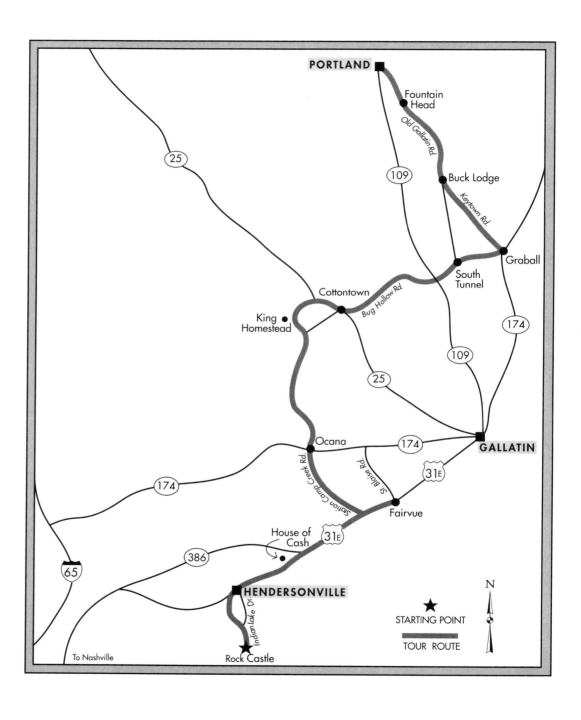

PORTLAND

Fountain Head

Old Gallatin Rd.

109

Buck Lodge

Keytown Rd.

Graball

South Tunnel

174

Cottontown

Bug Hollow Rd.

King Homestead

109

25

Ocana

174

GALLATIN

St. Blaise Rd.

31E

Station Camp Rd.

Fairvue

House of Cash

31E

386

65

HENDERSONVILLE

Indian Lake Dr.

To Nashville

Rock Castle

N

★

STARTING POINT

TOUR ROUTE

174

25

The Hendersonville–Portland Tour

This tour visits historic homes in the Nashville suburbs as well as lush bluegrass horse country before it ends at the pleasant upland town of Portland. It starts at Rock Castle, the home of General Daniel Smith, and stops at the House of Cash, the headquarters for singer Johnny Cash. The tour travels up lovely Station Camp Creek to Cottontown, then along the Highland Rim escarpment—called "The Ridge"—before it levels out in the highlands.

Total length:
approximately 35 miles

This tour starts in the Nashville suburb of Hendersonville at Rock Castle, the historic home of General Daniel Smith. To reach Rock Castle, turn south off U.S. 31E onto Indian Lake Drive and go 1.9 miles. Note that along this tour, U.S. 31E is known by at least four names—Main Street, Gallatin Road, Johnny Cash Parkway, and Nashville Pike.

Rock Castle is one of the oldest houses in Middle Tennessee. Daniel Smith, a graduate of Virginia's William and Mary College, and his wife, Sara Michie, started building Rock Castle as early as 1784, shortly after they settled on Smith's large Cumberland River grant. Daniel Smith played many important roles in the development of Middle Tennessee, including serving in the 1790–96 territorial government, one of several governmental phases during the first fifteen years of permanent settlement.

Isolated as they were from any organized government, the first settlers created their own local government on May 1, 1780, when they gathered at Fort Nashborough to sign the "Articles of Agreement, or Compact, of Government Entered Into By Settlers on the Cumberland River 1st May, 1780." Written by Richard Henderson, the land speculator who masterminded the Cumberland settlement, the Cumberland Compact established a representative body of men from each of the few stations in existence in those early months.

The Cumberland Compact was the first governing charter of any kind west of the Appalachians. It is notable for another reason as well. Of the 256 men who signed it, only one could not write his name. This level of literacy is evidence of the relative sophistication of the earliest Middle Tennessee pioneers. The compact stipulated that it was only a "temporary method of restraining the licentious" and a means of achieving "the blessings flowing from a just and equitable government."

Temporary government under the Cumberland Compact ended in 1783, when the North Carolina legislature placed all of today's Middle Tennessee in a new county, Davidson. While still under North Carolina jurisdiction, two more counties were carved out of Davidson—Sumner County in 1786 and Tennessee County, comprising today's Montgomery and Robertson counties, in 1788.

The settlers living along the Cumberland were never satisfied with their relationship with North Carolina. They briefly flirted with the Spanish authorities headquartered at New Orleans. The Spanish and the British were promoting many of the Indian attacks, and the settlers hoped that perhaps the Spanish authorities could put an end to them. When the North Carolina legislature included the three Cumberland counties in one administrative district in 1788, James Robertson, representing Davidson County in the legislature, suggested the name Miro for the new district. Don Estevan Miro was the Spanish governor, and Robertson's recommendation was intended to flatter him. A clerk's error changed the name to Mero, and for a little over a decade, Middle Tennessee was known as the Mero District.

North Carolina wanted to rid itself of the responsibility of protecting the settlements in present-day Tennessee, so in late 1789, it ceded its vast holdings from the Appalachian crest to the Mississippi River to the young government of the United States. Congress then established the Territory of the United States Southwest of the River Ohio—the Southwest Territory—creating a territorial government that lasted six years. President George Washington appointed William Blount governor and named Rock Castle's Daniel Smith lieutenant governor and secretary of the territorial government.

Leaders in the territory wanted to create a state, so a convention met at

Knoxville to consider statehood early in 1796. Daniel Smith was named chairman of the committee that drafted a state constitution. Statehood proponents got caught in a political crossfire in Congress, and it was not until June 1, 1796, that the act admitting Tennessee as the sixteenth state was signed by President Washington.

Smith was away much of the time while Rock Castle was being built, so responsibility for construction rested on Sara. No one knows for sure how long it took to build Rock Castle, but it was a long time. Finding skilled workers was not easy on the frontier, and the place was under constant threat of Indian attack; at least two construction workers were killed in Indian raids. Rock Castle was probably not completed before the raids ended around 1795.

Daniel and Sara Michie Smith's Rock Castle

Like most of the earliest Middle Tennessee houses—including Cragfont, near Castalian Springs, and Meeting of the Waters, near Franklin—Rock Castle is often described as a mixture of the Georgian style popular until around 1780 and the similar, but later, Federal style. Located on the frontier and isolated from the latest trends, the Cumberland settlers built what they remembered from back east. The result was a Georgian-Federal blend that has been called "glorified pioneer" architecture.

The houses are rectangular, have a central hallway that extends the width of the house, and have one or two rooms on each side of the hallway on each of the two floors. They usually have an L- or T-shaped wing extending to the rear.

Rock Castle is among the finest examples of glorified pioneer architecture. Pedimented porches were often added in later years to the plain fronts of these homes, and Rock Castle is no exception. The two-story porch supported by cedar posts was built in the 1830s.

General Smith, a strict disciplinarian, was not pleased with the attention his sixteen-year-old daughter, Polly, was getting from Samuel Donelson. Donelson was the son of John Donelson, leader of the 1780 Cumberland flotilla, and the brother of Rachel Donelson, Mrs. Andrew Jackson. The general determined to put an end to the relationship. He would send Polly to boarding school in faraway Philadelphia.

But Polly had ideas of her own. One night, with the help of Andrew Jackson, she climbed out a second-story window and descended on a makeshift ladder. She slipped on the way down but was able to break her fall by grabbing a maple tree. Once safely across the river, Polly and Samuel were married at Jackson's place, Hunter's Hill. General Smith was furious. He boarded up the window and cut down the maple. It was not until after the birth of the couple's first child that the general reconciled with Polly.

Daniel Smith lived at Rock Castle until 1818. Sara, his wife, lived until 1831.

A state historic site, Rock Castle is open to the public year-round except during January.

When you are ready to leave Rock Castle, head north on Indian Lake Drive through this suburban neighborhood. After 0.5 mile, turn left (W) onto Ridge Drive. Go 0.1 mile on Ridge, then turn right (N) on Berrywood Drive. After 0.3 mile, you will reach Eventide, the old house at 178 Berrywood.

Daniel Smith Donelson built this house around 1830. It is a one-and-a-half-story cottage of Virginia Tidewater design, rarely seen in Middle Tennessee. Eventide and its separate brick kitchen have been beautifully restored.

Named for his grandfather, Daniel Smith Donelson was the first child born to Polly and Samuel Donelson. Samuel died in 1806, just five years after Daniel's birth. Daniel and his brother, Andrew Jackson Donelson, became wards of Andrew Jackson, their uncle by marriage. Andrew Jackson Donelson was a member of the first class enrolled at the United States Military Academy at West Point, and Daniel followed him there, graduating at the top of the class of 1825. Later, while visiting his uncle Andrew—then president of the United States—Daniel Smith Donelson met and married Margaret Branch, the daughter of Secretary of the Navy John Branch, a former North Carolina governor and United States senator.

Daniel cut short his military career and returned to Sumner County to begin an active life in politics and farming on land inherited from his grandfather. A staunch Democrat in the tradition of his uncle Andrew Jackson, he was an influential political leader in the turbulent period before the Civil War.

When civil war came, Daniel immediately assumed an important role in the Confederate army. It was he who selected the site for the fort on the

Cumberland River near Dover. (For the story of Fort Donelson, see The Lower Cumberland Tour, pages 86–87.) Following his service as a brigade commander in the Army of Tennessee at the Battle of Stones River in January 1863, General Donelson was promoted and placed in charge of Confederate forces in Union-sympathizing East Tennessee. He died at the Montvale Springs resort near Maryville in April 1863.

From Eventide, turn left (W) off Berrywood Drive onto Trousdale Drive, then make an immediate right onto Cherokee Drive. After 0.7 mile, turn right into the Hazel Path office complex just short of U.S. 31E.

Not too long ago, Hendersonville was a quiet country village about midway between Nashville and Gallatin. As late as the 1920s, the town's telephone system required just one switchboard operator, Lily Hudgins, who ran it out of her house. The creation of Old Hickory Lake on the Cumberland River in the early 1950s made this part of Sumner County an attractive place for new homes. It was not long before Hendersonville began its evolution into Nashville's most populous suburb. The town is named for William Henderson, a Virginia Revolutionary War veteran who came to this area in 1790 and served as the community's first postmaster.

Hazel Path

After turning into the Hazel Path office complex, follow the road for 0.1 mile to the mansion for which the complex is named; it is located on the right at the crest of the hill. Daniel Smith Donelson, his wife, and their eleven children outgrew Eventide, so they moved into Hazel Path, which they completed in 1857.

Daniel Smith Donelson's stature as a Democrat who had backed Andrew Johnson for governor—even against his own brother-in-law—came in handy to the former Margaret Branch after the Civil War. She returned from a Deep South exile to discover Hazel Path occupied by Federal troops commanded by Clinton B. Fisk, the Tennessee-Kentucky head of the Freedmen's Bureau. Fisk refused to let Mrs. Donelson return to her plantation. She appealed to Andrew Johnson, by then president of the United States, who warmly remembered her father and husband. He saw that she was able to return.

The widow Donelson and General Fisk squabbled over who was going to control the place, so she again enlisted the aid of the president. She wired Johnson, "I appeal to you for protection. This day my home has been entered by colored soldiers living on my place, my life and that of my family threatened, my daughter cursed and my dog shot in my dwelling. Further violence is threatened tonight. From you alone can I expect justice." Fisk denied the charges to the president—except the one about the dog. "The dog was a vicious, mean dog," he noted. Fisk told the president that Mrs. Donelson caused him "more trouble than all the returned prodigals in Tennessee." The withdrawal of Federal troops ended the standoff.

Hazel Path is a splendid, well-preserved example of the Greek Revival style as interpreted in Tennessee. The original kitchen building, smokehouse, and springhouse are still standing. The home's interior was extensively renovated in the prevailing style by new owners Horatio and Nannie Smith Berry in the 1880s. Their daughter Sarah Berry, who inherited the property and lived in Hazel Path, died in 1982 at age 101. Sarah Berry made many contributions to Hendersonville, including donations of land for the high school and a grammar school named after her mother. In 1969, she gave Rock Castle to the state of Tennessee.

When you are ready to leave Hazel Path, continue the loop through the office park to U.S. 31E. Turn right. It is 0.5 mile to the Bradford-Berry House, set behind a grove of trees on the left.

Major Henry Bradford, a Revolutionary War veteran, came to the Middle Cumberland around 1784 and married a young widow, Elizabeth Chichester Payne Blackemore. They built this house in the mid-1790s. Their daughter, Cecelia, married William Carroll here in 1813. Carroll, a Pennsylvania native, was elected governor of Tennessee in 1821 and served in that office longer than any other person.

Bradford-Berry House

The Bradford-Berry House shares some history with Hazel Path down the road; the Bradfords named their house Hazel Patch. Horatio and Nannie Smith Berry owned Hazel Patch, too. It later passed to their daughter Sarah, who sold 241 acres to General Electric in 1969 for the construction of an automotive motor plant, with the provision that the house would never be destroyed.

General Electric has preserved the house for use by the Hendersonville Arts Council as a gallery, arts center, and office. It is open to the public. Henry Bradford's grave stands in the field to the right of the house.

When you leave the Bradford-Berry House, continue in your original direction on U.S. 31E.

The name of the country club on the left of the highway—Bluegrass—and the name of the local interurban railroad that once ran through here—the Bluegrass Line—are evidence that this is Tennessee's bluegrass country. The Volunteer State's Bluegrass Region—the Central Basin—though twice as large as the similar area in Kentucky, is not as well known for its horses. That was not always the case, for in the nineteenth century, Tennessee was unsurpassed as a breeder of thoroughbreds. The bluegrass that does well in the limestone soil here grows superior bone and sinew in horses.

Dr. Redmond D. Barry, a native of County Kildare, Ireland, is credited with introducing bluegrass and thoroughbreds to Middle Tennessee. Barry brought the first thoroughbred stallion into the Cumberland country from Virginia in 1804. That same year, his horse Polly battled Andrew Jackson's Indian Queen in the first race ever held at Gallatin. Back in Ireland, Barry had been classmates with a fellow named Packingham at Dublin University. Coincidentally, it was Jackson's 1815 victory at New Orleans over

British troops led by that same Packingham that thrust him onto the national stage.

Sumner and Davidson counties have traditionally been home to Tennessee's thoroughbred breeding. Andrew Jackson had a passion for horses and racing. During the long period of Jackson's dominance, the Tennessee thoroughbred had no superior in the nation. Sumner County was the home of many well-known studs throughout the nineteenth century, including Kennesaw and Fairvue. So why did the Kentucky Bluegrass eclipse the Tennessee Bluegrass as the place known for thoroughbred breeding? There were several factors, but the most important was the 1906 law that outlawed betting in Tennessee.

The Bluegrass Line was an electric railway that ran through Hendersonville between the courthouse squares in Nashville and Gallatin. Electric interurban railways—something akin to rural trolleys—began in the United States in 1889 and reached their peak in 1916 with 15,580 miles of main-line interurban track. A number of interurbans were planned for Middle Tennessee, but only two got off the ground, the Nashville-Gallatin line and the Nashville-Franklin line. The Nashville-Gallatin Interurban Railway began in 1913 on a line parallel to the main road. It was a convenient, clean, and inexpensive method of transportation, but competition from the automobile killed it and all the interurbans. The Bluegrass Line ceased operation in the 1930s.

It is 2.1 miles from the Bradford-Berry House to the House of Cash and the old Amqui railroad depot, located on the left. This is the headquarters of entertainers Johnny and June Carter Cash.

How can Johnny Cash's music be categorized? Is it country? Is it rhythm-and-blues? Gospel? Pop? The answer: all of the above. Born in 1932 and raised in the delta country of Arkansas, Johnny Cash was exposed to a variety of musical styles. He heard blacks sing the blues and gospel. He sang in his own church. Using his family's battery-powered radio—they did not have electricity until 1946—he listened to the Carter Family sing live on border radio from Del Rio, Texas. Listening to the broadcasts originating in Nashville's Grand Ole Opry, he heard male solo acts like Ernest Tubb, Hank Williams, and Hank Snow gradually replace string bands as the dominant form of broadcast country music.

After service in the air force in Germany, where he bought his first guitar, Cash wound up in Memphis, where he teamed up with musicians Marshall Grant and Luther Perkins to become Johnny Cash and the Tennessee Two.

Sam Phillips, a young music promoter, had a keen ear for blending the rich, diverse musical culture of Memphis. In 1952, he started Sun Records, concentrating at first on black artists. Then, between 1954 and 1958, he recruited Southern white boys—Elvis Presley, Carl Perkins, Jerry Lee Lewis, Charlie Rich, Roy Orbison, and Johnny Cash. Their unique blend of black and white music came to be known as "rockabilly."

Johnny Cash and his group had several hits. In 1956 came their first million-seller, "I Walk the Line," a big hit in the broader pop market as well as in the country market. From then on, Johnny Cash has been one of the giants in American music, not only as a writer and performer, but also as the creator of a unique style that reflects the diverse musical experience of his youth.

In 1968, Cash married into the very Carter Family he had listened to on the radio decades earlier. June Carter Cash is the daughter of Maybelle Carter, who, along with A. P. and Sara, made up the Carter Family, one of the first groups to record country music. Their initial recordings were made in a makeshift studio in Bristol, near their home in southwestern Virginia, in 1927. The second edition of the Carter Family featured Maybelle and her daughters.

Amqui railroad depot, relocated from Madison by Johnny Cash

The House of Cash contains a museum featuring awards, photographs, and other memorabilia from the long careers of Cash and Carter. It is open April though October.

Amqui was the name of the railroad station in Davidson County where the Louisville & Nashville Railroad's Evansville–St. Louis line split from the line to Louisville. When Johnny Cash heard that the depot was about to be destroyed, he acquired it and moved it to this location in Hendersonville. The depot dates from the late nineteenth century.

Continue toward Gallatin on U.S. 31E for 2.2 miles to the log house on the left. This is actually a collection of four old log structures joined together in the 1920s and 1930s by antique dealer Mary Felice Ferrell. The one building that was originally located on this property was a toll station on the Nashville-Gallatin Turnpike.

Log buildings collected by Mary Felice Ferrell in the 1920s and 1930s

Oakley

Continue on U.S. 31E across the Station Camp Creek embayment of Old Hickory Lake. The house on the right 0.3 mile past the Station Camp Creek bridge is Oakley, built in the Gothic Revival style in 1852 for physician-farmer John W. Franklin. It has long been speculated that Oakley was designed by noted architect William Strickland, who designed Tennessee's state capitol and other prominent Nashville buildings, but no one knows for sure.

U.S. 31E intersects St. Blaise Road 0.3 mile from Oakley. Turn left (N) onto St. Blaise and find a convenient place to turn around, as the tour will next retrace a portion of U.S. 31E.

Across the highway from St. Blaise Road is a gate opening onto a walnut-lined drive leading to Fairvue, the house Isaac Franklin built in 1832.

Fairvue is not visible from the road. That is unfortunate, for by all accounts, it is one of the most impressive homes in the area, described by some as the finest country home in Tennessee. Fairvue has lived several lives. First, it was the home of Isaac Franklin the bachelor. Then it was the home of Franklin and his young socialite wife. It was briefly a school. Decades later, it was home to a horse farm, then a horse club. Finally, it was restored by a business executive and his wife.

Isaac Franklin made his fortune as a slave trader. Working with his partner, John Armfield, his nephew by marriage, Franklin is believed to have made more money than any other American trading in slaves. A combination of factors made it profitable for the partnership to buy slaves in the East and sell them in Louisiana and Mississippi. From their headquarters in Alexandria, Virginia, Franklin and Armfield paid top dollar for slaves, then transported them to the old Southwest on their small fleet of ships. At their peak, they shipped a thousand to twelve hundred black people annually.

The Southern planters fought to preserve slavery, but slave trading was not looked on with favor in polite society. As one early writer put it, "Nothing . . . can reconcile the moral sense of the southern public to the character of a trader in slaves. However honorable may be his dealings, his employment is considered infamous. He can hold no rank in society, nor can he, by any means, push his family into favorable notice with persons of respectability." Isaac Franklin and John Armfield had good reputations as slave traders, and even ardent abolitionists complimented them for the way they cared for their slaves. But Franklin wanted respectability. He got out of the business.

He built Fairvue in 1832 and began devoting his time to planting here and on his considerable holdings in Louisiana. In 1839, when he was fifty, he married Adelecia Hayes of Nashville, the daughter of a New England–born Presbyterian minister. She was twenty-two.

Adelecia loved to entertain. When she and Franklin were at Fairvue, the place was a hub of social activity. Just seven years after their marriage, Isaac Franklin died in Louisiana. He had wanted to be buried at Fairvue. It took three barrels of whiskey to preserve his body for shipment back to Tennessee.

Franklin's fortune was so great that Adelecia was rumored to have the largest income of any woman in America. She later married Joseph A. S. Acklen and built her own mansion—Belmont—on a hill overlooking Nashville. It is now part of the university of the same name. As provided in Isaac Franklin's will, Adelecia lost Fairvue when she remarried, and Fairvue was briefly a school—Franklin Institute. In 1869, Adelecia bought the property back from Isaac's estate.

Fairvue began its third life in 1882, when Adelecia sold it to Charles Reed of New York, a man prominent in racing and gambling circles who was determined to own his own farm for breeding fine racehorses. The Reeds spent lavishly at Fairvue. They outfitted the house with furniture that once belonged to Marie Antoinette. At its zenith, the stud farm had 286 box stalls, some as large as twenty-four feet square, and all with piped-in water and oat sifters. Among the many buildings Reed constructed was a huge stone horse barn with a tin roof he imported from England. The barn still stands today.

In 1891, Reed bought St. Blaise, the 1883 winner of the English Derby, for a hundred thousand dollars, reportedly the highest price ever paid for a racehorse in the United States to that date. In 1902, Reed sold his breeding stock and retired from racing.

Fairvue took on another life in 1928, when a group of wealthy horsemen bought the property for a fox-hunting and racing club, the Southern Grasslands Hunt and Racing Foundation. The club eventually owned or leased around twelve thousand acres between the highway and the Cumberland River. Club members included some of the nation's wealthiest men. It was not unusual for them to reach the premises in their private rail cars. Colonel R. R. McCormick of Chicago arrived via a seaplane that landed on the Cumberland River.

One of the club's most ambitious projects was the construction of Grasslands Downs, a 4.5-mile steeplechase course. The first running of the Grasslands International Steeplechase was on December 6, 1930, before a crowd of eight thousand. The winner's trophy was presented by King Alphonso XIII of Spain. In their book, *A Pictorial History of Sumner County*, Walter T. Durham and James W. Thomas point out that the next year, Fox Movietone cameras were on hand to film the second running of what was already billed as "America's most famous steeplechase . . . the most prestigious event of its kind ever held in this country." That year, Glangesia, owned by Richard K. Mellon of Pittsburgh, won over twelve other horses. But even some of America's wealthiest horse enthusiasts could not weather the Depression. In March 1932, the foundation filed for bankruptcy.

Fairvue's latest life began two years later, when it was bought by William H. Wemyss, one of the founders of General Shoe Company, later Genesco, once the nation's largest apparel manufacturer. William and Ellen, his wife, restored Fairvue to its former grandeur.

The large house on the northwest corner of St. Blaise Road and U.S. 31E, diagonally across the highway from Fairvue, is Kennesaw, home of the famous stud of the same name. Albert Franklin, Isaac's brother, built the house in 1833.

From St. Blaise Road, turn right (W) onto U.S. 31E and backtrack toward Hendersonville for 1.3 miles to the intersection with Station Camp Creek Road.

The park located where U.S. 31E crosses Station Camp Creek is named for Nat Caldwell, a writer for *The Tennessean*, the Nashville newspaper. Caldwell lived in an 1867 log house overlooking this part of Old Hickory Lake. He was awarded a Pulitzer Prize in journalism in 1962 for disclosing undercover cooperation between the coal industry and union leadership.

Turn right (N) onto Station Camp Creek Road and follow it along the

Kennesaw

TOURING THE MIDDLE TENNESSEE BACKROADS

tree-shaded creek for 3.5 miles to Long Hollow Pike (TN 174) at the community of Ocana.

The frame siding of the house on Station Camp Creek's west bank at Ocana covers two log houses. It is believed that one of them was the meeting place of the first Sumner County Court in 1788. Two brothers, the Kirkendalls, known thereabouts as bullies, did not want the new county asserting authority over what they regarded as their territory. At an early session of the court, the Kirkendalls appeared and ordered it to disperse. The district attorney for the Mero District had heard the brothers might cause trouble. Andrew Jackson came prepared. He had his two bulldogs in court with him.

When the Kirkendalls started causing trouble, Jackson decided to restore order. He and one of the brothers wrestled their way out of the building and, rolling over each other, landed in the creek. Jackson then retrieved his bulldogs and faced down the Kirkendalls. He arrested them and brought them back before the court, which fined them heavily. Order in the court was restored.

Turn left (W) onto Long Hollow Pike, then right (N) onto Upper Station Camp Creek Road. Drive 2.9 miles to Vantrease Road, which leads to Station Camp Baptist Church, just to the right. The Baptist congregation that meets here is one of the oldest in Middle Tennessee. In 1796, this and the other four Baptist churches on the Middle Cumberland frontier formed the Mero Baptist Association, the first Baptist organization in Middle Tennessee.

Continue on Upper Station Camp Creek Road. After 1.5 miles, turn left (W) onto Watt Nolen Road. The road swings sharply to the right after 0.8 mile; the King Homestead is on the left. This large home is one of two beautifully preserved old log houses in the Cottontown area. William King and Caroline Hassell moved into this house following their marriage in 1798. They expanded the original building by adding a two-story addition.

Continue on Watt Nolen Road for 1.2 miles until it ends at TN 25. Turn right (SE) to enter the village of Cottontown. After 1 mile, you will reach the Bridal House, located on the right.

Thomas Cotton and his wife, Pricilla Knight, moved from North Carolina to this part of Sumner County in 1791 to claim Thomas's Revolutionary War grant. Thomas had been captured by the British; when he died, he still had scars on his wrists made by British chains.

King Homestead

Bridal House, built for Moore Cotton's daughter in 1819

Thomas and Pricilla had ten children. Moore Cotton was one of them. Around 1815, he built a brick house on property he inherited from his parents. This home still stands on TN 25 just before the Bridal House.

Moore Cotton did not approve of his daughter Elizabeth's marriage to a young blacksmith apprentice. He wanted her living close to his house, so he built the Bridal House for her. Constructed in 1819, this log house features hand-hewn poplar logs measuring three feet in width.

At the Bridal House, turn left (NE) off TN 25 onto Bug Hollow Road. The road is not named for insects, but for the Bugg family, early Sumner County settlers who had a hunting camp near here.

For the next 13 miles, the tour passes through The Ridge, the local name for the rugged hills separating the Central Basin from the Highland Rim.

It is 4.3 miles on Bug Hollow Road to TN 109, the main Gallatin-Portland road. Turn right onto TN 109, then make an immediate left onto South Tunnel Road. After 0.8 mile, South Tunnel swings right at its intersection with Old Gallatin Road; bear right and stay on South Tunnel Road as it descends to the crossing of the main line of the original Louisville & Nashville Railroad.

This railroad negotiates The Ridge through South Tunnel. Its destruction by John Hunt Morgan's Confederate cavalry in August 1862 was only one of many attacks on the L & N in this area by Confederates and their sympathizers. These attacks continued until the end of the Civil War.

Just east of the railroad, you will pass through the small village of attractive Victorian houses that grew up near the tunnel.

After 1.8 miles, South Tunnel Road ends at TN 174. Turn left (N) onto TN 174. After 0.1 mile, turn left (NE) onto Keytown Road. Stay on this rough road for 3.3 miles to where it makes a sharp turn to the left, then another to the right. After 0.1 mile, you will cross the railroad at an unsignaled crossing and reach Old Gallatin Road. Turn right (N) onto Old Gallatin Road.

Here at Buck Lodge, the Union army built Fort Mitchell, one of many stockades north of Gallatin that guarded the railroad from guerrillas—Southern-sympathizing outlaws who operated in areas of divided loyalty like Middle Tennessee. They clothed themselves in the cause of the Confederacy, but many of them were just plain bandits. Ellis Harper led a gang of guerrillas in this area. Over and over, Harper's men hit the railroad through these steep hills. But their worst brutality was saved for recently freed blacks and for whites they suspected of Union sympathies. Harper was hunted down by the Federals, and despite repeated reports to the contrary, they never got him. On May 9, 1865, after the war ended, Harper and twenty-four of his men met the Union provost marshal near South Tunnel and surrendered. They were all paroled.

The violence of the guerrillas was matched by that of the Union commander in the area, Brigadier General Eleazor A. Paine. From his Gallatin headquarters, Paine ruled the territory along the railroad with an iron fist. Summary executions of suspected Confederates were not unusual. Responding to complaints from prominent Unionists like Balie Peyton, Major General Ulysses S. Grant, Federal commander in the West, concluded in January 1864 that Paine was "entirely unfit to command a post." But the generals in the field did not want Paine, so he stayed on a little longer. Then, in April 1864, the new Western commander, William Tecumseh Sherman, removed Paine and sent him to guard the bridges across the Duck and Elk rivers between Nashville and Chattanooga.

The guerrillas derailed or attacked too many trains to count, but the worst rail catastrophe in these hills during the war was not caused by the outlaws. On May 5, 1864, a train carrying three hundred men of the Tenth Indiana Cavalry collided with a work train near South Tunnel. Ten soldiers lost their lives and nearly ten times that number were badly injured. The hatred aroused by Paine's authoritarian regime did not prevent the local citizens from aiding the injured Yankees. Many were nursed back to health by families in Gallatin.

Continue north on Old Gallatin Road. You will cross the railroad at an unsignaled crossing 1.5 miles from Buck Lodge; turn left to stay on Old Gallatin Road. Soon, the road crests The Ridge. You will reach Butler Bridge Road in the Fountain Head community 1.3 miles from the railroad crossing. Stay on Old Gallatin Road through this intersection.

Fountain Head was once the principal settlement in Sumner County north of The Ridge. The name comes from a large spring discovered by Joseph Drake, the long hunter and early settler for whom Drake's Creek is named. James Guinn, who came from Wales by way of Charleston, South Carolina, built the first house at Fountain Head in 1791.

An unusual Methodist church was built here in 1830. The congregation could not locate enough logs of sufficient length to build a rectangular building, so it decided upon a shape that made use of shorter logs—a twelve-cornered affair shaped like a cross. During the Civil War, Federal soldiers dismantled it and used the logs for barracks at Fort Mitchell.

After traveling 2.2 miles from Fountain Head, you will reach a stop sign at TN 52. Old Gallatin Road now becomes South Russell Street entering Portland. Cross TN 52 and turn right where South Russell makes a sharp right and parallels the railroad after 0.4 mile. If you have time, you may enjoy a stroll among the pleasant Victorian houses along South Russell, High, and Wheeler streets; there is ample space to park in front of city hall.

Victorian house in Portland

Portland is new by Sumner County standards. In 1858, as the railroad was being pushed south from Louisville toward Nashville, Thomas Buntin offered to build a depot on his property and deed it to the new railroad—that is, if the railroad would appoint him agent in charge of the station. The L & N accepted. The station was called Richland at first. After the Civil War, a town grew up around it. In 1888, the post office requested that the place change its name to avoid confusion with Richland in East Tennessee's Grainger County. No one seems to know why the name Portland was chosen.

Turn east off South Russell Street onto Wheeler Street. After 0.3 mile, you will reach McKendree Memorial United Methodist Church, on the left. Organized in 1877, the church later merged with the congregation at Fountain Head. The beautiful stone building was completed in 1947.

McKendree Memorial United Methodist Church

William McKendree was the first American-born Methodist bishop. He was born in Virginia in 1757 and consecrated a bishop at Baltimore in 1790. A frequent visitor to this area, he died in 1835 at the home of his brother at Fountain Head.

The Elmer Hinton Public Library is straight ahead. Elmer Hinton was mayor of Portland and edited the local newspaper. He is best remembered as the author of more than three thousand Mark Twain–style "Down to Earth" columns that appeared in *The Tennessean* beginning in 1952.

This library holds one of the hidden treasures of Middle Tennessee, the Bailey Room. Local native Jim Bailey was an official with the Tennessee Department of Conservation from 1937 until 1976. The year he started with the department, he founded *Tennessee Conservationist* magazine. It is fortunate that "Mr. Jim" saved everything, for the Bailey Room houses his valuable book collection and is decorated with his antique furnishings, including a 1790 grandfather clock. After historian Stanley Horn identified the twenty most important books on Tennessee history, Bailey determined to acquire all of them. He managed to get nineteen original copies on Horn's list of twenty. They are included in the collection.

The Cold Springs School stands in Richland Park just past the library. From 1857 until 1933, this building served as a one-room school north of Portland. During the Civil War, it was a hospital for nearby Camp Trousdale, a training camp that was abandoned when Union troops swarmed into Middle Tennessee early in 1862. The structure was moved to the park in 1975. It houses a small museum open from June through September.

Cold Springs School

Portland is famous for its strawberries. It still has its Strawberry Festival each May, but the crop is no longer a staple in northern Sumner County. From the 1920s and into the 1950s, Portland was a major strawberry-producing area, with over thirty-five hundred acres in berry patches and several processing plants. By 1994, only about a hundred acres were left, and all the plants had closed.

The tour ends at Portland. Interstate 65 is 4.4 miles west of town via TN 52.

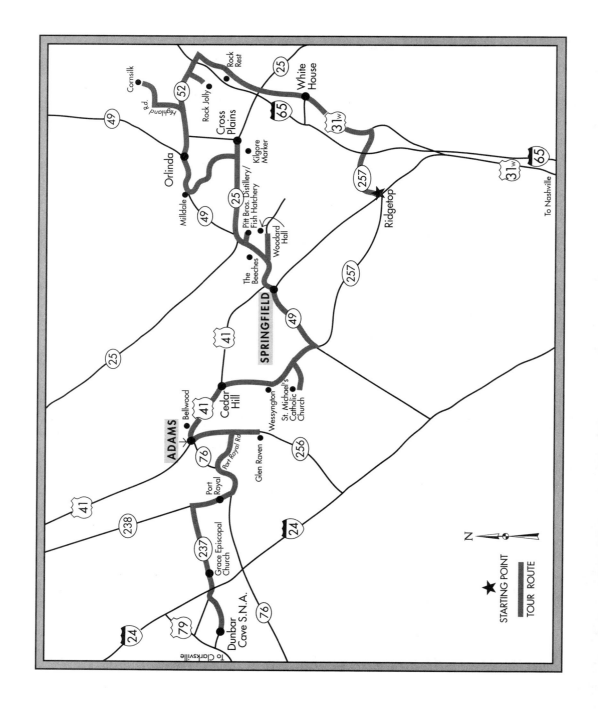

The Red River Tour

This tour goes through the rich farmland of Robertson and Montgomery counties, called the "Black Patch" because it produces most of America's dark-fired tobacco. The tour passes two of Middle Tennessee's largest estates—Wessyngton, founded by George Washington's cousin Joseph, and Glen Raven, another Washington family estate. It visits the pleasant small towns of Cross Plains, Orlinda, and Cedar Hill. The tour goes to Springfield too, and to Port Royal State Historic Area and Dunbar Cave State Natural Area. Also included is the lovely rural church of St. Michael's, the oldest Catholic church in Tennessee.

Total length: approximately 110 miles

This tour starts at Union Church in the old summer colony of Ridgetop. To reach the church, turn left (W) off U.S. 41 onto TN 257 (Greer Road), drive 0.2 mile, and turn left onto Highland Avenue.

A change of a few degrees in temperature does not seem like much today, but before air conditioning, or even before electric fans, people noticed. Sitting as it does on the edge of the Highland Rim, Ridgetop is slightly cooler than Nashville, and from the 1890s into the 1920s, Ridgetop was a summer colony for wealthy Nashvillians fleeing the city to escape the heat. It was an easy commute on the railroad, which passed right in front of Union Church. Ridgetop's stature improved in 1905, when the railroad completed its tunnel under the town. The summer colony reached its peak between then and 1915.

Following the railroad relocation, the summer residents built this nondenominational—or union—church. In 1920, the church began an affiliation with Vanderbilt University Divinity School, whose students served as its ministers. The church bell was donated by Nashville's Westminster Presbyterian Church, where many of the summer residents were members.

In front of the church, take the left fork, O'Brien Avenue. After less than 0.1 mile, you will reach the O'Brien Cottage, located on the left.

Most of the summer residents of Ridgetop stayed in their own cottages,

Union Church

though the Gray Gables Hotel—built in 1896 and later called the Villa Crest—had a main building and eleven cottages. Fewer than a dozen of the original summer houses remain. George O'Brien's 1893 summer house was in "the enclosure," a strip along Highland and O'Brien avenues considered the most prestigious part of the resort.

O'Brien was a Nashville apparel manufacturer who started the Duck Head brand of clothing. His sister, Martha O'Brien, known for her tireless efforts on behalf of underprivileged children, founded a Presbyterian community center that is named for her and that still serves Nashville. In later years, George and his family, and Martha as well, made Ridgetop their permanent home. Martha died in 1910 and George two years later.

Continue on O'Brien Avenue for 0.2 mile to U.S 41. Turn left (N), drive to the junction with TN 257 (Woodruff Avenue), and turn right (E). It is 6.3 miles on TN 257 to the junction with U.S. 31W. Turn left (N) and proceed 5.1 miles to the junction with TN 76 in the town of White House.

U.S. 31W follows the path of old Louisville and Nashville Turnpike, an important stage route in the first half of the nineteenth century. A stagecoach inn located in a white house built in 1796 gave this town its name. The house no longer stands, but a replica of it contains a library and a small museum; the replica is located on TN 76 between town and Interstate 65.

From White House, continue north on U.S. 31W for 7.8 miles to the crossing of the North Fork of the Red River. Just past the bridge, a historical marker commemorates the stagecoach inn visible on the left through a break in the trees.

The Louisville stage line was a favorite for stagecoach gamblers, men who made their living riding the stages and engaging other passengers in games of chance. It could be a hazardous occupation. One professional gambler on this line was Sam Austin, "known to have a flair for dealing from the bottom of the deck," according to Deborah Kelly Henderson in her book *"It Is a Goodly Land."* Austin tried the trick one time too many and got caught. The other passengers were not amused. Pistols were drawn. The driver, determined to keep to his schedule, had no time for this disturbance, so he put the men off. Behind him, he heard shots. Some men were wounded and were picked up by a later stage. Austin was killed.

The 1837 log inn is the second one on this property. Daniel F. Carter, one of the owners of the stage line, bought it in 1847 and named it Rock Rest. It is a wonder that Carter was able to make a go of it at Rock Rest, for the place had a reputation of the worst sort.

Robbery and murder are believed to have been the fate of some guests who stayed at the inn Elisha Cheek ran here from 1797 to 1818. In *Old Sumner*, Walter T. Durham quotes an early writer's characterization of Cheek as "dark of countenance—and dark of soul. He looked at once from under brushy eyebrows with eyes that foretold the savagery of his heart." Cheek supposedly disposed of his victims' bodies in a nearby cave. Long after Cheek died, rumors persisted of human bones being washed out of the cave, and a farmworker for a later owner reported finding "half a shoe box full of human teeth."

Continue north on U.S. 31W for 1.6 miles to the junction with TN 52. Turn left (W) on TN 52.

A 1934 monument near this junction marks the spot where Jenny Lind, "the Swedish Nightingale," sang to an excited crowd gathered near a roadside spring.

In 1849, Lind gave up her opera career and began a two-year tour of the United States under the management of showman P. T. Barnum. While she was on her way to a Nashville engagement, a large crowd assembled on Clarksville's river front hoping to catch a glimpse of the star as her steamboat made a brief stop. Perhaps she would even sing, the crowd hoped. But as a contemporary news account reported, she "did not show herself . . . and the crowd were much disappointed." The people along the Louisville and Nashville Turnpike were more fortunate. When the stage carrying her from Nashville to Louisville stopped at the spring, Jenny Lind sang for them.

Drive 1.5 miles on TN 52, then turn left (S) on Rock House Road. After 1.3 miles, you will recross the North Fork of the Red River in a shaded bottom that is covered with bright bluebells in the spring.

The old stone house above the river is Rock Jolly, built by William and Mary Derrington Johnson around 1830. The walls are eighteen inches of solid rock quarried on the property. No one knows for sure how the house got its name. Some say it was originally called *Roche Jolie*, after a house in France. Others say a 1930s visitor named it after having a jolly time at the place.

Return to TN 52 and turn left (W). After 2.4 miles, turn right (N) onto Highland Road and drive 3.6 miles to Stringer Road; on the way, bear right at the fork at 1.8 miles. Turn left (N) on Stringer Road. After 0.5 mile, you will reach Cornsilk, the two-story house on the left.

This house, built by Thomas Stringer in 1850, is unusual for its recessed two-story front porch. Stringer's two marriages produced fifteen children, so he built the one-room schoolhouse across the road to educate his and his neighbors' children.

Andrew Lytle moved here in 1939. Lytle was one of twelve Southern writers who in 1930 published *I'll Take My Stand*, a collection of essays that attempted to define the essence and soul of the South. The group came to be called the Agrarians. Lytle was one of the most prominent members, along with Donald Davidson, John Crowe Ransom, Allen Tate, and Robert Penn Warren.

I'll Take My Stand and their other writings urged a return to what they argued was the traditional Southern way of life, and a rejection of the

Plantation school at Cornsilk

trend toward attracting Northern industry that swept the South in the 1920s. Some dismissed the Agrarians as hopeless romantics, while others accepted them as serious writers. Whatever the opinion, they certainly sparked a debate about the nature of the Southern character.

Andrew Lytle was a Vanderbilt graduate who had studied drama at Yale and acted briefly in New York before moving to Cornsilk. He eventually settled at the University of the South, where he edited the *Sewanee Review*.

Cornsilk

From Cornsilk, retrace your route to TN 52 and turn right (W). The William Stringer House, located on the left, was constructed by Thomas Stringer's brother in 1858. William planned to build a two-story veranda across the front, but he ran out of money. That explains the second-story door.

Continue on TN 52 through the rich, productive Robertson County farmland for 4.9 miles to the pleasant little town of Orlinda. Turn right (N) onto TN 49 and drive a short distance to the mill that rises above the road on the right.

The first settlers in this area are reported to have been an Indian family, the Redferrins. The Crocker family dominated the commercial and social life of this village in later years. Sometime around 1890, the people of Crocker's Crossroads sought to establish a post office, but Crocker's Crossroads sounded too much like Tucker's Crossroads in Wilson County, so they needed a different name. Centerville, their next choice, was already taken. Orlinda was selected from a list provided by the United States Post Office Department. It is said to be the only Orlinda in America.

In 1902, W. G. Crocker and H. E. Wright founded the mill that came to be called the Orlinda Milling Company. The existing mill was built in 1939. Wheat growers deal with the mill on a deposit basis, which means that the mill grinds their grain and keeps part of it as payment. The mill produces flour under its own brand names and ships it to other producers as well.

Milldale Presbyterian Church

Turn around and head southwest on TN 49, toward Springfield. It is 3.1 miles to Milldale, a small village just past the crossing of Red River's South Fork. Turn left off TN 49 and ascend the hill above the river. After 0.3 mile, you will arrive at Milldale Presbyterian Church. This distinctive 1868 church, perched beautifully on a bluff above the Red River, houses a congregation that began in 1858.

Turn left (E) at the church onto Draper Road. After 1.7 miles, turn left (N) onto Doss Ford Road. Make an immediate right (E) onto Bob Carr Road. After 1.6 miles, Couts Carr Road comes in from the right at the foot of the bridge across Honey Run. Rather than crossing the bridge, follow Couts Carr Road up the hill. After 0.3 mile, you will arrive at one of the most unusual places in Middle Tennessee, the federal government's Wild Horse and Burro Adoption Center.

Wild horses and burros have long roamed the vast public lands in the West that are managed by federal agencies such as the Forest Service and Bureau of Land Management. They are descendants of animals that were turned loose by, or escaped from, ranchers, prospectors, Indian tribes, and the United States Cavalry beginning in the late 1800s. If left unchecked, the wild horse and burro population will exceed the capacity of the arid West to support the animals and will conflict with other uses, so wild animals are rounded up and made available for adoption. This facility, run by a government contractor, is the adoption center for the eastern United States.

Continue past the adoption center on Couts Carr Road; you will reach TN 25 after 1 mile. Turn left (E) and drive 0.4 mile to the Thomas Kilgore marker and cemetery, on the right. This spot and the stone-and-bronze marker on the right of TN 25 approximately 0.2 mile farther east note the location of Kilgore's Station.

In the spring of 1778, alone and on foot, sixty-three-year-old Thomas Kilgore set out for the Cumberland wilderness from his home in North Carolina. He spent the summer living in a cave near this spot. He believed that if he harvested the corn he had planted, he would have an undisputed claim to the land, so he stayed until the fall. Then, taking a few ears of corn with him, he walked back to North Carolina.

He returned with his family and several others in the spring of 1779 to settle for good. They built a stockaded fort. Their station was here even before James Robertson's party left for the Cumberland country in November 1779. It is believed that at least some of Robertson's group stopped here at Kilgore's Station on their way to start what would become Nashville.

Like all the early settlers, those at Kilgore's Station were under constant threat of Indian attack. In 1782, two men—Sam Martin and Isaac

Johnson—were captured by Creeks. Johnson got away, but Martin stayed with the Indians for two years. He was not missed. In his classic 1859 book, *History of Middle Tennessee*, A. W. Putnam has this to say about Martin: "Sam was a quarrelsome person, and of bad character. There were no tears shed because Sam was a prisoner. . . . 'A happy riddance! Hope he will do them as much harm as he did us'."

When the hostilities ended in 1795, the settlers spread out and continued the tasks of building homes and clearing the land. Thomas Kilgore's daughter, Lydia, married James Yates, and they settled on the high plain just east of the station.

Continue east on TN 25 for 1.2 miles to the four-way stop at Cedar Street in Cross Plains. This is a convenient place to park if you care to enjoy a walk in Cross Plains.

No one knows for sure how, but it was during the War of 1812 that Cross Plains got its name. One theory is that James Yates often remarked that he was going "across the plains" when he went from place to place. Another theory is that the name comes from the crossing of two roads on the plain. Whatever the source of the name, Cross Plains is a beautifully preserved, quiet country village.

The two-story building next to the United Methodist church was a combination home and inn built by William and Mary Hinton Randolph in 1816. William Villines bought the log structure in 1830, expanded it, and covered it with siding. According to the 1850 census, the combination house and inn was occupied by the Villineses, their ten children, and nine boarders.

Thomas Kilgore died here. It is said that Kilgore never rode a horse or rode in a wagon. One day in 1822, he needed to have his gun repaired, so he walked all the way to Gallatin—a distance of about 20 miles. On the way back, he stopped to rest at Villines' Inn, and while there danced a jig. He died that night. He was 107.

The structure is a private residence today.

Thomas Drugs is in the northeast corner of the TN 25–Cedar Street intersection. The building, dating to 1915, had been home to a number of mercantile establishments when the Thomas family bought it in 1935. It has since been used continuously as a drugstore, and is famous for its original

Villines' Inn

old-fashioned soda fountain. The small addition on the right has been used as a doctor's office since it was built in 1935.

After exploring Cross Plains, leave town by backtracking west on TN 25.

After 5.1 miles, you will pass the Martin Walton House, on the right. The original part of this impressive house dates to 1809. Continue for 1.1 miles to the junction with TN 49. Head straight (SW) toward Springfield on TN 49. After 1.1 miles, turn left onto Louis Draughon Road. Drive 0.5 mile to the Arthur Pitt House, then another 0.2 mile down the hill on the right to the Springfield Hatchery and the former site of the Pitt Brothers Cave Spring Distillery.

Middle Tennessee is famous the world over for sour mash whiskey. Before Prohibition, Robertson County was home to a booming whiskey business. The people of Scotch and Scots-Irish descent who settled this area knew about distilling and had a taste for good whiskey. Robertson County's sulphur-free and iron-free springs, its abundance of corn to grind into mash, and its plentiful forests for charcoal and barrels made the area ideally suited for the manufacture of whiskey. Early settler Thomas Woodard began the first distillery. Wilson Pitt started in the business on this property in 1840.

Pitt Brothers Cave Spring Distillery

Following the disruption caused by the Civil War, the Robertson County whiskey business rebounded stronger than ever, thriving until the end of the century. In 1870, for example, eleven whiskey and ten brandy distillers produced the forty thousand barrels of product shipped out of the county. Wilson Pitt's sons, John and Arthur II—named for his grandfather—operated the Pitt Brothers Cave Spring Distillery, which produced some of the most sought-after whiskey in America.

The rising tide of prohibition killed the industry in Robertson County. Over the veto of Governor Malcolm Patterson, the legislature enacted statewide prohibition that took effect on July 1, 1909. The Pitt brothers' operation was the last of the many Robertson County distilleries to close, but the revival of Tennessee sour mash distilling after prohibition that produced today's famous brands never took hold in Robertson County.

The brick house you passed on the way to the distillery was built by Wilson Pitt's father, Arthur, on land he acquired in 1798. Wilson added the frame portion to the rear in 1856.

The fish hatchery operated by the Tennessee Wildlife Resources Agency using the Pitt brothers' spring water is actually a rearing station that receives baby fish, or fry, from the hatchery at Clinton in East Tennessee. Rockfish, or striped bass, do not reproduce naturally in Tennessee's lakes, so they are grown from fry here at the Springfield Hatchery. When they are over two inches long, they are transported to area lakes, where they grow to as much as thirty or forty pounds.

From the hatchery, return to TN 49 and turn left (SW). Drive 1.8 miles, then make a sharp left onto Owen Chapel Road (Eden Corner Road). Woodard Hall is on the left after 1.2 miles.

The original part of this house on Beaver Dam Creek was built by Thomas Woodard and Elizabeth Pitt before 1792, making it the oldest house in Robertson County. It was substantially enlarged by Thomas's son, Wiley, in 1854. That same year, Wiley built the detached office for the distilling business he had assumed upon his father's death in 1836. Wiley's business reached its peak on the eve of the Civil War, when he sold whiskey to dealers as far away as St. Louis and New York. Following the war, he resumed his business and also produced the apple and peach brandies for which Robertson County was famous.

Continue on Owen Chapel Road for 0.4 mile to the large white house called Westview. Wiley Woodard's third son, Daniel, also a distiller, and his wife, Julia Young, built this house in 1878.

Retrace your route to TN 49 and turn left (SW). The large Victorian-style house sitting close to the road on the right after 0.6 mile was built by Springfield whiskey wholesaler John W. Stark for his son William around 1880.

After another 0.5 mile on TN 49, you will come to an enormous house on the right. Called "The Beeches," this large Italian villa is unique in the area. Another Woodard, John, built it in 1867. Like his uncle Wiley, John Woodard did well as a distiller. One of his employees at the Silver Spring Distillery was J. C. Napier, who went on to become one of America's most prominent black lawyers and businessmen. Among his accomplishments was the founding of Nashville's Citizens Bank, the nation's oldest continuously operating black-owned bank.

Stay on TN 49. At 0.5 mile from The Beeches, turn right onto Blackwood Drive at the sign for J. Travis Price City Park. Follow this scenic, winding road past the park entrance; you will reach Memorial Boulevard (U.S. 41/U.S. 431) after 1.7 miles. Cross Memorial diagonally to the right and travel down a short lane 0.1 mile until it ends at North Main Street in front of the Dorris Milling Company. Turn left, cross Sulphur Fork, and climb the hill to enter Springfield proper. You will reach Third Avenue after 0.7 mile.

The area from here to the square on North Main Street is lined with substantial houses that date to the late 1800s. If the house at 300 North Main Street looks familiar, there is a good reason—when John Stark built the house in the country for his son William, he duplicated this house, which he had built for himself in 1879.

Continue to the square, located at the intersection of North Main and Fifth Avenue (TN 49). This is a convenient place to park if you care to enjoy a walk along scenic North Main Street, around the square, and in the lovely neighborhood west of the square. Fifth Avenue West in particular is noted for its magnificent houses in a variety of styles. There are impressive houses as well on Seventh Avenue and the cross streets.

Robertson County was one of the two counties created out of Tennessee County when Tennessee became a state in 1796. It is named for James Robertson, the Father of Tennessee. Springfield was selected as the county seat and was laid out on land acquired from Archer Cheatham, Jr. The town takes its name from the many area springs.

The 1879 courthouse, located on the square, is one of Tennessee's most impressive. It is the third one on this spot. The distinctive clock tower and the wings are 1930 additions.

The square also holds a well-preserved collection of commercial buildings built between 1890 and 1925. The building at 516 South Main Street was once the Pitt Brothers Wholesale and Retail Whiskey House.

When you are ready to leave Springfield, follow TN 49 (Fifth Avenue West) west from the square for 5.4 miles, then turn right (NW) on Ridgetop–Cedar Hill Road; note that this road is marked as TN 257 on the left (SE) of TN 49. Drive 2 miles northwest on Ridgetop–Cedar Hill Road to the crossroads at Flewellyn, then turn left onto Catholic Church Road. After 1.2 miles, turn right onto Carter Road. Drive 0.4 mile to St. Michael's Catholic Church, which rests peacefully in the quiet, rolling countryside.

Robertson County Courthouse

This is the oldest active Catholic church in Tennessee. In 1842, the small congregation obtained an acre of land from Wessyngton Plantation

St. Michael's, Tennessee's oldest active Catholic church

and built a simple log church. In 1934, clapboards from the dismantled Episcopal church at the nearby Glen Raven estate were brought here and used for an addition and as siding on the original log structure. The brick bell tower was added in 1942. The bell, too, came from the Glen Raven church.

Among the church's relics are a candlesnuffer, an iron bread baker, and bread cutters that date to 1842. An altar missal printed in 1762 in Antwerp, Belgium, was an 1850 gift from Gustave Bouchard, a native of France.

St. Michael's Male and Female Academy began here in 1846 and lasted until 1855, when it closed due to lack of funds.

Retrace your route to Flewellyn and turn left (NW) on Ridgetop–Cedar Hill Road. You will reach an intersection after 2 miles; keep to the right to stay on Ridgetop–Cedar Hill Road. At the crest of the hill 0.2 mile from the intersection, you will arrive at the entrance to Wessyngton, one of the most celebrated houses in Middle Tennessee.

In 1796, President George Washington's twenty-six-year-old cousin, Joseph Washington, came to Robertson County and purchased sixty acres along Sulphur Fork on the Red River. By the time he finished acquiring land, he had accumulated over fifteen thousand acres. In 1812, he married sixteen-year-old Mary Cheatham, daughter of the man on whose land Springfield started.

Joseph and Mary completed construction of the original part of their home in 1819 and gave it the name Wessyngton, the original Saxon version of Washington. It took four years to build the home. The original brick structure is in the Georgian-Federal "glorified pioneer" style, but over the years, there have been many additions in a variety of styles.

When Joseph Washington died in 1848, management of the plantation passed to his only son, George Augustine Washington, who first married Margaret Adelaide Lewis, daughter of the secretary of war in Andrew Jackson's administration, and later married Jane Smith of Alabama.

The place thrived under George Augustine Washington. By 1860, Wessyngton was the world's second-largest grower of tobacco—250,000 bushels that year. Only the Khedive of Egypt produced more tobacco. And "Washington hams" were prized throughout America. In 1840, for example, the plantation cured over a thousand hams and shipped them out of Middle

Tennessee on steamboats. The furnishings in the house were splendid. Fortunately, most were sent north during the Civil War and were safely returned afterwards. They decorate the house to this day.

Wessyngton barely survived the Civil War. On a cold December day in 1864, George Augustine Washington got word that one of the many bushwhackers roaming the area was coming to rob him. He sent for help from the regiment of black troops stationed in Springfield. In the meantime, the robber came, and Washington shot him in the act of stealing a horse. A rumor quickly spread to a detachment of Federal troops at nearby Turnersville that Washington had killed a soldier. When the troops came to arrest him, a scuffle broke out, and Washington was shot in the arm. The soldiers then began looting the place. They set fire to the servants' houses and other outbuildings and were about to burn the main house when Colonel Downey arrived with his regiment of black soldiers. Order was restored.

Upon George's death in 1892, the vast estate was divided among his surviving children by drawing lots. His second son, Joseph E. Washington, drew the house. After finishing law school at Vanderbilt, Joseph was active in politics. In 1887, he began ten years' service in the United States House of Representatives.

Joseph's son George, born in 1879, was a graduate of Yale and Harvard Law School. He practiced law in New York from 1903 until the Depression, when he returned to Wessyngton. He died in 1964.

Continue driving on Ridgetop–Cedar Hill Road; you will soon cross Sulphur Fork. You will pass the grand entrance to Washington Hall 1.1 miles from the bridge. This was one of the Washington family's estates created when Wessyngton was partitioned following George's death in 1892. The massive house that stood here was destroyed by fire in 1965.

Continue toward Cedar Hill. Go straight at the intersection 0.6 mile from the Washington Hall entrance; you will reach Cedar Hill United Methodist Church on the left after 0.8 mile. This congregation has its origins in the log meeting house James Gunn erected near here in 1793. The elaborate building on the site today was built in 1899.

Past the church, you will reach Cedar Hill, a pleasant small town of tidy Victorian houses, and arrive at U.S. 41 after 0.3 mile. Turn left (NW) on

U.S. 41, heading toward Adams. At 3.6 miles from Cedar Hill, turn right into Bellwood, a cemetery marked by an impressive monument erected in the 1950s.

Among the Bell family members buried here are the patriarch, John Bell, and his son John Bell, Jr., an influential political figure for three decades leading up to the Civil War. John Bell, Jr., served as Speaker of the House and was a major candidate for president in the fractious election of 1860 that sent Abraham Lincoln to the White House. But the most famous person associated with the Bell family is not even a real person. It is a ghost—the Bell Witch.

Bellwood, the cemetery of the family thought to be haunted by the Bell Witch

The stories and theories about the Bell Witch are endless. One theory is that the witch is the ghost of Kate Batts, an eccentric neighbor with whom the elder John Bell had a boundary-line dispute. Another is that the witch began to appear as the result of Bell's killing of a plantation overseer in North Carolina before the family migrated to Tennessee in 1804.

The witch's pranks were directed toward John Bell at first, then stopped for seven years following his death—by poisoning—in 1820. Then the pranks began again, with daughter Betsy Bell the target. The pest supposedly sabotaged Betsy's romance with Joshua Gardner. Lucy Bell, John Sr.'s wife, was on the good side of "Old Kate," so one story goes, and received many favors from the invisible spirit.

A favorite Bell Witch tale involves Andrew Jackson. As the story goes, the wheels on a wagon carrying the general suddenly and inexplicably locked during a visit to the Bell home.

Bell Witch phenomena—strange noises, falling chairs, pulled hair—resurface from time to time. The witch has even been given a home—a cave just outside Adams. A longstanding amateur music show is held in Adams each Saturday night. It is called the "Bell Witch Opry."

Leaving Bellwood, return to U.S. 41 and continue northwest to the town of Adams. After 0.5 mile, turn left on Murphy Street. Cross the railroad at an unsignaled crossing, then turn right on Main Street. Main Street ends at TN 76 (Church Street); turn left (S). Red River Baptist Church, located on the right, houses one of Middle Tennessee's oldest Baptist congregations. It began meeting as early as 1791 and met at different places until 1872, when construction of this church in Adams was completed.

At 0.2 mile from the church, turn left (E) at the junction with TN 256. Follow TN 256 where it turns right (S) onto Glen Raven Road after 2.5 miles. You are now in the middle of the vast Glen Raven estate. The entrance to the Glen Raven House is on the right 1.1 miles past the intersection.

Lavish. Extravagant. Unprecedented. These are among the many words used to describe Glen Raven. Here, in the rolling countryside along Sulphur Fork, Jane Washington and her husband, Felix Grundy Ewing, did on a smaller scale what George Washington Vanderbilt did at Biltmore in North Carolina's Blue Ridge Mountains. They built a self-contained community on their 2,500-acre estate, complete with a school, a church, a store, a gristmill, a sawmill, their own electrical and telephone systems, forty-two spacious tenant houses, and too many outbuildings to count.

One of Glen Raven's distinctive tenant houses

The crown jewel of their barony was the Glen Raven House itself, barely visible through the trees on the right side of the road. Completed in 1900, it took over three years to build. In addition to its twenty-four rooms, the mansion has ten baths, a ballroom that covers the entire third floor, and a huge, 24-by-40-foot solid oak paneled entrance hall. It is said that Felix personally inspected each piece of the yellow poplar used as siding, rejecting any with even the smallest knot.

Jane, one of George Augustine Washington's children, received this land by lot in the partition of Wessyngton following her father's death. She and Felix, a Nashville carriage maker, expanded Jane's original grant to twenty-five hundred acres. The Ewings lived as lavishly as they built—too lavishly, in fact, for the place seldom, if ever, made a profit. They gradually exhausted Jane's fortune and ultimately lost the estate to foreclosure in 1935. Jane and Felix lived out their lives in relative poverty in a Nashville hotel.

Robert D. Moore's father had a farm near Glen Raven. As a boy, Moore was fascinated by the place. His dream came true in 1941, when he acquired the entire Glen Raven estate. Under the Moore family's ownership, Glen Raven has prospered. It is said to be the largest family farm in Tennessee today.

The store and the gristmill still stand on opposite sides of Glen Raven Road 0.1 mile past the entrance to the mansion; the store is on the left

and the mill on the right. The mill was operated by electricity generated by a power plant behind it on Sulphur Fork. One of Glen Raven's well-preserved, distinctive tenant houses is located next to the store.

After visiting Glen Raven, retrace your route on TN 256 to the intersection 0.2 mile past the sharp turn. Turn left here onto Port Royal Road; notice the stone marker for Glen Raven on the left of this intersection. Port Royal Road intersects Goodman Road after 1.2 miles. Turn right, then left; you will reach TN 76 after another 1.2 miles. Turn left (S) onto TN 76 and head for Port Royal.

Robertson County is in the Black Patch, an area embracing five Tennessee and Kentucky counties that produces most of the world's dark-fired tobacco. In the early 1900s, a dispute over the price paid to farmers rose to a level approaching civil war—the Black Patch War. The source of the controversy was the monopoly created by James B. Duke's American Tobacco Company and a few other buyers. Called "the Trust," Duke's organization cornered the market and intentionally depressed prices. Growers banded together in 1904 to form a protective association to fight the Trust. Glen Raven's Felix Ewing was its chairman and driving force.

To accomplish its goal, the association encouraged farmers to market their tobacco through the association rather than through the Trust. Not all of the farmers wanted to go along with the association. They wanted to continue to sell to the Trust. Association members derisively referred to them as "hillbillies." Neighbor turned against neighbor. Businesses unfriendly to the association were boycotted. Before long, some association members resorted to "nightriding," intimidating the hillbillies with threats of violence. Sometimes, the threats were carried out. Hillbillies were beaten and in a few cases even killed. In nearby Hopkinsville, Kentucky, on December 7, 1907, 250 heavily armed nightriders invaded the town, whipped their enemies, then burned and dynamited two large Trust tobacco warehouses.

New laws passed by the Tennessee legislature helped curb the nightriding in Robertson County, but the association's unrelenting pressure ultimately produced victory. State laws were passed to help the growers fight the monopoly without violence, and the Trust was forced to start buying tobacco from the association. Final victory came in 1911, when the United States Supreme Court ordered the dissolution of Duke's monopoly.

An interesting sidelight of the Black Patch War was the way it united farmers across economic and racial lines. Growers from the very wealthiest landowners like the Washingtons to the poorest sharecroppers were active in the association. And despite the nightriding—a tactic perfected elsewhere by the Ku Klux Klan—Robertson County's substantial number of black farmers joined the association, which claimed to go to great lengths to include them as equals.

Continue on TN 76 across Sulphur Fork Creek.

The 1809 Joshua Gardner House, which still stands upstream, played host to an awkward meeting in 1839. Future president James K. Polk's cousin Mary Polk Gardner lived in the house the year Polk, a Democratic member of Congress, was embroiled in a bitter election campaign with the Whig governor, Newton Cannon. The two candidates delighted a crowd in Springfield with a heated debate, then went their separate ways toward Clarksville for another round the next day. Cannon made arrangements to spend the night at the Gardner home, located between the two county seats. Polk, a frequent visitor to his cousin's house, had the same idea, but he had not bothered to tell his cousin in advance. He and Cannon arrived at the house almost simultaneously. The candidates set aside their differences long enough to enjoy a delicious feast together at the Gardners'. The next day, they resumed their attacks on each other before the crowd gathered in Clarksville.

At 2.6 miles from the Sulphur Fork crossing, you will reach the junction with TN 238; turn right (N). You will pass the house known as Maple Hill on the right after 0.8 mile. This distinctive house with its unusual dormer windows and rounded porch dates to the 1840s.

From Maple Hill, it is 0.2 mile to the headquarters for Port Royal State Historic Area. Turn left and park in the visitors' parking lot. You are now in the middle of what was once an important town with a population of over twelve hundred.

An ancient buffalo trail and Indian path once came through here, where Sulphur Fork empties into the Red River. Kasper Mansker, the long hunter and explorer, camped here in the mid-1770s. (For information about Kasper Mansker, see The Middle Cumberland Tour, pages 5–6.) Permanent settlement began in 1782, when a group of settlers came from Port Royal, South Carolina, and named the place. In 1797, a town was laid out, and Port Royal was on its way to becoming an important river town. It first served as a jumping-off place for the flatboats carrying products down to Natchez and New Orleans and later became a destination for the *Matt Gracey*, a little steamboat that ran the Red River during high water down to Clarksville and back.

Among the more interesting businesses at Port Royal were a silk mill and a broom factory.

The charter for the silk mill was granted in 1842. Soon, mulberry trees were planted by the thousands around the countryside to feed the silkworms. A mill and a dam—the remains of which still stand—were built on the Red River. Money was raised to buy machinery. One of the new enterprise's officers, A. D. Carden, was dispatched to England to make the purchase. He was never heard from again. The silk mill never got started, and it was converted to other uses.

R. L. Reding's factory produced brooms of such high quality that he was awarded the gold medal at the 1904 St. Louis World's Fair.

Situated as it is at the confluence of two major steams, Port Royal had several bridges built around it. The most famous was the covered bridge across the Red River. Construction started in 1903, but on December 3 of that year, the bridge collapsed, killing one worker and injuring three others. An additional center pier was added, and the bridge was completed the next year. A new highway bridge bypassed the covered bridge in 1955. Then, in 1972, when it was one of fewer than ten covered bridges remaining in Tennessee, it collapsed. The reconstructed bridge is part of Port Royal State Historic Area.

As a town, Port Royal slowly died. The railroad bypassed it. The steamboats quit running. Finally, the automobile made it easy to travel to nearby

Bridge over the Red River
at Port Royal
(Courtesy of the Tennessee
Tourist Development)

Clarksville. But the area has been beautifully resurrected. Today, the small park along the banks of the Red River and Sulphur Fork provides a pleasant place to walk and picnic.

Continue north from Port Royal on TN 238; you will soon cross the Red River. At 1.9 miles from Port Royal, turn left (W) onto TN 237 (Rossview Road), which follows the meandering Red River west toward Clarksville. You will arrive at Grace Episcopal Chapel, located on the left, after 4.4 miles.

This lovely chapel was built as an Episcopal mission in 1866. Like the 1850s log structure previously on the site, it doubled as a school and community center. Though there were substantial renovations in 1897, the original wood pews and molded window casings remain.

From Grace Episcopal Chapel, stay on TN 237 for 2 miles, then turn left onto Dunbar Cave Road. After 3 miles, you will come to Dunbar Cave State Natural Area, on the right.

A paved trail leads from the visitor center along the shore of the lake to the entrance to the cave; when you climb the steps, you can feel the cool air coming out of the cave. The concession area and elevated bandstand may seem out of place in a natural area, but they are remnants of one of Dunbar Cave's several lives. From 1931 until America's entry into World

Grace Episcopal Chapel

War II, Dunbar Cave was a favorite spot for big-band dances. Huge crowds came to hear some of the biggest acts in the land, among them Benny Goodman, Tommy Dorsey, and Kay Kyser. The cave-entrance area, the lake, a hotel, summer cottages, a concrete swimming pool, tennis courts, and a bowling alley were among the attractions.

After the war, singer Roy Acuff acquired the property and constructed the golf course across the lake. For a time, Dunbar Cave's former popularity was restored, but it did not last long. In 1950, the hotel burned, and the place gradually ceased attracting visitors. The swimming pool closed in 1967.

Dunbar Cave's latest life began in 1973, when it was acquired by the state of Tennessee. Today, visitors can take guided tours through the 8-mile-long cave to such places as Independence Hall, Counterfeiters' Room, and Crystal Palace. Back on the surface, they can enjoy picnicking, fishing, and walking.

The tour ends here, on the outskirts of Clarksville. This early town, settled by members of John Donelson's party as they came up the Cumberland River in 1780, is a storehouse of architectural treasures. Indeed, very few cities its size contain as many well-preserved buildings of such differing styles. Tour maps and information are available at the chamber of commerce, located at 312 Madison Street, and at the Clarksville-Montgomery Historical Museum, located at 200 Second Street.

To get to downtown Clarksville from Dunbar Cave State Natural Area, follow Dunbar Cave Road to Wilma Rudolph Boulevard (U.S. 79) and turn left (SW).

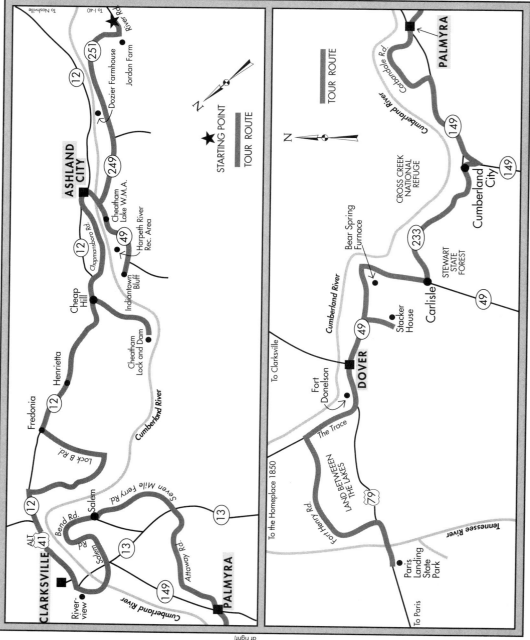

Left panel:

To Nashville

To I-40

River Rd.

12

251

Dozier Farmhouse

Jordan Farm

N

STARTING POINT

TOUR ROUTE

ASHLAND CITY

249

12

Chapmansboro Rd.

Cheatham Lake W.M.A.

49

Harpeth River Rec. Area

Indiantown Bluff

Cheap Hill

Cheatham Lock and Dam

Henrietta

12

Fredonia

Cumberland River

Lock B Rd.

12

Seven Mile Ferry Rd.

Salem

Bend Rd.

Salem Rd.

13

13

ALT 41

CLARKSVILLE

River-view

Cumberland River

149

Attoway Rd.

PALMYRA

Right panel:

PALMYRA

Cordonaple Rd.

Cumberland River

149

CROSS CREEK NATIONAL REFUGE

149

Cumberland City

N

TOUR ROUTE

Bear Spring Furnace

233

STEWART STATE FOREST

49

Carlisle

Cumberland River

Stacker House

To Clarksville

Fort Donelson

49

DOVER

The Trace

To the Homeplace 1850

LAND BETWEEN THE LAKES

Fort Henry Rd.

79

Tennessee River

Paris Landing State Park

To Paris

The Lower Cumberland Tour

This tour follows the scenic course of the Cumberland River downstream from Nashville all the way to the narrow land between the Cumberland and Tennessee rivers and Barkley and Kentucky lakes. Along the way, it stops at the mouth of the Harpeth River, Cheatham Dam, and Cumberland City, where the last ferry on the river still operates. The tour visits Fort Donelson National Battlefield, site of one the Civil War's pivotal battles, and ends at Paris Landing State Park, overlooking Kentucky Lake and the Tennessee National Wildlife Refuge.

Total length: approximately 144 miles

This tour begins along the Cumberland River west of downtown Nashville at the intersection of River Road (TN 251) and River Road Pike. To reach the intersection, take Exit 199 off Interstate 40 and follow TN 251 north. Follow River Road north, heading away from Nashville.

For the first 20 or so miles, the tour travels through the narrow valley the Cumberland River has carved through the Western Highland Rim. It is a scenic drive along a fertile bottom bordered in places by towering bluffs. Though much of the valley covers Davidson County—the state's second most populous—it is amazingly undeveloped.

You will swing away from the river and crest a ridge before reaching Indian Creek Road, located on the left 1.6 miles along River Road.

John Donelson's party came up this stretch of the Cumberland River on its 1780 voyage to The Bluff by French Lick—today's Nashville—where it joined the group James Robertson had led there on Christmas Day 1779. Like Robertson, Donelson was a native Virginian. Twenty-four years older than Robertson, he was an educated, versatile man. He was a surveyor and soldier and had served in Virginia's House of Burgess, the colonial legislature. To be sure, the Robertson party's overland trek was difficult and dangerous, but it was mild compared to the hardships faced by Donelson's group.

It was a 1,000-mile trip into the unknown wilderness. Donelson's plan was to float down the Holston River to the Tennessee, then down the Tennessee to the Ohio. Somehow, the party would navigate upstream on the Ohio to the mouth of the Cumberland, then struggle upstream on the Cumberland to the future site of Nashville.

Things went badly from the start. Their departure from Fort Patrick Henry, at the site of today's Kingsport, was delayed; they did not start until December 22, 1779. Rough water and bitter cold immediately forced the flotilla of about forty boats to pull up and stay for two months. In February 1780, they started again.

John Donelson's journal provides a vivid, if understated, account of the harrowing voyage. He describes the loss of life to disease and Indian attacks, the birth and death of a baby, and the group's passage through two treacherous rapids—the Suck, at the foot of what is now called Signal Mountain near Chattanooga, and Muscle Shoals, in what is now northern Alabama.

The trip up the Ohio from the mouth of the Tennessee to the mouth of the Cumberland was only a short one, but the high water of the great Ohio that spring was enough to convince some of the Donelson party not to attempt to travel upstream. Some departed for Illinois and some for Natchez. On March 21, 1780, Donelson wrote, "Set out, and on this day labored very hard, and got but a little way: camped on the south bank of the Ohio. Passed the two following days as the former, suffering much from hunger and fatigue."

Travel up the Cumberland was not quite as difficult, but it was still hard. The boats were poled up the river, sometimes with the assistance of sails. At times, they were pulled by men walking along the bank. Food was scarce and consisted mostly of game. Toward the end of the journey, Donelson wrote, "We are now without bread and are compelled to hunt the buffalo to preserve life. Worn out with fatigue, our progress at present is slow."

But they persevered. One can only imagine the joy when the survivors were reunited with their friends and families at The Bluff. Donelson's entry for April 24, 1780, reads as follows: "This day we arrived at our journey's end at the Big Salt Lick, where we have the pleasure of finding Capt. Robertson and his company. . . . Though our prospects at present are dreary, we had found a few log-cabins which have been built on a cedar bluff above the Lick by Capt. Robertson and his company."

About thirty people perished on the voyage of Donelson's fleet.

Continue on River Road past Indian Creek Road.

Here, in the small valley of Indian Creek, is a homestead that has been in continuous use for over 150 years. Drury Jordan, an uncle of Charlotte Reeves Robertson, the wife of James Robertson, brought his family to the Cumberland country from Virginia in 1806. The house, located just down Indian Creek Road but visible from River Road, was built by Drury Jordan, Jr., in about 1825.

River Road soon parallels the river again. It is 5.2 miles from the Indian Creek Road intersection to the Dozier Farmhouse, located on the right.

Like many of Middle Tennessee's farms, this one started on a North Carolina Revolutionary War veteran's land grant. Some of the veterans came to the Cumberland country to claim their grants, but most did not. Instead, they traded them. North Carolinian Enoch Dozier got his land on the Cumberland River through such a trade.

Sometime after 1801, Enoch and Margaret Ethridge Dozier built two cabins

Dozier Farmhouse, on the Cumberland River downstream from Nashville

in this rich bottom—one for their family and one for their slaves. After the Doziers' later frame house burned around 1840, they constructed this handsome two-story brick house. Enoch died soon after it was completed in 1842. One of the Doziers' original log cabins—since covered with weatherboard—also sits on the property, along with some original outbuildings.

Continue on River Road. Just past the Davidson County–Cheatham County line, you will see Nashville Bridge Company's barge-building facility across the river. This operation is evidence of the continued importance of navigation on the Cumberland River. The company is one of America's largest builders of river barges.

Navigation on the Cumberland reached its peak during the steamboat era, which began in 1819 with the landing of the *General Jackson*, the first steam-powered boat to reach Nashville. But the Cumberland River had been a path of commerce even before then. *Chaouanon* was the name the French gave the river. It was their word for the Shawnee, the Indian tribe that claimed the Middle Cumberland when the first Europeans arrived. The river Chaouanon first appeared on a 1674 map by the great French explorer-trader Louis Joliet.

The first white man recorded on the Cumberland River was Martin Chartier, a Frenchman who had deserted La Salle's army in 1680. As early as 1692, Chartier and his Shawnee wife lived at the Shawnee village near the great salt lick—today's Nashville. For several years before 1715, young Jean du Charleville and an older Frenchman whose name is not known ran a trading post at the French Lick. Feuds with the Chickasaws drove out the Shawnees and their French storekeepers. There were no full-time settlements along the Cumberland between 1715 and the arrival of James Robertson's party in 1779, but explorers and hunters traveled up and down the river.

As the area began to fill with settlers after 1779, the Cumberland and its tributaries, along with the Ohio and the Mississippi, became the main avenues for frontiersmen taking products to market in New Orleans and Natchez. The flatboat trade thrived during the last decade of the eighteenth century and the first two decades of the nineteenth. (For more information about the downriver flatboat trade and the boatmen's return on the Natchez Trace, see The Harpeth River Tour, pages 136–38.)

Steamboats replaced flatboats after 1820. In 1825, a steamboat made the New Orleans–Nashville trip in just under nine days; the fastest upstream flatboat trip had been sixty-seven days. The 1820s and 1830s saw a rapid rise in steamboat traffic, as the "packets"—the term for the steamboats that plied the inland waterways—came up the Cumberland in increasing numbers. In the 1850s, some 341 different packets are known to have landed at Nashville alone. On the Lower Cumberland, Clarksville and Dover became important stops.

On November 1, 1859, an event occurred that foretold the end of the steamboats—the first train traveled all the way from Louisville to Nashville. Now, goods and passengers could be transported overland between the Ohio River and the Middle Cumberland on a shorter, faster, and more dependable route. Eventually, competition from the railroads killed the steamboats.

Other factors led to the decline of steamboat traffic as well. Before the Civil War, cotton was the largest and best cargo on the packets. Following the war, agriculture in this region grew more diversified. Cotton was no longer king; by 1870, it had all but vanished from the packets. By 1880, much of the iron business had shifted from Middle Tennessee to a new city in Alabama—Birmingham. Shipments of tobacco also declined.

Because of the area's remoteness, people of the Upper Cumberland had no other way to ship goods, and the steamboats roamed the Cumberland above Nashville well into the twentieth century. But on the Lower Cumberland, not much packet business was left by 1900.

Commerce on the Cumberland River did not die with the steamboats, of course. Today, barges travel up and down the river hauling mostly bulk commodities, such as sand, gravel, coal, and oil. Nearly five million tons of cargo pass along this stretch of river each year.

River Road crosses the Sam's Creek embayment of Cheatham Lake 3.4 miles from the county line.

The navigable portion of the Cumberland River is actually a series of lakes created by four locks and dams built by the United States Army Corps of Engineers. Cheatham and Barkley are the two dams on the Lower Cumberland.

TN 251 ends at the junction with TN 249 in Lillamay 0.6 mile from

Sam's Creek. River Road continues as TN 249 before it ends 3.9 miles from Lillamay at TN 49. Turn left (NW) onto TN 49. You will reach the turnoff to the Bluff Creek Launching Ramp after 1.4 miles; the turnoff is on the right. This ramp is located in Cheatham Lake Wildlife Management Area, one of many such areas where the Tennessee Wildlife Resources Agency manages land owned by the federal government—in this case the Corps of Engineers. This site—Hudgen's Slough—and two others on Cheatham Lake are convenient areas for viewing wildlife, particularly waterfowl and other birds.

Continue on TN 49 for 2.7 miles. You will pass the entrance to Harpeth River Recreation Area. This site offers facilities for picnicking, camping, and boat launching below some impressive bluffs on Cheatham Lake.

Stay on TN 49 across the Harpeth River. Turn right onto Dozier Boat Dock Road 0.5 mile from the bridge. This road ends at Pardue Recreation Area, located where the Harpeth finishes its 185-mile journey across the Middle Tennessee heartland.

Indiantown Bluff

The narrow bluff across the Harpeth's mouth is known as Indiantown Bluff because of its ancient Indian site. A number of circular-shaped mounds and graves extend along the ridge for several thousand feet. Little is known about the original inhabitants of this site, surveyed in 1920 by pioneer Tennessee archaeologist William Edward Myer. In his book *Indian Trails of the Southeast*, Myer identifies a major trail that began here at what he calls the "old citadel and town."

When the Chickasaws ran the Shawnees and the French out of Middle Tennessee in 1715, their last confrontation occurred here, at the mouth of the Harpeth. As the last of the Shawnees came down the river, they were attacked by Chickasaws waiting on the bluff. Supposedly, all the Shawnees were killed in the attack.

Retrace your route to TN 49, turn left, and recross the Harpeth. Continue past the junction with River Road (TN 249) and cross the Cumberland River to enter Ashland City, the Cheatham County seat.

Cheatham County was created out of parts of neighboring counties in 1856 and named for Edward S. Cheatham, speaker of the Tennessee State Senate from 1855 to 1861 and a partner in the nearby Sycamore Mills.

The huge facility you will see on the right as you head toward the square in Ashland City is State Industries. Each year, over three million water heaters are manufactured here, to be marketed under several familiar brand names.

You will reach the intersection with TN 12 at the square. The Cheatham County Courthouse is directly ahead. The original 1869 Italianate building is in the rear of the main structure, which was built in 1914.

Cheatham County Courthouse

Turn left (NW) onto TN 12, drive 1.1 miles to Chapmansboro Road and a sign for Sycamore Creek Recreation Area, and turn left. Chapmansboro Road passes an abandoned railroad trestle, a remnant of the Tennessee Central's line connecting Nashville, Clarksville, and Hopkinsville, Kentucky, which opened in 1904. (For information on the Tennessee Central, see The Caney Fork Tour, pages 365–66.) Plans are under way to convert this abandoned railroad into a riverside path for hiking and biking.

Continue along Chapmansboro Road, which hugs the bank of the Cumberland River in places. You will cross Sycamore Creek 3.5 miles from TN 12. At the end of the bridge, take a sharp right turn and drive 2.2 miles to TN 12. Turn left (NW) onto TN 12. You will arrive at Cheap Hill—also known as Chapmansboro—after 0.6 mile.

There is nothing cheap about the large house on the northwest corner of the TN 12–Cheatham Dam Road intersection. Littleton John Purdue came to Middle Tennessee from North Carolina and married Martha Ann Williams in 1837. Their carefully preserved house is a good example of the frame, Greek Revival plantation houses of the 1840s and 1850s.

Purdue House at Cheap Hill

This home was fortunate to survive the Civil War. After taking anything they could find of value, a detachment of Federal troops debated whether to burn the place. They took a vote. The house won by a single vote.

Turn left (SW) on Cheatham Dam Road. After 2.9 miles, you will arrive at one of the most beautiful spots on the Cumberland River, the Lock A Recreation Area, a popular place for swimming, boating, camping, and picnicking.

Turn right at the river and drive parallel to it for 1.5 miles to Cheatham Dam.

Since it was created by the Continental Congress in 1775, the Corps of Engineers has had the dual mission of military construction and civil works. Congress first appropriated funds for navigation improvements on the Cumberland in 1832. In a survey that year, Corps of Engineers officers

Barges and tow passing through Cheatham Lock and Dam

reported obstructions to navigation from overhanging trees, snags, logs, rocks, and shoals. During 1833 and 1834, the army cleared driftwood out of the river downstream from Nashville. A similar effort was undertaken on the Upper Cumberland in 1837.

Over the centuries, the Harpeth River's waters deposited rocks and gravel in the Cumberland, creating Harpeth Shoals, the worst obstruction to navigation on the lower river. In 1904, the Corps of Engineers built Lock A near the current Cheatham Dam site. The lock backed up enough water to cover Harpeth Shoals year-round. Lock A was replaced by Cheatham Lock and Dam in 1952.

Three unusual boats passed through Cheatham Lock in August 1976—the *Adventure II*, the *Rachel*, and the *Charlotte*. As part of America's bicentennial celebration, a group of citizens from Nashville and Kingsport reenacted the Donelson party's 1780 voyage. *Adventure II* was a smaller version of John Donelson's boat. *Rachel* was named for Donelson's daughter, who later became the wife of Andrew Jackson. *Charlotte* was named for Charlotte Robertson. Both women were part of the original Donelson party.

Due to the impoundments on the Tennessee and Cumberland rivers, the tiny flotilla had to resort to motor power. It left Kingsport on June 6 for a journey of 1,006 miles. On August 7, 1976, dressed in a pioneer costume reminiscent of what James Robertson wore in 1779, Nashville mayor Richard Fulton led the crowd of two thousand people that greeted the twentieth-century pioneers as they landed at Nashville's river front.

Retrace your route from Cheatham Dam to TN 12 and turn left (NW). You will reach the crossroads at Henrietta after 6.2 miles.

A sign announces that Henrietta is the hometown of Pat Head Summit, the most successful coach in the history of women's college basketball. As of 1994, her teams at the University of Tennessee had won three national championships. In the 1984 Olympics, she also won a gold medal as coach of the United States team. Summit actually came from nearby Clarksville but moved to Henrietta, just inside Cheatham County, to play for Cheatham County High School. Clarksville High did not have a girls' team at the time.

You will enter Montgomery County just past Henrietta. The county is named for John Montgomery, who explored the Cumberland country in 1777, accompanied John Donelson on the 1780 voyage, and was a founder of Clarksville, the Montgomery County seat. Montgomery was killed by Indians in 1794.

Stay on TN 12. At 2.4 miles from Henrietta, take Old Ashland City Road where it angles off to the left just before the village of Fredonia. After 0.3 mile, you will come to an intersection with Lock B Road North; the 1840s Sanford Wilson House is on the right at the intersection. Turn left (SW) on Lock B Road North. You will pass through a succession of attractive, prosperous farms before reaching the Cumberland River at Holt's Landing after 3.3 miles. As the road's name suggests, this is the site of old Lock B, built in 1916, the second lock and dam on the Cumberland. Follow the road as it parallels the river.

The road swings away from the river, passes some remains of the Tennessee Central Railroad, then becomes Gholson Road. At the intersection with Johnson Road 2.6 miles from Holt's Landing, keep to the left on Gholson.

After 1.8 miles, you will arrive at Bethlehem United Methodist Church, one of the most beautiful of the many white frame churches in rural Middle

Bethlehem United Methodist Church

Tennessee. The first church here was organized in 1836. This impressive structure was completed in 1899.

Continue past the church on Gholson Road until it ends at Hickory Point Road after 1.9 miles. Turn left (N); you will reach TN 12 almost immediately. Turn left (NW) and follow TN 12 for 2.2 miles to the U.S. 41A bypass around Clarksville. Turn left (W) and follow the bypass for 4.5 miles to its intersection with TN 13. Turn left onto TN 13. After 0.4 mile, take Zinc Plant Road as it angles off to the right. You will cross the Cumberland River.

Ahead on the bluff to the right of the bridge stands Riverview, a house built around 1828. It is best known as the home of husband-and-wife writers Allen Tate and Caroline Gordon in the 1930s and 1940s. Tate and another man who lived for a time in Clarksville—Robert Penn Warren— were members of a group of writers associated with Vanderbilt University that came to be known as "the Fugitives," a name taken from their literary magazine, *The Fugitive*, which they published for three and half years starting in 1922.

It was through Warren that Tate met Caroline Gordon, whose writings he admired, particularly her published assessment of the Fugitives. They married in 1924 and lived in New York. Tate wrote for *The Nation*, *New Republic*, and the *New York Herald-Tribune*. Caroline wrote fiction. Tate continued with the poetry he started in Nashville, including "Ode to the Confederate Dead," which he revised over the next ten years.

Tate was in France when two other Fugitives, Donald Davidson and John Crowe Ransom, began to seriously consider mounting a counterattack against people they perceived were heaping contempt and ridicule on the South. The result was the 1930 publication of *I'll Take My Stand* and the formation of a new group of Southern writers, the Agrarians. Both Tate and Warren were members of this group. (More information about the Agrarians is included in The Red River Tour, pages 52–53.)

Although best known as Allen Tate's wife, Caroline Gordon was a respected novelist and short-story writer in her own right. Her best-known books are *Aleck Maury, Sportsman*, based upon the life of her father, and *The Strange Children*, a 1951 work in which she recreates her life in Clarksville from 1930 to 1938.

At the end of the bridge across the Cumberland River, turn left onto River Road, which follows the Cumberland's south bank upstream atop some high bluffs.

The Shawnees—the last Native Americans to inhabit the Cumberland country—called the river *Warioto*. It was first called the Cumberland in 1750. A Virginian, Dr. Thomas Walker, was employed to survey the lands beyond the Great Valley, which slices diagonally through the Old Dominion and what is now East Tennessee. Walker named the mountains that rise on the valley's west the Cumberlands. He also named a gap through the range the Cumberland Gap and gave the same name to the small river north of the gap, all in honor of the duke of Cumberland, a favorite son of, and prime minister to, King George II of England.

It is 1.1 miles on River Road to where Mayhew Drive veers to the left as River Road swings right, away from the river. Continue on Mayhew above the river. You will pass under the TN 13 bridge before reaching Salem Road after 1 mile. Turn left on Salem Road.

From here to Palmyra, the tour meanders through the beautiful, rolling Montgomery County countryside on several rural roads past a number of substantial farmhouses and lovely churches. Built in the second half of the nineteenth century, these structures stand as evidence of the prosperity that quickly returned to this productive land following the devastation of the Civil War.

The Edmondson House is on the left 1 mile from the intersection of Salem Road and Mayhew Drive. Robert Henry Edmondson built this unusual-looking house in the 1880s. His father, William Edmondson, ran a ferry across the river near this point. During the Civil War, when Federal troops attempted to enter William's house, he met them with his shotgun. He might be killed, William said, but he would take at least one Yankee with him. The Union officer in charge was impressed with Edmondson's bravery and ordered his men to leave. But not before taking the chickens.

Continue 1.2 miles past the Edmondson House to Seven Mile Ferry Road and turn left (N). As the name suggests, this road leads to the site of a ferry that once crossed the Cumberland River. Mule power ran this ferry. A mule fitted with blinders was hitched to a heavy beam, which in turn was attached to a wheel. The mule walked in endless circles to furnish the power for the ferry.

Seven Mile Ferry Road now ends short of the Cumberland River. After a sharp turn, the road continues as Bend Road. The lovely Beach Bend Farmhouse, built in 1873, stands on the left 0.4 mile from the sharp turn.

Stay on Bend Road. You will reach Salem 2.7 miles from Beach Bend Farmhouse.

Bend Road ends at Salem. Turn left (S) onto Seven Mile Ferry Road and drive 5.7 miles through farm country to where the road ends at TN 13/TN 48. Along the way, you will cross old TN 48 and then Martha's Chapel Road, where there is a charming rural church.

At TN 13/TN 48, make a dogleg by turning left onto the highway, then right (W) onto Attaway Road. It is 2.8 miles through remote, forested country to the old Attaway Farm. Built in the 1880s, this frame house was expanded in the 1960s with brick from two old Clarksville warehouses—the 1856 Elephant Warehouse and the 1878 Biggers Loose Floor building.

It is another 1.6 miles to the intersection with Vernon Creek Road. Turn right, then make an immediate left on Palmyra Road. You will reach TN 149 after 3.3 miles. Cross the highway and proceed 0.2 mile into Palmyra.

Palmyra's name was changed from Blountville when the town was officially established and laid out in 246 lots in 1797. It was once an important river town, designated by Congress in 1797 as the first official port of entry in the West. The town thrived as a steamboat landing before the Civil War, when tons of iron, tobacco, and cotton were shipped from its banks. But Palmyra was ruined during the Civil War.

Beginning with Nashville's surrender on February 24, 1862, and continuing to war's end, the Tennessee capital was a major supply base for the Union army. Commander LeRoy Fitch was placed in charge of the gunboats assigned to protect the shipping that brought most of the supplies. During the massive Federal buildup in the first half of 1863, it was not unusual for forty or fifty steamboats a week to arrive at Nashville in convoys protected by Fitch's gunboats. On April 2, Confederate artillery at Palmyra nearly sank the gunboat *St. Clair* and badly damaged three transports. In retaliation, Fitch sent gunboats to Palmyra, shelled the town, then reported to his superior that not a single house was left standing when he finished.

Stay on Palmyra Road up the hill. At 0.8 mile from Jarman Hollow Road, veer right onto Corbandale Road where Palmyra Road swings left. Continue on Corbandale Road as it drops off the ridge and parallels the Cumberland River. The abandoned railroad visible between the road and the river was the Louisville & Nashville Railroad's Memphis line, which connected with the main line to Louisville at Bowling Green.

The idea for a Memphis-Louisville railroad started in the late 1840s as an alternative to steamboats, which were at the mercy of water levels on the Mississippi and Ohio rivers. Political squabbling and intrigue delayed construction. It was not until April 15, 1861—the day Fort Sumter was fired upon—that the first train made it from Memphis to Louisville.

There were other problems as well. Both the Tennessee and Cumberland rivers had to be crossed. Amid the push to get across the Cumberland at Clarksville, it seems that little attention was paid to the height of the bridge. Steamer after steamer had its stacks ripped off as it passed under the structure. One vessel, the *Minnetonka*, was nearly demolished when she hit the bridge at high water. The railroad had no choice but to remove the bridge and build a new one.

Corbandale Road makes a sharp left turn at Birchfield Place, climbs the ridge away from the river, and at 1.1 miles ends at Tarsus Church Road. Turn right on Tarsus Church Road and drive 0.2 mile to TN 149. Turn right (W) again. TN 149 crosses the Yellow Creek embayment of Lake Barkley, passes through the Sailors Rest community, and enters Stewart County.

Cumberland River Lock C, built near Sailors Rest in 1918, was rendered obsolete in 1966, when the Corps of Engineers completed Barkley Dam in Kentucky, creating a 118-mile-long lake. Barkley Dam and Lake Barkley are named for Alben W. Barkley, who served as a United States senator from Kentucky and as vice president under Harry S. Truman from 1949 to 1953.

Sailors Rest is said to be named for a spot on the river where boatmen rested during their long flatboat journeys down the Cumberland, Ohio, and Mississippi rivers to New Orleans.

Stewart County, formed from Montgomery County in 1803, is named for a Revolutionary War veteran and early settler, Duncan Stewart. Following the 1818 Chickasaw Cession of West Tennessee, Stewart County stretched west all the way to the Mississippi River and took in about one-fourth of Tennessee. Its size was gradually reduced as new counties were created.

It is 6.1 miles on TN 149 to the junction with TN 46. Turn right (N) onto TN 46 and crest the hill to enter the town of Cumberland City. You will reach the Cumberland River 0.5 mile from the junction.

Though not as important as Palmyra, Cumberland City was a "call" for the packets during the steamboat era. The town was called New Lisbon in 1814, then Bowling Green in 1815, and finally Cumberland when the Memphis rail line came through in 1860. The addition of the word *city* is evidence of the aspirations local people had when the railroad came.

Here at Cumberland City, TN 46 crosses the Cumberland River on a ferry. At one time, there were dozens of ferries crossing the Cumberland and Tennessee rivers in Stewart County. This is not only Stewart County's last remaining ferry, it is the only remaining ferry on the entire Cumberland River in Tennessee.

Cumberland City Ferry

Where TN 46 stops just shy of the ferry, turn left (W) onto TN 233. After 0.5 mile, veer right to stay on TN 233. The huge complex on both sides of the highway is the Tennessee Valley Authority's Cumberland Steam Plant. TVA is the nation's largest producer of electricity, and this plant has the largest generating capacity of any in the TVA system. The plant, which burns 1,010 metric tons of coal per hour, went into operation in 1973.

Past the TVA plant, the route passes through the 8,862-acre Cross Creek National Refuge, which encompasses both sides of the Cumberland River for 12 miles. The refuge includes impounded water, marshes, farmland, and upland hardwood forests. Its primary purpose is providing feeding and resting habitat for migrating waterfowl. The walks and drives available here allow visitors to observe some of the 271 bird species recorded. Bald eagles returned to the refuge in 1983 and now hunt and fish here year-round.

Stay on TN 233 as it leaves the river, turns west, and passes the edge of 4,000-acre Stewart State Forest, established in 1935 on land deeded to the state in lieu of delinquent taxes on a 9,000-acre estate.

The TVA's power plant at Cumberland City

It is 8.4 miles from Cumberland City to where TN 233 ends at TN 49 at Carlisle. Many of the men prominent in the Western Highland Rim iron industry came to Middle Tennessee from Pennsylvania, including the greatest iron master of them all, Montgomery Bell. Carlisle is named for the

Pennsylvania town of the same name. (For more information about the iron industry, see The Western Highland Rim Tour, pages 236–38.)

Turn right (N) on TN 49 and head for Dover.

In 1898, the 14-mile Tennessee & Cumberland Railroad was built from Tennessee Ridge on the Louisville & Nashville Railroad's Memphis line to the Bear Spring Furnace near the Cumberland River. This was one of several short lines constructed to serve the iron industry. It was abandoned in 1921. Now, TN 49 follows its route north from Carlisle before it passes along the Cross Creek Reservoir portion of the national wildlife refuge.

Bear Spring Furnace

TN 49 swings west 3.6 miles from Carlisle; the main entrance to the wildlife refuge is on the right. Stay on TN 49 for 0.9 mile to the Bear Spring Furnace.

The Bear Spring Furnace is one of the best-preserved iron-industry sites in Middle Tennessee. Still standing are a stack, a pylon, and three company houses. Look closely at the side of the stack facing the highway and you will see a bear and lettering carved into the huge limestone blocks.

It was 1832 when the first furnace was built here by Woods, Yeatman and Company, the same company that owned the nearby Cumberland Iron Works. The furnace was abandoned in 1854 but was built anew by the Cumberland Iron Works in 1873, the date carved in the base of the stack.

Where the road curves west of the stack, you will see the company doctor's house on the left. Two workers' cottages are located along the road between the doctor's house and the stack.

Continue on TN 49. Turn left (S) onto Long Creek Road 2.6 miles from the stack at Bear Spring. After 1.2 miles, you will reach the Stacker House, located on the left. Samuel Stacker, one of the Pennsylvania iron masters, arrived in Middle Tennessee in 1819 and was one of the founders of the giant Cumberland Iron Works. He built this house around 1859. The fountain in front of the house was imported from France.

Home of Samuel Stacker, one of the many iron masters who came from Pennsylvania

Backtrack to TN 49 and turn left (W). The road to the wildlife refuge visitor center is on the right after 0.2 mile. Continue on TN 49. You will arrive at U.S. 79 in Dover after 2.4 miles.

There was a settlement at Dover as early as 1795, but the town was not laid out until 1805. It was initially called Monroe. Sitting on a cliff above the Cumberland, it reminded someone of England's White Cliffs of Dover;

it took on its new name in 1806. For a quarter-century before the Civil War, Dover prospered as a packet call. Its importance was exceeded only by Nashville and Clarksville. The Cumberland Iron Works had nearly cornered the regional market for nails, chairs, shovels, castings, and other iron products shipped from the town. At its peak, the Cumberland Iron Works owned 63,000 acres along an 8-mile stretch on both sides of the Cumberland River.

In Dover, turn left on U.S. 79 and head for Fort Donelson National Battlefield. It is 1.6 miles to the turnoff for the fort. The visitor center and museum are just inside the park. Information on a driving tour of the national battlefield is available at the visitor center. Note that the driving tour will later return to Dover.

When the Civil War came to Dover, it did so with a vengeance. Here, on February 16, 1862, the North won its first major victory. It was also here that a previously unheard-of Union officer started along a path that took him to the White House.

The Cumberland and Tennessee rivers provided avenues for Northern troops to penetrate the heartland of the new Confederate States of America. To defend against river advances, the Confederates constructed two forts—Fort Donelson on the Cumberland and Fort Henry on the Tennessee—separated by 12 miles of the "land between the rivers." Brigadier General Ulysses S. Grant devised a plan for combined Union naval and land attacks on the forts. Assisted by gunboats under Flag Officer Andrew Hull Foote, Grant's men easily took Fort Henry on February 6, 1862. Fort Donelson was next.

Grant's reinforced troops marched east toward Fort Donelson on February 12. Confederate reinforcements were sent to the fort. By the time Grant's men in blue arrived, eighteen thousand or so Southerners were entrenched in a large semicircle around Dover and Fort Donelson with their backs to the river. From Dover, Confederate brigadier general Gideon J. Pillow wired Governor Isham G. Harris at Nashville, "I will never surrender the position, and with God's help I mean to maintain it."

But he did surrender. After three days of fighting in bitterly cold weather, the Federals had the Confederates surrounded by the night of February 15. The four Confederate brigadiers in charge bickered among themselves during the night. Should they stay and fight another day or should they evacuate? Someone mentioned surrender.

Two of the Confederate generals fled, leaving Simon Bolivar Buckner in charge. Buckner was taken aback by Grant's response to a messenger sent to propose a discussion of surrender. "Unconditional surrender," Grant replied. On Sunday morning, February 16, 1862, Grant accepted Buckner's surrender at the Dover Hotel. Fifteen thousand Confederates went north to prison.

There was one Confederate—an unknown cavalry lieutenant colonel—who would have none of this. He had not come to Fort Donelson to surrender, he said. Taking eight hundred men with him through the frozen waters of Lick Creek, he got away. This would not be the last time Nathan Bedford Forrest did the bold and unexpected.

Grant was an unlikely hero. Named Hiram Ulysses at birth, he was by mistake listed as Ulysses Simpson when he arrived at West Point. He decided to keep the name. His new initials came in handy later, it turned out.

Grant had a weakness for whiskey, so much so that he had left the army nearly eight years before the surrender at Dover. Between then and the war, he did not accomplish much of anything in civilian life. When he left the army, he was broke. A good friend and fellow officer loaned Grant money to get home. He was Simon Bolivar Buckner.

It is difficult to overstate the importance of the fall of Forts Henry and Donelson. The Tennessee and Cumberland rivers were now unobstructed. Within weeks, Nashville—one of the Confederacy's principal cities—was in Union hands for good. The next stop for "Unconditional Surrender" Grant was a landing on the Tennessee River near a little country church called Shiloh.

The driving tour at Fort Donelson National Battlefield goes to the river batteries where the Confederate gunners repulsed the Union gunboats and to other sites at the fort, then heads to the Dover Hotel, where Buckner surrendered. The hotel, built around 1852, was one of the few structures in Dover to survive the war. The national battlefield also offers a pleasant walking trail that starts at the visitor center and loops down to the river.

The Dover Hotel

When you are ready to leave Fort Donelson, turn right (W) on U.S. 79 and drive 1.4 miles to the turnoff on the right for Land Between the Lakes (LBL). Head north on the Trace (formerly TN 49) for 3.7 miles to the South Welcome Station, located at the intersection with Fort Henry Road.

Development of this national recreation area started in the mid-1960s, when Barkley Dam was being constructed on the Cumberland across the narrow strip of land from Kentucky Lake on the Tennessee River. LBL's 170,000 acres offer an abundance of activities, including hiking, bicycling, hunting, and fishing.

If you care to take a side trip, it is 13 miles north from the South Welcome Station to where the TVA has reconstructed an 1850s homestead using sixteen log structures from the area. Here, staff dressed in period costumes demonstrate the daily living of that period.

Though the Trace extends up the length of LBL for 40 miles, the tour now heads west toward Kentucky Lake. Leaving the welcome station, cross the Trace and head down Fort Henry Road. After 6.1 miles, you will pass the road to Boswell Landing, which takes off to the right in the direction of the Civil War fort on the Tennessee River.

The site of Fort Henry is now completely under Kentucky Lake. Indeed, the fort was so close to the Tennessee River that it flooded during the Civil War, too. That is one reason it was so vulnerable to attack.

Continue on Fort Henry Road for 4.4 miles to where it ends at U.S. 79. Turn right (W). You will cross Kentucky Lake before arriving at the entrance to Paris Landing State Park after 4.1 miles.

The state park is located at the old steamboat landing for the town of Paris, 18 miles to the southwest. Its 841 acres are beautifully situated overlooking the wide expanse of Kentucky Lake at the confluence of the Tennessee and Big Sandy rivers. When it was impounded, Kentucky Lake was the world's largest man-made lake.

The peninsula between the two rivers is part of the Tennessee National Wildlife Refuge, which encompasses 50,000 acres in three units along 80 miles of Kentucky Lake. Each fall and winter, over 150,000 ducks and 75,000 Canada geese visit the area.

The tour ends with this slight venture into the edge of West Tennessee.

U.S. 79 heads southwest to Paris and east to Dover and then Clarksville, 50 miles distant.

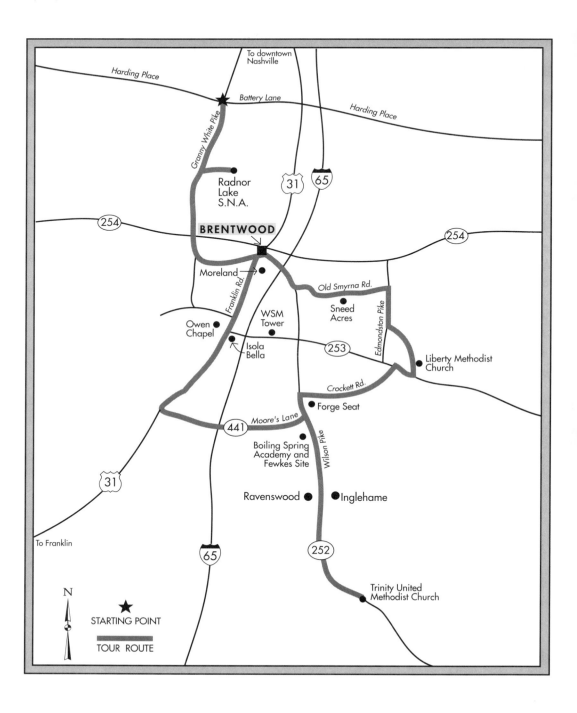

To downtown Nashville

Harding Place

Battery Lane

Harding Place

Granny White Pike

31

65

Radnor Lake S.N.A.

254

BRENTWOOD

254

Moreland

Old Smyrna Rd.

Franklin Rd.

Sneed Acres

Edmondston Pike

WSM Tower

Owen Chapel

253

Liberty Methodist Church

Isola Bella

Crockett Rd.

Forge Seat

Moore's Lane

441

Wilson Pike

Boiling Spring Academy and Fewkes Site

31

Ravenswood

Inglehame

To Franklin

65

252

Trinity United Methodist Church

N

★ STARTING POINT

▬▬▬ TOUR ROUTE

The Brentwood Tour

This tour through the Nashville suburbs includes some of the region's most impressive antebellum homes, each with a fascinating story to tell, and passes the prehistoric Indian site at Boiling Springs. It takes in Radnor Lake State Natural Area as well.

Total length: approximately 30 miles

This tour begins south of downtown Nashville at the intersection of Granny White Pike and Harding Place. Travel south on Granny White.

Harding Place roughly follows the Confederate line on the second day of the Battle of Nashville. The Union rout of General John Bell Hood's Confederates on December 16, 1864, ended Hood's ill-fated invasion of Tennessee. And for all practical purposes, it ended the Civil War in the West, though it would be five more months before Robert E. Lee's surrender at Appomattox, Virginia.

Following the battle at Franklin on November 30, 1864, the Federals fell back to Nashville's impregnable fortifications. (For information on the Battle of Franklin, see The Franklin Tour, pages 117–19.) Hood's depleted, hungry, and ragged Army of Tennessee followed the Federals north and dug in along a 4-mile front south of the city; the Confederate line ran parallel to the current route of Interstate 440. Hood hoped to lure the Federals out of their fortifications for a fight.

Union forces in Middle Tennessee were commanded by Major General George H. Thomas—the "Rock of Chickamauga"—a Virginian who remained loyal to the Union. Hood, the Confederate general, was fifteen years younger than Thomas, had been Thomas's student at West Point, and had served under Thomas in the Second Cavalry before the war.

His former student was only one of the problems George Thomas faced. The other was Ulysses S. Grant.

Grant's success in the West had landed him command of the entire United States army. He was the first person to hold the rank of lieutenant general since George Washington. From his headquarters near Petersburg, Virginia, where he had Robert E. Lee's army under siege, Grant had been trying to get Thomas to attack Hood's army. But Thomas had good reasons for not going after the Southerners entrenched on the outskirts of Nashville.

Thomas had no real army, just a collection of troops of various sorts, including four thousand noncombat personnel who worked in the huge Nashville supply depot. Reinforcements were on the way. Thomas wanted to wait, but Grant was unrelenting. "Attack Hood at once," he wired Thomas on December 6.

The weather then figured into Thomas's delay. Temperatures fell below zero by December 11—"Cold Sunday," as it came to be called. The Confederates particularly suffered from the cold, especially the three thousand or so men who were barefoot. More than a few froze to death. On December 13, Thomas informed Grant that the snow and ice made an attack impossible. From his vantage point far removed from the misery around Nashville, the impatient Grant decided to relieve Thomas of command.

On December 14, Grant left City Point, Virginia, for Washington, intending to continue to Nashville and take command himself. Grant prevailed upon President Lincoln and Secretary of War Edwin Stanton to approve of Thomas's removal. They did so reluctantly, for by all accounts except Grant's, George H. Thomas was one of the finest generals in the entire army. Grant wrote out the telegram relieving Thomas and gave it to Major Thomas T. Eckert of the telegraph office.

But Eckert could not send the wire. The lines to Nashville were down. Grant retired to the Willard Hotel to prepare to leave for Nashville. Meanwhile, back in Tennessee's capital city, the weather improved. On December 15, the Battle of Nashville began when the Federals moved out of their defenses and attacked Hood's Southerners. They overcame the Confederates, pushing them back a mile to the line along today's Harding Place.

That evening, the telegraph line to Nashville reopened. Eckert was under orders to send the telegram removing Thomas. But he hesitated. He knew the president and the secretary of war were uneasy with Grant's decision. Eckert held up sending the telegram until he heard some word from Nashville. At about eleven o'clock that night, a message arrived from Middle Tennessee—the battle had begun and the Federals were winning.

Eckert tore out of the telegraph office and rushed to Secretary Stanton's house. The two of them then hurried to the White House to rouse the sleeping president and give him the good news. On the way, Major Eckert confessed to Stanton that he had never sent the telegram. Stanton replied, "Major, if they court-martial you, they will have to court-martial me. . . . The result shows you did right." Lincoln, too, was pleased with Eckert's insubordination. By just a few minutes, the career of George H. Thomas was saved by a junior officer whose instincts told him to disobey an order of the nation's highest-ranking officer.

On the second day of the battle—December 16—the Confederate left flank was anchored on Shy's Hill, the high point that rises just west of Granny White Pike. (For a discussion of how Shy's Hill got its name, see The Harpeth River Tour, pages 133–34.) The right flank was anchored on the high ground east of the Franklin Pike. Troops in the Confederate center were protected by a stone wall that ran east to west.

By the end of the day, it was all over for Hood's Army of Tennessee. Those men not killed, wounded, or captured fled south on the Granny White and Franklin pikes. To the tune of "Yellow Rose of Texas," the dejected Southerners sang,

> So now I'm marching southward,
> My heart is full of woe;
> I'm going back to Georgia
> To see my Uncle Joe.
> You may talk about your Beauregard
> And sing of General Lee,
> But the gallant Hood of Texas
> Played hell in Tennessee.

Sewanee Road is the first street to the left off Granny White Pike. The stone wall used for cover by Lieutenant General A. P. Stewart's Confederate

Corps still stands behind the houses on Sewanee Road and Stonewall Drive, the street named for the famous wall.

Lucinda White ran an inn on this old road—the Middle Road to Franklin. Long after her death, "Granny" White became a national celebrity.

A frequent visitor to the inn during the first decade of the 1800s was the young Franklin lawyer Thomas Hart Benton. (For information on Benton's life in Tennessee, see The Harpeth River Tour, pages 155–56.) Years later, as a senator from Missouri, Benton was a major promoter of westward expansion. In a speech on the Senate floor pleading for legislation to give land to Western settlers, he referred to Granny White, a widowed innkeeper who had struggled from North Carolina to Tennessee with two orphaned grandchildren and an old slave. Why, Benton exclaimed, the land upon which Granny White settled was so steep that she had to prop up her pumpkins to keep them from rolling down the hillside. Yet she prospered, Benton went on, through industry, diligence, and perseverance.

Granny White had died in 1815 at seventy-three. Her celebrity status following the speech is recognized in the name of this lovely road. Her inn was located on the steep hillside where the pike enters the gap through the Harpeth Hills.

It is 1.8 miles on Granny White Pike to the intersection with Otter Creek Road. Turn left (E) and enter Radnor Lake State Natural Area.

The Louisville & Nashville Railroad built this eighty-acre lake in 1914 to supply water for steam engines at its new Radnor Yard. Very quickly, the lake became a stopover for migratory birds. In 1923, the L & N made the area a wildlife sanctuary.

When development threatened the pristine area, a massive grass-roots fund-raising effort led by state senator Douglas Henry resulted in its 1973 acquisition by the state of Tennessee. It became the first area acquired under the state's new Natural Areas Preservation Act. Expanded to 1,048 acres, the lake and surrounding hills are now home to a wide variety of wildlife, trees, and wildflowers. Hiking trails extend from parking lots at both the west and east entrances.

The road passes along the shore of the lake to the east parking area. Turn around and retrace Otter Creek Road to Granny White Pike. Turn left and go south on Granny White for 2 miles to Maryland Way. Turn left again.

You are now in Brentwood, the sprawling Williamson County suburb of Nashville. Though settlement of the area within the current limits of Brentwood began as early as the 1780s, the town did not form until the 1850s, when the railroad came through. It remained a quiet village on Franklin Road until the 1960s, when it began its transformation into a prosperous suburb.

The slavery-based agricultural economy of the area around Brentwood collapsed after the Civil War. Many of the magnificent antebellum mansions that line the main roads fell into disrepair. From the 1920s through the 1940s, a rebirth occurred, as affluent families bought and restored the mansions during what local history writer Vance Little calls the "Brentwood Renaissance." This community of new wealth centered around horses. The Hillsboro Hounds, a fox-hunting group, was organized in 1932. The Iroquois Steeplechase was first run in 1941.

The splendid mansions still stand out, though much of the rich land around them has been lost to development. Maryland Farm was a working horse farm started in 1937 by Truman Ward and named for his wife, Mary. The farm is now an office park. The Wards' 7,500-square-foot house is beautiful, but it is not one of the historic homes. It fronts Maryland Way on the right 0.7 mile from Granny White Pike.

Continue through the office park to Franklin Road (U.S. 31). Turn right (S).

Starting in Brentwood and extending through Franklin, Spring Hill, Columbia, and Mount Pleasant—a distance of about 50 miles—an unbroken chain of splendid antebellum homes lines the highway. This is not only the largest concentration of rural antebellum homes in Tennessee, but it is believed to be the largest concentration anywhere in the South. Most of these homes are visited on this tour, The Franklin Tour, and The Maury County Tour.

The first Brentwood antebellum house is Moreland, located on the left off Franklin Road 0.2 mile from the Maryland Way intersection. Moreland has been beautifully preserved by the owners of the office complex that surrounds it.

Moreland

Often incorrectly referred to as "colonial mansions," houses like those in Brentwood are characterized by their most prominent feature—their columns. Most of the antebellum houses in Brentwood are blends of the Georgian-Federal "glorified pioneer" style and the Greek Revival style popular in the three decades before the Civil War. Moreland is an exception. It is pure Greek Revival. The front-gabled roof and two-story full-width colonnaded porch beneath it give the home the appearance of a miniature Greek temple.

Moreland was built in 1838 on Robert Irvin's Revolutionary War grant by his grandson Robert Irvin Moore, a successful Nashville merchant.

The enlistment of Hugh Campbell Moore, son of Robert Irvin Moore, in the Second Tennessee Infantry was hardly ordinary. At age fourteen, young Moore slipped out a front bedroom window one night, took a waiting horse, and made off for the Confederate army. William B. Bate, the general who later served as Tennessee governor and United States senator, told the boy to go home. When Moore refused, Bate threatened to whip him as well as send him home. "I will come back if you do!" the boy replied. Bate allowed Moore to stay as a water boy. He eventually became a member of the regiment and served to war's end.

Continue south on Franklin Road to the intersection with Murray Lane.

Off to the left stands Green Pastures, barely visible when there is no foliage. This home, built in 1840, was originally called Hadleywood. Denny Porterfield and Elizabeth Smith Hadley built this house on two hundred acres granted to Elizabeth's grandfather, Captain James Leiper.

The story of James Leiper is one of joy and tragedy typical of those who lived—and died—on the frontier. Shortly after the April 1780 arrival of John Donelson's flotilla—which brought the women and children—the settlers on The Bluff above the French Lick were treated to their first social event, the wedding of James Leiper and Susan Drake. James Robertson performed the ceremony, the first known marriage west of the Cumberland Mountains. Unfortunately, the marriage was short-lived.

James Leiper was one of the casualties at the Battle of The Bluff, fought at Fort Nashborough on April 2, 1781. (For information about the Battle of The Bluff, see The Western Highland Rim Tour, pages 234–35.) In October of that year, Susan Leiper delivered their baby, Sarah Jane. Three years later, Susan died a tragic death. A gun fell from a rack, exploded, and killed the young mother. Sara Jane was raised by the Drake family and

later claimed her father's grant here along the Little Harpeth River. It was her daughter Elizabeth Smith who built Green Pastures.

The home underwent a thorough restoration during the Brentwood Renaissance. The new owners added a wrought-iron entrance gate that came from Killarney Castle in Ireland, along with a sundial in the garden that reportedly belonged to Anne Boleyn, one of Henry VIII's wives.

Stay on Franklin Road. Just past Murray Lane, the heavy, square columns of Mountview rise on the right. If Mountview has a different look from the other Brentwood antebellum mansions, there is a good reason for it. Completed in 1861, it was the last to be built, and it incorporates some details of the Italianate style, which was beginning to replace Greek Revival as the dominant American house style.

One night in the fall of 1865, a lone rider stopped at Mountview and asked the owner, William A. "Buck" Davis, if he might spend the night. When Davis found out that the man was on his way to Franklin to see about buying an estate, he talked him into buying Mountview. The next day, Ashley Rozell left owning a new house. Rozell, of French Huguenot descent, was a noted Methodist minister who retired from the clergy and accumulated considerable wealth before his death in 1886.

Ashlawn, the elegant, columned mansion across Franklin Road from

Ashlawn, built in the 1830s but substantially made over during the Brentwood Renaissance

Owen Chapel

Mountview, traces its beginning to the Leiper grant, as does Green Pastures. The house was built in the 1830s by another daughter of Sara Jane Leiper Smith, Mary Emeline Smith, and her husband, Richard Christmas. For a time, it was owned by the famed iron master Montgomery Bell. The full two-story Corinthian columns were added to the house in the 1940s by the Stirton Oman family.

Continue on Franklin Road to the next main intersection, Concord Road (TN 253).

Owen Chapel is the charming old meeting house on the right. Built in 1860 on land donated by James C. Owen, the building now houses a Church of Christ congregation that has had many prominent ministers. Among them was David Lipscomb, a gifted speaker and writer who edited the *Gospel Advocate*, a church periodical, and was a founder of Nashville Bible College, now known as David Lipscomb University. Owen Chapel was built with two doors, one for men and one for women. For many decades, a partition kept the genders separated at services.

Look down Concord Road and you will see the WSM radio tower. Beginning with the completion of the tower in 1932, WSM's Grand Ole Opry was beamed from this spot for many years. Started in 1925, America's longest-running radio show played a major role in the rise of country music as a popular art form.

The tower sent out another show, too, not as well known now as the Opry, but a big hit in its day. It was the daily passing of the Louisville & Nashville Railroad's passenger train, the Pan-American. On August 15, 1933, announcer Jack Harris reported, "We take you now to a point 12 miles south of Nashville to hear the actual sound of the L & N crack passenger train, the Pan-American, as it passes the 878-foot tower of WSM." The original pickup point for the broadcast was a small shed along the tracks within sight of the tower.

From that first broadcast until June 1, 1945, the afternoon passing of the Pan-American was a daily feature on WSM. It proved to be a great advertising gimmick for both the radio station and the railroad. Veteran engineers took pride in the music they made with the locomotive whistle, and the railroad could brag about the punctuality of the train, though the L & N did resort to recordings in later years, after the pickup point was changed to the Melrose tower, located closer to Nashville's Union Station.

Continue south on Franklin Road.

Past the southeast corner of Franklin and Concord roads stands yet another splendid antebellum home, Isola Bella, built around 1840 by James and Narcissa Merritt Johnson. The house is unusual in that it has two imposing main entrances, one facing north and the other west, each decorated with two-story columns. Its renovation by the John Oman family included a 1,500-light Waterford crystal chandelier and a white onyx mantel in the parlor that came from Victor Hugo's Paris apartment.

Isola Bella

Stay on Franklin Road past Isola Bella. This is an ancient route. When the first Europeans came to Middle Tennessee, they found a number of broad paths radiating out from what is now Nashville, site of the great salt lick. Salt is an essential ingredient in the diet of man and animals alike. Buffalo and other animals migrating to the great salt lick beat down these paths. The Indians used them, as did the explorers and the long hunters. They then became the main roads as Middle Tennessee began to fill with settlers after 1779. West End Avenue and Franklin, Murfreesboro, Dickerson, and Gallatin roads all follow the old buffalo paths.

The state began chartering and giving financial aid to private turnpike companies in the 1830s. Soon, a system of turnpikes radiated out of Nashville along the existing routes. The Nashville-Franklin Turnpike Company was the first to receive a charter. The road was built in 1834. As on the other turnpikes, toll gates stood along Franklin Road at regular intervals.

State aid to the turnpikes ended in 1840. For many years after that, there was no organized effort by the state to build and maintain roads. The construction and maintenance of main roads was almost exclusively in the hands of private companies. At one time, nine hundred private road companies operated in Tennessee. In 1915, the newly created Tennessee Highway Department began assuming responsibility for the main roads, most of which were rebuilt during the 1920s. These state and federal highways were the main roads until construction of the interstate highway system began in the 1950s as a result of legislation sponsored by Tennessee senator Albert Gore, Sr.

Franklin Road crosses a range of hills through Holly Tree Gap before intersecting Moore's Lane (TN 441). Turn left (E) on Moore's Lane. You will recross the range of hills, then cross the tracks of the old Nashville & Decatur Railroad. Moore's Lane passes the sprawling Cool Springs commercial development, named for nearby Cool Springs Farm.

The original log house at Cool Springs Farm, built by Dr. James Carothers, was enlarged and remodeled by his son Robert in 1850. In 1993, the city of Brentwood acquired the Cool Springs house and moved it to Crockett Park, where it has been carefully restored by volunteers.

Continue on Moore's Lane past Interstate 65. Maplelawn stands on the left 1 mile from the interstate. Built by Nathan Owen in 1830, the house was substantially made over in the Italianate style by Nicholas N. Cox in the 1870s. Cox represented Williamson and neighboring counties in Congress in the 1890s.

A road leads to the right into a golf-club development 0.2 mile past Maplelawn. The large structure visible from the road was built as a log house by Joseph Crockett, who came to the area from Virginia in 1808.

Continue 0.3 mile to an island of green pastures in this crowded suburban area.

The Owen-Primm House, on the left, was originally a log house built by

Maplelawn

Jabez Owen in 1806. New owner Thomas Perkins Primm contributed the larger frame addition in 1845. The house is notable for the slave cabins on the property, which share a common chimney.

The great spring here, Boiling Spring, and the fertile land along the Little Harpeth River's headwaters guarantee that this area was inhabited long before settlers began arriving around 1800. As Moore's Lane swings into an S curve past the Owen-Primm House, you will see a large mound in the pasture on the right. This is the site of one of the largest prehistoric Indian villages in the region, the Fewkes Group Site, named for Dr. J. Walter Fewkes, chief of the United States Bureau of American Ethnology. Fewkes visited the site in 1920, about the time Carthage, Tennessee, native William Edward Myer investigated it for the bureau.

The site and over two hundred like it were inhabited by a vanished culture that once flourished in this region. Estimates of the Middle Cumberland Culture's viable period vary, but it seems to have been from around 1000 A.D. until about 1700. The culture had disappeared by the time settlers came to Middle Tennessee; no one knows why it vanished or where its people went. The prehistoric villages that remain are characterized by large mounds, called temple mounds because they were used as pedestals for religious temples.

Of the five mounds Myer identified on the 14.6-acre site, only one is clearly visible today. Myer measured it at 23 feet, 8 inches high, 179 feet long, and 166 feet wide. Rectangular stone-lined graves containing remains in the prone position are common at Middle Cumberland Culture sites. But Myer found something different here. The remains at the Fewkes Site were in a flexed position, with the knees drawn up to the chest. And they were in hexagonal—almost circular—graves. This method of burial is found at a few sites in the Tennessee Valley to the south, but not in Middle Tennessee. Myer also found customary rectangular graves, leading him to conclude that the site was occupied twice, first by people who buried their dead in the flexed position and later by people who used the prone position.

Myer's digging uncovered pottery, tools, fabric, and even some charred grains of corn. These and animal bone fragments offer considerable insight into the habits of these ancient people. The vast majority of bones came from deer, but there were also remains of wild turkey, turtle, black bear, raccoon, skunk, gray fox, squirrel, rabbit, and small birds.

Myer also found the remains of an important house—the House of Mysteries, as he called it. The floor was a beautiful, smooth, black, glossy one, made so by the use of fire. The walls and roof were made by implanting poles in the ground about eighteen inches apart, bending them, and tying them together at the top. Cane was then woven in and out among the poles, after which the walls were covered with clay plaster on both the interior and exterior.

Boiling Spring Academy, located next to the Middle Cumberland culture mounds

The two-story brick building at the Fewkes Site is the former Boiling Spring Academy, a private school that operated from 1832 until about 1900, when it was replaced by public schools. The building also doubled as a Presbyterian church, whose congregation met here until the 1920s.

Moore's Lane ends at Wilson Pike (TN 252). Turn right (S).

Begun as the Harpeth Turnpike—a toll road—in the 1840s, the pike later took on the name of the turnpike company's major stockholder, James Hazard Wilson II. The Wilson family dominated this part of Williamson County from settlement until the Civil War.

A native of Ireland, James Hazard Wilson and his North Carolina wife, Ruth Davidson Wilson, settled in this area around 1800. Each of their nine children achieved prominence. Samuel D. Wilson was the secretary of state of Texas, and James Hazard Wilson II was one of the wealthiest men in the South when the nation divided in 1861. It was he who lent his name to the turnpike and who built the fine homes along it.

It is 1.8 miles on Wilson Pike to Ravenswood, on the right.

Co-lon-neh. It is the Cherokee word for raven. It was also Sam Houston's Cherokee name. When James Hazard Wilson II married Houston's cousin Emeline in 1821, Sam Houston was the best man. When Wilson built his first substantial home in 1825, he named it Ravenswood in honor of his friend. The house is magnificently preserved today.

"I could make money if I was chained to a rock," Wilson once declared. Indeed he did. In a time when wealth was measured in thousands of dollars, Wilson was worth millions in plantations, slaves, a steamboat line on the Mississippi, and other assets. Each year, Wilson brought fifty or so slaves to Middle Tennessee on boats from his Deep South

TOURING THE MIDDLE TENNESSEE BACKROADS

plantations in Mississippi and Louisiana, supposedly so they could benefit from a more healthful climate.

But wealth could not insulate Wilson from tragedy. His son Samuel died in 1851. The next year, his only daughter, Emeline, died. His sons Jason and George Washington died in 1854. Walter, age fourteen and a deaf-mute since infancy, was accidentally killed in 1856. His greatest blow came in 1860 with the death of his wife, Emeline. Wilson died a broken man at the home of one of his four surviving sons in 1869.

Continue south on Wilson Pike. The railroad that runs parallel to the pike—which you will cross and recross in narrow one-lane tunnels—is the last major railroad constructed in Middle Tennessee, completed between Brentwood and Athens, Alabama, by the L & N in 1914. It replaced the older Nashville & Decatur Railroad route through Franklin and Columbia as the main line south from Nashville.

After tunneling under the railroad a second time, you will reach Clovercroft at the intersection with Clovercroft Road West. Just down Clovercroft stands the James Wilson House, a typical frame, two-story Greek Revival home from the 1840s. Its builder was blind, and it is said that he inspected each piece of lumber by hand during the construction.

Approximately 1.2 miles from Clovercroft, turn left into the parking lot at Trinity United Methodist Church. This interesting Victorian-Romanesque structure was built in 1897. The original cast-iron hoop-and-dart fence in the front was made by the Stewart Ironworks in Cincinnati.

From the church, backtrack north on Wilson Pike to Ravenswood.

Across the pike from Ravenswood, the columns of Inglehame are visible through the trees. Using his considerable wealth, James Hazard Wilson II constructed substantial houses for his surviving sons. He built Inglehame, originally known as Harpeth, for James Hazard Wilson III in 1858 upon the son's marriage to Virginia Zollicoffer. Inglehame was substantially rebuilt by the Vernon Sharp family in the 1930s. The columns are twentieth-century additions.

Trinity United Methodist Church

The Zollicoffers were a prominent Nashville family. Felix, Virginia's father, was the first Confederate general killed in the Civil War. In both North and South, it was not unusual for politically prominent men to be appointed to high-ranking positions even though many had little or no military experience. Felix Zollicoffer, formerly a newspaper editor and congressman, was one of them. The winter of 1862 found Zollicoffer in the eastern part of Kentucky, a Confederate brigadier in command of the eastern end of the thin gray line across the Bluegrass State.

Zollicoffer was killed in a small battle on January 19, 1862—a battle known variously as Mill Springs, Logan's Crossroads, and Fishing Creek. Clad in a white raincoat that not only hid his uniform but made him an easy target, Zollicoffer found himself between the lines. He encountered a colonel from Kentucky. The two began to talk. Trouble was, it was a Union colonel. Zollicoffer had gotten himself into the area occupied by the Fourth Kentucky Infantry—the *Union* Fourth Kentucky. According to one version of the events, when the colonel realized who Zollicoffer was, he leveled his pistol and killed the Tennessean with a single shot to the chest.

The general's horse, recognized by the hole in its ear sustained in the battle, survived and was stabled at Ravenswood during the rest of the war. It became a favorite children's pet.

When West Point–educated James Hazard Wilson III left to fight in the Civil War, Virginia Zollicoffer Wilson's father-in-law, no doubt lonely following the deaths of his wife and children, invited her to move across the pike to Ravenswood and stay with him. She, her five motherless sisters, and her infant daughter spent the war years with James Hazard Wilson II.

Continue north on Wilson Pike and pass back under the railroad. Turn right into the Oak Hall subdivision 1 mile from Inglehame. Cross the railroad grade and take an immediate left onto Oak Hall Road. The house just ahead is Oak Hill, later known as Century Oak.

James Hazard Wilson II was not afraid to say that his oldest son, Samuel—the first of his children to die in the 1850s—was his favorite. When Samuel married Lucy Ann Marshall in 1845, the elder Wilson built this house for them. Lucy married one of Samuel's brothers following his death—a common occurrence in those days—and the couple continued to reside in the house. The many massive oak trees that once surrounded the place are gone now. Most were taken when the railroad came through.

Return to Wilson Pike and turn right (N). It is 1.1 miles from the Oak Hill subdivision to one of Brentwood's oldest and best-known landmarks, on the right. Forge Seat gets its name from Samuel Crockett's forge, which thrived here in the early days.

There is an interesting story about how Crockett's grandfather met his grandmother. They supposedly met as immigrants on the ship that brought them to America in 1715. Crockett the grandfather—also named Samuel— was twenty-one years old at the time. He met the family of a minister, John Thompson, and relieved the boredom of his long passage by watching the Thompson children play. When Samuel Crockett told the minister he would like to someday marry his five-year-old daughter, Esther, Thompson laughingly agreed. When Esther was grown, Crockett did just that.

One of their children was Andrew, a Revolutionary War soldier who came from Virginia to claim his grant. Andrew Crockett was living in this area by 1799. His son Samuel built the original two-story house, Forge Seat, in 1808 and later made some additions. The forge operated in a log building that still stands.

Samuel Crockett was best known as a gunsmith. Frontiersmen considered themselves fortunate if they owned a gun engraved "S. & A. C.," initials that stood for Samuel and his business partner–brother Andrew. It is said that Andrew Jackson visited Forge Seat to acquire weapons for his troops during the War of 1812. The forge operation was discontinued following Samuel Crockett's death in 1827.

Just past Forge Seat, turn right (E) onto Crockett Road. Crockett Park is on the left after 0.3 mile. The original Cool Springs Farmhouse is located in the back of the park.

It is another 0.4 mile on Crockett Road to Holtland, nestled in the trees on the hill. Built in 1840, this Georgian-Federal house with Greek Revival detailing is one of the best preserved in the region. Like the other old houses, its bricks were fired on the premises, and its woodwork comes from the ancient trees cut on the property. Holtland boasts two-inch-thick solid-walnut doors.

Holtland

Continue past Holtland to where Crockett Road ends at Concord Road (TN 253). Turn right (E). After 0.4 mile, turn left (N) off Concord onto Liberty Church Road. You will reach Liberty Methodist Church after 0.3 mile; bear left.

This building, constructed as a school in 1900, is typical of the frame schools built all over Tennessee during the advent of public education.

Liberty Methodist Church

Cottonport

Sneed Acres

Liberty Methodist Church began using the building when its days as a school ended in 1940. Liberty Church is one of the oldest Methodist congregations in Tennessee. Bishops Francis Asbury and William McKendree presided over the first Methodist conference west of the Appalachians near here in 1808.

Continue on Liberty Church Road to where it ends at Edmondston Pike. Turn right (N) and drive 1.3 miles to Old Smyrna Road. Turn left (W). As it passes through an island of rural tranquility in a sea of suburbia, Old Smyrna Road is surely one of the most lovely lanes in Middle Tennessee. It is not the old road to the town of Smyrna. Rather, it is named for Smyrna Church, organized in 1823, which once stood in the area.

After traveling through the cedars for 0.8 mile, you will reach Cottonport, the brick house on the right.

Early settler Sutherland Mayfield and his extended family built a station here. In 1788, Creek Indians attacked them as they worked outside the fort. Mayfield, one of his sons, and another man were killed. Another son, George Mayfield, was taken captive; he stayed with the Indians for twelve years. Following the attack on the Mayfields, the remaining settlers abandoned the site and moved to Raines' Station, closer to Nashville.

John and Rhoda Miles Frost were part of an exodus of Quakers from South Carolina in the early 1800s. Most of them went to Ohio, but the Frosts bought property from the Mayfields and settled in Williamson County. They built Cottonport around 1810. It is named for the community that grew up around it. Cottonport had a store, a gristmill, and a cotton gin. Its post office was located in the house.

Continue past Cottonport for 0.5 mile to Sneed Acres.

Sneed Acres is the oldest house on Old Smyrna Road and one of the oldest in Williamson County. James Sneed married Bethenia Harden Perkins, sister of Nicholas Tate Perkins and a member of the Perkins family that settled along the Harpeth River. (For the story of the Perkins family, see The Harpeth River Tour, pages 132–36.) The Sneeds built this log structure shortly after their arrival in 1798. It has since been covered with frame siding and lovingly restored.

Continue on Old Smyrna Road. The Sneeds' children constructed three fine homes along this route. Constantine Sneed built Windy Hill in 1825; it is on the left 0.2 mile past the original Sneed house. Across from Windy

Hill stands Foxview, built by Alexander Ewing Sneed shortly after his marriage to Elizabeth Guthrie in 1834.

William Temple Sneed's elegant 1830 two-story log house has been moved from its original site to Crockett Park. One of his children, William Joseph Sneed, a physician, played a prominent role in the establishment of one of Middle Tennessee's best-known educational institutions, Meharry Medical College.

While serving in the Confederate army, Dr. Sneed became acquainted with a Federal medical officer, Dr. George Whipple Hubbard. Hubbard conceived the idea to establish a medical school for blacks. When Samuel Meharry learned of Hubbard's search for funds for the new school in 1875, he and his brothers offered the initial contribution that made the school possible. Dr. Sneed served as an early member of the Meharry faculty.

Old Smyrna Road makes a sharp right turn at a stop sign on the edge of a subdivision, then curves back to the left to Wilson Pike. Turn right (N) on Wilson Pike and continue to where it ends at Church Street. Turn left. After passing under Interstate 65, turn right on Frierson Street and drive to Mount Lebanon Missionary Baptist Church, on the right.

East of Wilson Pike, Church Street was once called Hardscuffle Road, named for the early black community that formed here after the end of slavery. During the Union occupation of Middle Tennessee, slaves reacted differently to the opportunity for freedom. Some chose to remain with their masters. Some who were abandoned by their masters ran their former masters' farms for their own profit. Some moved to the city and thrived as craftsmen and businessmen. Some were mired in poverty in the city. Some were forced to work for the Union army without pay. But whatever economic route the freed slaves followed, they shared a common desire to control their social institutions.

Black churches were the first institutions to arise from emancipation, and Mount Lebanon Missionary Baptist Church was one of these early churches. It was founded in 1863 by liberated slaves led by the Reverend Larry Thompson. In 1908, the church purchased an abandoned school; that building still houses the venerable church.

Return to Church Street and turn right (W). The tour ends where Church Street meets Franklin Road. Nashville is to the right (N) and Franklin to the left (S).

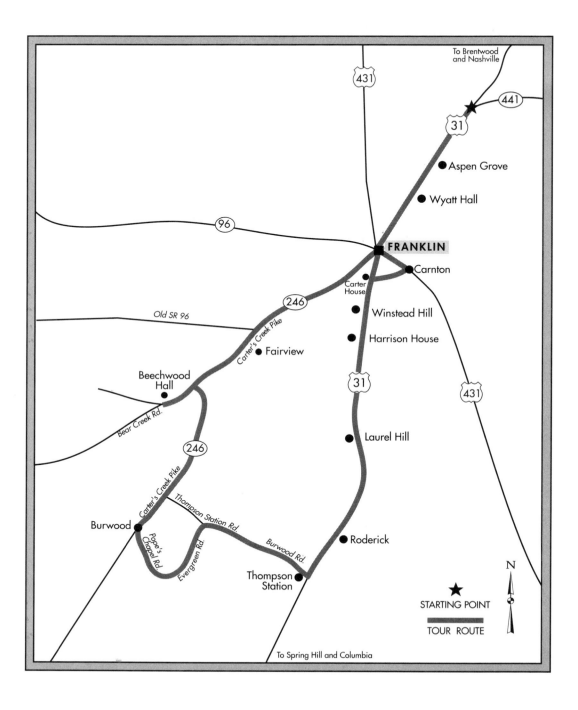

The Franklin Tour

This tour visits Franklin, Middle Tennessee's most beautiful town. It includes the site of the Civil War Battle of Franklin and two houses associated with it, Carnton and the Carter House. South of Franklin, the tour passes through the rolling Williamson County bluegrass and the quiet villages of Thompson Station and Burwood.

Total length: approximately 37 miles

This tour starts between Brentwood and Franklin at the intersection of Franklin Road (U.S. 31) and Moore's Lane (TN 441). Travel south on Franklin Road toward Franklin.

It is less than 20 miles from Fort Nashborough on Nashville's river front to the Harpeth River at Franklin, yet it took nearly twenty years for the tide of settlement to rise into the heart of what is now Williamson County. During the two decades following the Christmas Day 1779 arrival of James Robertson's expedition, the settlers stayed fairly close to the Cumberland River, mostly in Davidson and Sumner counties.

By 1796—the year of Tennessee's statehood—the constant threat of Indian attack was over, and there was rapid expansion into the countryside. In 1798, the families of four men—George Neely, Andrew Goff, William McEwen, and David McEwen—crossed Holly Tree Gap on the Old South Trail, the ancient buffalo path that is now Franklin Road. They joined the handful of settlers already living in the fertile Harpeth Valley. Others soon followed. Within a year, enough people had arrived to form a new county.

Williamson County was established in 1779 and named in honor of Dr. Hugh Williamson, surgeon general of the North Carolina militia, member of the Continental Congress, and signer of the Constitution. The county seat was named for his good friend Benjamin Franklin.

After 1.6 miles on Franklin Road, you will reach Aspen Grove, on the left.

Christopher McEwen was only eight years old when his family came over the gap into the Harpeth Valley. David, his father, built a log cabin as shelter for the family, a cabin that still stands on the golf course east of the highway. With the area rapidly filling with settlers, there was a demand for all sorts of implements and fixtures—hoes, axes, plows, hinges, nails—and David McEwen did well as a blacksmith. Christopher went off to war with Andrew Jackson, returned in 1815, married, and settled down here near his father. Christopher and his second wife, Narcissus Newsom, built this house in 1834 and named it for the aspen poplars they planted.

Aspen Grove took on a new, interesting life in 1994, when the Tennessee Golf Foundation renovated it for use as a hall of fame and museum. The additions to the rear include offices for several golfing organizations. The nine-hole "short course" that surrounds Aspen Grove doubles as the foundation's turf research center.

Continue south on Franklin Road past several of the substantial, well-preserved, old houses for which Williamson County is noted. At 0.7 mile from Aspen Grove, you will pass Creekside, on the left. Thomas Shute built this house around 1845 on land his father bought in 1801.

Wyatt Hall is the house on the left 0.3 mile past Creekside. No one knows for sure who built it, but it is one of the oldest houses in this part of Tennessee. It was completed around 1800. The walls are finished with plaster made of hog's hair, lime, and sand. Two original log outbuildings—a smokehouse and storage shed—also stand on the property.

As you enter Franklin, you will pass Truett Place, the large, columned house on the left 0.6 mile from Wyatt Hall. Alpheus Truett came to this area in the 1840s to establish his nursery business. Using glass imported from Philadelphia, Truett built Tennessee's first greenhouse. His frame house, built in 1846, served as the Union headquarters during the Battle of Franklin and survived the Civil War quite well, but the greenhouse was destroyed. The nursery business was rebuilt, and the Truett Floral Company stayed in business at this location until 1969.

Just past Truett Place, turn right (W) onto Myles Manor Court, the grand

Wyatt Hall

Jasmine Grove, formerly called Myles Manor

circular drive to impressive Jasmine Grove, formerly called Myles Manor. You will reach the house after 0.1 mile.

Though the rounded two-story portico supported by four columns fits the image of an antebellum plantation house, it was actually added in 1916. The house itself was built by William Maney and Martha Murfree—daughter of the man for whom Murfreesboro is named—in about 1840. Myles Manor is one of many buildings that doubled as a hospital following the Battle of Franklin. Being north of the river, it was used by Union troops. An inscription on an upstairs windowpane—"S. M. Frazer, February 25, 1867"—is thought to have been made by a Yankee veteran who returned after the war to marry one of his caregivers.

Myles Manor's most famous resident was a horse. When the Harlin family operated Harlinsdale Farm here in the 1940s, its walking horse, Midnight Sun, won two world championships and is said to have been the sire or grandsire of practically every champion for the next two decades. Known as a gentle stallion who allowed a mother cat to raise kittens in his stall, Midnight Sun lived until 1965.

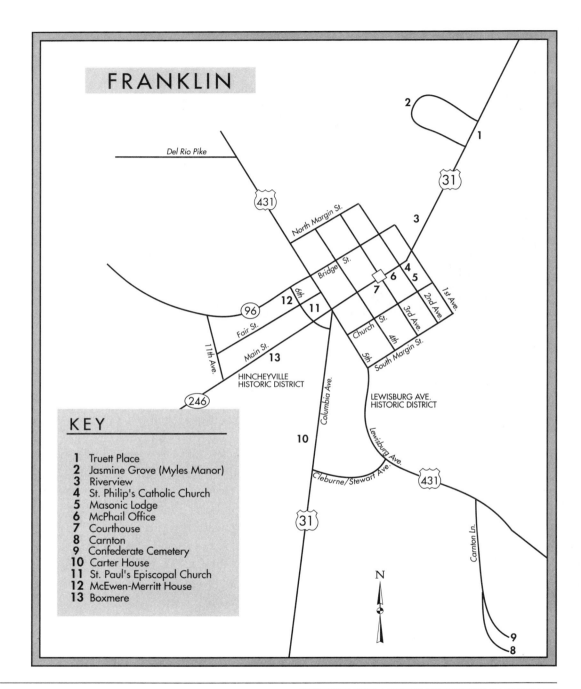

FRANKLIN

Del Rio Pike

431

31

North Margin St.

Bridge St.

6th

96

12

11

Fair St.

11th Ave.

Main St.

13

HINCHEYVILLE
HISTORIC DISTRICT

246

Church St.

5th

4th

3rd Ave.

2nd Ave.

1st Ave.

South Margin St.

LEWISBURG AVE.
HISTORIC DISTRICT

Columbia Ave.

Lewisburg Ave.

Cleburne/Stewart Ave.

431

10

31

Carnton Ln.

2

1

3

4

5

6

7

9

8

N

KEY

1 Truett Place
2 Jasmine Grove (Myles Manor)
3 Riverview
4 St. Philip's Catholic Church
5 Masonic Lodge
6 McPhail Office
7 Courthouse
8 Carnton
9 Confederate Cemetery
10 Carter House
11 St. Paul's Episcopal Church
12 McEwen-Merritt House
13 Boxmere

Continue past Jasmine Grove back to Franklin Road. Turn right. After 0.2 mile, you will pass Riverview, the large, columned mansion on the right above the Harpeth River. This is Franklin's "house of firsts." When Henry Hunter Mayberry and his wife, Marietta Watson, built the house in 1902, it was the first in town to have what was described as "a water works system," the first to have electric lights, and the first to have central heating. Mayberry was the man responsible for Middle Tennessee's two electric interurban railways, the Nashville-Gallatin and Nashville-Franklin lines.

Riverview

Past Riverview, Franklin Road becomes Main Street; from Riverview, it is 0.3 mile to the intersection of East Main Street (U.S. 31) and Second Avenue in the heart of Franklin. Founded in 1799, Franklin is without question Middle Tennessee's most beautiful town. Partly out of fear of being overrun by Nashville's sprawl, Franklin's citizens have gone to great lengths to preserve and display their considerable heritage.

At East Main Street and Second Avenue stands St. Philip's Catholic Church. The original part of the church was built in 1871, but the church's history at this location dates to 1847, when Bishop Richard P. Miles acquired the John Henry Eaton property.

John Henry Eaton was an important man in his day. From 1818 until 1829, he served in the United States Senate, then as secretary of war under his friend Andrew Jackson, the first president who was not from either Virginia or Massachusetts. Eaton was governor of the Florida Territory from 1834 to 1836, then minister to Spain until 1840. All his lofty offices notwithstanding, Eaton is best remembered for one of Washington's early scandals—the Peggy Eaton Affair.

"In case anything should happen to me, there is only one man to whose hands I should be willing to entrust you, and that is John H. Eaton." With those words, navy officer John Timberlake said good-bye to his wife in a letter he wrote from a Mediterranean island. Within four months of his death—possibly by suicide—Peggy Timberlake married one of Washington's most handsome, sought-after bachelors, Franklin's John H. Eaton.

It didn't take long for the gossip to start. During his Senate career, Eaton boarded at the hotel run by Peggy's father, William O'Neale, and became a close friend of the O'Neale family. Peggy was pregnant with Eaton's child when they married—or so the rumor went.

It was untrue—Peggy and John never had children together—but by the time Andrew Jackson arrived in Washington for his March 1829 inauguration, it was a full-blown scandal. The Eatons were shunned in polite society. Cabinet wives refused to attend functions if the wife of the secretary of war was on the guest list. One foreign ambassador went so far as to invite every cabinet member except Eaton to a formal dinner.

If not promiscuous, Peggy Eaton was certainly provocative. At a ball, she would head straight for a crowd of her detractors just to watch them scatter. But pretty Peggy Eaton tired of being an outcast, so she decided to get to the source of the rumors. She traced them to a minister in Philadelphia and, with her mother, traveled there to confront him. He admitted being a source but said he had heard the stories about Peggy and John's premarital liaisons from a Washington minister. "Good God!" Peggy exclaimed. "Can it be possible that . . . the clergy have taken upon themselves to tear reputations to pieces rather than to perform the part of the peace maker?" Peggy made the ministers promise to recant the rumors, but the scandal raged on. It was the biggest news in Washington.

Secretary Eaton and his famous wife spent the second summer of Jackson's administration at Eaton's Franklin home. By then, everyone in the country had an opinion about Peggy Eaton, and the people in Franklin were no exception. But for the most part, she was well received in town. President Jackson later recorded his pleasure when, on an unannounced trip to Franklin that summer, he came upon a barbecue given in Eaton's honor by several hundred of his old friends.

Andrew Jackson was no stranger to the type of rumor that was destroying his young presidency. For years, he and Rachel, his wife, had been hounded by endless gossip over their marriage, which took place before she was legally divorced from her first husband. Rachel's recent death no doubt heightened Jackson's sensitivity. He was solidly on Peggy's side.

As might be expected in Washington, there was a political cast to the furor. Jackson's enemies—and there were always plenty of them—kept the scandal alive. Vice President John C. Calhoun split with Jackson over the issue of national sovereignty, but Peggy Eaton played no small part in their breach. Mrs. Calhoun was among the most prominent of the Peggy Eaton haters. Partly in response to Jackson's steadfast support of the innkeeper's daughter, Calhoun was the first of only two vice presidents in our nation's history to resign his office.

The controversy over Peggy Eaton split Jackson's own family, too. In the absence of a first lady, Emily Donelson, the wife of Rachel's nephew Andrew Jackson Donelson, was the hostess of the White House. The Donelsons actually left Washington for a time in 1830 rather than accept Peggy Eaton. Jackson's cabinet was badly split over the matter, but Jackson was reluctant to dismiss the dissidents for fear of alienating their allies in Congress.

The controversy swirling around Peggy Eaton dominated the first two years of Jackson's eight years in office. It finally ended in the spring of 1831, when Secretary of State Martin Van Buren and John H. Eaton both resigned, paving the way for Jackson to pick a whole new cabinet. Van Buren's loyalty to Jackson in the Peggy Eaton affair earned him Jackson's support in Van Buren's own quest for the White House. He succeeded Jackson as president.

In 1831, the Eatons returned to make their home in Franklin. They later left for John's service as governor of the Florida Territory in 1834, then went on to four glorious years at the court in Madrid. After Spain, they lived in Washington, where John died in 1856.

Peggy became a rather pathetic character in her later years. At age sixty-one, she married her grandchildren's nineteen-year-old dance instructor. After seven years of lavish living, he tricked her out of her property and ran off with her sixteen-year-old granddaughter. Peggy died in poverty in 1879 at age eighty.

The 1823 Masonic Lodge is located on Second Avenue behind St. Philip's. This structure has hosted many important gatherings over its long life, including religious gatherings that had a part in the birth of two Protestant denominations in Tennessee.

The Masonic Lodge

Like John H. Eaton, James H. Otey attended the University of North Carolina. In 1821, at age twenty-one, Otey and his young bride arrived in Franklin, where he succeeded Presbyterian minister Gideon Blackburn as headmaster of Harpeth Academy. After returning to North Carolina to study for the ministry, he was ordained into the Episcopal priesthood in 1827. He then returned to Franklin and organized St. Paul's, the first Episcopal congregation in Tennessee. The Franklin congregation, too small for

Dr. McPhail's office, now home to the Heritage Foundation

The iron columns of the Williamson County Courthouse

its own church building, met at the Masonic Lodge until St. Paul's Church was completed in 1834. For a time, music was provided by none other than Peggy Eaton, an accomplished pianist. Otey later served as the first Episcopal bishop of Tennessee.

Alexander Campbell was at the opposite end of the Protestant spectrum. From his Virginia home, he launched a movement based upon Biblical literalism. By the 1830s, the Disciples of Christ emerged as a major independent denomination. Located mostly in the West—which included Tennessee in those days—the Disciples numbered an estimated two hundred thousand by 1860. Campbell made several trips to Franklin to preach at the Masonic Lodge. At one gathering in 1851, he converted four hundred people to his branch of the faith.

A schism began developing before the Civil War, as congregations gradually left the Disciples movement one by one, a process accelerated after the Civil War under the leadership of pacifist David Lipscomb. By 1900, the schism was complete. In Tennessee, most Campbellite congregations began calling themselves Churches of Christ. The Disciples eventually became known as the Christian Church.

The little building on the left of Main Street just past Second Avenue is the 1813 McPhail doctor's office. It is now home to the Heritage Foundation, the place to park your car for a walking tour of Franklin. The Heritage Foundation offers a brochure for a thirty-eight-stop, fifteen-square-block walking tour; the brochure can also be obtained at city hall, located one block away at Third and Main. The walking tour takes in houses, churches, and commercial and public buildings, almost all of them built before the Civil War.

After you have enjoyed your walking tour of Franklin, drive south from the Heritage Foundation office on Main Street. You will circle the square and pass through the restored commercial district.

The Williamson County Courthouse, located on the square, may look like it was built yesterday, but it is among the oldest in the state, one of only seven antebellum courthouses in Tennessee's ninety-five counties. The pediment on the 1858 building is supported by four thirty-foot fluted iron columns forged at the Caney Fork Furnace near Fernvale and hauled by wagon to Franklin.

One of the highlights of old Franklin is its commercial district. In 1993, the National Trust for Historic Preservation and other organizations hosted a conference on downtown revitalization—and for good reason, they held it in Franklin. As businesses fled to strips and malls in the 1960s and 1970s, a determined group of merchants and property owners vowed to keep downtown Franklin alive. Their success is apparent from the thriving businesses around the square, along the nineteenth-century Main Street, and on the side streets as well.

Franklin's Square

When you reach Five Points—the U.S. 31/U.S. 431/TN 96 junction— turn left (SE) onto U.S. 431 (Fifth Avenue). After 0.2 mile, stay on U.S. 431 as it threads its way through another intersection. U.S. 431 follows Lewisburg Avenue through the lovely Lewisburg Avenue Historic District, a "new" part of Franklin developed after the Civil War.

After 0.7 mile, turn right onto Carnton Lane. At the fork after 0.6 mile, go right to Carnton Plantation House, one of two Franklin houses prominently associated with the Battle of Franklin. The left fork goes to the Confederate cemetery on the Carnton grounds.

The arrival of Major General John M. Schofield's Federal army corps and the prospects for witnessing a battle excited fifteen-year-old Hardin Perkins Figuers. When the battle came, the boy climbed a tree near his Franklin house and watched. Any romantic thoughts about war left him early in the morning on December 1, 1864. As he later wrote, "It might be said without exaggeration that one could walk upon the dead and never touch the ground." Death and suffering surrounded him. Of all the horror Figuers saw that day, nothing affected him as much as the sight of a dead Union soldier who looked to be about his own age.

Stupid. Irrational. Stubborn. And above all, *aggressive.* Men on both sides of the great conflict used such words to characterize John Bell Hood. Smarting from being outfoxed the night before in "The Affair at Spring Hill," the young Confederate general was looking for a fight on November 30, 1864. (For information about the Spring Hill affair, see The Maury County Tour, pages 191–94.) John M. Schofield, Hood's old West Point classmate, did not want a fight at Franklin. His goal was to get his Federal army across the Harpeth River and join his commanding general, George H. Thomas, in Nashville.

But the Army of Tennessee caught up with Schofield's army at Franklin. Schofield ordered his wagon trains across the Harpeth and on to Nashville. He told his soldiers to dig in south of Franklin and hold off any attack. It proved to be a good defensive position. The bends in the Harpeth River protected Schofield from what he feared most, a flanking movement. Franklin was also well fortified with entrenchments built during nearly three years of Union occupation. And Schofield had plenty of artillery to rip through Southern flesh if there was an attack.

To Hood's subordinate generals standing on Winstead Hill some 2 miles south of town, it looked like a disaster waiting to happen. Their hungry, ragged veterans, exhausted from the forced march up from Spring Hill, would have to cross a 2-mile plain and make a frontal assault on an entrenched enemy. On top of that, one-third of Hood's infantry and practically all of his artillery were still on the road to Spring Hill. It was a suicide mission. But Hood insisted.

Shortly after four in the afternoon, the Southerners threw themselves against the Franklin fortifications.

Sam Watkins, a foot soldier from nearby Columbia, went through the entire Civil War with the Army of Tennessee and lived to tell about it. Franklin, Watkins writes, was "the blackest page in the history of the war of the Lost Cause . . . the bloodiest battle of modern times in any war . . . the finishing stroke to the independence of the Southern Confederacy."

He describes the assault this way: " 'Forward men,' is repeated all along the line. A sheet of fire was poured into our very faces. . . . 'Forward, men!' The air loaded with death-dealing missiles. . . . It seemed that the very elements of heaven and earth were in one mighty uproar. 'Forward, men!' And the blood spurts in a perfect jet from the dead and wounded. The earth is red with blood. It runs in streams, making little rivulets as it flows. . . . We advanced on toward the breastworks, on and on. I had made up my mind to die."

"Five tragic hours" is how Civil War historians James Lee McDonough and Thomas L. Connelly describe the Battle of Franklin. As they note, it was not one of the biggest battles of the war, but it was one of the most intense. Accurate statistics are hard to come by, but it is estimated that of the 23,000 Southern infantrymen engaged in the assault, a staggering 7,000 were lost, including 1,750 killed, 3,800 seriously wounded, and 702 missing. These losses exceeded those at some of the better-known battles, where three to four times as many Southern soldiers were engaged. Schofield, on the other hand, lost 2,326 men, including 189 killed.

One sobering feature of the Battle of Franklin is the number of Confederate generals lost—six killed, five wounded, and one captured. This gruesome record was unmatched in any other Civil War battle.

Carnton

Many of the Confederate wounded were taken to Carnton, John McGavock's fine two-story plantation house built in 1826 by his father, Randall McGavock. Caroline Winder McGavock, John's wife, labored with others nursing the wounded. She used up her linens for bandages, then her husband's shirts, and finally her own undergarments. It was a chaotic scene. Surgeons were kept busy, and before long, wagonloads of severed limbs were being hauled away. At one time, the bodies of four dead generals—Adams, Cleburne, Granbury, and Strahl—lay on Carnton's veranda.

The bodies of four Confederate generals once lay on Carnton's back veranda.

The Confederate dead were hastily buried on the battlefield in groups according to their states. The crude wooden markers erected at the mass graves did not last long, for Franklin's desperate poor began to take them for firewood. In 1866, Carnton's John McGavock donated two acres of land for a cemetery. Money was raised from most of the states whose sons were buried at Franklin, and the remains were reinterred here at this peaceful spot.

Today, Carnton is owned by a nonprofit association. It and the cemetery are open to the public year-round.

When you are ready to leave Carnton, backtrack to Lewisburg Avenue and turn left. After 0.3 mile, turn left (W) onto Stewart Avenue. Stewart crosses Adams after 0.1 mile, where it becomes Cleburne. Continue west 0.2 mile to Columbia Avenue (U.S. 31) and turn right (N). It is 0.2 mile to the turn on the left for the Carter House.

The Confederate cemetery at Carnton

If the Union line had a weak point, it was here at the Carter House. The Northerners left a gap through the earthworks to permit passage of their wagon trains fleeing the Confederate advance. The Federal commander in the area, Brigadier General Jacob Cox, made up for the breach by placing several artillery batteries along the road. It was a deadly arrangement. The fighting around the Carter House was the most desperate of the day.

Carter House

Young Hardin Figuers describes what he found the next morning: "In front of the Yankee battery which faced the Columbia Pike you would find a man with his head shot off. Others had arms and legs shot off, and some were cut in twain, or almost so."

At one point during the fighting, some Southerners made it over the Federal entrenchments. But night came early on that last day of November, and the shooting that had begun at four that afternoon ended by nine. During the night, Schofield gave the order to withdraw. He had accomplished his goal of protecting his trains. By daylight, the Union soldiers were well on their way to Nashville's secure fortifications.

Fountain Branch Carter and his wife, Mary Armistead Atkinson, built this distinctive house between 1828 and 1830. Their farm eventually grew to 288 acres. Mary and five of their twelve children died before the Civil War.

The Carters' three surviving sons all joined the same Confederate company in 1861. Two of them were back home recovering from wounds and sickness and seeking protection in the cellar with the rest of the family at the time of the battle. The third son, Tod, was on his way home. He was in Hood's army. From the hill south of town, he could see the house he had not seen in three and a half years. He would be there before long, he remarked to his comrades.

At daybreak after the battle, word came to the Carters that Tod lay wounded near the house. Family members made their way through the death and destruction and found the young captain. He was lying on the Federal breastworks. Using an overcoat as a litter, the family took his limp body to the house. He lived only forty-eight hours.

The Carter House was acquired by the state of Tennessee in 1951 and fully restored to its Civil War appearance. The separate brick kitchen, the frame farm office, and the brick smokehouse survive, but the cotton gin across the road was lost. The Carter House includes a museum and is open to the public all year.

Leaving the Carter House, turn right (S) on Columbia Avenue. You will pass through Franklin's industrial area. After 2 miles, turn into the Winstead Hill parking area, on the right.

The steps at this site climb steeply to an overlook that offers the same view John Bell Hood had when he got his first look at the Federals digging in around Franklin. A small shelter covers a metal relief map describing the action on November 30, 1864, and a hillside monument honors Major General Patrick Cleburne, one of the six Confederate generals lost at Franklin.

Patrick Cleburne marker at Winstead Hill

If there was anyone who should have been in command of the Army of Tennessee that day, it was Cleburne. He never owned a slave. He was not a secessionist. Yet when the Civil War erupted, he joined his friends from Arkansas in the Southern cause. He was an exemplary general in every respect, referred to once by Confederate president Jefferson Davis as the "Stonewall Jackson of the West." Twice he had been honored by resolutions passed by the Confederate congress. When a vacancy at the corps command level occurred around the beginning of 1864, this division commander was the logical choice to receive the promotion to lieutenant general. But it never happened.

Cleburne was not a West Point man. He was not even a native of the United States. He came from Ireland. At age seventeen, he had run away from his County Cork home and joined the British army. After three years

in Her Majesty's Forty-First Regiment of Foot, he left the army. He migrated to the United States in 1849 and settled in Helena, Arkansas, where he was a successful pharmacist and lawyer. He joined the Confederate army as a private. Within a year, he was a brigadier general.

The Confederate president may have admired Pat Cleburne's ability, but the Mexican War hero and former secretary of war was not likely to appoint to corps command a foreigner who was not trained at the United States Military Academy. Davis felt strongly about that. Then, too, Cleburne was on the wrong side of Braxton Bragg, the unsuccessful former commander of the Army of Tennessee, a man who had the president's ear.

But it was probably Cleburne's dramatic proposal of January 1864 that sealed his fate with Davis. It was Cleburne's opinion that, from a military standpoint, slavery was the Confederacy's greatest weakness. It would be only a "concession to common sense" to give blacks their freedom and enlist them in the Confederate army. When fellow general W. H. T. Walker—a hard-core Georgia secessionist—asked Cleburne to put his proposal in writing, the politically naive Irishman was unaware that the general intended to mail it to Jefferson Davis, along with a biting comment. A shocked Davis ordered that all such discussions cease. That was the end of it. And that was the end of any chance for promotion for Patrick Cleburne.

Cleburne counseled Hood against the Franklin attack. But when he saw that it was inevitable, he did as ordered and rode to a meeting with his brigade commanders. One of them, Daniel C. Govan, wrote of the meeting after the war, "General Cleburne seemed to be more despondent than I ever saw him. I was the last one to receive any instructions from him, and as I saluted and bade him good-bye, I remarked, 'Well, General, there will not be many of us that will get back to Arkansas,' and he replied, 'Well, Govan, if we are to die, let us die like men'."

Continue south from Winstead Hill. The tour follows U.S. 31 through prosperous Williamson County farm country lined with antebellum homes, each with an interesting story to tell. The Harrison House is on the right 0.4 mile past Winstead Hill.

Harrison House

Situated as it is on the road between Spring Hill and Franklin, this stately 1848 mansion was destined to play a role in the battle. It was here that John Bell Hood met with his generals after his first look from Winstead Hill and outlined his plans for the frontal attack. Nathan Bedford Forrest, commanding Hood's cavalry, had a better idea—take the cavalry and some infantry, cross the Harpeth River upstream from Franklin, and block the road to Nashville at Holly Tree Gap. Schofield's Federals would be trapped. But Hood was resolute. Forrest was less restrained than taciturn former British soldier Patrick Cleburne. Following a sharp exchange with his army commander, Forrest left "in a towering rage," as it was later reported.

Like the houses closer to Franklin, the Harrison House was a place to bring the wounded. "Tell her that I have always loved her devotedly and regret leaving her more than I can express"—these were among the last words of John Carpenter Carter, spoken in response to a chaplain's request for a message to Carter's wife. When the twenty-seven-year-old brigadier general from Memphis died here ten days after the battle, he became the sixth Southern general lost at Franklin.

Carter was not the first general to die at the Harrison House. Earlier in the fall of 1864, Confederate calvary leader Joseph Wheeler brought his men up from the Atlanta area on one of his sensational but ineffective raids behind enemy lines. John Herbert Kelly, the youngest brigadier

Laurel Hill

general in the Confederate army, was shot nearby and brought to the Harrison House, where he died two days later.

Continue south through the rolling bluegrass. After 3.4 miles, you will pass Laurel Hill, on the right. This home was completed by James P. Johnson in 1834. Laurel Hill's thin columns, added later, are unusual in this area, where two-story porticoes are usually supported by heavy square or round columns. Laurel Hill boasts floors of ash, poplar, and walnut that are two and a half inches thick. Mountain laurel once grew on the Middle Tennessee hillsides—that is how the house got its name.

At 2.5 miles from Laurel Hill, you will see the house called Roderick in the trees on the hill to the left.

This house is named for a horse. Long before the Army of Tennessee was pushed into Georgia and defeated around Atlanta in September 1864—the event that set the stage for Hood's Tennessee invasion—the army was in Middle Tennessee. On March 5, 1863, Union colonel John Coburn led a force out from Franklin on a scouting and foraging mission and was met by Nathan Bedford Forrest's Confederate cavalry in what came to be called the Battle of Thompson Station. Forrest's men carried the day, but not without a severe loss to the Memphis general—his favorite horse, Roderick, with him since the beginning of the war, was killed. It was buried on this property.

Homestead Manor is the impressive house on the right 0.7 mile from Roderick. Francis and Mary Giddens came to this southern part of Williamson County from Virginia in 1800 and completed a Georgian-Federal house in 1819. It was uncommon for houses to have a third floor in those days, but the Giddenses built one so their house could double as an inn. The home was later made over in the Greek Revival style, giving it the appearance it has today.

U.S. 31 intersects Thompson Station Road 0.2 mile past Homestead Manor. Here, the tour leaves the heavily traveled highway and circles back to Franklin on quiet rural roads. Along the way, it passes through several pleasant villages and past a number of historic houses and commercial buildings, as well as a century-old one-room schoolhouse.

Turn right off U.S. 31 onto Thompson Station Road. Keep alert to the fact that the road makes a number of right-angle turns before the next turn at Evergreen Road.

You will pass the lovely 1876 Thompson Station United Methodist Church before reaching the Thompson Station Bank building, located across from the restored railroad depot 0.4 mile from U.S. 31.

The first two decades of the twentieth century were great times for farmers in America, and little towns like Thompson Station thrived. Most had a bank, and Thompson Station was no exception. This building was built in 1913 and housed the bank until the late 1920s.

One of the strangest events in Thompson Station occurred when T. H. "Daddy" Timmons brought a wheelbarrow to the bank and told President C. B. Alexander he wanted all his money. Alexander gave the man his ten thousand dollars, and Timmons went on his way, pushing his wheelbarrow full of money. Ten thousand dollars was a good deal of cash in those days, and Alexander had to make a quick trip to Franklin to replenish his supply. The next day, Timmons returned, pushing his wheelbarrow of money. He had just wanted to see if it was all there, he told Alexander.

Railroads were the principal source of transportation before the highway expansion of the 1920s. Thompson Station was an important shipping

Thompson Station

Plaque on Thompson Station Bank

Thompson Station Bank

point for the hogs, cattle, sheep, and grain raised in its fertile environs. The pleasant little town is no longer the hub it once was, but the region is still one of Tennessee's most prosperous farming areas.

Continue on Thompson Station Road. After 0.6 mile, you will pass a substantial farmhouse, located on the right. To the left on a rise across the pasture stands the Moss Side Farmhouse.

This house has seen many changes since the first part of it was built in 1815, but it has remained in the same family since that time. The land on which it rests originally belonged to Homestead Manor's Francis Giddens, who deeded it to his son James. In her valuable book *Historic Williamson County*, Virginia McDaniel Bowman points out that the marriages of the children of James and Priscilla Buford Giddens make the work of a genealogist confusing, if not impossible. The three Giddens daughters married three Moss brothers. And three Giddens sons married Bufords.

Thompson Station Road intersects Evergreen Road 1 mile from Moss Side Farm. Turn left on Evergreen and follow it through the open fields and forested hillsides. It is 1.3 miles to the 1835 Jacob Critz House, on the right. At 0.9 mile from the Jacob Critz House, bear right on Evergreen where it intersects Lavender Road.

The steep ridge rising to the south is Duck River Ridge, part of the Tennessee Valley Divide, which separates the watersheds of the Tennessee and Cumberland rivers. Here, the ridge rises three hundred feet above the fertile valleys and hollows of the West Harpeth River and its feeder streams.

Turn right onto Pope's Chapel Road 1 mile from the Lavender Road intersection.

Eastview, the house facing Pope's Chapel Road just past Evergreen Road, was built by John Pope, one of the most influential men in the early days of this part of Williamson County. In addition to being a major landowner, Pope was a lay Methodist minister who had no use for bishops and other forms of church hierarchy. He preached regularly around the countryside, drawing large crowds to his camp meetings.

The original part of Eastview was built of logs in 1806.

After 1.1 miles on Pope's Chapel Road, you will arrive at the pleasant village of Burwood. Turn left into the parking area between the church and Huff's Store.

John Pope provided land for a church here in 1818. It came to be called Pope's Chapel and was used by several denominations. The chapel was destroyed by a tornado in 1910. The current Burwood United Methodist Church was erected in 1912.

Huff's Store

Huff's Store is one of the last full-service general stores in Middle Tennessee. Built in 1911, it served the needs of a population limited in its ability to travel great distances. Rural general stores carried just about everything anyone needed—food, clothing, hardware, medicine. When automobiles and paved roads made it easier to get to larger towns, the general stores started closing, and most are no longer standing. Huff's Store is more akin to a convenience market now, but visitors can get the feel of what a general store was like by lingering a bit in its spacious interior.

Carter's Creek Pike (TN 246) is the main road in front of Huff's Store. Turn right (NE) onto it for a drive through the rich Williamson County countryside.

The old, one-room Forest Hills School stands on the side of the hill to the right 4.3 miles from Burwood. Like Liberty School in Brentwood, this is a fine example of the hundreds of one-room schools built in Tennessee with the advent of widespread public education after 1900. It continued as a school until the arrival of consolidated schools in the 1940s.

Beechwood Hall

Turn left onto Bear Creek Road 0.1 mile past Forest Hills School. After 0.3 mile, you will reach the drive to Beechwood Hall, the magnificent mansion that caps the hill on the right at the end of the drive.

Sophronia Hunter Mayberry and Henry George Washington Mayberry built this house in the twilight of the antebellum South on land given to them by Henry Hunter, Sophronia's father. The Mayberrys wanted nothing but the best, and in the latest style, so the detailing on the 1856 house is in the Italianate style, rather than the Greek Revival style. Among its distinctive features are an entrance hall forty feet long and twenty feet wide and a circular stairway that has no visible means of support. The Mayberrys' neighbors were impressed with the stairway, but they were also suspicious about its strength. To prove its safety, the biggest and strongest workers on the place were brought in to stand in pairs on each of the twenty-five steps. The stairway passed the test.

Continue past Beechwood Hall a short distance to Bailey Road. Turn

Fairview

around and backtrack to Carter's Creek Pike. Turn left (NE). After 0.3 mile, you will pass the house Samuel S. Morton built in 1850, located on the left. Another splendid antebellum mansion, Fairview, will come into view on the right after 0.4 mile.

Edward Swanson was a member of James Robertson's exploratory trip to the Middle Cumberland in 1779. He returned with Robertson later that year to begin the permanent settlement of Middle Tennessee. Swanson eventually acquired considerable land in this area. Before he died in 1840, he sold some of it to Claiborne H. Kinnard. Kinnard and his wife, Elizabeth Fleming, built Fairview in 1850. The home's columns give the appearance of the style popular in that day, but they were actually added by the Kinnards' son during remodeling in 1898. The porches the junior Kinnard added nearly surround the house. In fact, they caused one family member to remark that the junior Kinnard had a "porch fit" when he was planning the additions.

Stay on Carter's Creek Pike for 1.6 miles past Fairview to the stop sign at Southall. Continue north on Carter's Creek Pike as it enters Franklin and becomes West Main Street. West Main rounds a curve and climbs a small rise 3.2 miles from the stop sign at Southall.

The two impressive Greek Revival houses that flank the street just short of Eleventh Avenue signal the entrance to Hincheyville. This part of town gets its unusual name from Hinchna Petway, the man who in 1819 developed this first addition to Franklin. Today, Petway's development forms a historic district embracing West Main and Fair streets and several numbered avenues connecting them.

Continue on West Main for several blocks until it becomes a one-way street at Seventh Avenue at the 1877 Cumberland Presbyterian church; St. Paul's Episcopal Church is located diagonally across the street. Park here to enjoy a brief walking tour of this part of Franklin.

A walk through Hincheyville is a walk through a living history museum displaying a century of American residential architecture. Some ninety-two residences have construction dates ranging from 1828 to the 1930s. The district includes a wide variety of styles—Federal, Greek Revival, Italianate, Queen Anne, Four Square, Bungalow, and Tudor.

From St. Paul's, walk up Sixth Avenue North to Fair Street. Turn left

on Fair. The impressive Italianate house at 612 Fair Street was built by John B. McEwen, son of Aspen Grove's Christopher McEwen. Until recently, it was the home of Gilbert S. Merritt, chief judge of the United States Sixth Circuit Court of Appeals.

Walk west on Fair Street past several well-preserved Victorian-era houses until Fair ends at Eleventh Avenue. Turn left on Eleventh, return to West Main, and head east.

The house at 903 West Main is Boxmere, the home of young Hardin Figuers during the Battle of Franklin. It was from a tree near this house that the boy watched the opening of the battle. John Bell Hood's fateful decision to attack on November 30, 1864, without any significant artillery support cost the lives of many of his men. But it spared much of Franklin from devastating shelling, and houses like Boxmere are the legacy of Hood's decision.

Boxmere

Take time to stop and inspect the impressive houses in a rich variety of styles that line West Main Street.

Return to your car to end the tour.

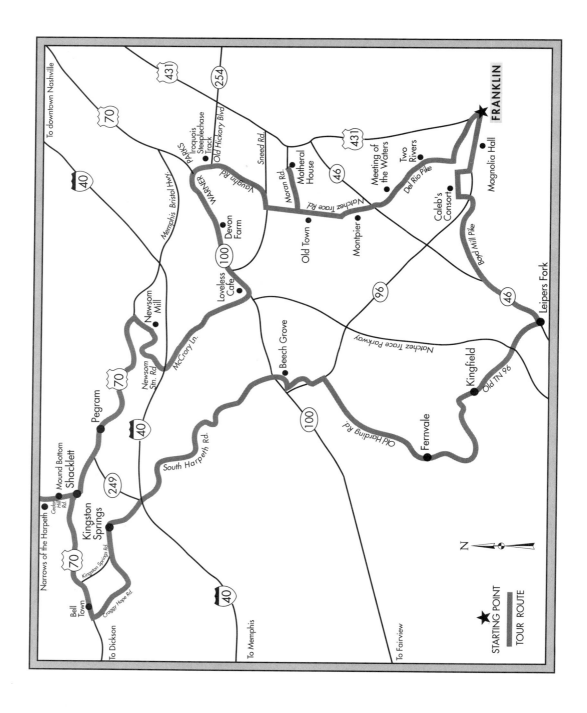

FRANKLIN

To downtown Nashville

431

254

70

40

Iroquois Steeplechase Track

Sneed Rd.

431

PARKS

WARNER

Yauolin Rd.

Old Hickory Blvd

Moran Rd.

Motheral House

46

Meeting of the Waters

Two Rivers

Del Rio Pike

Memphis Bristol Hwy.

Devon Farm

100

Old Town

Montpier

Natchez Trace Rd.

Caleb's Consort

Boyd Mill Pike

Magnolia Hall

Loveless Cafe

Newsom Mill

McCrory Ln.

96

Beech Grove

Natchez Trace Parkway

46

Leipers Fork

70

Newsom Stn. Rd.

40

Pegram

100

Old Harding Rd.

Kingfield

Old TN 96

South Harpeth Rd.

Fernvale

Mound Bottom

Shacklett

249

Narrows of the Harpeth

Cedar Hill Rd.

Kingston Springs

70

Kingston Springs Rd.

Craggy Hope Rd.

Bell Town

40

To Dickson

To Memphis

To Fairview

N

STARTING POINT

TOUR ROUTE

The Harpeth River Tour

This tour follows the meandering of the lovely Harpeth River through prosperous farmland and along the river's narrow valley through the Highland Rim. Included are four stately houses built by the Perkins family in the early 1800s and several popular recreation areas, among them Nashville's Warner Parks and the Narrows of the Harpeth, where Montgomery Bell built his iron forge. The old resorts of Craggy Hope, Kingston Springs, and Fernvale are on the tour, as is the pleasant country village of Leipers Fork.

Total length: approximately 88 miles

This tour begins in Franklin at the junction of U.S. 431 (Fifth Avenue North) and TN 96. Head north, away from downtown Franklin, on U.S 431. On the right after 0.3 mile, you will see two historic markers and a Battle of Franklin marker in a grassy area on the bluff above the Harpeth River.

One of the historic markers describes Harpeth Academy, the school founded near this spot in 1810. Middle Tennesseans love the name Harpeth as much as the river itself. Countless natural and man-made features bear the name—churches, schools, businesses, housing developments.

The origin of the name is obscure. It has been reported that this lovely stream is named for the infamous Harpe brothers—Big Harpe and Little Harpe—two murderous outlaws who terrorized Tennessee and Kentucky in the late 1790s and early 1800s. They would rob or kill anyone, including their own family, but they were especially noted for preying on the "Kaintucks," boatmen returning home on the Natchez Trace with the money they'd received from selling the flour, pork, tobacco, hemp, and iron they'd transported on their downriver flatboat voyages.

Another theory—more plausible and certainly more appealing—is that the name Harpeth comes from a character in English literature. In the August 23, 1714, edition of *The Spectator*, a popular London periodical edited by Joseph Addison, there was a story about an oriental legend involving two brothers who lived in China, Harpath and Shalum. The brothers became rivals for a woman named Hilpa. Harpath won, but Shalum cursed him, and Harpath eventually drowned in a river that was forever named for him. The earliest settlers in Middle Tennessee were for the most part a literate group, so it is possible this story and the name Harpath were known to them.

The stream first appeared—spelled Harpath—on maps in the 1780s. That tends to support the *Spectator* theory. In his splendid little book, *The Harpeth River: A Biography*, James A. Crutchfield points out that the bloody Harpe brothers did not begin their crime spree until over a decade after the first use of the name Harpath. This further supports the *Spectator* theory. By the early 1800s, the common spelling had changed to Harpeth.

From the markers above the river, continue north on U.S. 431 to the next light and turn left (W) onto Del Rio Pike. The tour follows Del Rio Pike through a series of right turns until the pike ends at Old Hillsboro Road. As the developed part of Franklin gives way to farmland, notice that Del Rio Pike is a sunken road, worn down by nearly two centuries of foot, hoof, and vehicle traffic.

You will reach the Del Rio Pike–Carlisle Lane intersection 1.6 miles from U.S. 431. Turn right, staying on Del Rio Pike. You are now in the domain of the Perkins family.

Shortly after Thomas Hardin and Mary Magdalene Perkins arrived in the newly established Williamson County from Virginia in 1800, they began the construction of a fine two-story brick house they named Meeting of the Waters. Over the next forty years, members of the Perkins family built six of the most beautiful homes imaginable here, within sight of the Harpeth River. Five are still standing, each impeccably restored.

It is not easy to keep up with the Perkins family. Thomas Hardin Perkins was the son of Nicholas Perkins. Two of Thomas Perkins's daughters married men named Nicholas Perkins. Another Nicholas Perkins—Nicholas Tate Perkins—married Ann Perkins, the daughter of yet another Nicholas Perkins. And many descendants of Perkins daughters with different last names were given the name Nicholas.

At 1.1 miles from the Carlisle Lane intersection, Del Rio Pike makes another sharp turn, this one to the left (W). Ahead and to the right is River Grange, the first of the Perkins houses on this tour. It is barely visible through the trees.

In 1820, twenty-two-year-old Virginia native Thomas Moore—himself the son of a Perkins mother—was riding west from the village of Franklin in search of the home of his relative Nicholas Tate Perkins. He encountered a slave girl drawing water from a spring and asked directions. The girl told Moore that the nearby house was the Perkins house. As Moore rode on, she added that Perkins had a mighty pretty daughter, too. Three years later, Moore married the pretty daughter, Mary Price Perkins. Nicholas Tate Perkins built this fine home for Mary and Thomas in 1826.

Del Rio Pike intersects Cotton Road 1 mile from River Grange. Turn left (W), staying on Del Rio Pike. After 0.2 mile, you will come to Two Rivers, the home of Nicholas Tate Perkins.

Nicholas Tate and Ann Perkins came from Guilford County, North Carolina, to buy this land on the Harpeth on Christmas Eve 1802. Originally called Poplar Grove, Two Rivers was completed around 1820. In 1849, ownership passed to Simeon and Amelia Shy, whose son, Colonel William M.

Two Rivers

Shy, lent his name to a prominent Civil War site; on December 16, 1864—the second day of the Battle of Nashville—he was killed defending a hill that has been known as Shy's Hill ever since. (The Battle of Nashville is described in The Brentwood Tour, pages 91–93.) Shy's body was brought back here to the family home, where it rested peacefully for 113 years.

In December 1977, it was discovered that graverobbers had opened Shy's grave, broken through the iron coffin, and made a frightful discovery—Shy's intact body. The ghouls—probably looking for Civil War relics—pulled out the body, knocking off its head in the process. Having had enough, they abandoned their pursuit and left Shy's headless torso sticking out of the grave.

The remains were so well preserved by embalming fluid—Shy's last meal was still in his stomach—that the sheriff thought the body might be that of a recent murder victim. An anthropologist from the University of Tennessee at Knoxville was called in to aid in the investigation, and it was conclusively established that the body was in fact that of Colonel Shy. With full military honors provided by the Sons of Confederate Veterans, Shy was reburied at Two Rivers in January 1978.

Two Rivers takes its name from the two rivers that meet nearby, the Big Harpeth and West Harpeth. There are actually four Harpeth Rivers—the Big Harpeth (or just plain Harpeth), the West Harpeth, the Little Harpeth, and the South Harpeth. This tour takes in all of them. The Big Harpeth rises in Rutherford County, flows across the middle of Williamson County, and meets the West Harpeth near this point. The West Harpeth rises in southern Williamson County and eventually flows northward parallel to the Big Harpeth for several miles, creating a peninsula cut in the middle by Del Rio Pike.

Continue on Del Rio Pike as it crosses the West Harpeth. You will reach the first Perkins home, Meeting of the Waters, 0.3 mile from the bridge.

After settling in the area in 1800, it took Thomas and Mary Perkins nine years to assemble the materials and the skilled workers needed to complete this handsome house, which they named for the adjacent meeting of the West and Big Harpeth rivers.

The house is in the Georgian-Federal "glorified pioneer" style typical of the earliest houses built in Middle Tennessee. Nashville businessman-historian Ridley Wills II and his wife, Irene, acquired Meeting of the Waters in 1989. As a result of their restoration, the house boasts a level of beauty unsurpassed in Middle Tennessee.

After the death of Thomas and Mary Perkins, their daughter Mary Hardin Perkins and her husband, Nicholas—the one called Bigbee—moved from their equally fine home, Montpier, into Meeting of the Waters. Montpier then passed to the other daughter of Thomas and Mary Perkins, Elizabeth, who was married to Leland Bradley.

Leland's nephew Robert Bradley fell in love with a daughter of Bigbee and Mary Hardin Perkins, Margaret Ann Perkins. Bigbee disapproved of the relationship because young Robert was not a Perkins, but the couple courted over his objection, often meeting in secret and with the aid of house servants. Bigbee decided to put an end to the affair once and for all. On August 1, 1844, he and Margaret Ann struck out in a carriage for the long journey to Philadelphia, where Margaret Ann was to be enrolled in boarding school. They stopped in Nashville the first night. Robert Bradley, it turns out, was in the Tennessee capital. He and Margaret Ann

Meeting of the Waters

secretly met and eloped to the home of the Reverend R. B. C. Howell, a Baptist minister, who married them.

The year Bigbee Nicholas Perkins died, his son Nicholas Edwin Perkins married Martha Thomas Maury, granddaughter of Abram Maury, on whose land Franklin was established. Meeting of the Waters passed to Nicholas Edwin Perkins. By the Civil War, the younger Perkins had several children.

Following the Battle of Franklin on November 30, 1864, a group of Union soldiers happened upon Meeting of the Waters. They planned to burn the house after they finished plundering it and stealing the livestock. Nicholas Edwin Perkins was not in a good position to resist. His right hand was permanently crippled. Years earlier, while he was a student at Centre College in Kentucky, another student had wounded Perkins in a duel. But he was determined to resist the Yankees. Nicholas Edwin Perkins locked his wife and daughters in a room, stood guard, and sent his son out to try to find a Union officer. "You can tell an officer because he will be on a horse and wearing a sword," he instructed his son. The son returned with an officer, who drew his sword and ran the marauding soldiers out of the house. A thankful Nicholas Edwin Perkins could not believe what he saw. The helpful Union officer was the same Centre College mate who had wounded him in the duel years earlier.

Del Rio Pike ends at Old Hillsboro Road (TN 46) 0.7 mile from Meeting of The Waters. Turn right (NE) on Old Hillsboro Road. After 0.1 mile, make a left (NW) turn onto Natchez Trace Road, also known as Old Natchez Trace.

This area is known as Forest Home. Though just a rural crossroads with an abandoned store today, the community was once the home of two stores, a blacksmith shop, and a distillery.

You will notice a stone monument at the intersection next to the old store. It is one of the Natchez Trace markers erected by the Daughters of the American Revolution early in the twentieth century. The DAR played a key role in keeping alive the memory of the ancient road.

It is no accident that this county road is called Natchez Trace Road, for it follows one of the routes of the old Natchez Trace. When people think of the Natchez Trace today, they generally envision a single route from Middle Tennessee to Natchez, Mississippi. In truth, the location of the

Nashville-Natchez overland route shifted often to meet the changing needs of the Southwest, as the region was called around 1800.

When the first European-American explorers came to the old Southwest, they found a network of Indian trails—paths that tended to follow ridge tops and watershed divides in an effort to avoid stream crossings and swamps. The early settlers named one of them the Chickasaw Trail because it extended from the Cumberland settlements toward the Chickasaw nation, centered near today's Tupelo, Mississippi.

A small boat loaded with flour arrived in 1785 at the Spanish town of Natchez on the Mississippi River. It had come all the way down the Ohio and Mississippi rivers from Fort Pitt—today's Pittsburgh, Pennsylvania. Thus began the thriving downriver flatboat trade, by which people on the frontier took their products to market at Natchez and New Orleans. This trade grew rapidly as the frontier in the Ohio River watershed filled with settlers.

The old Indian trails provided a convenient route for the traders to return north. Soon, the Chickasaw Trail became the Boatman's Trail. It is estimated that by 1810, as many as eight to ten thousand boatmen a year walked north on the trail. They were from all over the Ohio Valley, but they came to be called "Kaintucks." The Boatman's Trail, like the Chickasaw Trail before it, kept to the high ground when possible. It left Nashville on the route of today's West End Avenue, continued along the current route of TN 100, then climbed out of the Harpeth Valley and traversed Backbone Ridge a few miles west of Natchez Trace Road, the country road you are now traveling.

As the river trade increased after the Spanish withdrew from the Mississippi Territory in 1798, there was pressure to improve communication and transportation in the old Southwest. Also about this time, treaties with the Chickasaws and Choctaws gave the young United States government permission to build a road through Indian territory. In 1801, President Thomas Jefferson ordered the army to build a road from Nashville to Natchez. Constructed between 1801 and 1803, the northern end of the "Government Road" bypassed the heights of Backbone Ridge and instead followed the Harpeth River along the very route you are now traveling. It intersected with the old high-ground trail south of the current village of

Leipers Fork, visited later on this tour. In all, the army improved over half the Natchez Trace route.

The Natchez Trace was used as a post road beginning in 1800, with one trip each month between Nashville and Natchez. Postal service grew steadily. By 1816, there were three deliveries each week. The route the post riders took between the two growing towns changed often, reflecting the shifting nature of the route of what is now called the Natchez Trace.

In 1812, a boat arrived at Natchez from Pittsburgh, site of old Fort Pitt, from which the flatboat loaded with flour had been sent downstream twenty years earlier. It was the steamer *New Orleans*, piloted by Nicholas Roosevelt. Before long, the power to navigate upstream provided by steam engines rendered the overland Nashville-Natchez route obsolete. By the 1820s, regularly scheduled steamboat traffic ran between Pittsburgh and New Orleans, and by 1830, extended journeys on the Natchez Trace were rare. The Natchez Trace faded into history, only to be revived a century later.

Montpier, built by Bigbee Nicholas Perkins, is on the left 0.8 mile from the Old Hillsboro Road intersection.

Before this Nicholas Perkins moved to Tennessee from Virginia, President Jefferson appointed him register of lands in the new Mississippi Territory—today's states of Alabama and Mississippi. His nickname, "Bigbee," comes from land he owned along the Tombigbee River.

While in the Mississippi Territory, Perkins was involved in one of the great dramas of American history, the treason trial of Aaron Burr.

Burr had been vice president during Jefferson's first term, but his promising political career began to decline after he killed the influential Alexander Hamilton in a duel. Burr was later indicted for treason, charged with conspiring with the Spanish to annex the Southwest. He was a fugitive, and the whole Southwest was in an uproar about his whereabouts.

It was late at night on February 18, 1807. Perkins and some other men in a backwoods tavern in the Mississippi Territory were startled when two travelers passed by their remote location. One asked directions to the home of Colonel John Hinson. The other remained silent and did not look at the men in the tavern. Perkins became suspicious. He and some of the men followed the two strangers to Hinson's place. There, they found what Perkins suspected. One of the travelers was Aaron Burr.

Bigbee Nicholas Perkins was placed in charge of a detachment to take Burr back east, a long and arduous trip in those days. Perkins completed his mission and received praise and a handsome reward for his efforts.

In a Virginia trial presided over by Chief Justice John Marshall, Burr was acquitted on the treason charge.

Bigbee Nicholas Perkins's sister Ann married Nicholas Tate Perkins of Two Rivers. While on a visit there, Bigbee met Mary Hardin, the daughter of Thomas and Mary Perkins, the first Perkinses to settle in Williamson County. Bigbee and Mary married in 1808. He was twenty-nine. She was fourteen.

Bigbee Nicholas Perkins became the largest landowner in the area, eventually acquiring some twelve thousand acres. He built Montpier around 1821. The two-story central portico was added during the Greek Revival fad in the 1850s. When Bigbee and Mary moved to the home of her parents, Meeting of the Waters, after Thomas and Mary died, Bigbee's daughter Elizabeth and her husband, Leland Bradley, took possession of Montpier.

Past Montpier, Natchez Trace Road soon parallels the Harpeth River. After 0.9 mile, you will arrive at one of the Harpeth River's most beautiful houses, Old Town, located on the left.

Old Town

Thomas Brown immigrated to the Harpeth region from Virginia in 1822 and built Old Town in 1846 along the old Government Road. Some of the log buildings beside the house are not original. They were added by singer Jimmy Buffett during his ownership of the property in the late 1980s.

Old Town takes its name from the archaeological site on the grounds. When Dr. Joseph Jones excavated it in 1868–69, he found the remains of a large, prehistoric Middle Cumberland Culture village. (The Middle Cumberland Culture is described in The Brentwood Tour, pages 101–102.) At Old Town, a crescent-shaped fortification 2,470 feet in length enclosed the twelve-acre village bordering the Harpeth River. The remains of two mounds are visible in the field to the right of the house at Old Town. In addition to the temple mounds, fifty stone-lined graves were discovered along the riverbank.

On the left 0.2 mile beyond Old Town are the stone abutments of a bridge across Brown's Creek. Remnants of a bridge the army built in 1801,

these sturdy structures held a succession of wooden platforms until 1913, when the existing bridge was constructed. Only recently have these old limestone blocks started to tumble. It is said that this bridge is the only one remaining from the old Natchez Trace route along the Harpeth, but the next bridge rests on stone abutments identical in appearance to the ones at Old Town.

Continue along this beautiful route by the Harpeth River. You will soon pass the 1850 Stokley Davis House, on the left. Turn right on Moran Road 1.3 miles from the Old Town bridge.

The ropes that drop from overhanging trees at swimming holes on the Harpeth are evidence that the river is popular for all sorts of outdoor recreation—canoeing, fishing, swimming, wading, and bird-watching.

It is remarkable that the four Harpeth Rivers are as well preserved as they are, for all of the 866-square-mile Harpeth watershed is within the Nashville metropolitan area, an area with a 1990 population of about one million. And three of the five Harpeth River counties—Cheatham, Rutherford, and Williamson—grew faster than any other Tennessee counties in the 1980s. The riverside is heavily developed in Franklin and at Bellevue in Davidson County, and new subdivisions spring up all the time. Only time will tell whether the Harpeth will hold its character as a charming, pastoral river.

Moran Road is a lovely lane through lush bluegrass pastures between ancient stone fences. The several historic homes dating to the early 1800s include Blue Springs Farm, the log house on the right 1.1 miles from Natchez Trace Road; Locust Guard, built in 1823, located on the left just before the Harpeth River; and the John Motheral House, which sits beautifully on the river's opposite bank. Motheral, a Revolutionary War veteran from Pennsylvania, built this log house when he settled here in 1800. The 1870 Italianate additions included covering the log exterior with siding.

John Motheral House

Turn around at the John Motheral House. Backtrack to Natchez Trace Road and turn right (N). You will reach Sneed Road after 1.1 mile. Turn right (E) on Sneed Road and cross the Harpeth River.

This area, once known as Ash Grove, boasted a store, a sawmill, a school, and several churches. But the best-known Ash Grove landmark was the Union Bridge, the last covered bridge along the Harpeth. The original bridge here was not called the Union Bridge because Union soldiers burned it during the Civil War. Rather, its name came from the economic union of Davidson and Williamson counties symbolized by the structure.

After the Civil War, there was no bridge crossing the Harpeth at this point until 1881. That year, a covered bridge was built that rested on one center pier in the river. The sturdy oak floor provided safe passage over the Harpeth for more than six decades.

A record flood on the Harpeth occurred on the night of February 13, 1948. The average flow at the nearest gauging station is 544 cubic feet per second (cfs). That night, a flow of 40,000 cfs was recorded. It was too much for the old bridge, and the Harpeth claimed it all, including the center pier.

Sneed Road intersects Vaughn Road 0.5 mile from the Harpeth crossing at Union Bridge. Turn left (N) onto Vaughn Road.

Vaughn, Sneed, and Natchez Trace roads and Del Rio Pike comprise the most popular bicycle route in the Nashville area. Having just driven it, you can understand why. The route from the Warner Parks on Nashville's edge to Franklin is about 15 miles, a perfect length for a leisurely bike ride.

Vaughn Road continues on the route of the old Government Road and crosses the Little Harpeth River 1.6 miles from Sneed Road. The Little Harpeth follows a westerly course for 14 miles along the northern edge of Williamson County before it empties into the Big Harpeth a mile or so downstream from this bridge.

As the tour crosses the Little Harpeth, it enters Davidson County and Nashville's incomparable Warner Parks. A range of rugged hills—an outlier of the Highland Rim—stretches across the southern boundary of Davidson County. Often called the Harpeth Hills or Overton Hills, the range is home to two remarkable urban preserves—Warner Parks and Radnor Lake State Natural Area. (For information on Radnor Lake, see The Brentwood Tour, page 94.)

Percy Warner was an electric-utility pioneer who had attained a great deal of wealth and influence by the time he became chairman of Nashville's park board in 1926. A lifelong outdoorsman and nature lover, he wanted to establish a park to emphasize recreation as well as land and wildlife conservation. He persuaded his son-in-law, Luke Lea, to donate 868 acres of his property in the Harpeth Hills to the park board. This initial acreage became the nucleus of the 2,664-acre preserve. In 1927, Percy Warner died unexpectedly, and Lea convinced the board to name the new park after his father-in-law. The park board then honored Lea by naming the park's highest point, now called Lea's Summit, in his honor.

Edwin Warner assumed his late brother Percy's place on the board. After twelve years, he was elected chairman, a position he held until his death in 1949. Edwin Warner made a substantial donation that allowed the expansion of the park. Part of the park was then named for Edwin. Thus the Warner Parks, for Percy and Edwin.

Edwin and Percy personally surveyed much of the 20-mile road system, designed to take full advantage of the terrain. Eight more miles were added by the Works Progress Administration (WPA) during the Depression. These roads are so carefully laid out that it is often possible to be on one road just a few feet from another and never know it, a characteristic that contributes to the feeling of solitude most park visitors seek.

The WPA also built stone entrance gates and retaining walls, bridle paths, hiking trails, playgrounds, and picnic shelters of such quality that many are still in use today. The stonework, handcrafted from limestone quarried in the park, blends in nicely with the natural environment, though some of it has deteriorated in recent years due to lack of maintenance.

Iroquois Steeplechase Track

Vaughn Road ends at Old Hickory Boulevard (TN 254). Directly across the intersection is the Iroquois Steeplechase Track, built by the WPA in 1941—the only racetrack ever constructed by the federal government. The track is named for Iroquois, a horse raised at nearby Belle Meade Plantation. In 1881, Iroquois became the only American horse to win the prestigious Epsom Derby in England. The annual running of the world-class Iroquois Steeplechase in May is a major event in Nashville, attracting thousands of spectators who fill the box seats and perch on the hillside to watch an afternoon of races.

Turn left (W) onto Old Hickory Boulevard. You will reach TN 100 after 0.7 mile. Turn left (W). Immediately on the left is the Warner Parks Nature Center, a pleasant spot offering a small museum and nature activities. A sunken road—a section of one of the original Natchez Trace routes— runs just inside the woods west of the nature center.

Original WPA construction in the Warner Parks

Luke Lea, the man who donated the original land, is one of the most interesting, albeit controversial, figures in Tennessee history. He was a descendant of an early pioneer family that came to own much of the land in southern Davidson County. From 1906, the year he literally took over the fractious state Democratic convention at age twenty-seven, until the financial collapse of 1929–30, Lea was a major force in Tennessee business and politics. At one time, he owned three major daily newspapers—the *Memphis Commercial Appeal*, the *Knoxville Journal*, and *The Nashville Tennessean*. At age thirty-one, he was elected a United States senator, the youngest Tennessean ever to hold that office.

Lea is perhaps best known for his bizarre attempt to capture Kaiser Wilhelm II, the defeated German leader, after World War I. Lea, a colonel commanding a volunteer artillery regiment he formed, devised a scheme to enter neutral Holland, where the kaiser had taken refuge, and kidnap the monarch. On New Year's Day 1919, Lea and eight of his Tennessee associates left on their mission through France, Luxembourg and Belgium and into Holland, fast-talking their way past military and civilian guards.

View of Nashville from Lea's Summit

They made it to the house that was the kaiser's refuge and all the way to his door before they were finally stopped.

After the war, Luke Lea began a long association with financier Rogers Caldwell, equally flamboyant and equally controversial. The effects of the collapse of Caldwell's financial empire in 1930 were felt for years. For Lea, it led to a conviction for defrauding a bank in Asheville, North Carolina. Lea's long fight to avoid extradition to North Carolina was about as dramatic as his failed plot to kidnap the kaiser, but eventually, he served his time and returned to Nashville to a hero's welcome. He died in 1945.

Continue west on TN 100. You will reach the drive to Devon Farm 0.7 mile from the nature center.

The house above the confluence of the Big and Little Harpeth rivers is considered by many to be among the most beautiful in Davidson County. For years, the original structure was thought to have been built around 1796 by pioneer surveyor John Davis, an early settler who eventually owned just under seven thousand acres of Harpeth Valley land. Davis's daughter, Fannie, married Morris Harding and lived on the place until she died in 1865. Fannie and Morris enlarged the house considerably and added the porches and columns visible today.

Morris was the son of Giles Harding, the original Harding who settled the area in 1798, and the brother of John Harding, founder of Belle Meade Plantation. Recent research indicates that Giles Harding, not John Davis, built the first house at this location.

Morris and Fanny owned slaves, as did most of the plantation owners along the Harpeth. Though there was only one male slave under age forty-five on the property during much of the 1820s, ten children were born to slave Priscilla Harding. Their father was Morris Harding. Fanny Harding never bore any children, but she took particular care of her husband's children by Priscilla, as well as of Priscilla herself, ensuring that they were taught to read and write. Morris provided for the emancipation of Priscilla and the children in his will. Fanny even prevailed upon him to leave half the plantation to Priscilla and her children.

By the time of Morris's death in 1854, the slave states had enacted restrictive laws regarding the rights of free blacks, mostly in response to the abolitionist sentiment that was building in the country. Priscilla sold her land for a considerable sum and moved to Ohio with two of her children in 1858. She bought a valuable farm adjoining Wilberforce College, an early school for free blacks.

Edward Dickson Hicks II, Fanny's nephew, inherited the property upon Fanny's death at the end of the Civil War, and it has been in the Hicks family ever since. Hicks imported Devon cattle from England and devoted most of his adult life to promoting the breed. He changed the name of the place from Oak Hill to Devon Farm.

Less than a mile from Devon Farm, TN 100 crosses the Harpeth River. The canoe access at the west end of the bridge is the first of four state-maintained public-access areas from this point downstream. The 15-mile stretch of river in Davidson County is protected under Tennessee's 1968 Scenic Rivers Act, the first such act in the nation. It authorizes the state to acquire conservation easements, a form of regulation that allows riverbank land use compatible with scenic integrity.

You will reach the intersection with Old Harding Road 1.8 miles from the bridge. Harpeth Valley School is across Old Harding Road. It is ironic that songwriter Tom T. Hall thought up the title for Jeannie C. Riley's 1968 hit, "Harper Valley P.T.A.," from the name Harpeth Valley. Yet another theory of the origin of the name Harpeth is that it is a corruption of Harper.

Continue on TN 100. On the right 0.9 mile from Old Harding Road is one of Middle Tennessee's best-known landmarks, the Loveless Motel and Cafe. Indeed, when it comes to hearty Southern-style breakfasts, the Loveless is one of the best-known restaurants anywhere.

Lou Loveless built this little twelve-unit tourist court and cafe in the 1950s. Americans were becoming more mobile in the post–World War II years, and the location was well situated on the main route between Nashville and Memphis.

Loveless Motel and Cafe

The motel has faded, but the cafe has remained much the same under three subsequent owners. Specialties at the Loveless include country ham, fried chicken, biscuits, and fresh homemade preserves. The owners are careful about what they buy and serve. In a given year, they buy as many as three thousand hams, all from a single supplier, and all slow-cured the old-fashioned way, aged for a minimum of six months.

McCrory Lane comes into TN 100 from the right just past the Loveless. Turn right onto McCrory.

The Natchez Trace Parkway intersects TN 100 just past McCrory Lane. This is the northern terminus of the 445-mile linear park, a unit of the National Park Service that extends all the way to Natchez, Mississippi.

The movement to commemorate the Natchez Trace began in 1909, when the Daughters of the American Revolution began erecting commemorative markers along the route of the old Trace in Alabama, Mississippi, and Tennessee. The marker back at Forest Home is one of them. The northernmost marker is in Nashville's Centennial Park.

Like so many of America's parks and recreation areas, the parkway got its start as a Depression-era public-works project. Under the sponsorship of Representative Jeff Busby of Mississippi, Congress passed the act authorizing the parkway in 1938. Construction has been slow, as Congress has dribbled out appropriations over the years. The last Tennessee section to be built is the final 5 miles, a stretch over the heights of Backbone Ridge between TN 96 and TN 100. This construction had to await the 1994 completion of the bridge over TN 96.

And what an impressive bridge it is. The 1,648-foot span passes 155 feet over the highway and rests on two massive arches 582 and 460 feet in length. The bridge—the first segmental concrete-arch structure ever built in North America—has become an attraction in its own right; the tour later passes near this bridge.

This area of Davidson County is known as Pasquo. The first families to settle here came from Pasquotank County, North Carolina. Apparently, the long name was too much for the early settlers. Since their arrival in the Harpeth Valley, this area has been know as either Pasquo or Tank. The Tank Store was started here in 1851 by William B. Knight and stayed in business at two locations until 1975, an incredible 124 years. It was located near the TN 100–McCrory Lane intersection.

The ridge McCrory Lane crosses is a spur of the Western Highland Rim. It marks the point where the Harpeth River leaves the Central Basin and begins its course through the Highland Rim. The valley that the river has carved out of the uplands is lined with steep hills and sheer vertical bluffs, some rising as high as two hundred feet. For the next several miles, the tour alternates between the Harpeth Valley and the high ridges before returning to the Central Basin near Franklin.

It is 4.4 miles on McCrory Lane to the intersection with Newsom Station Road just past Interstate 40. Turn right onto Newsom Station Road. After 2 miles, turn right into the Newsom Mill Historic Site just past the railroad underpass.

From the time the Newsom family came to the Harpeth Valley around 1800, there had been a mill here on the river. Joseph Morton Newsom wanted a more permanent structure for his mill, so he completed this impressive structure in 1862, using limestone quarried on his property. Newsom Mill was a gristmill where farmers traded on a share basis—the miller would take part of the ground meal and the farmer would take part.

Before he constructed the mill, Newsom built Harpeth Heights, a magnificent house in which he used the same type of limestone blocks as in the mill. Three years in the making, the home was completed in 1861. Unfortunately, Harpeth Heights was destroyed in the 1960s to make way for construction of the interstate. The venerable house did not go down easy. First, a wrecking ball was tried, and when that did not work, a large quantity of dynamite was used.

In 1905, ownership of Newsom Mill passed to the Ezell family, who rebuilt the dam two years later using concrete. During the construction, a skeleton was found wedged in the old log-and-stone dam. It was thought to be the remains of an escaped convict, but no one knew for sure.

When you are ready to leave Newsom Mill, continue on Newsom Station Road across the Harpeth River. You will reach U.S. 70 after 1.3 miles. Turn left (W). It is 7.8 miles through Pegram to the turnoff onto Cedar Hill Road in Shacklett. This stretch of U.S. 70 is particularly scenic, as it plays tag with the Harpeth River, meandering around one giant bend after another.

Turn right on Cedar Hill Road just before the bridge over the Harpeth River. It is 1 mile to the historical marker at Scott Cemetery announcing the location of one of the region's largest prehistoric Indian habitations, Mound Bottom. Like Old Town and the Fewkes Site, visited in The Brentwood Tour, this site was inhabited by the long-vanished people now called the Middle Cumberland Culture.

Mound Bottom—a river bottom covered with huge temple mounds—is part of a larger complex that also includes the Great Mound site, located south of U.S. 70. Together, the two sites cover around five hundred acres. William Edward Myer, the pioneer archaeologist who surveyed the Fewkes Site near Brentwood, studied these sites in 1923.

The central point of the site south of the highway is its great mound. The natives leveled a natural hilltop, creating a broad plaza measuring about five hundred feet by a thousand feet. For defense, they relied upon the Harpeth River on two sides and on a stockade lined with watchtowers on the other two sides. Myer was overwhelmed by what he found at the Great Mound. He was not tentative in his description. "No other remains of ancient man have been found in our southeastern United States which approached this Great Mound group in an artistic sense," he wrote in his 1924 report.

Here at Mound Bottom, a large pyramidal mound is surrounded by several smaller mounds. The bend in the Harpeth offered protection on three sides, and earthen fortifications protected the fourth side. Myer found the remains of an ancient roadway connecting the two sites leading out of these fortifications.

The mounds in this state-owned site have survived the centuries remarkably well and are clearly visible in the bottom across the river when there is no foliage.

Ancient petroglyphs, no doubt left by the Middle Cumberland people, are found on several bluffs along the Harpeth River. High on the bluff above Mound Bottom, someone pecked or scraped an image of what appears to be a baton. Farther down the river, above Corlew Bend, an extensive series of petroglyphs appears to have been painted. One image seems to be of the sun. It is five feet across. These petroglyphs give the bluff its name, Paint Rock Bluff.

From the Scott Cemetery across from Mound Bottom, continue on Cedar Hill Road for 1.9 miles to the left-hand turn to the Narrows. Follow the steep, narrow road 0.5 mile to the parking area.

At the Narrows of the Harpeth, natural and man-made features combine to form one of the most pleasant and interesting places in Middle Tennessee. Here, the Harpeth flows hard against a bluff, swings out around

Bells Bend, and, after 5 miles, flows within two hundred feet of itself on the opposite side of the bluff. It was here that Montgomery Bell built an iron forge and constructed what is believed to be the first man-made tunnel in the United States.

Montgomery Bell is rightly regarded as Tennessee's first capitalist and industrialist. Described as wily and sharp—and sometimes unscrupulous—he was the dominant force in the iron industry that thrived on the Western Highland Rim during the first half of the nineteenth century. (For more information about the iron industry, see The Western Highland Rim Tour, pages 236–38.)

Bell remains to this day a mysterious person. He was known as a ruthless master of the slaves who labored hard in his furnaces and forge. Yet he had an intimate friendship with one of them, James Whorley, for whom he named one of his iron furnaces. When the American Colonization Society began a move to free slaves and resettle them in Africa, Bell responded by freeing as many of his slaves as wanted to go and by financing their resettlement.

The crusty old bachelor was known as a person who would go to great lengths to avoid paying a just debt, even a small one. Yet it was through his generosity that funds were made available to start a school in Nashville that was eventually named for him.

Bell was born and raised in the iron-producing country of southeastern Pennsylvania. By the time he came to Middle Tennessee around 1800, he was well acquainted with the business. He acquired the area's earliest ironworks, Cumberland Furnace, from James Robertson in 1804 and from there built a remarkable industrial empire.

He had always been intrigued by water power, and the Narrows of the Harpeth seemed to be a perfect site for a project. Here, he would build an iron forge. Power was needed to turn the wheels and lift the heavy hammers that forged the crude pig iron into a more refined product. To obtain the power, Bell bored a tunnel through the Narrows to create a drop of sixteen feet. Water was diverted from the upstream side into the tunnel, then released on the downstream side to turn the wheels. No one knows for sure how his slaves built the tunnel, but it took three years. Completed in 1820, the tunnel is three hundred feet long, fifteen feet wide, and six feet high.

Water flowing through Montgomery Bell's 1820 tunnel at the Narrows of the Harpeth

Bell called the site Patterson Forge, or Pattison Forge, after his mother's maiden name. Before long, a small industrial city grew up here on the banks of the Harpeth. Pig-iron bars were brought in from the furnaces and refined into bars that were shipped out to be forged into steam boilers and other heavy equipment. Further refining produced bars of a higher grade for use by blacksmiths, locksmiths, and gunsmiths. The forge also produced its own finished products, among them axes, rakes, hoes, shovels, hinges, chains, and other tools.

Montgomery Bell died a recluse in 1855. He is buried nearby. His nephew, James L. Bell, took over the forge, which continued to operate until Federal troops overran the area following the fall of Fort Donelson in February 1862. The tunnel is about all that remains of this once-thriving industrial site.

Leave the upriver side of the Narrows on the one-way road and turn left (N) on Cedar Hill Road. It is 0.5 mile over the ridge to the downriver side of the Narrows. Turn into the access area on the right just short of the picturesque Harris-Street Bridge.

This is the takeout point for the 5-mile float around Bells Bend. The

Harris-Street Bridge

TOURING THE MIDDLE TENNESSEE BACKROADS

Harpeth River downstream from Shacklett is used by canoeists year-round. In fact, it is the most popular float stream near Nashville. The wide bends make it possible to take long floats with a minimum of car shuttling, or, in the case of Bells Bend, no shuttling at all. It is an easy walk across the Narrows.

From the Narrows, return on Cedar Hill Road to U.S. 70. Turn right (W). It is 4.7 miles to Craggy Hope Road. Along the way, the route climbs from the Harpeth Valley to the top of the Highland Rim and passes through the ridge-top community of Belltown. The first residents of this mostly black settlement were former slaves of Montgomery Bell.

Turn left onto Craggy Hope Road, where the route drops off the ridge. After 1.6 miles, you will come to Craggy Hope United Methodist Church, on the left. The Campbell family came from Texas to settle here in the 1870s and named the place after its ancestral home in Ayrshire, Scotland. The charming church set back against the ridge was built in 1910.

Craggy Hope United Methodist Church

Craggy Hope was a popular resort in the early 1900s. A 1904 brochure promoted it as a place where a Nashville businessman might send his family for the summer while he worked in the city and commuted on one of the five daily passenger trains. It advertised a new thirty-two-room hotel and an existing fourteen-room hotel, as well as cottages, a swimming hole, a bowling alley, and a dance pavilion. By 1915, the hotels at Craggy Hope had closed. Several of the cottages still stand on the right of the road just past the railroad crossing.

Stay on Craggy Hope Road as it parallels Turnbull Creek before ending at Kingston Springs Road 1.3 miles from the church. Go straight on Kingston Springs Road; you will come to the main intersection in the town of Kingston Springs after 1 mile. Along the way, the route crosses Turnbull Creek.

"Turn the bull! Turn the bull!" That is the exclamation said to be the origin of the name of this major Harpeth River tributary. Some early settlers were driving cattle when the big bull leading the way charged into the swollen stream. The herd master's command to the drover prompted him to turn the bull around and cross the creek at a safer place.

Turn right to stay on Kingston Springs Road. It is 0.4 mile through two sharp turns to the old Kingston Springs Hotel. You will pass the library,

located next to the 1903 Kingston Springs Methodist Church. When the citizens of this fast-growing part of south Cheatham County asked for a library, they were told public funds were lacking. So in 1989, they built a library themselves. A local building firm donated the materials for the handsome log structure, which was built entirely with volunteer labor.

The Kingston Springs Hotel stands on the right of the road. As early as 1849, there was a resort near the mineral springs here on the bluff above the Harpeth River. The original log building burned in the 1880s. It was replaced in the 1890s by this Victorian hotel, which has changed little over the years. Of the thirteen cottages that flanked the main hotel in 1860, two remain today. There are also two cottages built in 1900.

The Kingston Springs resort, advertised as a "well known and popular watering place," reached its peak around the turn of the century. Guests arrived at the railroad station in town and were driven here to the resort. The hotel closed when the United States entered World War I in 1917. It never reopened.

From the hotel, it is 0.5 mile to an unusually large, well-preserved log house on the right. This home was built by James M. Dunn, son of the first settler in the area, in the 1850s.

Continue another 0.5 mile to the stoplight near the Interstate 40 junction. Turn right (S) and drive 0.9 mile across Interstate 40 and up a ridge to the intersection with South Harpeth Road. Turn left. Where South Harpeth intersects Poplar Grove Road after 5.2 miles, keep right, staying on South Harpeth. It is another 2.1 miles to TN 100. The route travels up the lovely, isolated valley of the South Harpeth River. As you return to Davidson County, you may find it difficult to believe that this remote area is within the state's second-most-populous county.

At TN 100, cross the highway onto Old Harding Road. The house on the hill on the left 0.1 mile from the highway is called Beech Grove.

This property was once owned by James Robertson, who, in addition to being the founder of Nashville, was one of the region's largest landowners. Hugh Allison bought this land from Robertson in 1801 and eventually established sawmills and gristmills on the South Harpeth. Hugh's son, Thomas Jefferson Allison, took over the Allison family business and built Beech Grove in 1850. The house was enlarged after the Civil War, when Allison moved a plantation schoolhouse that had been damaged by Union soldiers and attached it to the main dwelling.

Beech Grove on the South Harpeth River

It is 0.1 mile from Beech Grove to where Old Harding Road returns to TN 100. Turn left (W) onto TN 100 and cross the South Harpeth River. This area, located where the old Richland Turnpike crossed the South Harpeth, is called Linton. It is named for the family of Johanna Linton, a Virginia widow who came west to claim a Revolutionary War grant given for the service of her husband, Silas Linton.

At the west end of the bridge over the South Harpeth, turn left (SE) onto Old Harding Road and follow it as it runs parallel to the river for 0.6 mile before ending at TN 96. Turn left (E) on TN 96 and cross the South Harpeth. After 0.2 mile, turn right (S) off TN 96 onto Old Harding Road. Note that the Natchez Trace Parkway double-arched bridge is 2.5 miles ahead (E) on TN 96.

Old Harding Road heads up the pleasant, narrowing valley of the South Harpeth River and arrives at the site of the long-vanished Fernvale resort after 4.9 miles. A sign on the left marks the location of Mayfield Spring, one of the three springs that provided water for the resort.

It is difficult to imagine now, but this is the site of one of the largest and best known of the many mineral-spring resorts that thrived in Middle Tennessee in the late 1800s and early 1900s. Visitors came from the low-lying, damp areas of the Deep South to avoid the humid weather they believed caused the yellow fever prevalent in those days. Arriving by train at Franklin or Bellevue, they traveled by horse or carriage to Fernvale.

The first hotel here burned near the end of the century, and a new one opened for business in June 1901. It boasted 114 rooms in buildings on either side of the road, connected by an arched breezeway. Cabins scattered around the site offered quarters for visiting families.

The climate may have drawn visitors from the Deep South, but others came for the mineral water, which was thought to have medicinal qualities. An advertisement for the resort read, "For all diseases of the stomach, kidney, bowels, skin, and eyes, these Springs have no superior, if an equal. For dyspepsia and kidney troubles they are almost a specific. For teething children in their second summer, it is a paradise. For nervous and physical exhaustion, from whatever causes, a few weeks sojourn and rest in this place will work wonders."

In addition to the advertised health benefits, Fernvale offered all sorts of activities, including fishing, hunting, hiking, bowling, and dancing to the music of Professor De Pierrei and his orchestra from Nashville.

The popularity of the resort began to wane in the first decade of the new century. In March 1906, the hotel caught fire and burned to the ground. Now, all that remains are the springs.

Continue 0.1 mile to the three-way stop at "downtown" Fernvale. Old Harding Road ends here at Old TN 96. Continue straight on Old TN 96. After 1.7 miles, continue straight (S) where South Harpeth Road comes in from the right; note that this is not the same South Harpeth Road traveled earlier. You will reach the church in the ridge-top settlement of Kingfield 3.5 miles from the South Harpeth Road intersection. The Seventh-Day Adventists established this church early in the twentieth century. From 1918 until 1923, the church ran a school here, the Kingfield Industrial School.

Kingfield is located in a remote part of Williamson County. Electricity first came here around 1930. Telephones were installed in the 1950s. Noble King, who with his wife, Vera, ran the local store from 1943 until 1977, brought the first car to Kingfield, a used 1918 German-made Metz he purchased in Franklin.

Continue on Old TN 96 through Kingfield, descending the ridge back into the Harpeth Valley and passing under the Natchez Trace Parkway after 2.3 miles. You will enter the village of Leipers Fork where Old TN 96 ends at Old Hillsboro Road (TN 46). The tour goes left (N) here, but to the right, this interesting village extends for about a mile along the road. Farther down the road is the point where the old Government Road joined the original Natchez Trace. Access to the Natchez Trace Parkway is provided on TN 46.

Leipers Fork, a major tributary of the West Harpeth, is named for a family whose three brothers contributed heavily to the early Cumberland settlements. All three brothers—George, Hugh, and James Leiper—signed the Cumberland Compact at Fort Nashborough in 1780. (See The Hendersonville-Portland Tour, pages 31–32, for information about the Cumberland Compact.)

One of the Leiper brothers is said to have killed the outlaw Big Harpe up in Muhlenberg County, Kentucky. After Big Harpe was beheaded, his head was placed on a pole as a deterrent to others with tendencies toward his occupation. His brother, Little Harpe, was eventually caught, too, near Natchez, Mississippi. On February 8, 1804, he was ordered to be "hung up by the neck, between the hours of ten o'clock in the forenoon and four in the afternoon, until he is dead, dead, dead."

Leipers Fork is the third name of this village. First, it was called Bentontown, for the family whose most famous member was Thomas Hart Benton. The Bentons were a prominent, prosperous family in North Carolina before the American Revolution. When young Thomas Hart Benton was expelled from the University of North Carolina in 1799 after being accused of stealing, he remarked as he left Chapel Hill, "You will hear from me again." He was right.

Benton's widowed mother moved to the Leipers Fork area around 1800. The intellectually gifted Thomas quickly grew tired of the backbreaking work of a frontier farmer. After a short stint at teaching, he took up the study of law and began his practice in 1806, first in Franklin and later in Nashville.

Thomas Hart Benton and Andrew Jackson had crossed paths back in North Carolina when Jackson visited the Benton home. In Tennessee, Benton's brother Jesse became a bitter enemy of Andrew Jackson as Jackson began his rise to power in the second decade of the 1800s. At first, Thomas shared Jesse's hostility toward Jackson. In fact, the Benton brothers and Jackson were involved in a shootout and brawl at Nashville's City Hotel following Jackson's return home from the War of 1812.

Thomas Hart Benton was already into politics himself, having been elected to the Tennessee General Assembly, but the disturbance with Jackson convinced the family to leave Tennessee. So in 1815, the Bentons moved to Missouri. Thomas Hart Benton was one of Missouri's first United States senators when the state was admitted to the Union in 1821; he served in the Senate for thirty years. Benton overcame his family's difficulty with Jackson, becoming a staunch and invaluable supporter of President Jackson. For twenty-five years, Benton was one of the foremost political figures in America.

Hillsboro was the name chosen for the village after the Bentons left for Missouri. They and other original settlers came from Hillsborough, North Carolina. The road to the south from Nashville toward this settlement became known as Hillsboro Road or Hillsboro Pike, and the name Hillsboro has been applied to a host of places south of downtown Nashville. There is another Hillsboro, Tennessee, in Coffee County on U.S. 41. The post office insisted that there be only one. Leipers Fork thus acquired its current name, though many people still call it Hillsboro.

Residents of Williamson County consider themselves lucky if they own Poynor chairs. Dick Poynor was a former slave from the Leipers Fork area who made a variety of sturdy chairs. For his ladder-back chairs, he used green maple for the posts, seasoned oak for the rungs, seasoned maple for the slats, and hickory strips for the splits. When the green wood of the posts dried around the seasoned wood of the rungs and slats, the chairs could not be pulled apart, making them almost indestructible. A free black, Dick Poynor supposedly used the money he made from the chairs to purchase the freedom of his wife. A Poynor chair is on permanent display in the Tennessee State Museum.

After turning left (N) onto Old Hillsboro Road at Leipers Fork, you will be following the route of the old Government Road and the later route of the Hillsboro Turnpike, an early toll road. Tolls were collected as late as 1927, but after that, the road became a free public road maintained by the county.

At 2.6 miles from Leipers Fork, turn right (E) off Old Hillsboro Road onto Boyd Mill Pike just past the carefully preserved 1843 Henry P. Gray House, located on the left. Cross the West Harpeth River.

Henry P. Gray House

This area, known as Bingham, is where Hog Eye Church once stood. Organized in 1857, the church got its unusual name because children could look through holes in the floor and see pigs under the building.

The limestone foundation of Boyd's Mill can still be seen on the riverbank upstream. William A. Boyd built the mill around 1840, and it continued in operation until 1910, when it collapsed in a storm.

The home of William Irby Boyd is located on a hill to the right where the road makes a left-hand turn 0.2 mile from the bridge. Boyd, father of the man who founded the mill, built the original one-and-a-half-story log house around 1800. William, his son, added to the original house in 1850 and covered the existing log structure with frame siding. The house is known as All Bright Hill.

Boyd Mill Pike continues along the bends of the West Harpeth before the river finally swings away from it for good. After traveling 2.1 miles from the Boyd House, look to the field to the left, where there is a clearly defined Indian mound with a clump of trees growing out of it. This is another of the Middle Cumberland Culture sites in the Harpeth Valley.

Boyd Mill Pike ends at TN 96 after another 0.5 mile. Turn right (E). After 0.1 mile, turn left (N) onto Short Lane. On the rise off to the left stands the Samuel Glass House, sometimes known as Pleasant View. Construction on this home began in 1859 but was interrupted by the Civil War. The house was not completed until 1869.

Short Lane ends at Old Charlotte Pike, the early road west from Franklin toward Dickson County and its seat of Charlotte. Turn right (E) onto Old Charlotte Pike.

Caleb's Consort

Magnolia Hall and its widow's walk

The house on the hill to the left after 0.2 mile was reportedly built in 1800, making it one of the oldest brick houses in this region. A graveyard near the house contains only one marker. The name is broken and the dates are faded, but one line says the stone is in memory of the "consort of Caleb Garrett," a prominent Franklin citizen in the 1820s. The house is now known as Caleb's Consort. It was once known as Cottonwood.

Continue on Old Charlotte Pike for 0.8 mile from Caleb's Consort. Turn right (S) onto Carlisle Lane and drive 0.4 mile to TN 96.

Perched on the hill on the northwest corner of the Carlisle Lane–TN 96 intersection is a building with a glass dome that looks strangely out of place. It is the Knights of Pythias Pavilion, built by the fraternal organization for the Tennessee Centennial Exposition, held at Nashville in 1897. The exposition should have been held in 1896—the hundredth anniversary of Tennessee's admission to the Union—but it was one year late.

The buildings at the exposition in what is now Centennial Park were of temporary construction; the current edition of the Parthenon is not the one built for the exposition. After the exposition, Joseph Parks bought the Knights of Phythias Pavilion, dismantled it, and reconstructed it on his property west of Franklin. Parks supposedly accomplished this feat to impress a woman he wanted to marry, Sophia Phipps. He brought Miss Phipps to the building before he had completed the reconstruction, showed her around, then proposed matrimony. She threw up her hands—so the story goes—and said, "Never!" She is said to have later remarked, "That old fool wanted me to leave my nice, comfortable house and move out to that monstrosity."

Neither Parks nor Sophia Phipps ever married, but they were often seen together in Franklin.

Turn left (E) on TN 96 and head for Franklin. Magnolia Hall is the house on the right behind the small lake 1.4 miles from Carlisle Lane.

William S. Campbell built this imposing structure. He came to Franklin from Belfast, now in Northern Ireland, in 1839, and worked for a bank until the Civil War. He then started what is said to be the first national bank to open in Middle Tennessee after the war. The beautiful view of Magnolia Hall from the highway is actually of the back of the house.

The cupola of this Italianate house is rare in this part of the country, as is the widow's walk around it. Cupolas are often seen in houses along the New England coast, where anxious women are said to have stood on their roofs scanning the horizon for a hopeful glimpse of returning ships.

Continue on TN 96 for 0.7 mile to the junction with U.S. 431 in Franklin, where this tour started and now ends.

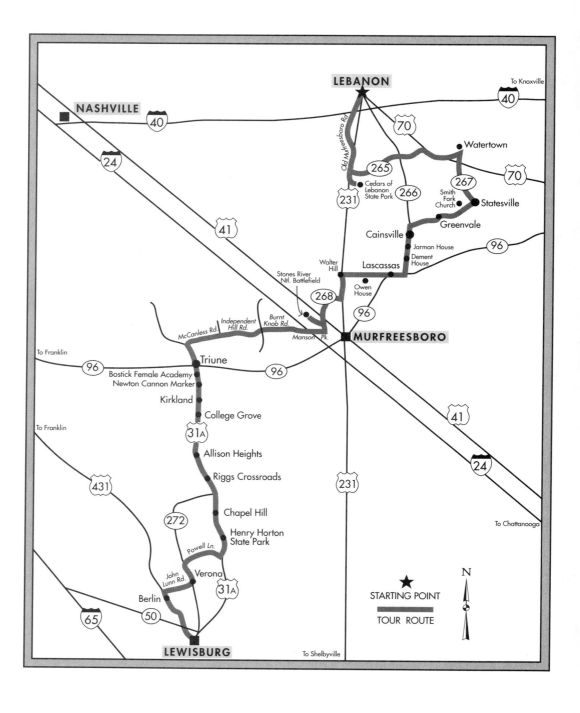

The Cedar Forests Tour

This tour takes in areas once covered by vast stands of cedars and includes the site of one of the Civil War's major battles. It starts in Lebanon and goes to the nearby state park, which holds the world's largest stand of eastern red cedars. After visiting the lovely little towns of Watertown and Statesville, it stops at Stones River National Battlefield near Murfreesboro. It then visits the pleasant small towns of College Grove and Chapel Hill before ending at Lewisburg.

Total length: approximately 121 miles

This tour begins on the square in the Wilson County seat of Lebanon. To reach the square, take Exit 238 off Interstate 40 east of Nashville and follow U.S. 231 into Lebanon.

The area that comprises Wilson County, like most of the rest of Middle Tennessee, remained free of settlers for fifteen years after Christmas Day 1779, when James Robertson led his weary followers across the frozen Cumberland River to start a permanent settlement. (The first settlement of Middle Tennessee is discussed in The Middle Cumberland Tour, pages 3–4.) It was not that the land was poor. The opposite was true. And it was not that no one wanted to come to the Cumberland country. Plenty of people wanted to come.

It was the unrelenting threat of Indian attacks that kept people away. The Chickamaugas—often called "renegade" or "outlaw" Cherokees—and their allies, the Creeks, sometimes aided by mainstream Cherokees, made one deadly raid after another on the isolated Cumberland stations.

One of their most vicious attacks was in June 1792 at Ziegler's Station, across the Cumberland River in Sumner County. Five settlers were killed, four wounded, and eighteen taken prisoner. (The Ziegler's Station attack is described more fully in The Middle Cumberland Tour, pages 27–28.)

Following a route through what is now Wilson County, the attackers with their captives fled south, back to the Indian towns along the Tennessee River. The militia was called out to give chase. Led by General James Winchester, the party picked up the attackers' trail south of the Cumberland. It followed footprints that included the pitiful outlines of the abducted children's little bare feet.

Winchester's men made a discovery near a big spring. Littered around the ground where the Indians had stopped to build a fire to light their pipes were unused strips of deer hide. At the next muddy spot, the pursuers saw something for which, as one militia man later wrote, they "rejoiced." The little bare footprints had been replaced by little moccasin prints. The Indians had made moccasins for the children. "There was that much of kindness in them," the pursuer wrote of the Indians. The big spring, later called Town Spring, is now covered by Lebanon's Public Square.

The militia camped for the night at another spring 8 miles south of Lebanon. Near the site stands a giant red oak thought to be over three hundred years old. Where part of its bark is missing from a lightning strike, a perfect arrow is carved in the bare wood about shoulder high. It points south. It has been speculated that a captive from Ziegler's Station carved it hoping that it would be seen by rescuers.

The next day, Winchester called off the pursuit. It would be safer, the general reasoned, to let the captives be taken alive to the Indian nation, and perhaps be ransomed, than to risk their lives in a fight.

The captives held at the Chickamaugas' towns were indeed ransomed. They included the three daughters of the slain Jacob Ziegler. Sarah Wilson, taken by the Creeks, remained in their custody for many years. Reports circulated that when she was finally freed, she had nearly forgotten how to live in civilized society. It was many years before she lost her Indian ways.

More blood was shed on the Cumberland frontier through 1792, 1793, and 1794. It was widely believed that the Spanish were behind the attacks. They wanted to keep settlers away from the Mississippi River, which was claimed by Spain.

Home for the Chickamaugas was the Lower Towns on the Tennessee River around today's Chattanooga. The Creeks lived south of the river in what is now Alabama. Pressure grew in the Cumberland country for an attack on the Lower Towns if that would stop the violence. But the government ordered Cumberland settlers to stay put. This was during Tennessee's territorial period, between 1790 and 1796, between the time it was part of North Carolina and the time it was a state. President George Washington wanted to stay on good terms with the Spanish. The territorial governor, William Blount, wrote James Robertson, "With respect to destroying the Lower Towns, . . . whatever good the consequences might result from it, I am instructed specially, by the President, to say that he does not consider himself authorized to direct any such measure."

The people on the Cumberland frontier respected George Washington, but they could wait no longer. James Robertson organized an expedition of about 275 men to destroy the Lower Towns. "Spare women and children, and . . . treat all prisoners who may fall into your hands with humanity, and thereby teach those savages to spare the citizens of the United States, under similar circumstances," he instructed his men.

Taking a route from Nashville that roughly follows today's Interstate 24, the force reached the Tennessee River on September 12, 1794. It attacked the Lower Towns of Nickajack and Running Water the next day, killing about fifty Chickamaugas. After the Nickajack expedition, there were more murders on the Cumberland that fall. A second invasion was planned, this one against the Creeks. Meanwhile, a meeting with the mainstream Cherokees in East Tennessee brought peace with them.

Next, an opportunity to neutralize the Creeks came when the Chickasaws, allies of the Cumberland settlers, asked James Robertson for help against their old enemies. In May 1795, Robertson sent two companies of militia to help the Chickasaws defeat the Creeks near today's Memphis. Also in 1795, the United States and Spain negotiated a treaty by which Spain settled its claims to the old Southwest. By the end of 1795, fifteen years of Indian attacks on the isolated Cumberland settlements were nearing an end. People now felt secure to move into the surrounding countryside.

The first settler to bring his family to the site of today's Lebanon was Needy Jacobs. Jacobs was born in Ireland around 1769. At age ten, he was rescued from a shipwreck off the coast of North Carolina by an Indian tribe, who subsequently raised him. Jacobs married an Indian girl, Layula, in 1785. A child, Sallie, was born to them the following year. Needy, Layula, and Sallie wound up in the Cumberland country around 1790.

Jacobs and his family left Nashville and built a sturdy cedar cabin by a big spring, the same spring where the Indians fleeing Ziegler's Station had stopped to light their pipes and make the moccasins. Needy and Layula were not alone long, for settlement of the area was rapid and widespread after the Indian hostilities ceased.

Needy Jacobs was a well-known character in Lebanon's early days. He was said to have retained many of the skills learned years earlier living with the Indians. When Sallie married, he killed a dog, tanned the hide, and made her a dressy pair of wedding slippers. When the 1835 cholera epidemic hit Lebanon, Jacobs is reported to have cured people with "Indian medicine"—an herbal concoction.

Layula Jacobs was visited by some Indians late in her life. She left with them and never returned. No one knows for sure who her visitors were, but it is speculated she might have joined the Cherokees while they were being driven off their lands in northern Georgia. The infamous Trail of Tears passed quite near Lebanon. She would have been nearly seventy at the time.

In 1799, the settlers in this area petitioned the legislature meeting at Knoxville to sever Sumner County at the Cumberland River and create a new county. It is curious that the county was named for David Wilson, since the Revolutionary War veteran had no connection with the new county or the lands that comprised it. And little is known of his military service.

Town Spring, the big spring where Needy Jacobs built his cabin, was chosen as the site for the county seat in 1802. Impressed with the vast stands of cedars in the area, the founders named the town after the cedars of Lebanon mentioned in the Bible.

Lebanon quickly grew into an important trade center. For a time, Andrew Jackson ran a store here. And Sam Houston practiced law in a small cedar building east of the square for about ten months before he moved to Nashville in 1819. Today, Lebanon has found its niche as the "Antique City of the South." Over eighty-five antique dealers have their shops around the square and at other locations in town.

The people of Wilson County thought enough of Robert Hopkins Hatton to erect a monument to him in the center of the square in 1912. Hatton was killed in action near Richmond, Virginia, eight days after he was promoted to brigadier general in the Confederate army in May 1862. But he was not always so popular. In fact, on a night in March 1861, an angry crowd hung him in effigy in front of his West Main Street house.

The Tennessee congressman was strongly against secession. As he wrote to a Lebanon friend from Washington in December 1860, "If the Union we cannot preserve, the *dream* of the Revolution is over, and the melancholy fact will have to be announced to the world, that a truly free government is *too good* for mankind. To preserve it . . . I could, this night, *cheerfully* lay down my life." What an irony it is that he gave his life for the opposite cause.

From the square, drive east on Main Street for one block and turn north. It is one block to Market Street. Turn right on Market and drive one block to Pickett Chapel.

The Methodists built this, the oldest brick building in Lebanon, in 1829. They outgrew it and built a new church on East Main in 1856. From 1866

Hatton Monument on Lebanon's square

Pickett Chapel

Fite-Fessenden House, now the Wilson County Museum

Former home of Robert L. Caruthers

to 1974, this structure housed a congregation of black Methodists. They named it for Calvin and James Pickett, trustees of the Methodists' Tennessee Conference who assisted in forming the congregation. Lately, Pickett Chapel has served as Lebanon's community theater.

Return to the square. Drive west on Main Street, a pleasant tree-shaded thoroughfare with several historic houses. Two of them face each other 0.2 mile west of the square.

The Wilson County Museum is in the Fite-Fessenden House, located on the left. Dr. James Leonidas Fite built the original part of this house in 1852.

The large white house across the street—now a funeral home—was built by Robert L. Caruthers in 1828. Joseph Reiff, the builder, also built Andrew Jackson's Hermitage. Caruthers served one term in Congress in the 1840s. He was later selected to be the Confederate governor of Tennessee in 1863, but he never took office because almost all of Tennessee was under Federal occupation by then.

Isaac William Pleasant Buchanan's house

Caruthers's best-known contribution to Middle Tennessee was the founding of Cumberland Law School, which operated here from 1847 until it relocated to Samford University in Birmingham in 1961. Cumberland Law School boasts that among its graduates were one secretary of state—Cordell Hull—two justices of the United States Supreme Court, forty-two Tennessee Supreme Court justices, nine United States senators, and sixty-six United States congressmen.

Continue west on Main Street. The Isaac Buchanan House, one of Middle Tennessee's most distinctive homes, is on the left after 0.3 mile.

Isaac William Pleasant Buchanan was a man of many talents. He organized the Wilson County Bank in 1884. In 1902, he and David Mitchell founded the school that became Castle Heights Military Academy. Buchanan was an inventor who held many patents, including one for an automobile self-starter and another for an automatic spray gun for painting. He lived until 1943.

Buchanan selected nationally prominent Knoxville architect George F.

Castle Heights Military Academy

The 1906 Mitchell House

Barber to design this house, completed in 1897. Buchanan himself personally supervised the construction. The house stands today as one of the finest examples anywhere of the elaborate Queen Anne style.

Stay on Main Street for another 0.3 mile, then turn right into the grounds of Castle Heights Military Academy.

The school Buchanan and Mitchell started in 1902 became a military academy in 1914 and was taken over by Bernarr Macfadden in 1930. A local foundation assumed ownership of the school in 1974, but decreasing enrollment and rising costs finally forced it to close. Its fascinating old buildings stand empty today.

David Mitchell built his massive Neoclassical house to the left of the campus drive in 1906. Saddened by the death of his wife, Mitchell mysteriously left Tennessee in 1919. The academy bought the house and converted it to a junior school in the 1920s. It is now unoccupied.

When you are ready to leave Castle Heights Military Academy, cross Main Street onto Castle Heights Avenue and drive 0.2 mile to Spring Street. Turn left (E) and go 0.6 mile to Greenwood, passing the campus of Cumberland University. Turn right (S) on Greenwood.

The towered building that sits beautifully behind a grove of trees and is the focal point of the campus is Memorial Hall. Nashville architect W. C. Smith, the designer of Vanderbilt University's Kirkland Hall and the original Parthenon in Nashville's Centennial Park, is the man responsible for Memorial Hall. The building's cornerstone was laid in 1892.

Cumberland University traces its origin to the decision of the General Assembly of Cumberland Presbyterian Church to relocate its college here in 1842. Fanceway Ranna Cossitt served as the college's first president. The original board included Robert L. Caruthers, founder of Cumberland Law School; "Lean Jimmy" Jones, the Lebanon Whig who defeated James K. Polk for governor in 1841; and Jordan Stokes, Speaker of the Tennessee House of Representatives.

Memorial Hall at Cumberland University

The university has seen its ups and downs over the years. It was completely destroyed during the Civil War, and its sponsoring institution has changed often. The school was taken over by the Presbyterian Church, USA, in 1906, then by the Tennessee Baptist Convention, and finally by a nondenominational board in 1951. Cumberland was reduced to a two-year junior college in 1956 but later regained its status as a four-year college.

Cumberland University has an athletic record it would probably just as soon forget. In 1916, Georgia Tech beat the small school 220–0, the most lopsided score in the history of college football.

In front of Memorial Hall, turn left (E) off Greenwood onto University Drive. Go 0.2 mile to Maple Avenue and turn right (S). It is 5.4 miles to U.S. 231. Along the way, Maple Avenue becomes Old Murfreesboro Road.

It was not far from here that the first train chugged into Lebanon in 1870. The name of this short line to Nashville reflects the grandiose plans of its promoters—the Tennessee & Pacific is what they called it. A solicitation for the bonds to finance the project proclaimed that the line "will extend to the East and will be the shortest and cheapest road to New York City, and also to Memphis and New Orleans."

But within a year after it opened, the railroad defaulted on its bonds and was taken over by the Nashville, Chattanooga & St. Louis. A competing railroad, the Tennessee Central, opened in 1902. The two lines paralleled each other through Mount Juliet, the Nashville suburb that was then a quiet village; it was not unheard of for engineers on the two railroads to challenge each other to races. Competition from the Tennessee Central and improved highway transportation killed the old Tennessee & Pacific. The last train left Lebanon in 1935.

Turn right (S) on U.S. 231. Drive 2.8 miles and turn left into Cedars of Lebanon State Park. It is 0.3 mile to the park headquarters.

The story of the creation of this park is a familiar one. Once, there was a great forest. Then it was destroyed by reckless exploitation. Finally, a small part of the forest was restored as a Depression-era conservation project.

Red cedar—actually a juniper, not a true cedar—is the most widely distributed evergreen in the eastern United States. The trees tend to grow in shallow, rocky soil, and there is plenty of that at middle elevations southeast of Nashville. For a hundred years, local residents cut the cedar they needed for their cabins, shingles, fences, and furniture. The wood was easy to split and resistant to rot.

It was later that commercial exploitation of the vast forest got under way. Red cedar was particularly prized for use in pencils, for it is light and sharpens easily. But pencil manufacturing was also wasteful. The industry used only straight, knot-free heartwood and threw away 70 percent of every log cut. Three million board feet of cedar logs were shipped out of Middle Tennessee in 1900. Within ten years, the cedar forests were practically gone. The restoration that began in 1935 on 8,817 acres of dissipated farmland evolved into the largest stand of red cedars anywhere in the East.

Cedars of Lebanon is actually three areas managed by the state of Tennessee—a park for recreation, a natural area set aside for preservation, and a multiple-use state forest. Cedars of Lebanon offers something unusual for a state park—a Frisbee golf course. Eight miles of hiking trails and 12 miles of horse trails meander through the forest and glades.

The cedar glades of Middle Tennessee are unique. Found in Wilson, Rutherford, and Davidson counties and to a lesser extent in six other contiguous counties, they consist of rocky openings in the forest where the soil is too shallow to permit the growth of woody plants. In the summer, soil surface temperatures are often ten to thirty degrees hotter than in the woods. The cedar glades—so named because they are in the cedar forests, not because cedars actually grow in them—are really minideserts. One of the most common plants is the prickly pear cactus.

The 350 different species of plants that grow in the glades have adapted to their harsh environment, resulting in unique plant communities as well as several plants that occur nowhere else in the world. The Tennessee coneflower is found at only ten sites. Guthrie's ground-plum, even rarer, is found at only three sites. Leafy prairie clover is found at about eighteen sites.

To the uninformed, cedar glades look like barren, worthless wasteland, and for that reason, they have been abused over the years, particularly as places for dumping. Augustin Gattinger, a German-born physician and botanist who settled in Nashville during the Civil War, was the first to recognize and document the unique plant life of the glades. In more recent times, Elsie Quarterman, a Vanderbilt University biology professor, has heightened public awareness of this special resource. An increasing number of landowners recognize the uniqueness of the glades and take pains to protect them. Glades are protected here at Cedars of Lebanon and at nearby Long Hunter State Park on Percy Priest Lake. Naturalist programs at both parks offer an introduction to these uncommon areas.

From Cedars of Lebanon State Park, backtrack a short distance on U.S. 231 to TN 265 (Chicken Road) and turn right (E); you will reach Doak Cross Road at 3.4 miles. Continue on TN 265 for 2.7 miles to U.S. 70. Turn right (SE) on U.S. 70. It is 2.8 miles to Mount Zion Baptist Church and the left turn into Watertown. As you enter Watertown, you will pass a trio of lovely brick churches before reaching the town square 1.4 miles from U.S. 70.

First called Three Forks because of its location near where the three forks of Round Lick Creek meet, Watertown is named for Wilson Lawrence Waters, the town's leading citizen in the nineteenth century.

Waters was a farmer, a merchant, a miller, and a leader in the formation of the Lebanon and Sparta Turnpike Company, which built a road through here in the 1840s. He freed his slaves before the Civil War and was one of the rare Republicans in these parts; he attended the 1860 convention that nominated Abraham Lincoln. Late in his life, Waters was instrumental in bringing the Tennessee Central Railroad through Watertown.

The railroad helped Watertown develop into a thriving little industrial center in the first quarter of the twentieth century. One of the town's several textile mills was the Williams Manufacturing Company, which in 1928 operated the world's largest wooden pin mill. Today, Watertown is a well-kept, pleasant small town noted for its mile-long yard sale, held each April, and for being a destination for train excursions out of Nashville sponsored by the Tennessee Central Railway Museum.

Leave Watertown by heading south on Depot Street. After crossing U.S. 70 at 0.1 mile, Depot Street changes to TN 267 (Statesville Road).

Geologists assure us that there are no real mountains in Middle Tennessee west of the Cumberland Plateau, but you would never know it here. Broken, detached pieces of the Eastern Highland Rim create ranges of rugged hills that rise hundreds of feet above the valleys below.

After crossing a high gap in the ridge, the route drops into the fertile valley of the Smith Fork River. Bear left at the fork 6.1 miles from U.S. 70, staying on TN 267 as it swings east. Turn right (S) on Hardin Hollow Road 0.3 mile from the fork. Cross the Smith Fork on the little Veterans Memorial Bridge—marked by a handsome 1993 plaque—and make an immediate right (W) onto Statesville's Main Street.

Statesville is a picture-perfect out-of-the-way village nestled among the hills. The first settlers came here in 1797 and later started a town called Maryville in honor of the wife of the tavern keeper. The story of its name change should be familiar by now. When the local people applied for a post office in 1828, there was a conflict with Maryville in East Tennessee. They chose the name Statesville because a number of the settlers came from the town of that name in North Carolina.

At the intersection at the west end of Statesville, go straight (W) on Greenvale Road. After 0.8 mile, you will pass the picturesque 1906 Smith Fork Baptist Church, located on the right. Bear right at the intersection in Greenvale after another 4.1 miles. Greenvale Road ends at TN 266 (Cainsville Road) after another 2.7 miles. Turn left (S) on TN 266.

The steep hills recede into the background now as the route returns to the gentler Central Basin, dotted with thick cedar groves. The route goes through the pleasant community of Cainsville, founded around 1829, enters Rutherford County, and passes two historic houses.

General Griffith Rutherford has the distinction of having two counties named for him—this one, established in 1803, and another in his native

Smith Fork Baptist Church

TOURING THE MIDDLE TENNESSEE BACKROADS

North Carolina. The general came to the Cumberland country after 1783 and settled in Sumner County, but it is doubtful that the Revolutionary War hero ever visited his namesake county.

The house on the right 3 miles from the Greenvale Road intersection was built by Robert Hall Jarman about 1855. Jarman's father, also named Robert, came to Middle Tennessee from North Carolina in 1796 with his brother and his widowed mother and settled on this land.

The Dement House, located 2.1 miles past the Jarman House, was built entirely of logs in 1817. It was expanded in 1833 and later covered with the four-inch yellow poplar weatherboard siding visible today. The Dements were French Huguenots who arrived in Middle Tennessee in 1798.

Continue south on TN 266. At 0.5 mile from the Dement House, you will reach the junction with TN 96. Stay on TN 266 as it turns right (E), then turns right again and enters the village of Lascassas after 0.8 mile. The lovely Methodist church in the middle of town was built in 1910 as a Presbyterian church. The congregation's membership dwindled until it finally disbanded, and the Methodists bought the building in 1930.

Leave Lascassas by heading west on TN 266, known both as Jefferson Pike and Barlow Lane.

On the left 3.3 miles from Lascassas is a beautiful old farmhouse that has seen its share of joy and tragedy. The place is best known for the massive pine tree that towers over the house. Shortly after the house was built in 1860, William B. Owen, a Baptist minister, and his bride, Betty M. Nance, planted two pines—one for him and one for her—as symbols of their love. One was lost long ago, but the other, surely one of Middle Tennessee's tallest trees, still stands. Tragedy came to the Owens in April 1883 with the death of their two daughters within twenty-four hours of each other of complications from measles while they were away at boarding school.

Pine tree planted in 1860 dwarfs the Owen Farmhouse.

It is another 2.1 miles to Walter Hill. Turn left (S) onto U.S. 231. Drive 0.6 mile across the East Fork of the Stones River and turn left into the park at Walter Hill Dam.

Uriah Stone was a member of a party of long hunters and explorers who ventured into the vast Middle Cumberland wilderness in 1766. The men were enticed by a large stream emptying into the Cumberland a few miles from where Fort Nashborough would be established over a decade later.

Stone led a party nearly 40 miles up the smaller river to the point where it forks, hunting and setting traps along the way. From then on, the river carried Stone's name.

By the time Rutherford County was established in 1803, the downriver flatboat trade had begun, so it was only logical that a site on Stones River be selected for the county seat. The town of Jefferson, named for President Thomas Jefferson, was laid out on a rise where the river's east and west forks join. A brick courthouse was built, and before long, Jefferson was a full-fledged town with houses, stores, taverns, wharves, and warehouses.

Money was hard to find on the frontier, and a system of barter evolved at Jefferson and places like it. Merchants obtained scarce goods needed by the settlers—such as cloth, nails, hinges, coffee, lead, and gunpowder— and took items like hides and pelts in exchange. Large ox hides would buy $4.00 worth of goods, wolf scalps $2.50. Deerskins brought $.50. The merchant would then ship the products of the forest downriver on the flatboats. Silver coins did show up from time to time, and dollars would be cut in pieces as a method of making change, hence the terms *two bits* and *four bits*.

Rutherford County took in much more territory in those days, and Jefferson, located in its northwest corner, was too distant for many of the citizens to get to. After a bitter competition, the site for a new county seat was selected in 1811, to be built on land donated by Captain William Lytle. Newton Cannon, a rising young politician from neighboring Williamson County who represented the area in the state senate, was honored by having the new town of Cannonsburgh named for him. But after only a month, at William Lytle's suggestion, the name was changed to Murfreesboro in honor of Lytle's friend Hardy Murfree, who had recently died.

Jefferson continued as an important port for the flatboats bound for faraway New Orleans and Natchez. Later, it was a major departure point for log rafts, the method by which the area's abundant cedar logs were exported. The little town eventually dwindled in importance after it was bypassed by the railroad. Today, Jefferson is nothing more than a memory.

From the time of the arrival of the earliest settlers, the Stones River has been a valuable source of water power. A mill was established here at Walter

Walter Hill Dam, an early hydroelectric site on the Stones River

Hill in 1804. The Southern Cities Power Company purchased the site in 1918 and built a hydroelectric generating station in the building across the river. When the TVA took over private power interests in the 1930s, it bought the Walter Hill generating station, which continued to produce electricity until 1941.

Leave the park at Walter Hill Dam by heading south on U.S. 231. It is 2.1 miles to the intersection with Thompson Lane (TN 268) at the beautifully landscaped Alvin C. York Veterans Hospital. Murfreesboro proper is straight ahead. Turn right (W) onto Thompson Lane and drive 4.4 miles to Northwest Broad Street (U.S. 41).

There is much to see in Murfreesboro, even though it is not on this tour. The splendid 1857 courthouse is one of the oldest in the state. The first part of Oaklands, one of the Tennessee's best-known historic houses, dates to around 1815, when it was built by Sally Hardy Murfree, daughter of the man for whom Murfreesboro is named, and her husband, Dr. James Maney. Significant additions were later made to the house by Lewis Maney and his wife, Rachel Adeline Cannon, daughter of Newton Cannon. Oaklands houses a museum and is open to the public year-round.

Two other Rutherford County landmarks not on the tour—the Sam Davis Home and the huge Nissan Motor Manufacturing Plant—are at Smyrna, located on U.S. 41 toward Nashville. Davis was a young Confederate soldier who was hanged. The Sam Davis Home is open to the public year-round. (For more information about Davis, see The South Central Tour, pages 267–69.) The Nissan plant houses facilities for assembling pickup trucks and two automobile models. Tours are offered to the public.

Information about these and other points of interest can be obtained at the Cannonsburgh Pioneer Village, a reconstructed nineteenth-century town in the heart of Murfreesboro.

Stay on Thompson Lane across Northwest Broad Street; you will cross the railroad on a bridge. At the end of the bridge, 0.3 mile from Broad, turn left off Thompson Lane at the sign for Stones River National Battlefield. This short connector intersects the Old Nashville Pike. Turn left (NW). At 0.9 mile from Thompson Lane, turn left to reach the battlefield's visitor center.

It was at Murfreesboro in December 1862 that the Old South had its final fling in the Mid-South. General Braxton Bragg had brought the South's principal western army to Murfreesboro following his failed Kentucky invasion that fall, and the citizens of this former Tennessee capital, overwhelmingly Confederate in their sympathies, were happy to see the Army of Tennessee. Something of a social scene evolved, as the ladies of the town hosted the officers at parties and balls and as wives and sweethearts came for visits.

The most noted visitor was Confederate president Jefferson Davis. In mid-December 1862, he came to Murfreesboro to confer with Bragg and to get his first look at the big western army. The Army of Tennessee staged a massive, colorful review for the Mississippian. But the social highlight of this lull in the fighting was the wedding of Brigadier General John Hunt Morgan.

Morgan was one of the dashing cavalry leaders in the West, famous for his daring raids behind enemy lines, which usually produced more show than results. The summer before, a Murfreesboro girl, when asked her name

Stones River National Battlefield

by some Union occupation soldiers, had answered, "It's Mattie Ready now. But by the grace of God one day I hope to call myself the wife of John Morgan." She had heard of the flashy Kentuckian and was hoping some-day to meet and even marry him.

This story made its way to John Hunt Morgan, a young widower. When the Confederates were back in Murfreesboro that fall, he called on Miss Ready. It was a short courtship. They were married the day after Jefferson Davis left, December 14.

It was an impressive ceremony. Outfitted in clean gray uniforms, with their swords at their sides, many of the ranking officers were in the wed-ding party. General Bragg was in attendance, as was the rest of the high command. Leonidas Polk commanded half of Bragg's infantry. He was also the Episcopal bishop of Louisiana. Wearing his bishop's vestments over his lieutenant general's uniform, the "bishop-general" performed the ceremony. (For more information about Polk, see The Maury County Tour, pages 215–16.) Following the wedding, a lively Christmas social season started with balls and parties held for the Confederate officers.

The social swirl was short-lived. William S. Rosecrans saw to that. The Ohio engineer who commanded the Army of the Cumberland at Nash-ville was using this quiet time to gather men and material for a Union push south. On December 26, after considerable prodding from Washing-ton, the long blue lines marched out of Nashville toward Murfreesboro. Within days, the opposing forces would meet along the Stones River in one of the Civil War's major battles.

This campaign signaled the opening of nearly two years of fighting along the vital rail line that stretched from Nashville to Atlanta via Chatta-nooga. The first Union goal was simple—take the pivotal rail junction of Chattanooga and free Union-sympathizing East Tennessee from Confeder-ate control. The second goal was to move on to Atlanta. The Confederate goal was equally uncomplicated—stop the Yankees. It took nearly two years, but Atlanta finally fell in September 1864. Along the way, blood was spilled at Chickamauga, Lookout Mountain, Missionary Ridge, Resaca, Kennesaw Mountain, Peachtree Creek, and here at Stones River.

As the new year approached, both Rosecrans and Bragg consolidated their forces northwest of Murfreesboro. On the night of December 30, everyone knew there would be a battle the next day. The orders had been issued. Tension was broken by the serenading of regimental bands from both sides. The armies were close enough to easily hear each other's bands, and a competition broke out—a battle of the bands, Civil War–style. Then one band started playing "Home Sweet Home." Soon, another joined in, then another, and before long, all the bands in both armies played the song in unison. The men started singing. A massive chorus went up in the cold Middle Tennessee night. Tomorrow, they would kill each other. Tonight, they sang together of home.

On December 31, Bragg launched his attack on Rosecrans's right. By the end of the day, the Confederates had pushed the Federals all the way back to the Nashville Pike. "The enemy has yielded his strong position and is falling back. We occupy the whole field and shall follow him. . . . God has granted us a happy New Year," Bragg wired Richmond.

But the new year turned out to be not so happy after all. The exhausted survivors of the bloodshed on December 31 were idle on New Year's Day. Then, on January 2, Bragg launched another offensive, but it was soundly repulsed. By darkness, his men had not gained any ground to speak of.

Braxton Bragg still believed he had won, and was encouraged by reports of long lines of wagons leaving in the night for Nashville. Rosecrans was retreating, he thought. He was wrong. Rosecrans held fast. The wagons were merely hauling off the wounded. The next day, Bragg received reports that Rosecrans, who already had more troops than the Southern army, was being reinforced. And a train of fresh supplies was coming from Nashville.

Bragg ordered a retreat. His disheartened soldiers, still believing they had won a victory, left behind their dead and wounded on January 3 and started out on an miserable, muddy, aimless march through sleet and rain. They ended up haphazardly scattered along the Duck River in the Shelbyville-Tullahoma area.

From a purely military standpoint, the Battle of Stones River was a draw, albeit a bloody one. Southern casualties were 11,739. The North lost 13,249. But the Confederates, who retreated, were the real losers. Morale was already low following the failure in Kentucky, and now it was even lower. Bragg was not well liked by his men to begin with. He came to be despised. In fact, no one in the Confederacy thought that Bragg should still be commanding the army. That is, except one person—Jefferson Davis.

The national battlefield preserves only a fraction of the land on which the Battle of Stones River was fought, but it is enough to get a feel for how difficult it must have been to fight in the thick cedar forests. The visitor center offers programs and publications describing the battle. There is also a driving tour, as well as a walking path. Across the Old Nashville Pike from the visitor center is a national cemetery where many of the Union dead are buried.

From Stones River National Battlefield, retrace your route to Thompson Lane. Turn left (S) on Thompson and drive 0.5 mile to Manson Pike. Turn right (W). It is 4.2 miles to Blackman. At Blackman, follow a dogleg to the left, then turn right onto Burnt Knob Road. The route continues west through a remote, hilly part of Rutherford County. You will reach Almaville Road (TN 102) after 4.4 miles. Turn left (S). After 0.3 mile, turn right (W) onto Independent Hill Road. You will cross more hills before reaching McCanless Road after 3.5 miles. Here, the land becomes gentler and opens up into prosperous Williamson County farms. Turn left (S) onto McCanless. This stretch of road passes several historic houses, including the Abram Glenn House, located on a hill to the left after 0.5 mile.

There are not too many old log houses like this left in Middle Tennessee, but these were the norm for pioneers in the early days. The two-story section built in 1815 was joined by a one-story log kitchen in 1825. They were connected by the familiar dogtrot breezeway.

Abram and Martha Glenn migrated from Virginia and bought part of the land that had been granted to General Jethro Sumner, the man for whom Sumner County is named. Martha lived until 1848 and Abram until 1851. Their son, James, then took over the place.

A son born to James and his second wife, Ruth Ann, was just a baby when the first Federal troops arrived in the area during the Civil War. James had just sold some farm produce for a hundred dollars, a goodly sum in those days. When the Federal troops got wind of it, they descended upon the Glenn place. The troops had been tipped off by Union-sympathizing neighbors—"homemade Yankees," they were called. The Glenns denied that they had any money, but when the troops started rummaging through the house looking for it, they began to fear for the safety of their infant. Ruth Ann finally took the money from under the mattress in the baby's cradle and gave it to the soldiers.

Continue 1.7 miles on McCanless Road to U.S. 31A/U.S. 41A. Turn left (S). It is 1.7 miles to the old Triune Methodist Church, on the left, and another 0.6 mile to the junction with TN 96.

Triune is named for the church, rather than the other way around. Hardeman Cross Roads was the town's original name, then Flemingsburg. When the first local church was built in 1849 to house a congregation that dates to at least 1804, the minister gave it the name Triune. On the eve of the Civil War, Triune was a thriving town with several businesses, including a weekly newspaper.

The church was destroyed by Union troops in 1863, as was the adjacent Porter Female Academy. The academy was one of five schools in this area built between 1820 and 1845, making Triune something of an educational center in this prosperous part of Middle Tennessee before the Civil War. The current church, started right after the war on the foundation of the old one, was not completed until 1874.

Dr. Jonathan Bostick, a trustee of Porter Female Academy, left Tennessee after the Civil War, but he obviously remembered it fondly. In his will, he provided for the creation of a new school. Bostick Female Academy was built in 1892. It stands on the rise to the right 0.2 mile south of the junction at Triune.

Bostick Female Academy

The school accepted both day and boarding students and offered classes in liberal arts, music, and art. Classrooms, a dining room, and a kitchen occupied the first floor, while the second floor was taken up by nine dormitory rooms. As many as seventy-five girls attended the academy, with overflow boarders housed in neighboring homes. With the advent of universal public education around 1900, the private school closed. The building housed a public school until 1957. The former Bostick Female Academy has since been restored for use as a private residence.

Continue south on U.S. 31A/U.S. 41A for 2.9 miles to where Taliaferro Road comes in from the left. A historic marker notes that Newton Cannon lived and is buried just down Taliaferro Road. Sadly, his house, part of which was built of logs as early as 1800, was burned by arsonists in 1989.

Cannon County, east of Murfreesboro, is named for Newton Cannon. So was Murfreesboro, at least for a month. Aside from that, most Tennesseans have never heard of Newton Cannon. Yet he was an important political figure in the first half of the nineteenth century.

It was inevitable that a man as forceful, dominant, and hot-tempered as Andrew Jackson would have enemies. Cannon was one of them. Cannon's first bad experience with Jackson supposedly happened at the Clover Bottom racetrack, owned by Jackson and brothers William and Patten Anderson. Newton Cannon lost a good deal of his money and possessions wagering with Jackson. The three owners were heavy gamblers themselves, and the widespread suspicion that races were fixed apparently figured into Cannon's hostility.

Cannon and Jackson then had an unpleasant encounter in one of the three trials that resulted from the killing of Jackson's friend and Clover Bottom partner Patten Anderson. David Magnes, who killed Anderson, and his brothers Jonathan and Perry were tried separately at Franklin in 1810, 1811, and 1812. Newton Cannon happened to be on the jury in the third trial. After Jonathan Magnes was found not guilty, Jackson approached Cannon. Shaking his fist under Cannon's nose, Jackson said, "I'll mark you, young man."

But it was Cannon's experience serving under General Jackson in the war against the Creeks that most embittered him. Cannon, the leader of a detachment, came to believe that Jackson had purposely exposed him and his men to almost certain death.

Newton Cannon ran for Congress against Jackson ally Felix Grundy in 1813. Cannon lost, but he ended up replacing Grundy when he resigned due to his wife's poor health. Cannon then won election to Congress three times, over Jackson's objection.

Cannon ran for governor in 1827 but lost to Jackson's handpicked candidate, Sam Houston. Cannon served briefly in the state senate a second time, then retired from politics, or so he thought. When a constitutional convention was selected in 1834 to consider revising Tennessee's original 1796 constitution, Cannon's fellow citizens prevailed upon him to serve as a delegate. He ended up being the leader of the convention. Many of the progressive provisions in the new charter were passed on Cannon's initiative.

While Andrew Jackson was serving as president, the Whig Party emerged as the opposition to Jackson's Democrats. Cannon was a natural choice to carry the anti-Jackson banner. In the governor's election of 1835, as the Whig candidate, he defeated incumbent William Carroll, Jackson's man. Cannon was elected to another two-year term in 1837. He was known as a progressive governor and an early advocate of free public education, pushing for legislation calling for "common schools."

Jackson and his allies could take it no more. They needed a strong candidate to challenge Cannon in the 1839 election. A reluctant James K. Polk of Columbia was persuaded to give up his national office as Speaker of the House to return to Tennessee and run for governor. It was one of the most celebrated campaigns for governor in Tennessee history, marked by the stormy debates the candidates held around the state. Polk won by 2,616 votes. Cannon lived just two more years after his defeat.

His house is only one of the many historic homes here in the eastern part of Williamson County. Another sits on the hill across the highway from Taliaferro Road. It took James and Margaret Webb three years in the 1850s to build this house, which combines the Greek Revival and the emerging Italianate styles. They called it Sylvan Retreat for the many trees around it.

Stay on U.S. 31A/U.S. 41A for 0.7 mile to the junction at Kirkland, where the two routes split. Bear right on U.S. 31A. Before the days of interstate highways, Kirkland was an important stopping point south of Nashville. Look closely and you will see the remains of a "tourist court" or two around the junction.

It is 1.5 miles to the pleasant town of College Grove. As you come into the village, the beautiful College Grove United Methodist Church is on the left. It was built in 1888.

First called Poplar Grove, College Grove takes its name from two early schools, one for boys and one for girls. The boys' school, Cary and Winn Academy, stood on the site of today's elementary school. Nearly one hundred students attended the school at its peak, but it could not survive the ravages of the Civil War. Most of the students went off to fight for the Confederacy, and so did Professors Cary and Winn. Cary spent much of the war in a Northern prison. Winn was killed in action.

College Grove United Methodist Church

Continue south on U.S. 31A through College Grove. Two miles south of town, you will pass Allison Heights, the house perched atop the steep hill to the right.

James Allison came to this far corner of newly established Williamson County around 1800 and bought enough land to make him the area's largest landowner. When he died in 1821, he left this property to his son, William Allison. In 1827, William and his wife, Louisa Perkins, started building this handsome Federal house, the most imposing home in this area in its day. They completed it in 1832.

William died just two years after Allison Heights was completed. The property eventually passed to his son Thomas F. P. Allison. Thomas served as a major in the Confederate cavalry during the Civil War, lived through it, and went on to become one of Tennessee's best-known and most progressive farmers. He served as the state's commissioner of agriculture from 1893 until 1897 and was chief of the Agricultural Department at the 1897 Tennessee Centennial Exposition.

Thomas Allison's first wife died before the Civil War. At the end of the war, he married Clara Bills, whom he had met while serving in West Tennessee. They posed quite a contrast. He was a tall, large man and she was "as small as a child," according to Virginia McDaniel Bowman, author of the exhaustive *Historic Williamson County*. He loved horses. She was afraid of them. In fact, the only horse she would ride was an old swayback named Ben. Old Ben seldom moved faster than a walk, much to the embarrassment of Thomas—but much to the satisfaction of Clara.

Continue 3.5 miles south to Riggs Crossroads, marked by a small graveyard on the right of the highway. As the plaque on the stone wall notes, Gideon Riggs, born in 1790, outlived three wives: Mary Reynolds, who died in 1825; Sophia Campbell, who died in 1836; and Catherine F. Holden, who died in 1865. Gideon Riggs lived until 1871.

Between Riggs Crossroads and Chapel Hill, a distance of 6 miles, the highway enters Marshall County and passes the community of Holt's Corner.

There was once a little town called Gideonville about 2 miles from Holt's Corner. It got its start through a fraud committed about 1820 by John DeFreese, a man who had married into the Riggs family and named his only son for Gideon Riggs. DeFreese believed that he could accumulate a fortune by dividing his land and starting a town. But he needed a gimmick to attract people. Salt was a valuable commodity in this remote country in those days, so he came up with a scheme: salt a spring. He placed a sack of salt in a spring, then made sure a Mrs. Dickson—described as "a reliable lady"—got some of the water. She discovered the salt, and before long, word spread that this area was the site of a valuable salt spring.

The town DeFreese hoped for did grow up around the spring. He named it Gideonville, after his son. At one time, there was a hotel, a store, a blacksmith shop, a cabinet shop, a saddler's shop, a hatter's shop, and three whiskey stores. The town died out, though, and was gone by 1833. Nothing remains of it today.

North of Chapel Hill, another little town existed for a while bearing the curious name of Civil Order. Nothing of it remains either.

The name Chapel Hill was suggested by John Laws. Shortly after finishing college, he headed west. By the time he arrived here on the Duck River frontier, he was nearly broke. He decided to stay and started a school. Laws liked the idea of naming this town after his hometown back in North Carolina.

As you enter town, Chapel Hill Cumberland Presbyterian Church is the

Chapel Hill Cumberland Presbyterian Church

TOURING THE MIDDLE TENNESSEE BACKROADS

brick building on the left near the high school. This handsome structure in simplified classical temple style was built in 1866.

It is 0.1 mile from the high school to a monument on the right marking the birthplace of Nathan Bedford Forrest, the famed Confederate cavalry general. Forrest was actually born on a farm west of town near a community now called Thick.

Middle Tennessee's best-known tale of the supernatural is that of the Bell Witch of Robertson County. But Chapel Hill has its tale, too. People crossing the railroad tracks west of town at night—particularly on damp, drizzly nights—report seeing a bright light moving down the tracks. And this is at times when there is no train nearby.

The legend stems from an incident when the track was weakened by torrential rains. A man with a lantern was sent to warn a train coming from Nashville. As he signaled the approaching train, he slipped and fell onto the tracks, and his head was severed by the locomotive's wheels. The mysterious light seen moving up and down the tracks is, they say, the man with his lantern looking for his head.

Monument to Nathan Bedford Forrest

Stay on U.S. 31A through Chapel Hill. You will pass the TN 99 junction and cross the Duck River.

The highway south from Nashville—today's U.S. 31A—follows an ancient route. It was first a well-worn Indian path used by the tribes living south of the Tennessee River to access the vast uninhabited hunting ground between that river and the Ohio, to the north. The earliest white settlers named the route Fishing Ford Road. It crossed the Duck River at a ford near this spot. A bridge replaced the ford as early as 1838.

The entrance to Henry Horton State Park is 0.2 mile past the bridge over the Duck River. The park is noted for its fine public golf course. Henry Horton served as governor of Tennessee from 1927 to 1933. This park was developed on land that was once his farm. His grave is on the left 0.2 mile past the park entrance.

The lovely Mount Carmel Missionary Baptist Church is on the left 0.6 mile from Horton's grave. This area was once called Smyrna, and the church was built in 1872 as the Smyrna Church.

It is 1.2 miles from the church to Powell Lane. Turn right (W) on Powell and drive 4.6 miles to TN 272 (Verona-Caney Road) through a

Mount Carmel Missionary Baptist Church

landscape alternating between fertile pastures and rocky cedar forests and glades.

Turn left (S) on TN 272 and drive 2.7 miles to Verona. As the historical marker notes, Verona was the home of Buford Ellington, who served as Tennessee's governor from 1959 to 1963 and from 1969 to 1971. The golf course at Henry Horton State Park is named for Ellington, an avid golfer, during whose administration the park was created.

Just past Verona, turn right (W) onto John Lunn Road, also known as Berlin-Verona Road. At the intersection with Gray Road 1.8 miles from Verona, bear right, staying on John Lunn Road. It is another 1.5 miles to U.S. 431. Turn left (S). Old Berlin Road takes off to the right just ahead.

This is the historic Berlin community. When the first settlers came here, they found a huge spring gushing out of the cedar-covered ridge and named it and the community that grew up around it Cedar Spring. The name was changed at the request of the post office in 1835. Families of German origin lived here—it is speculated that they gave the place its current name, but no one knows for sure. Several well-preserved houses dating to the 1840s face U.S. 431 and Old Berlin Road. The 1857 Methodist church is down the road just west of the highway.

The Berlin Rock

TOURING THE MIDDLE TENNESSEE BACKROADS

The Berlin Rock is the community's landmark. It rests in the southwest corner of the U.S. 431–Old Berlin Road intersection in the small park where the spring flows out of Berlin Ridge. James K. Polk literally used this as a steppingstone to the presidency. Two local men, James Finley and Robert Fields, erected a little rock rostrum in this natural amphitheater, where Polk made his first speech after he received the Democratic nomination for president in 1844. (For the story of how Polk was nominated, see The Maury County Tour, pages 204–205.)

The Berlin Rock was later moved to Lewisburg. As the plaque next to it notes, Andrew Johnson was the second president to use it for a rostrum. Two United States senators, four United States congressmen, six governors, and seven judges also made speeches from this rock. The Berlin Rock and the plaque were later returned here to the site of Polk's speech.

From Berlin, continue south on U.S. 431 for 4 miles to the junction with TN 50, where there is a beautiful antebellum mansion on the left. Turn left, staying on U.S. 431. Franklin Road comes in from the right after 0.6 mile. Turn right onto Franklin Road. It is 1.6 miles to Second Avenue in Lewisburg. Turn right (S) and go 0.2 mile to Church Street at Lewisburg's square. The 1929 courthouse stands in the middle of the square.

Marshall County Courthouse

Marshall County got its name through a mistake. A bill passed the general assembly in 1836 creating two new counties—this one and another county east of Murfreesboro—out of established counties. This county was supposed to be named for Governor Newton Cannon, who lived just up the road. The other was to be named for Chief Justice John Marshall. Due a copying mistake, the names got reversed.

A site for a courthouse and jail was selected on land donated by Abner Houston, and the new town of Lewisburg was laid out. It was named for Meriwether Lewis, the famed leader of the Lewis and Clark expedition, who mysteriously lost his life in Middle Tennessee in 1809. (For information about Lewis's death, see The South Central Tour, pages 255–57.)

Lewisburg evolved into an important trade center in a region noted for fine Tennessee Walking Horses and Jersey cattle. The Tennessee Walking Horse Breeders and Exhibitors Association has its headquarters here, and the United States Department of Agriculture and the University of Tennessee run a dairy-experiment farm in the beautiful hills south of town on

Ladies Rest Room

U.S. 31A. Located as it is near cedar forests, Lewisburg is home to several pencil-manufacturing plants.

Circle around the square to Third Avenue. What is surely one of the most unusual buildings in Middle Tennessee is located just north of the square on Third. It is the Ladies Rest Room. In the days when whole families would come to town for a day of shopping and activities, members of the county court became concerned over the lack of rest-room facilities for women. In 1924, they appropriated funds to build the Ladies Rest Room.

A grateful woman sent an unsigned letter to the county court. It reads,

> In behalf of the ladies of the county, I desire to thank the gentlemen of the County Court for the beautiful restroom they have given us. I need not speak of its specific beauties for it stands where all may see them and take advantage of their benefits. Rather I would speak of that to which it bears eloquent though silent testimony, the courtesy and chivalry of the men of the Court and the County. Men show their own natures by the way they treat women. The savage man makes of his woman a beast of burden, the brutish man holds her a "little" better than his dog, a little dearer

than his horse, but the enlightened man delights to honor and elevate his woman and in so doing honors and elevates himself. And so we praise this beautiful gift, not merely for its beauty and many conveniences but because it shows that we the women of the county are held in love and honor by our men. Again we thank you.

The Cedar Forests Tour ends here in Lewisburg.

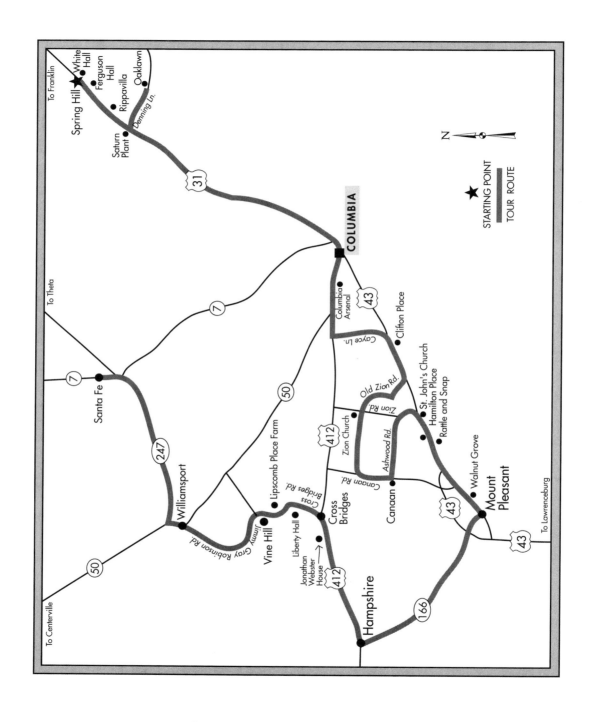

N

STARTING POINT

TOUR ROUTE

COLUMBIA

To Franklin

White Hall

Ferguson Hall

Rippavilla

Oaklawn

Spring Hill

Saturn Plant

Denming Ln.

31

To Theta

7

7

Santa Fe

247

Williamsport

50

To Centerville

50

Columbia Arsenal

43

Clifton Place

Cayce Ln.

Old Zion Rd.

St. John's Church

Zion Rd.

Hamilton Place

412

Rattle and Snap

Zion Church

Ashwood Rd.

Walnut Grove

Canaan Rd.

Canaan

43

Mount Pleasant

Lipscomb Place Farm

Cross Bridges Rd.

Cross Bridges

Jimmy Gray Robinson Rd.

Vine Hill

Liberty Hall

Jonathan Webster House

412

Hampshire

166

43

To Lawrenceburg

The Maury County Tour

This tour includes the many splendid antebellum houses for which Maury County is famous, among them Rattle and Snap, Rippavilla, Clifton Place, and the home of President James K. Polk. It visits the picturesque small towns of Spring Hill, Mount Pleasant, and Santa Fe. A walking tour of Columbia includes the well-preserved downtown and historic residential neighborhoods. The tour also visits the old Zion community and its historic church.

Total length: approximately 60 miles

This tour starts at the library at the corner of U.S. 31 (Main Street) and Depot Street in Spring Hill, which is located between Franklin and Columbia. You can pick up a brochure describing a twenty-stop walking and driving tour of the Spring Hill area from a box just outside the library entrance.

Spring Hill is a lovely small town, rich in history. First called Peters' Campground for the Methodist camp meetings held here, the town on Maury County's northern boundary is named for its location on a hill above a spring.

When Spring Hill, Tennessee, is mentioned, most people think of the massive Saturn automobile assembly plant General Motors built in the rolling bluegrass south of town. But mention Spring Hill to people knowledgeable about the Civil War and they think of two of the war's great mysteries. The unexplained events of November 29, 1864, came to be called "The Affair at Spring Hill." The mysterious killing of Confederate major general Earl Van Dorn on May 7, 1863, had its genesis in an affair, too, only of a different sort.

At age thirty-three, John Bell Hood was the youngest full general in the Confederate army. He was given command of the Army of Tennessee in July 1864, as the Confederacy's principal western army tried in vain to save Atlanta from William Tecumseh Sherman. After Atlanta fell that September, Sherman decided to ignore Hood's defeated army and launch his famous— or infamous—March to the Sea. Hood took the Army of Tennessee in the opposite direction on a hastily conceived, poorly planned invasion of Middle Tennessee—a desperate, last-gasp attempt to save the Confederacy.

When Hood's men came into Middle Tennessee, they were confronted by Federal troops under Major General John M. Schofield. Hood and Schofield were no strangers. They were among the fifty-two graduates in the West Point class of 1853. Schofield's orders were to use his Union troops to slow down Hood's advancing army and to gradually fall back to the secure fortifications of Nashville. Schofield first retreated from Pulaski north to Columbia.

General Hood devised a plan that avoided a direct confrontation with the Federals at Columbia. On November 29, his army went around Columbia and headed for Spring Hill on the good road to Nashville via Franklin. From Spring Hill, the Confederates could march on Nashville or attack Schofield's men at Columbia from behind. When darkness fell that day, Hood's army bivouacked for the night. But the Southerners had stopped short of the vital road north. To this day, no one knows for sure why.

Meanwhile, Schofield figured out he was being trapped and marched his men north from Columbia toward Spring Hill. A fight was sure to result. But it did not. Schofield's Federals walked right up the road within talking distance of the encamped Confederates. By midnight, they had marched safely past Hood's army and were well on their way to Franklin. "The Affair at Spring Hill" was one of the great missed opportunities of the Civil War.

How did it happen? Hood himself has been implicated. His left arm had been shattered at Gettysburg, and he had lost his right leg at Chickamauga. Just that day, he had fallen off his horse. John Bell Hood was a man in pain. Laudanum, an opium derivative used for pain in those days, was known to induce euphoria. Hood may not have grasped what was happening.

Strong drink has also been mentioned. One Confederate soldier said in a postwar interview that the owners of the house where Hood was headquartered for the night "spread a big feast" for the ranking Southern officers and that some grew "full drunk." It is also suspected that one general enjoyed the company of the "beguiling temptress" Jessie McKissack Peters.

Jessie McKissack Peters was no stranger to the Confederate generals at Spring Hill that night in November 1864. She was part of the triangle that produced the other Spring Hill mystery, the May 7, 1863, killing of General Van Dorn by Dr. George B. Peters, Jessie's husband.

In the spring of 1863, Van Dorn was commanding the Confederate cavalry in the Columbia area from his Spring Hill headquarters. He loved to show off, especially in his splendid tailored uniform, often staging reviews and parades. One of his troopers grumbled that the cavalry wasted its time in dress parades for the benefit of "a few lonesome and garish young ladies." When it came to the ladies, the Mississippi general definitely "had a great weakness in such matters," as one colonel later reported.

Dr. Peters spent a good deal of time away from his Spring Hill home for reasons that have never been clear. Some suspect he was a Union spy. In any event, Mrs. Peters and General Van Dorn were frequent companions. Once, upon Dr. Peters's return to Spring Hill, he was, by his own later account, "alarmed at the distressing rumors which prevailed in the neighborhood in relation to the attentions paid by General Van Dorn to my wife." He sent word to Van Dorn that he would "blow his brains out" if the general set foot on his lawn again.

After returning from another short trip, Peters was "exceedingly mortified" to learn that Van Dorn had visited his house every night in his absence. Peters then feigned another trip, hoping to catch the rakish general in the act. He did. Accounts of their encounter—which took place at two o'clock one morning—vary, but less than two days later, Peters paid a visit to Van Dorn at his headquarters. After he left, Van Dorn was discovered shot in the back of the head. Dr. Peters fled.

Did Peters kill Van Dorn in cold blood? Did they fight and Peters get the best of Van Dorn? No one will ever know.

Van Dorn's passing was not met with much sorrow in the Confederacy. One Southern paper called his death a "happy riddance." One of his fellow generals said there was little regret in the army "for a man whose willful violation of social rights led him to such an inglorious end." Even the "wicked libertine" Jessie McKissack Peters was heard to remark, "Now ain't that the devil, a sweetheart killed, and a husband run away, all in the same day."

Spring Hill's Civil War mysteries are kept within the walls of several structures in and around town. From the library, head two blocks north on U.S. 31 to Duplex Road (TN 247).

The large, columned home on U.S. 31 between the library and Duplex Road is the first brick house in Spring Hill, built by William McKissack in 1845. McKissack's three marriages produced nine children. One of them, Jessie Helen, became the famous Mrs. Peters.

White Hall is on Duplex Road 0.2 mile east of U.S. 31. It was here, in the 1844 home of Dr. Aaron White, that General Van Dorn set up his first headquarters. The general was asked to leave because the house was too crowded. But that was not the real reason. Margaret Fain White confided to her husband, "You must get the General out of this house. You *know* Mrs. Peters. There is going to be trouble between Dr. Peters and the General. It must not happen here."

From White Hall, return to U.S. 31. A Spring Hill landmark with a more peaceful history is Grace Episcopal Church, at the corner of Duplex Road and U.S. 31. It was built in 1878 in the Carpenter Gothic style. John Henry Hopkins, an Episcopal bishop from Vermont, was determined that the charm of Gothic architecture should be available for small churches, so he published books containing simple designs that could be built inexpensively with local materials and labor. His style, which came to be called Carpenter Gothic, can be seen in numerous rural and small-town churches.

Ferguson Hall

Head south on U.S. 31 past the library. The 1835 Martin Cheairs House, otherwise known as Ferguson Hall, stands on the left of the highway on the grounds of the Tennessee Children's Home. This is where Van Dorn moved his headquarters from White Hall. Dr. Peters killed the general in this house.

After enjoying Spring Hill, head south toward Columbia on U.S. 31. It is 1.6 miles from Ferguson Hall to Rippavilla, the magnificent mansion on the left.

Here, in the house built by Nathaniel and Susan McKissack Cheairs in 1851, over breakfast provided Mrs. Cheairs, John Bell Hood blamed his subordinate generals the morning after "The Affair at Spring Hill." Historian Stanley Horn writes, "There were angry accusations of neglect, followed by flashing swords and demands for apology, as the edgy commanders stewed in impotent exasperation." One general wrote of Hood in his diary, "He is wrathy as a rattlesnake this morning, striking at everything."

This was the last breakfast for several of the officers. Later that day, Hood did strike at Franklin, spending the lives of thousands of his men. (For information about the Battle of Franklin, see The Franklin Tour, pages 118–21.)

Nat and Susan Cheairs had been involved in controversy before that fateful morning. And they would be again. Indeed, even their wedding was controversial, at least in the Cheairs family.

Nat was from a well-to-do family descended from French Huguenot Jan de la Chaire, who came to the New World in 1662. Nat's father, also named Nathaniel, moved from Maryland to Maury County in 1811 and soon became one of the area's largest landowners.

All six previous men by the name of Nathaniel Cheairs had married women named Sarah. The father opposed Nat's marriage to Susan for no better reason than that the sister of Jessie McKissack Peters was not named Sarah. The father even offered Nat a bribe of five thousand dollars, no small sum of money in those days, to break the engagement! Love prevailed. The couple was married in 1841.

Like many other Southerners who opposed secession, Nat Cheairs took up the Confederate cause when civil war came. February 1862 found Major Cheairs commanding a regiment at Fort Donelson. He had the dubious honor of being selected to carry the white flag of surrender to Ulysses S. Grant and to return with the demand of unconditional surrender that contributed to Grant's fame. (For information about Fort Donelson, see The Lower Cumberland Tour, pages 86–87.)

After six months in a prison on an island in Boston Harbor, Cheairs was released, only to be captured again in November 1863 in West Tennessee while serving on the staff of General Nathan Bedford Forrest. It was suspected that Cheairs was a spy, and he barely escaped execution.

Following the war, a vindictive Reconstruction government charged him with treason. He fled his substantial Maury County home, hid out in "the barrens"—the rough land to the west—then made his way to Washington.

Rippavilla

He managed to get in to see the president, fellow Tennessean Andrew Johnson. Johnson pardoned him on the spot.

Cheairs returned to Rippavilla and survived the Civil War by nearly fifty years. In January 1914, he died while visiting his daughter in Waco, Texas. He was in his ninety-sixth year.

Nat and Susan Cheairs named their house Rippo Villa, corrupted over the years to Rippavilla. The origin of the name is unknown. General Motors acquired the property when it was buying land for the Saturn plant. Plans call for the mansion to be open to the public as a regional visitor center.

The nucleus of the land General Motors bought in the 1980s for the Saturn plant was Haynes Haven, a noted horse farm. The columned mansion across the road from Rippavilla is the 1938 Haynes Haven House.

Continue on U.S. 31 from Rippavilla. It is 0.2 mile to Denning Lane. Turn left (E) onto Denning. After driving 2.5 miles through this rich farmland, you will arrive at Oaklawn, the large house on a rise to the left.

Absalom Thompson's 1835 house looks much as it did when an exhausted John Bell Hood arrived here on the afternoon of November 29, 1864.

Oaklawn

When General Hood set up his headquarters at Oaklawn, he had been up since three in the morning. Crippled and in pain, strapped onto his horse, he was attempting to lead what he later said was to have been "the best move of my career as a soldier." But he never continued toward Spring Hill to see for himself that his army had stopped short of its goal, the road north.

Oaklawn was again in the news in the 1970s. Country singers Tammy Wynette and George Jones lived here during their stormy marriage.

Retrace your route to U.S. 31. You will notice a road curving off to the right. It leads to the visitor center at the Saturn plant. Though Saturn does not offer public tours, the visitor center provides information about the facilities.

Through creative land-use planning, this stretch of highway past one of the world's largest manufacturing plants retains its historic, rural character. When it invested $5 billion in Saturn, General Motors acquired both sides of the highway. The company has preserved the land for its traditional agricultural use. Over eight thousand people work at Saturn, but man-made hills screen much of the plant from the highway. The main access to the facilities is from Interstate 65, so plant traffic stays off U.S. 31.

Across the highway from the visitor center entrance is the University of Tennessee's Middle Tennessee Experiment Station, one of eleven such agricultural research stations scattered across the state. Here, on 1,263 acres, research is conducted in beef and dairy cattle, commercial crops, fruit trees, and forage crops. The station was established in 1917.

Continue in your original direction on U.S. 31. It is 8 miles to downtown Columbia.

Maury County is justly famous for its large number of well-preserved old houses. They can be identified by the distinctive markers placed by the Maury County chapter of the Association for the Preservation of Tennessee Antiquities (APTA). These markers are handy references, particularly for houses not described on this tour. Several of the APTA-marked houses are between Spring Hill and Columbia.

U.S. 31 enters the old part of Columbia on the John Harlan Willis Memorial Bridge over the Duck River. Willis is the only Maury Countian ever awarded the Congressional Medal of Honor. It was awarded posthumously. He was killed saving the lives of other men on Iwo Jima in World War II.

At the top of the hill past the bridge, turn left (W) off U.S. 31 onto Fourth Street at Greenwood Cemetery, the old graveyard set aside when Columbia was first laid out. Fourth quickly turns right and becomes Main Street. Stay on Main for 0.2 mile to the square at the courthouse. This is a convenient place to park to see Columbia. The well-preserved commercial area around the square and the neighborhood to the west make for a pleasant walk along tree-shaded streets and among interesting houses, churches, and commercial buildings that hold much of Middle Tennessee's history.

Settlement of this area occurred rapidly following the 1805 and 1806 Indian treaties that made it legal. Maury County, created out of Williamson County in 1807, is named for Abram Maury, the pioneer surveyor, soldier, and politician on whose land Franklin was laid out in 1799. Columbia, named for Christopher Columbus, was laid out in 1809.

Columbia quickly grew into a major commercial center in this area of rich plantations. By 1850, its population had surpassed Knoxville's, making it the third-largest town in the state, behind Nashville and Memphis. Maury was the wealthiest county in Tennessee by 1860.

Though Columbia was an important town, it suffered from the lack of a navigable waterway. From time to time, various schemes were advanced to remedy this deficiency. They all failed. As early as 1813, the town provided funds to make the Duck River navigable from its mouth at the Tennessee River upstream to Gordon's Ferry, located west of Columbia on today's Natchez Trace Parkway. Nothing came of the plan.

In 1820, at a time when Columbia aspired to be the capital of Tennessee, a company was formed to construct a road west to the Tennessee River and to build a steamboat to run between there and New Orleans. The investors had the *General Green* built for forty thousand dollars. But after one season, the venture proved unprofitable. Following several more seasons on the Cumberland River, the boat was sold for nine thousand dollars.

In 1839, and with considerable difficulty, the steamer *Madison* made it all the way to Columbia, 125 river miles from the mouth of the Duck. The resulting excitement prompted an attempt to raise money to fund the Duck River Company, which would promote navigation. Nothing came of

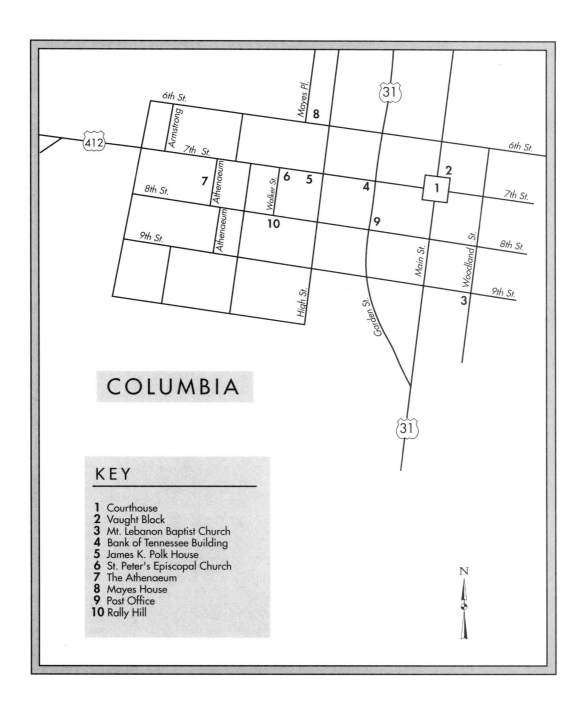

COLUMBIA

KEY

1 Courthouse
2 Vaught Block
3 Mt. Lebanon Baptist Church
4 Bank of Tennessee Building
5 James K. Polk House
6 St. Peter's Episcopal Church
7 The Athenaeum
8 Mayes House
9 Post Office
10 Rally Hill

N

it. The 1844 arrival of the *Lily of the West* prompted another company, but it, too, did not last long.

The grandest scheme came in 1848 with the incorporation of the Duck River Slackwater Navigation Company. Engineers hired to survey the river reported that it could be made navigable with a series of dams. The first one was built 16 river miles below Columbia. It was then discovered that the engineers had made a serious mistake in their calculations. It would cost twice the estimated amount to make the project work. Railroad fever was by then gripping Columbia. In 1851, the balance of the six hundred thousand dollars raised for the navigation company was transferred to a company that would promote a railroad.

The impressive courthouse that stands in the center of the square replaced an 1844 building built with slave labor. When the cornerstone of the new building was laid in 1904, Dick Porter, an elderly man who had worked on the earlier building as a slave, was invited to lay the first trowel of mortar.

From the square, walk south on Main to Ninth Street, then turn left and walk one block to Mount Lebanon Baptist Church.

Mount Lebanon Baptist Church

Established in 1843, the original Mount Lebanon was the first Baptist church for free blacks in Tennessee. Edmund Kelly was the first pastor and Dyer Johnson one of the first deacons. Johnson was a free black who saved enough money to purchase the freedom of his wife, Elizabeth. And it was Johnson who gave most of the money for the construction of the first church. The congregation moved to the present church in 1885.

Columbia did not escape the ugly aftermath of slavery that plagued much of the South for a century following emancipation. One early incident involved Dyer Johnson.

A school for blacks set up in the church following the Civil War became a target of the Ku Klux Klan. The Klan ordered it to disband. The teacher refused, and from then on he brought a gun to school. The teacher wisely left town when word got out that a group of nightriders was coming to hang him. When the hooded Klansmen arrived at the church, they found Johnson at his house next door. Assuming he was the teacher, they dragged him from his house and had the rope around his neck, ready to lynch him. In the meantime, a crowd had gathered. "You've got the wrong man! Turn Dyer loose. He's a good man," someone yelled. Dyer's life was spared.

Dyer Johnson had four children, all of whom went on to become prominent citizens of Columbia. Two of them were well-known educators.

Racial unrest in Columbia continued with lynchings in 1925, 1927, and 1933. There were disturbances during World War II between white and black workers in Mount Pleasant's phosphate plants. When black veterans returned home from the war with a new expectation for equality and a will to do something about it, racial tensions were high in the county.

Trouble broke out on February 25, 1946. As is so often the case, it started over a seemingly small incident. James Stephenson, a World War II veteran, and his mother, Gladys, went to the Castner-Knott Department Store to retrieve a radio they had left for repairs. When they found out the store had sold it, they demanded payment for it. In the ensuing scuffle, a store employee was injured when he fell through a window. His family had the Stephensons arrested.

Throughout the day, rumors spread and crowds gathered. There was talk of a lynching. Blacks retreated to their business district—called "Mink Slide," located around Mount Lebanon Baptist Church—and took up arms. When the police chief and three officers entered the area, all were shot and wounded, one seriously.

The Tennessee Highway Patrol was sent to Columbia at the request of the local sheriff. But the patrol quickly joined the white mob and turned on the blacks. The patrol asked the National Guard to arm the mob, a request that was refused. The patrol and the mob then entered the black area anyway. Most of the black businesses were damaged and many houses were entered. Over three hundred weapons were seized.

The situation was quiet but tense for several days. Then, on February 28, Tennessee Highway Patrol officers entered the jail to identify those who had shot at them during the raid. They brought some men from their cells. Supposedly, the prisoners grabbed the officers' guns and fired at them. The officers then returned fire, killing two of the black men.

This was the end of the violence but not the end of the affair. A Maury County grand jury indicted thirty-one blacks and four whites, and the defense of the blacks became a national cause. The NAACP established the National Committee for Justice in Columbia, co-chaired by Eleanor Roosevelt. Thurgood Marshall, later Justice Marshall of the United States

Supreme Court, took the lead in defending the blacks. There was only one conviction in the case.

Marshall himself became a target of resentful whites. While leaving Columbia after a trial, he was stopped by patrol officers. They had been tipped off that he had illegal liquor, they said. Finding no liquor, they let him go, only to stop him again. For the second time, he was let go. On a third stop, Marshall was arrested for drunk driving. He was escorted into the office of a local magistrate, an avid teetotaler renowned for his skill at smelling alcohol on the breath. Marshall passed the test, and the magistrate ordered him released. This time, he let someone else drive him to Nashville.

Fortunately, Columbia is not known for racial unrest today. It is, however, widely known for its mules. Mule Day is one of the biggest events of the year.

Beginning in the 1930s, Columbia started playing host to the world's largest mule market, hosting thousands of traders and mules. The event quickly turned into a festival, complete with open-air markets, medicine shows, and political speeches. The highlight of the market was the Mule Day Parade, an event that still takes place every April.

The biggest Mule Day of all was in 1940, when sixty thousand people crowded Columbia's streets. The festivities were covered by Universal News for theater newsreels and were broadcast live nationwide on the Mutual Broadcasting System's radio network. The guest of honor for the event was Postmaster General James A. Farley, who came to lay the cornerstone for the new post office.

Mule trading is not as important as it once was, but mules are still traded in Columbia. There is a market for them among the Amish, particularly those in Pennsylvania. Tennessee mules are shipped to the western United States, too; the mules that carry visitors into the Grand Canyon are Tennessee-bred. Show mules are also traded, a good pair bringing as much as six thousand dollars.

From Mount Lebanon Baptist Church, return to the square.

The buildings around Columbia's square and on the connecting streets comprise a well-preserved collection of commercial and public structures dating from the 1820s to the 1940s. The building on the square's northeast corner, built in 1858, is called the Vaught Block for the man who built it, Nathan Vaught.

Born in Virginia in 1799, Vaught came to Middle Tennessee as a child and was orphaned at an early age, at which time he and his brother became public charges. Nathan was "bound out" to cabinetmaker James Purcell until he was twenty-one. From Purcell, young Nathan learned how to make most anything.

He took time to educate himself—to "learn figures," as he put it—and in adulthood became the region's premier builder. He built many of the fine houses for which Maury County is famous, as well as commercial buildings. Becoming literate served him well, too. In 1871, Nathan compiled a manuscript entitled *Youth and Old Age*, which includes a diary as well as valuable information about the buildings on which he worked. Vaught lived until 1880.

Bank of Tennessee Building

Walk west from the square on Seventh Street.

The Bank of Tennessee Building, located at West Seventh and Garden streets one block from the square, is one of Vaught's best-known commercial buildings. Built in 1839–40, it is in the Greek Revival style. The Bank of Tennessee, established in response to the financial panic of 1837, provided credit for farmers and merchants ruined during that depression. But the Columbia branch got off to a bad start.

On October 22, 1839, the bank was robbed of several thousand dollars' worth of paper notes. The rewards that were offered underscore the magnitude of the loss. The bank put up five thousand dollars and the city another two thousand, considerable sums in those days. Then, the following year, the cashier embezzled thirty-four thousand dollars. The bank failed in 1843, but the building has remained in use by a variety of businesses since then.

The Bethel Hotel once stood across West Seventh Street from the bank building. This sixty-room hotel housed a theater and was the hub of Columbia's social life before it burned in 1949.

It was here that Hollywood's singing cowboy, Gene Autry, learned the truth of the slogan, "The show must go on." Autry was scheduled to give a show in the theater in 1938. A few hours beforehand, it was discovered that the sound system did not work. No one seemed to know how to repair it. Then someone mentioned that the man who operated the hotel's Western Union telegraph could probably fix it. Yes, he could, he said, but he could not leave the telegraph office without someone to "run the wire." And he was the only telegrapher in town. Or so he thought.

When the famous cowboy showed up to operate the telegraph, the operator thought it was a joke. He did not know that Gene Autry was a telegraph operator before he began his career as an entertainer. In fact, Autry was discovered by Will Rogers when Rogers came upon the telegrapher playing his guitar and singing in an Oklahoma railroad depot. In his 1978 autobiography, *Back in the Saddle Again*, Autry speculates that there are not "any other entertainers who were able to keep a booking because they knew the Morse Code."

Continue walking west on Seventh Street to the James K. Polk House, at 301 West Seventh.

It was almost by accident that the Democrats nominated James K. Polk for president in 1844. It was assumed that Martin Van Buren would be the nominee, since he had succeeded Andrew Jackson as president. Although Van Buren had lost the election of 1840, he was Old Hickory's choice in 1844. It was seven years since Jackson left the White House, but he was still a dominant force in Democratic politics.

Then Van Buren made a mistake. He got on the wrong side of Jackson on an issue important to the ex-president—the proposed annexation of Texas. Jackson began looking around for another candidate. Polk was not his choice; Jackson was promoting his fellow Tennessean for vice president. But Polk and his friends had ideas of their own.

That May, while James K. Polk stayed in Columbia, three of his closest associates went to the Democratic Convention in Baltimore. Led by Polk's Columbia law partner, Gideon Pillow, they worked behind the scenes promoting Polk as an alternative to Van Buren should the New Yorker's campaign falter. It did. Van Buren did not get the required two-thirds vote on the first ballot, and on each successive ballot, his strength slipped away. Polk's name first appeared on the seventh ballot. He drew only a few votes. Then, on the eighth ballot, Van Buren's supporters switched to the Tennessean. He won overwhelmingly on the ninth ballot, and the convention voted to make his nomination unanimous.

In many ways, Polk was an unlikely candidate. He was a brilliant man, educated at the University of North Carolina and trained as a lawyer by Felix Grundy, later the United States attorney general. But Polk had a stern disposition that did not endear him to many people. And his political life was a mixture of success and failure. He served in the United States House of Representatives from 1825 to 1839 and was elected Speaker of the House for two terms. But after only one two-year term as governor of Tennessee, he was defeated for reelection, then was defeated again when he tried a comeback. He was not a man of national prominence in 1844.

The Democrats were badly split over the Texas question and the emerging issue of slavery. The tariff issue split the party along sectional lines, too. The Whigs, on the other hand, were united behind Kentucky senator Henry Clay. It proved to be an unusually vitriolic election. Polk, a slave owner, was depicted as a cruel master. Clay was described as a vindictive, blasphemous man with a propensity for gambling. In the end, Polk won the 1844 election.

He vowed to serve only one term and then threw himself into it with a vengeance, working night and day and hardly ever taking time off. He once wrote, "No President who performs his duty faithfully and conscientiously can have any leisure. If he entrusts the details and smaller matters to subordinates, constant errors will occur."

James K. Polk is not a household name today, but he is well remembered by experts. In a poll of historians, Polk was ranked as a near-great, along with Theodore Roosevelt and Woodrow Wilson. He is best remembered for extending the United States to the Pacific Ocean. Texas, California, Oregon, and most of the West became part of the nation during his administration, when more territory became part of the United States than at any other time. A popular toast around the California gold-rush camps was given "to George Washington, who did more than any other man to establish our country; to James K. Polk, who did more than any other to enlarge it."

Polk was worn out when he and his wife, Sarah, left Washington in 1849. They were looking forward to a life of leisure at their new house in Nashville, located just a few blocks from the Capitol. But just three months after leaving the White House, the ex-president died. Sarah lived until 1891.

It is a bit misleading to call this classic Federal-style town house in Columbia the James K. Polk House, for it was really the home of his parents, Sam and Jane Polk. They built this, the oldest brick house in Columbia, in 1817, while James was away at college. After the future president married Sarah Childress of Murfreesboro in 1824, the new couple lived in their own house across and down the street until they left for the White House. It was destroyed in 1960 to make room for a funeral home parking lot.

The house next door to the James K. Polk House is called the Polk Sisters' House. James Walker, business partner of the future president's father, married one of James K. Polk's sisters, Jane Maria Polk. Walker hired James Purcell, Nathan Vaught's mentor, to build this house in 1818. Another of James K. Polk's sisters, the troublesome Ophelia, and her husband, Dr. Samuel Hayes, bought the house in 1849.

The James K. Polk House is a state historic site open to the public year-round. It is decorated with period furniture, much of it from the Polk family. The Polk Sisters' House is a visitor center and museum that contains Polk memorabilia, including Sarah's ball gown, made in Paris, and a beautiful fan the president had made for her to take to the inaugural ball.

Walk west on Seventh Street from the James K. Polk House.

St. Peter's Episcopal Church, at 311 West Seventh, was only partially completed when the Civil War came to Columbia. General Van Dorn's funeral was held here in May 1863, following his inglorious end at the hand of Dr. Peters at Spring Hill. The funerals of three of the six generals killed at Franklin—Cleburne, Granbury, and Strahl—were held here, too. Columbia changed hands several times during the Civil War; for a time the Union army used the building as a provost marshal's office. The church's tower was added in 1871.

From St. Peter's, continue walking west on Seventh Street. You will pass several of Columbia's most impressive homes. The house at 320 West Seventh was for a time the home of Senator Edward Ward Carmack. (For information about Carmack's career and his sensational 1908 killing, see The Middle Cumberland Tour, pages 28–29.)

At the intersection of West Seventh and Athenaeum streets, turn left to see one of Columbia's best-known landmarks, the Athenaeum.

This exotic blend of Gothic Revival, Greek Revival, Italianate, and

St. Peter's Episcopal Church

Rectory of the Athenaeum

TOURING THE MIDDLE TENNESSEE BACKROADS

Moorish styles was constructed in 1835 as a residence for Samuel Polk Walker. Nathan Vaught built it. Well-known Nashville architect Adolphus Heiman designed it.

It later became the home of the Reverend Franklin Gillette Smith of the nearby Columbia Female Insitute. Smith, a Princeton graduate, became dissatisfied with the quality of education at the institute, so he founded a competing girls' school, The Athenaeum, in 1852. It occupied a twenty-two-acre campus and grew into one of the most prestigious schools in the South, housing as many as 125 boarding students at its peak. This house served as the school's rectory—the home of the head of the school. The school closed in 1903, and the property was sold to the city of Columbia for use as a school. Only this structure survives.

Fannie Louise Smith Davis of Texas, Franklin Gillette Smith's granddaughter, eventually came to own the Athenaeum. She donated it to the local people in 1973. It is now open to the public and serves as the headquarters for the APTA's Majestic Middle Tennessee Fall Tour, held the last weekend of September each year.

In 1994, the Athenaeum hosted a one-week summer session for teenage girls, giving them an opportunity to experience life as it was at an exclusive boarding school in the mid-1800s. They wore period clothes and attended classes in etiquette, art, music, French, and writing. They learned the parlor games and dances popular in 1860. The program was a huge success, and plans are to make it an annual event.

From the Athenaeum, return to West Seventh Street and continue west. The shopping center on the left stands on the site of Columbia Female Institute, the school Smith left in 1852 to start the Athenaeum. The institute was founded in 1835.

Turn right onto Armstrong Street and walk up the hill to West Sixth Street. Turn right and walk east between the rows of beautifully restored Victorian-era houses.

Hardin Perkins Figuers was the fifteen-year-old boy whose witness to the Battle of Franklin is reported in The Franklin Tour. He ended up in Columbia, where he was a successful attorney. His 1890 house is at 408 West Sixth Street.

The massive house at 306 West Sixth was built around 1850 by Samuel

Mayes. This prosperous Maury Countian had a feeling that the abolitionist sentiment building in the country would eventually wipe out the fortune Southern planters had accumulated in human property, so he sold his slaves and invested in this house.

The Mayes-Frierson House, located across the street at 305 West Sixth, was built in 1833 by Patrick Maguire for his daughter Ellen as a wedding present upon her marriage to Roger B. Mayes.

Continue east to Halcyon Hall, the large two-story house at 211 West Sixth. Joseph Walker built this home in 1845 and moved into it with his new bride, Adaline Nelson. Legend has it that they lived here only six weeks. Adaline became homesick and insisted they move in with her family—across the street.

David Looney built the Looney House, located at 207 West Sixth, in 1835. Nathan Vaught enlarged it in 1839. At one time, this was the home of William S. Fleming, a judge-historian who gave the locally famous American Centennial Speech at Columbia on July 4, 1876, a historical sketch that provides a valuable history of Maury County.

Continue down the hill on West Sixth Street to Main Street. The square is one block to the right. Return to your car to resume the driving tour.

Drive south on Main Street to Eighth Street and turn right (W). On the corner of West Eighth and Garden streets is the post office started on Mule Day 1940. It is considered one of the best examples of the New Deal public-building style in Middle Tennessee.

Continue west on Eighth to the intersection with Walker Street. The impressive mansion on the left is Rally Hill. The little rise upon which the house sits was a rallying point for local recruits during the War of 1812. That is how the house got its name. James and Jane Maria Polk Walker built it in 1848 after they left the Polk Sisters' House. Today's Walker Street was once the carriage lane leading to Rally Hill.

President Polk's brother-in-law. That is the way James Walker is often described, but it overlooks his many contributions to early Columbia. Walker founded the county's first newspaper, the *Western Chronicle*, in 1811, co-founded Columbia's first bank, was one of the founders of St. Peter's Episcopal Church, served on the board of Columbia Female Institute, and was one of the owners of the ill-fated Tennessee River steamboat venture of

1820. He also served as Columbia's mayor in the 1830s and was instrumental in the political success of his brother-in-law.

Many of the Walkers' eleven children lived interesting lives, too. One son, Samuel, built what became the rectory at the Athenaeum. Another son, Joseph Knox, served as President Polk's personal secretary; two of Joseph's children were born in the White House. Another son, Lucius M., graduated from the United States Military Academy and was a general in the Confederate army; he was killed in a duel with another general at Little Rock, Arkansas, in 1863. The Walkers' daughter, Maria Polk, was married to Confederate general Frank C. Armstrong at Rally Hill in 1863.

From Rally Hill, continue west on Eighth Street for 0.3 mile until it ends; turn right to reach West Seventh. Turn left (W) on West Seventh. Here, West Seventh is designated U.S. 43/U.S. 412. Just ahead, Trotwood Avenue (U.S. 43) splits off to the left. Continue straight on West Seventh (U.S. 412).

To say that the road markings west of Columbia are confusing is an understatement. Pay close attention to the directions. The old highway from Columbia to Mount Pleasant is marked U.S. 43, but so is the new limited-access highway running parallel to it. To confuse matters even more, the old highway is marked in some places as TN 243; many names have been used for Columbia–Mount Pleasant highway over the years. The situation does not get any better on the side roads. Not only do roads change names, but several roads have the same name!

Beyond the Trotwood Avenue split, West Seventh is a beautiful street shaded by old trees and lined with well-kept houses. Note the 1858 Carpenter Gothic Pise-Parsons House, located on the left at 909 West Seventh. This home was built by David H. Pise, rector of St. Peter's Episcopal Church, partly out of logs from the original Zion Presbyterian Church, which will be visited later on this tour.

Guardhouse at the 1890 Columbia Arsenal, later Columbia Military Academy

You will reach the old Columbia Arsenal 0.3 mile from the Pise-Parsons House. The United States Army built the arsenal on sixty-seven acres about 1890. Its purpose was manufacturing, repairing, and storing ammunition and weapons. The nine original buildings still standing housed quarters and storerooms. Military use of the property did not last long. After being used for training soldiers in the Spanish-American War, the arsenal was declared surplus property and sold. It took on new life in 1904 as the Columbia Military Academy, a respected private secondary school that operated until the 1970s.

Continue past the old arsenal; West Seventh Street becomes Hampshire Pike (U.S. 412). Where TN 50 veers off to the right, keep to the left on Hampshire Pike. Turn left (S) onto Cayce Lane 2.2 miles from the arsenal. You will pass Columbia State Community College—dedicated in 1967 by President Lyndon Johnson—and reach Trotwood Avenue (U.S. 43, the Columbia–Mount Pleasant highway) after 2 miles.

The roads radiating out of Columbia all offer beautiful drives to interesting places like Bigbyville, Culleoka, Santa Fe, and Water Valley. And the parade of impressive homes continues on Pulaski Pike (U.S. 31), Campbellsville Pike (TN 245), Williamsport Pike (TN 50), Hampshire Pike, and Mooresville Pike. But the route that stands above all others is the road to Mount Pleasant.

Concentrated in this area, which historian John Trotwood Moore called "the Dimple of the Universe," are a dozen or so of the most impressive antebellum houses imaginable and two historic rural churches, all surrounded by what is arguably Tennessee's best farmland. The wealth of this land can be traced to three groups of early settlers—the Pillow family, the Polk family, and a group of stern South Carolina Presbyterians.

John Pillow was a Revolutionary War veteran from North Carolina who migrated to the Cumberland country with his sons William and Gideon in 1783. In 1806, Gideon Pillow acquired five thousand acres in Maury County, which he divided among his three sons, Granville, Gideon Jr., and Jerome. The three sons built splendid houses that still stand today.

Gideon Pillow, Sr., built his house on a rise overlooking Little Bigby Creek on today's Campbellsville Pike. Nothing remains of the home today, but his oldest son, Granville, built a fine house on the same spot in 1852. Like each of the three Pillow houses, it is noted for its monumental portico with four Ionic columns. Granville Pillow's house is not on this tour, but it can be reached from the Cayce Lane–Trotwood Avenue intersection by going straight across Trotwood onto Sunnyside

Lane. The house is on Campbellsville Pike just south of where Sunnyside ends.

Turn right (SW) off Cayce Lane onto Trotwood Avenue. It is 1 mile to Clifton Place, located on the left.

Clifton Place

"Few of Tennessee's ante bellum estates so perfectly express the spirit of the past as does Clifton Place," says the classic 1936 book *History of Homes and Gardens of Tennessee*. Completed in 1839 for Gideon Pillow, Jr., Clifton Place was Nathan Vaught's crowning achievement.

There is much of interest about Clifton Place besides its grandeur and beauty. It was built almost entirely of materials found on Pillow's property. The tons of stone for the foundation, the portico, and the bases for the Ionic columns were all quarried here. The bricks were made from clay dug here. And the cherry in the doors, moldings, and mantels all came from trees cut at Clifton Place. A large number of original outbuildings still stand, including a smokehouse, an office, an ice house, and several servants' houses. It is reported to be one of the most intact plantation properties in the nation.

Gideon Pillow, Jr., achieved fame in many areas—the military, politics, law, and agriculture. He was James K. Polk's law partner and political confidant. The West Point graduate's Mexican War service earned him hero status, and when Tennessee seceded from the Union in 1861, Pillow was placed in charge of the state's troops. However, the Civil War tarnished his reputation. He was one of the generals who abandoned Fort Donelson to U. S. Grant.

As a former Confederate military leader, Gideon Pillow was a target of the United States government, and his considerable properties in Tennessee and in Arkansas were confiscated. A decade after the Civil War, he declared bankruptcy. He lived out the remainder of his years practicing law in Memphis and died in 1878 at age seventy-two.

It is 0.8 mile from Clifton Place to a lane on the left leading to Bethel Place, the former home of the third Pillow son; this house is not visible from the highway. Jerome Bonaparte Pillow, the youngest brother, hired Nathan Vaught to build his house in 1855. Like the other two Pillow houses, it is graced with a portico supported by strong Ionic columns. Jerome's daughter and her husband, William Bethel, lived here, thus giving the house its name.

Turn right (N) onto Old Zion Road 0.2 mile past the lane leading to Bethel Place.

The Scots-Irish who settled the Zion community were members of a people who always seemed to be moving in pursuit of a better life. First it was from Scotland to Northern Ireland in the 1600s. Fleeing bad conditions there, they started migrating to the British colonies in North America around 1720. In 1732, a number of them relocated to the Williamsburg District in South Carolina. There, they lived under the strict discipline of the Presbyterian Church.

Newer Scottish settlers began arriving in the 1770s. They did not share the first group's zeal for such serious living. There was friction from the start. The early settlers found the newcomers given to amusements and frivolity and were horrified at their interest in horse racing, dancing, and drinking.

The unpleasant feelings between the two factions, by then split into two Presbyterian congregations, became so intense that the original group decided it was time to move again. In 1805, eleven families headed for the Cumberland country, hoping to buy one large tract of land. Fortunately for them, there was one available—the twenty-five thousand acres in Maury County granted to Revolutionary War general Nathanael Greene.

Ranked by many historians as second only to George Washington in military ability, Greene had settled on Cumberland Island, Georgia, following independence and never came to see his Tennessee property. He had died in 1786, so his large grant was owned by his heirs. In August 1807, the settlers bought 8 square miles, about one-fifth of the Greene tract.

To come up with the $15,360 purchase price, each family gave silver in an amount equal to the land it wanted. The entire sum was turned over to two men who made the long journey to pay Greene's heirs. They carried the whole amount in their saddlebags. To avoid arousing any would-be thieves, they would carelessly toss the saddlebags on the porch of their shelter when they stopped for the night, as if the contents had no value.

The group moved onto its land in 1808. Before long, the settlers were joined by others, then still others, some from South Carolina and some not. They named their community Zion.

Old Zion Road makes several sharp turns and crosses new U.S. 43 before it reaches Zion Road after 2.2 miles. Along the way, it passes several houses built by early members of the Zion community. They are marked with the familiar APTA signs.

Zion Church is directly ahead at Zion Road. Turn right briefly on Zion, then turn into the church parking lot.

Church had always been the center of life for these strict Presbyterians, so they built a church when they first arrived here. The log structure was too small by 1813, so they built a second, more permanent church. In 1846, they started work on their third church, which was completed in 1849. It has been in continuous use ever since.

Once settled in Maury County, the Scots-Irish continued the strict discipline they knew back in South Carolina. The church's governing body— the session, composed of elders and the minister—regulated the moral life of the community. Old records show that discipline was imposed for absence from church services, attendance at other churches—even other Presbyterian churches—use of profane language, stealing, lying, "drinking to excess," and, in the case of one married couple, "living unhappily together." One person who was tried for murder and acquitted in court had his case reviewed by the session. He was acquitted a second time. When the session found a person guilty of an offense, the punishment was often a public rebuke.

Zion Church

In addition to regulating moral life, the session also resolved disputes between Zion residents. One commentator noted that "the Church Session, prior to the Civil War, was practically the Supreme Court of the community and settled all differences without appeal to Civil Courts."

The interior of Zion Church has changed very little since 1849. Notable exceptions are the Tiffany stained-glass windows, installed in 1880; the pulpit, made in 1892 by a church member; and the Pilcher pipe organ, imported in 1899 from Louisville. The original lamps and chandeliers, some now outfitted for electricity, are still working. Among the valuable relics are pewter mugs and china plates brought from South Carolina and a Bible, a psalter, and a chair belonging to the first minister, James White Stephenson.

The design of the church says something about the importance the settlers placed on the religious life of their slaves. The balcony was built for slaves, who were taken into the church as members. At times after emancipation, the number of black members at Zion Church was equal to the number of white members. In the church graveyard is a monument erected to the memory of the slaves of the early Zion settlers—the unusual tombstone of a slave called Daddy Ben.

After visiting Zion Church, return to Old Zion Road and turn right (W). Go straight at the intersection 1.2 miles from Zion Church. You will reach Canaan Road after another 1.2 miles. Turn left (S) and drive 1.2 miles to Ashwood Road.

This is Canaan, an important community started by freed slaves after the Civil War. Emancipation gave blacks some measure of control over their lives. As their days of bondage slipped farther into the past, they wanted their own churches. They eventually left the congregation at Zion and formed their own here at Canaan. The congregation of Canaan African Methodist Episcopal Church dates to that early post–Civil War period. Canaan School for blacks was built here before 1917 and continued in operation until after World War II.

Turn left (E) onto Ashwood Road and drive 2.2 miles to Zion Road. Turn right (S). You will pass under new U.S. 43 before coming to the old village of Ashwood at the railroad. The little town that grew up around the railroad after the Civil War was an important shipping point for the area's plentiful agricultural products. A large mill operated here from 1900 to 1929.

Continue south on Zion Road for 0.4 mile to the Columbia–Mount Pleasant highway. Turn left, then pull into the small parking area on the right in front of St. John's Episcopal Church. Some steps climb over the ancient rock wall in front of the church. You are now in the Polk family domain.

William Polk came to the area—still part of North Carolina—as a surveyor in 1783. He went on to become one of Tennessee's largest landowners. The Revolutionary War hero gradually built up his holdings to over 100,000 acres, including a 5,648-acre tract just south of General Greene's vast grant in Maury County. Polk called this his "rattle and snap" land.

The pioneer period was over and the plantation era emerging in 1823 when the first of William Polk's sons came from Raleigh to Maury County. Lucius Janius Polk was followed by Leonidas Polk in 1833, by Rufus Polk in 1836, and finally by George Washington Polk in 1840. They divided

St. John's Episcopal Church

their father's tract, after which each established himself as a planter of considerable prominence. They built houses that rivaled the Pillows' up the road. Two of the Polk houses stand today.

Leonidas Polk is surely one of the most interesting figures in the history of the Volunteer State. After attending the University of North Carolina for one year, he secured an appointment to West Point. There, he made friends with a young Mississippian named Jefferson Davis. It would prove to be a fateful relationship for Polk. While at West Point, Leonidas Polk came under the influence of the chaplin. In 1826, he became the first cadet ever to be baptized at the citadel overlooking the Hudson River.

Polk's military career—at least the first part of it—did not last long, for he resigned from the army shortly after his graduation and enrolled in seminary. Within three years of completing his seminary training, he and his wife, Frances Ann Deveraux, moved to his share of the Polk property in Maury County. Polk completed his fine house, Ashwood Hall, in 1837, while serving as rector of St. Peter's Episcopal Church in Columbia.

He was appointed a missionary bishop in 1838 but continued to live at Ashwood Hall until 1841, when he was named bishop of Louisiana. From that position, he promoted the establishment of an Episcopal college in the South and was the moving force in the founding of the University of the South in Franklin County, Tennessee, on the eve of the Civil War. (For the story of the University of the South, see The Elk River Tour, pages 313–15.)

When the Confederate army was being organized after secession, President Jefferson Davis persuaded Polk to accept a commission—as a major general, no less. Polk was later promoted to lieutenant general and commanded a corps in the Army of Tennessee. As might be expected of a man whose adult life had been spent as a priest and planter, not as a soldier, Polk was not particularly effective as a general.

On a hot summer day in 1864, while standing atop Pine Mountain in Georgia pondering how to stop William Tecumseh Sherman's relentless push toward Atlanta, Polk was struck by an exploding shell and killed instantly. He had always hoped to be buried back in Middle Tennessee at the church he founded, but it was impossible. Middle Tennessee was in Union hands.

Long before the war, Leonidas Polk had talked his brothers into contributing to the church he wanted to build on his Ashwood Hall property. Constructed between 1839 and 1842, this Gothic-style church is modeled after a small chapel in Devon, England, and one in Chapel Hill, North Carolina. St. John's never fully recovered from the Civil War but remained an active congregation until 1915. The only regularly scheduled service held now is on Whitsunday—the last Sunday in May—and is often presided over by the Episcopal bishop.

The graveyard of the church is worth a visit. In late November 1864, a young Confederate general was moved by the serenity of this peaceful spot. "If I am killed in the impending battle I request that my body be laid to rest in this, the most beautiful and peaceful spot I ever beheld." Within days, Patrick Ronayne Cleburne, killed at Franklin on November 30, was laid to rest here at St. John's. Eventually, his remains were returned to Arkansas for reburial. By tradition, Tennessee's Episcopal bishops are buried at St. John's even to this day. The graves of several of them are just behind the church.

Leonidas Polk's house, Ashwood Hall, stood across the road from St. John's Episcopal Church. Jill K. Garrett, the prolific writer of Maury County history, recounts an intriguing incident from 1982 when a man showed up to see the house.

Melvin Weaver of Omaha, Nebraska, had a Bible that his grandfather, a Union soldier from Indiana, had brought back from the Civil War. "Got this book from Rebal [sic] general Popes Library at his Residence in the State of Tennessee December 8th, 1864," the young soldier had written in the Bible.

Weaver knew his grandfather had served around Columbia. And he knew that there was no General Pope from around here. There were two General Polks, Leonidas and his nephew Lucius E. Polk. The Bible was a working minister's Bible published in 1852. Lucius was only nineteen then, but Leonidas was a priest. From that, Weaver deduced that the Bible had once belonged to Leonidas Polk. He came to find General Polk's house—108 years too late. Ashwood Hall burned in 1874.

From St. John's Episcopal Church, turn around and head southwest on the Columbia–Mount Pleasant highway toward Mount Pleasant. Hamilton

Place is on the right 0.7 mile from the Zion Road intersection. With the help of workers his father sent from North Carolina, Lucius J. Polk completed Hamilton Place in 1832. It was the first of the Polk houses. Hamilton Place is said to be a perfect example of Palladian-style architecture.

Lucius Polk was a man held in high regard by his neighbors, so he decided to try his hand at elected office. He got himself elected to the state senate for a term that began in 1831, but he never sought a second, expressing his disgust for the "wire-pulling, log rolling, and jugglery" of politics.

About the time of his senate service, Polk met Mary Ann Eastin, grandniece of Rachel Jackson, Andrew's wife. In the spring of 1832, Lucius and Mary Ann were married in a ceremony at the White House. Mary Ann died at Hamilton Place in 1847 at age thirty after giving birth to twins, the couple's seventh and eighth children. Lucius lived until 1870 and is buried at St. John's Episcopal Church.

Continue 0.3 mile past Hamilton Place. On the opposite side of the road stands Rattle and Snap, one of the most impressive houses in the South, often referred to as "the most monumental house in Tennessee."

The trail of Middle Tennessee antebellum houses that began at the

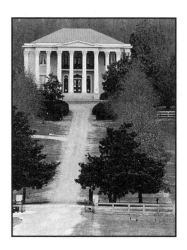

Rattle and Snap, considered the South's most magnificent antebellum plantation house

Bowen-Campbell House at Goodlettsville on The Middle Cumberland Tour ends here at Rattle and Snap. The former structure—Captain William Bowen's frontier house—is plain to the point of being severe, a reflection of the no-nonsense life of the early settlers, who were engaged in a deadly struggle for survival. By contrast, the house George Washington Polk completed here in 1845 seems almost frivolous. With its tall columns, heavy cornices, and refined classical trim, it was built not so much as a place to live but as a place to show off.

The ten Corinthian columns that flank the mansion were made in Cincinnati, shipped by steamboat to Nashville, then hauled by oxcart south to Maury County. The marble mantels were imported from Italy. The grounds were designed by a German landscape artist. The New Orleans–style grillwork on the east portico was cast in Pittsburgh. The main dining room is capped by an exquisite Waterford chandelier. The list goes on and on.

The house's unusual name has its origin in the way William Polk acquired his Rattle and Snap property. A game popular in colonial America was played with dried beans rattled in the players' hands and rolled with a snap of the fingers. Polk supposedly engaged in a high-stakes rattle-and-snap contest with the North Carolina governor at Raleigh and won the property in a wager. When George Washington Polk built his house, he gave it the name of the game that had brought the property into the family's possession.

A squad of Union troops was ready to burn the house in 1862 when its captain noticed a portrait of George W. Polk. Polk was wearing a Masonic ring. The captain reported this fact to his superior officer, and the house was spared. It has long been speculated that the commanding officer and maybe the captain, too, were Masons.

Rattle and Snap fell into disrepair over the years but was brought back in 1979. Amon Carter Evans, retired publisher of *The Tennessean*, the Nashville newspaper, bought the home and determined to restore it to its antebellum splendor. He assembled a team headed by Henry A. Judd, retired chief restoration architect for the National Park Service; Judd had previously restored Philadelphia's Independence Hall and other historic buildings. Working with John W. Kiser, a nineteenth-century design scholar,

Evans furnished the house with antiques from the period from 1845 to 1865. The restoration effort at Rattle and Snap took three years and reportedly cost $8 million. The estate has been open to the public in recent years.

How was it that the Pillows, the Polks, and others in the area were able to accumulate such wealth?

The quality of the soil is one reason. Its continuing productivity long after the plantation era offers evidence that this is good land. In the 1905 book *Century Review—1805–1905—Maury County, Tennessee*, it is asserted that this area was the best farming country in Tennessee. More produce was shipped from Ashwood Station than from any other station of its size on the entire Louisville & Nashville Railroad. This bounty included over 150 cars of potatoes and 25 cars of wheat. Then, too, Ashwood Mills used five times more wheat for its flour than was shipped as raw grain.

Crop diversification and innovation were also factors. Unlike the Deep South plantations where rice and cotton were king, these smaller plantations grew tobacco, cotton, hay, hemp, corn, oats, wheat, rye, and other grains. Orchards and gardens produced fruits and vegetables. Livestock, too, was emphasized. At Clifton Place, Gideon Pillow raised sheep, hogs, and cattle and experimented with new forage foods. Rattle and Snap's George W. Polk stated in 1859, "You must not be content with going on with the same old crop year after year, but it must be made a science and studied. . . . Farming is a science."

Of course, an abundant supply of cheap labor helped. Though there is considerable evidence that the plight of slaves here in the Mid-South was better than in the Deep South, slavery was still slavery. Workers were the property of their masters and did not have to be paid a wage.

Continue past Rattle and Snap for 1.6 miles to the intersection where U.S. 43 turns right to join the new U.S. 43. Go straight on the main road, now marked TN 243, which becomes Mount Pleasant's Main Street. It is 1.6 miles from the U.S. 43–TN 243 junction to Walnut Grove, the impressive mansion on the left.

When William Henry Boddie died in 1841, he left his property to his widowed sister, Sabra Lawrence. She was a strong, independent woman who managed one of Maury County's most extensive plantations on this site. Once, during the Civil War, when Union soldiers took twenty or so bales of her cotton, the seventy-six-year-old Sabra got in her buggy, followed them to Columbia, and demanded payment from their commanding officer. He paid her.

After her original house burned, Sabra Lawrence commissioned Nathan Vaught to build this beautiful home in 1858. She died in 1867. Around 1880, her daughter sold or leased the place for use as an Episcopal school, the Otey School, which operated here for less than a decade. The house was carefully restored in 1982.

Continue on Main Street to the square and the 1907 Confederate Monument.

Mount Pleasant's status as the county's second-largest town dates to the completion of the Military Road through here around 1820. Built under the supervision of General Andrew Jackson, the road led from Nashville all the way to Louisiana. When it replaced the Natchez Trace as the post road to the old Southwest, the Trace's days as a major route of travel were just about ended. The name Mount Pleasant comes from a real-estate development started by some Nashville speculators in 1822.

The beginning of phosphate mining in the area turned Mount Pleasant into a boom town in the 1890s. The "Phosphate Capital of the World" was almost renamed Phosphate City in 1896. By that year, around fifteen hundred men were employed in the business. Maintaining law and order was not easy. Fights and shootings were common. On one Sunday morning, thirteen bodies were found on Blue Grass Avenue between the square and the railroad.

In her collection of articles, *"Hither and Yon,"* Jill K. Garrett describes what the town's leaders did to restore order. A legendary lawman, a former Texas Ranger named Captain Russell, was hired to clean up the town. On the day he was to arrive by train, a large crown of ruffians gathered at the depot, intent on intimidating him. The train came. When no Captain Russell got off, a cheer went up from the crowd. Then the train left. Standing on the opposite side of the tracks was Russell. With a gun in each hand pointed at the crowd, he announced, "I'll kill the first damn man who moves. I'm Captain Russell." And, Garrett writes, it is said that Russell cleaned up the town.

With the arrival of TVA electricity in the 1930s, new methods of mining and washing phosphate for use as fertilizer were employed. Until the 1980s, phosphate was still big business around Mount Pleasant. Phosphate companies employed twenty-four hundred people in 1955.

Continue southwest on Main Street past the square for 0.1 mile to Merchant Street. Turn right and drive to Pleasant Street. Manor Hall, built by Martin Luther Stockard in 1859, is the Greek Revival plantation house at this intersection. Turn right on Pleasant, then left on Washington Street. Proceed 0.3 mile to College Street. Turn right and drive 0.3 mile to TN 166 (First Street). Turn left.

Manor Hall

It is 7.1 miles on TN 166 to the junction with U.S. 412 at Hampshire. The landscape changes as the rolling bluegrass of the Central Basin gives way to the high ridges and fertile valleys created by broken parts of the Western Highland Rim. Bright green pastures sweep up from the valleys to the edge of the forest on the ridges. In April, the soft green of the forest is broken by splashes of dogwood and redbud. The deep green of the summer forest gives way in late October to brilliant fall colors. This is a particularly beautiful part of Middle Tennessee.

At U.S. 412 on the edge of the lovely little village of Hampshire, turn right (E) and head toward Columbia. After 4.4 miles, you will pass the Jonathan Webster House, located on the left.

Jonathan Webster was a Revolutionary War veteran who settled here in 1807. He built this Federal-style house, the first made of brick in the region, around 1810. The front porch is a later addition. Webster came to own a good bit of this part of Maury County. His sons built four splendid plantation houses, two of which stand today, on land their father gave them. The Websters ran a mill on Bigby Creek. The community that grew up around it was called Webster's Mill before it came to be known as Cross Bridges.

Jonathan Webster House

Continue east on U.S. 412. After 0.5 mile, you will pass the distinctive 1907 Cross Bridges United Methodist Church, on the right. You will then cross Bigby Creek. Turn left (N) onto Cross Bridges Road 0.3 mile past the church.

At one time, there were supposedly four toll bridges here at Webster's Mill. Travelers spoke so often about "crossing the bridges" that the place soon took on that name. Bigby, the name of the creek, is derived from Tombigbee, the Choctaw word for box maker or coffin maker.

After 1.1 miles on Cross Bridges Road, you will reach Liberty Hall, on the left.

Jonathan Webster's son, George Pope Webster, hired Anthony Gholshon to build this house in 1844. Gholshon was a superstitious man. A well-known brick manufacturer and builder before the Civil War, he believed that if he made his bricks by following the signs of the zodiac, he would get a better product, so he always burned his brick "by the sign."

It seems strange that Gholshon sided with the Union during the Civil War, for he was a major slave owner before the war, using his slaves at his kiln and in his building trade. One of the slaves he bought was a twelve-year-old boy named Isaiah, who was destined to rival his master in his skill as a brick mason. After emancipation, Isaiah took on Gholshon's name, spelling it Gholston, and went on to become a prominent citizen in Columbia. The former master and former slave worked side by side in the construction of Columbia's First Methodist Church in 1875 and 1876.

George Pope Webster's fellow Maury Countian James K. Polk ran for president in the year Webster completed Liberty Hall. Webster took out a newspaper ad as a challenge to any local Whig. He would bet a thousand dollars on the outcome of the election, plus "one bale of cotton on each state from Maine to Louisiana." Whether anyone took up the Democrat's challenge is not known, but Webster would have had plenty of cotton if they had. Polk carried sixteen of the twenty-six states, including Maine and Louisiana, but not Tennessee. He lost his home state by just 113 votes.

Cross Bridges Road intersects Morel Road 0.3 mile past Liberty Hall; bear left, staying on Cross Bridges Road.

Lipscomb Place Farm, on the right, is impressive not just for its splendid 1830s mansion, but also for its beautiful barn and other well-kept buildings. George Lipscomb's fall from riches to rags at the time of the Civil War tells a great deal about what happened to many in the planter class in those turbulent times.

Lipscomb was an elderly veteran of Andrew Jackson's Seminole campaign. Two of his horses were Traveler and Prince Pulaski, both descended from the famous harness pacer Star Pointer. Prince Pulaski was just a colt when he and Traveler were confiscated by Union troops. Traveler did not survive the war, but Prince Pulaski did; he was sold by Federal authorities at Nashville after the war. Lipscomb was broke and could not buy the horse. To raise cash, he boarded horses here on his substantial place. A man from neighboring Marshall County bought Prince Pulaski, then hired Lipscomb to board what had once been his own horse.

Continue on Cross Bridges Road for 0.6 mile to Vine Hill, a large white house flanked by columns that sits high on the hill to the left. The house is visible from the road only when there is no foliage.

James Henry Webster, another of Jonathan Webster's sons, finished the first part of Vine Hill around 1837. This well-known landmark has a massive entrance hall measuring sixty feet by eighteen feet. The house is noted for features that were innovative in its day, including built-in closets. It is not that no one had thought of built-in closets before. Houses were taxed according to the number of rooms, and closets were considered rooms.

One of Vine Hill's two porticoes

Vine Hill fell into disrepair, only to be saved in 1963 when it was purchased by Mrs. Charles Deere Wiman, great-granddaughter of the builder. She refinished the poplar floors and the walnut and cherry doors and trim and filled the place with furnishings collected from the United States and Europe. She also replaced the missing columns on the south portico with ones obtained from a house being demolished on West Seventh Street in Columbia. Mrs. Wiman donated the property to the Maury County Historical Society in 1971, and the society in turn sold it to Mr. and Mrs. Randolph Jackson in 1993.

Jimmy Gray Robinson Road comes in from the left just past Vine Hill. Follow Jimmy Gray Robinson Road for 3.8 miles to where it intersects TN 50 (Williamsport Pike). Cross the highway onto Old Williamsport Pike to enter the village of Williamsport.

Edward Williams settled here in 1805, and the town grew up around the ferry he started across the Duck River in 1810. By 1850, it was an important commercial center. Williamsport was also home to Tom Jones, better known as "Free Tom," a Williams slave who operated the ferry.

The flood that occurred here in the spring of 1812 was the largest to date. Around midnight on the night of the flood, as Tom Jones was checking on his boat, he saw that water was all around his master's house. He rushed to the house and woke Williams, and the family members made their es-

Claborne Chapel African Methodist Episcopal Church

cape. They had been out of the house for only an instant when they saw it shaken from its foundation and taken away down the swollen river. A grateful Edward Williams gave Tom is freedom. He was fondly called "Free Tom" until his death in 1848.

On the western edge of Williamsport, take time to study Claborne Chapel African Methodist Episcopal Church, on the right. This interesting, well-preserved structure was built in 1923 to house a congregation that dates to the immediate post–Civil War period.

Old Williamsport Pike rejoins TN 50 after 0.6 mile. Turn right (W) and cross the Duck River, then make an immediate right (N) onto TN 247 (Snow Creek Road). It is 6.3 miles to TN 7 (Santa Fe Pike).

The route follows the lush, narrowing valley that Snow Creek has carved into the ridges of the Western Highland Rim. If you like traditional Middle Tennessee farmhouses, you will enjoy this stretch of road. It is lined with substantial, well-kept houses in a variety of styles.

This area just north of the Duck River marks the southern edge of the vast military reservation that North Carolina set aside in 1783 to provide land as payment to Revolutionary War veterans. (For information about the grants, see The Middle Cumberland Tour, page 9.) The surveyors marking the boundary got caught in a snowstorm here. That is how Snow Creek got its name.

Turn left (NW) onto TN 7 and drive 0.7 mile into the village of Santa Fe.

Pronounced Santa *Fee*, this pleasant town of tidy white frame houses and pretty churches is reminiscent of a New England village. It even has a little village green. The lovely little building just past the green was once Santa Fe's bank.

Santa Fe has not changed much since 1895, when it was described in a local history as being "cozily nestled down between the rugged and everlasting hills by which it is surrounded." One of the first areas of Maury County to be settled, it was initially called Pin Hook.

Thomas Hart Benton lived for a time just to the north in Williamson County. Later, when he was a senator from Missouri and one of America's most prominent men, this place changed its name to Benton in his honor. (For information about Benton's life in Tennessee, see The Harpeth River Tour, pages 155–56.)

Like so many of Middle Tennessee's small towns, Santa Fe got its permanent name when it applied for a post office. There was already a Benton in East Tennessee, so the post office said that the local people had to pick another name. Remarking that there was no town of this name "this side of Mexico," they chose the name of the territorial capital in today's state of New Mexico.

The congregation that meets in Santa Fe United Methodist Church, located just past the sharp turn at the green, is an old one, dating to around 1810. Like so many of the beautiful white frame Methodist churches in the Middle Tennessee countryside, this one was built in the 1880s.

The 1845 Masonic Hall, next to the church, is where a group of local men met in 1861 to form the Maury Light Artillery. A marker honoring the unit is located at Fort Donelson, near Dover.

This tour ends at Santa Fe. The Natchez Trace Parkway is about 5 miles ahead on TN 7. In the opposite direction, TN 7 leads to Columbia. Or you can go back to TN 247 (Snow Creek Road) and follow it north through the interesting ridge-top community of Theta to Carter's Creek Pike (TN 246). A left (N) turn here leads to Franklin. A right (S) turn on Carter's Creek Pike and then a left (E) turn on TN 247 will take you back to Spring Hill, where the tour began.

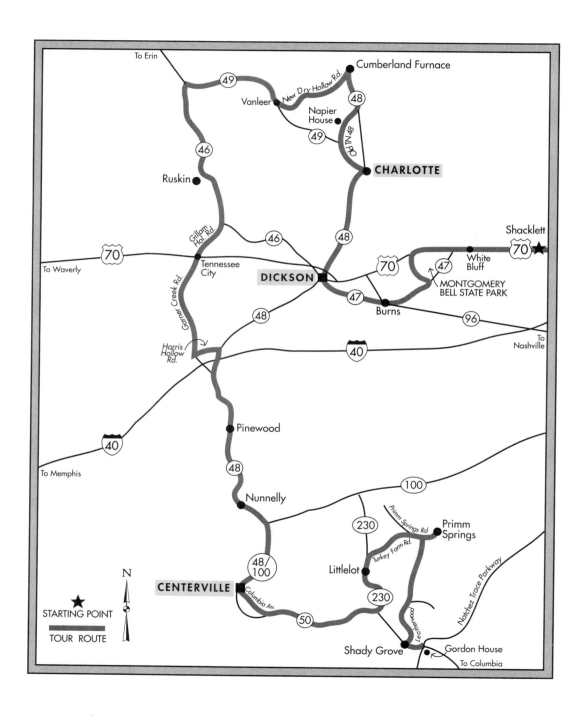

The Western Highland Rim Tour

This tour alternates between the Highland Rim's forested ridges and green valleys, taking in sites associated with Middle Tennessee's now-extinct iron industry. After visiting Montgomery Bell State Park, it stops at Dickson and the charming town of Charlotte, where Tennessee's oldest courthouse stands. Among the interesting communities along the route are Cumberland Furnace, home to the iron industry; Ruskin, a failed socialist colony; and Pinewood, an early industrial site. After stopping at Centerville, the tour goes to the old resort at Primm Springs and ends on the Natchez Trace Parkway.

Total length: approximately 116 miles

This tour begins where U.S. 70 crosses the Harpeth River at Shacklett. You can reach Shacklett by driving west on U.S. 70 for 10 miles from Exit 196 off Interstate 40 at the Nashville suburb of Bellevue.

From Shacklett, head west on U.S. 70 for 7 miles to the stoplight in White Bluff. Just past where the tour begins, you will climb the long hill that rises at the edge of the Harpeth Valley. This marks an important transition in the geography of Middle Tennessee from the Central Basin to the Highland Rim, from what historian Stephen V. Ash has labeled the "heartland" to the highlands. It is a transition from fertile farmland and rolling bluegrass to timbered ridges and narrow valleys. Historically, it has meant a cultural passage as well. Life was lived differently in the highlands.

The mass communication and swift transportation of the late twentieth century have homogenized local culture, but to alert observers, the cultural lines separating the distinct parts of Middle Tennessee can still be seen. Although the standard of living is no longer as dependent upon the quality of the soil as in times past, evidence of social patterns and habits has not been completely erased.

White Bluff, established along the railroad by Union soldiers during the Civil War, is named for a cliff on nearby Turnbull Creek. The small town is on the eastern edge of Dickson County, formed in 1803 and named for

Dr. William Dickson, a young Nashville physician who served in Congress from 1801 to 1807.

The railroad line through White Bluff played a major role in the development of the region west of Nashville. It began as the Nashville & Northwestern, linking Tennessee's capital city on the Cumberland River to the Mississippi River far to the west. The Cumberland was often plagued by water too low for steamboats to make it up to Nashville. A direct rail line to the Mississippi would afford year-round passage for goods and travelers.

By the time the Civil War came to Middle Tennessee in the winter of 1862, only the 25-mile section of the line to Kingston Springs had been completed. The Union army needed an alternative to the unreliable Cumberland River to get men and materials from the North to its huge base in occupied Nashville, so it completed the railroad west to the Tennessee River. After the war, the Nashville & Northwestern line was absorbed into the Nashville, Chattanooga & St. Louis Railroad, becoming part of that road's Nashville-Memphis main line. The Nashville, Chattanooga & St. Louis was in turn absorbed into the Louisville & Nashville in the 1950s.

From the stoplight in White Bluff, it is 3.7 miles west on U.S. 70 to the turnoff on the left for Montgomery Bell State Park. The park headquarters is on the right just past the entrance.

Named for the famed iron master who built his nearby forge at the Narrows of the Harpeth River, this park began as a 1930s New Deal effort of the National Park Service, with assistance provided by the Civilian Conservation Corps (CCC). (For information about Montgomery Bell and the Narrows of the Harpeth, see The Harpeth River Tour, pages 148–50.)

The 5,000-acre resort park offers a variety of activities including golf, swimming, and hiking on trails that range in length from 0.25 mile to 11.7 miles. A popular hiking destination is Hall Spring on the headwaters of Lake Woodhaven. The spring flows at a rate of eleven hundred gallons per minute and has an active beaver colony.

At the fork in the road 0.5 mile inside the park, take the right fork; continue 0.3 mile to the road's end. The short Ore Pit Trail starts here. A hardwood forest that includes some magnificent white oaks has reclaimed the old ore pits, but the remains of the 1815 Laurel Furnace can still be seen on Ore Pit Trail. This is an access point for other trails as well.

The chapel and reconstructed cabin just ahead commemorate the founding here of the Cumberland Presbyterian denomination. The denomination had its origin in what came to be called the Great Revival, the impassioned religious movement that swept across the frontier like wildfire. It began in 1800 in Kentucky and quickly spread into Middle Tennessee. James McGready, a dramatic Presbyterian evangelist, was the spark that ignited the revival. McGready stirred the normally staid Presbyterians into an emotional frenzy. Before long, he was drawing crowds much too large for the small pioneer churches. Other preachers, including Methodists and Baptists, quickly emerged to lead the large gatherings.

Shrine where Cumberland Presbyterian denomination started

Worshipers traveled great distances over roads that were nothing more than crude paths. After expending such an effort to get there, they wanted to stay, and the religious events soon turned into massive camp meetings. People would camp for days, listening to round-the-clock preaching and exhortations. Camp-meeting crowds often numbered in the thousands.

The religious excitement was manifested in conduct never before witnessed. Moans and sobs rose from the crowd. Worshipers were struck down with violent motions of the body. Jerking was the most common physical manifestation, followed by dancing, rolling, and barking.

The Presbyterians were the largest denomination in the region when the Great Revival started. It is ironic that a revival movement started by Presbyterians ended up splintering that denomination and significantly reducing the influence of mainline Presbyterianism.

The camp meetings were getting so big and were being held so frequently that there were too few educated Presbyterian ministers to go around. A deep rift developed over whether to ordain ministers who did not meet the denomination's educational requirements. And within a few years of the Great Revival's beginning, concern was also being expressed over the emotional and physical excesses of the movement. This alarmed McGready and other revivalist Presbyterian preachers as well. One of them was Samuel McAdow, who lived in a cabin here in Dickson County. McGready, McAdow, and other revivalists were ordaining men whom mainline Presbyterians called "illiterate exhorters." The general assembly of the denomination ordered them to stop.

But they were not about to stop. Some revivalists in the Cumberland

Replica of Samuel McAdow's cabin

Presbytery felt so strongly about it that they decided it was time to consider separating from the main church. Samuel King, Finis Ewing, and Ephriam McLean came here to Samuel McAdow's cabin on February 3, 1810, to talk things over.

Legend has it that they went out into the cold winter darkness and prayed the entire night. At the break of dawn, McAdow supposedly saw the light. He shared his vision with the others. They would renounce the authority of the Presbyterian Church and continue to ordain uneducated ministers. The men formed the nucleus of the new denomination, the Cumberland Presbyterian Church.

The chapel in Montgomery Bell State Park is a shrine built in 1961 to mark the founding of the church on this spot. A 1956 replica of Samuel McAdow's cabin is just beyond the chapel.

After visiting the chapel and cabin, return to the main park road and turn right. It is 1.1 miles to the park's rear entrance, located on TN 47 at the Bakersworks community.

Along the way, the road passes the turnoff to Lake Woodhaven and a memorial to the CCC workers who helped build the park.

Roosevelt's Tree Army—that is what they were called by some. But to most people, they were just "CCC boys," thousands of young men ages eighteen to twenty-five who were part of the Civilian Conservation Corps. The CCC was created by an act of Congress in 1933 during Franklin D. Roosevelt's first hundred days in office. Its goal was to take unemployed young men and put them to work reclaiming America's landscape. They earned thirty dollars per month, twenty-five of which they had to send home. They also received clothing and room and board. More than that, they got self-esteem and a new direction in life. Over forty thousand of them learned to read and write, and a host of others learned skills like carpentry, stone masonry, and mechanics from LEM—Local Experienced Men—who were put to work training the younger men. In the peak year of 1935, there were half a million CCC boys. Tennessee had seventy-seven camps. Over seventy thousand young men from the state joined the CCC.

They left behind enormous contributions, building or improving over 1,000 parks, constructing 3,470 fire towers and 97,000 miles of roads, and planting more than 2 billion trees. Tennessee benefited as much as any state from the work of the CCC boys, for most of the initial construction in Tennessee's state parks is CCC work. So, too, are the 600 miles of hiking trails in Great Smoky Mountains National Park. In those days of racial segregation, the CCC was segregated, too. The beautiful stone dams that impound Lakes Woodhaven and Acorn at Montgomery Bell State Park were built by CCC boys from an all-black camp near here.

The program lasted until World War II, when 85 percent of the CCC boys went into the military.

In 1990, the Tennessee chapter of the National Association of Civilian Conservation Corps Alumni embarked on a program to erect markers in the seventeen state parks the CCC helped develop. The memorial at Montgomery Bell is the first.

Turn right on TN 47 at the rear entrance of the park. It is 3.4 miles to the pleasant small town of Burns. Burns, like White Bluff, dates to the construction of the railroad during the Civil War. It is named for Captain John Burns, a Union officer.

Dam at Lake Woodhaven, built by the CCC

Turn right at Burns, staying on TN 47; where the road crosses TN 96 after 0.6 mile, continue straight on TN 47. You will pass through Colesburg before reaching TN 46 on the edge of Dickson after 3.5 miles.

The numbering of the state highways around Dickson is confusing. No fewer than four of them are numbered in the forties—TN 46, TN 47, TN 48, and TN 49—so pay careful attention to the signs.

Cross TN 46 onto Dickson's East Walnut Street and drive 0.7 mile to Main Street. Turn right (N) on Main to enter downtown Dickson. Where Main Street crosses the railroad, the depot is just to the right.

Like the smaller towns of White Bluff and Burns, Dickson owes its existence to the railroad the Union army built west from Kingston Springs. The town was first a work camp called Forty-Two because it was 42 miles from Nashville. Then it was Sneedsville—named in honor of a Federal engineer who supervised the construction—before the name Dickson was finally selected.

German and Irish immigrants brought in to build the railroad formed the nucleus of the new town, which was laid out in 1868. Dickson also became a popular destination for settlers from Pennsylvania and Ohio in the days when immigration into the devastated South was heavily promoted.

By 1870, the town eclipsed the county seat of Charlotte as the commercial and social center of Dickson County. It was inevitable that there would be an effort to relocate the seat of government to the larger town.

Bills to do that were introduced in the legislature in 1870 and 1873, but nothing came of them. The issue smoldered for several decades, then finally erupted with great fury in 1927. A courthouse—the second in town—had been built in Dickson years earlier, but it was in bad repair. So was the one in Charlotte. There was widespread concern over whether the county could afford to renovate two courthouses. To break the impasse, a referendum was called in August 1927 to decide whether to move the county seat to Dickson.

The county became embroiled in something of a cold war. Each faction campaigned actively and often bitterly. "The Historical Court House at Charlotte is the Object of Attack by a Ring of County and City Politicians at Dickson," a propaganda leaflet of the Charlotte faction proclaimed. When the vote was counted, Dickson won 2,734 votes and Charlotte 1,983. But a two-thirds majority was required to force the move. Charlotte is still the seat of Dickson County.

By the end of the first decade of the twentieth century, Dickson was a thriving town humming with mills, factories, tobacco warehouses, stores, and a well-respected college. The railroad continued to play a major role in the life of Dickson well into the twentieth century. Two important branch lines connected with the main line near town. The Nashville, Chattanooga & St. Louis built the existing brick depot in 1914.

Railroad workers, passengers changing trains, and traveling salesmen created a demand for lodging in Dickson. In 1913, J. T. Halbrook built a hotel across from the depot. In 1917, he rented it to a widow from Kentucky, Belle S. Goad. Mrs. Goad's daughter, Maybelle, helped her run the hotel.

Maybelle eloped in 1919 with a man six years her junior, nineteen-year-old Robert Clement. They returned to take up residence in a back bedroom of the hotel, where, a year later, a son was born to them. They named him Frank Goad. In 1952, Frank Goad Clement became the youngest man ever elected governor of Tennessee. And he served as Tennessee's chief executive longer than any other man save one, William Carroll.

Halbrook Hotel, birthplace of Governor Frank Clement

It is probably safe to say about Frank Clement what was said about another man who dominated Tennessee politics in his day, Andrew Jackson: on the subject of Frank Clement, very few people were neutral. Clement did indeed have a large and devoted following. But his detractors were many, too. Chief among them was the Evans family, publishers of *The Tennessean*, the Nashville newspaper. Their attacks on the governor were unrelenting.

It was his ability as an orator that first drew people to the brilliant, young Frank Clement. As a child, he attended the Shipp School of Expression, run by his aunt, Dockie Shipp Weems. He learned a style of speaking guaranteed to draw and please crowds. And in 1956, the young governor planned to use his gift to make himself a contender for national office.

Outmaneuvering Senator John F. Kennedy of Massachusetts, Senator Hubert Humphrey of Minnesota, Governor Edmund Muskie of Maine, and a host of other rising stars, Clement was selected to give the keynote address at the Democratic National Convention in Chicago. The eventual presidential nominee, Adlai Stevenson, was pleased. Clement was "one of those wonderful young men who is reinvigorating the Democratic party," Stevenson remarked.

Clement's strategists hoped a rip-roaring oration would land him the number-two spot on the ticket. Then, win or lose, he would be a contender for the presidential nomination four years later.

It is doubtful that anyone ever worked harder to prepare a convention speech. Clement consulted with party leaders, including former president Harry Truman and Senator Lyndon Johnson, and even received advice from evangelist Billy Graham.

Frank Clement lived up to his billing. In a rousing speech reminiscent of an old-style evangelist, he spoke for forty minutes about the GOP—the "Gilded Old Party"—and the "Vice-Hatchetman" Richard Nixon. President Eisenhower, an able battlefield leader, had exercised little leadership, Clement argued. Over and over, he yelled, "How long, O how long America?" "Come home," he pleaded to Americans, "before it is too late. Your lands are studded with the white skulls and crossbones of broken Republican promises. How long, O how long, America, shall these things endure?"

The governor's supporters were euphoric. Amidst favorable reviews by the likes of the *New York Times* (which said Clement "set the . . . convention on fire") and the *Los Angeles Herald and Express* (which called the speech "one of the finest . . . in decades") and enthusiasm from party leaders like James A. Farley and Speaker of the House Sam Rayburn, the Tennessee delegation started talking about Clement as the presidential nominee.

But within twenty-four hours, it was apparent that the intended groundswell of support for Frank Clement would not materialize. The age of television was emerging. The stock of old-fashioned orators like Frank Clement was declining. Stevenson, the presidential nominee, let the convention pick the nominee for vice president, and in a tremendous blow to Clement, fellow Tennessean Estes Kefauver was the choice.

Historical writer Robert E. Corlew III notes that the failure of the speech "was a bitter and traumatic experience" for Clement, "a blow to his spirit from which he never completely recovered." Clement completed his term as governor. Then, after four years out of office, he was elected to another four-year term in 1962. But, as Corlew argues, Frank Clement's later successes "did not completely heal the Chicago wound."

After unsuccessful tries for the United States Senate in 1964 and 1966, Clement left office in 1967. When the 1970 governor's election approached, his many friends were gearing up for yet another campaign. But his career—and life—ended tragically on the night of November 4, 1969. Clement was killed in a Nashville automobile accident. His father, Robert, directed that the body be brought home that night to Dickson.

After visiting downtown Dickson, drive north on Main Street, away from the railroad. Main Street becomes TN 48 and crosses U.S. 70. It is 7.2 miles on TN 48 from U.S. 70 to a three-way stop in the Dickson County seat of Charlotte.

The town is named for Charlotte Reeves Robertson, wife of James Robertson, the "Father of Tennessee." An important person in her own right, this woman of courage and fortitude is best remembered for winning the April 2, 1781, Battle of The Bluff at Fort Nashborough.

Early that morning, a small party of Cherokees attacked the fort, perched on the Cumberland River bluff. They then retreated down the hill. The men at the fort grabbed their flintlocks and gave chase. It turned out to be a trap. A larger group of Indians sprang from its hiding place and rushed the fort, intent on battering down the gates and massacring the remaining inhabitants, most of whom were unarmed.

The fifty or so fierce hunting dogs in the fort were stirred by the commotion, and they clawed at the gates. Charlotte Robertson opened the gates and set the dogs on the Indians. The attackers were caught completely by surprise and lost their advantage. The armed men returned to the safety of the fort and repelled the attack, though there were several casualties. Charlotte Robertson's cool-headed response saved the fledgling settlement on the Cumberland.

Charlotte survived this and many more encounters with the Indians, encounters which took the lives of her brother-in-law and two of her sons. She also experienced the horror of seeing her twelve-year-old son, Peyton, beheaded before her very eyes.

It is reported that an alert Charlotte Robertson made a dress on the day she died in 1843. She was ninety-two.

Turn right (E) onto TN 49 at the three-way stop in Charlotte and drive 0.1 mile to Charlotte Cumberland Presbyterian Church. Turn left (N) to reach the Charlotte Courthouse Square Historic District.

This charming small town looks and feels more like a town in the Middle Tennessee heartland than one on the Highland Rim. One reason is its age—it was laid out in 1804 on fifty acres Charles Stewart donated for a county seat. Another reason was the location of the railroad—it bypassed Charlotte. Following the Civil War, Charlotte never regained its status as a trade center.

Only one of the historic buildings around the square dates to Charlotte's earliest period, for a tornado struck on May 30, 1830, and nearly destroyed the town. The oldest building, the two-story 1806-vintage brick structure on the northwest corner of the square and Dunning Street, was designed for use as a store and residence. It later became the home of Jacob Voorhies, who came here from New Jersey around 1820, married a prominent local girl, and was a prosperous merchant and landowner who helped establish the town's first school.

The courthouse was rebuilt in 1833. This beautiful structure stands today as the oldest courthouse in Tennessee.

Voorhies Building on Charlotte's square

The 1833 courthouse in Charlotte, Tennessee's oldest

Ironworks at Cumberland Furnace

Two other buildings around the square were built in 1849—the Greek Revival–style Collier Store at the northwest corner of the square and Humphreys Street and the three-story brick building at the southwest corner of the square and Dunning Street. Most of the other buildings around the square date from the 1850s to 1900.

The lovely Charlotte Cumberland Presbyterian Church, located just off the square, was completed in 1850 and is furnished with the original poplar pews and some other original furniture. The bell in the tower came from the Cumberland River steamboat *Sarah Blayden*. For a time during the Civil War, the Union army used the church as a field hospital.

Leave the square on Spencer Alley on the square's northwest corner and return to TN 48. Turn right (N), then turn left (W) on TN 49. Where TN 49 swings left after 1.8 miles, go straight onto Old TN 48.

This road follows the fertile valley of Barton's Creek, one of the earliest parts of Dickson County to be settled. One of the area's earliest houses, the Napier House, is on the hill to the left after 1.4 miles. It is visible only when there is no foliage.

Richard C. Napier was a pioneer in the iron industry. He married Charlotte Robertson, the youngest daughter of James and Charlotte Robertson, in 1789 and managed Robertson's iron interests until he sold them to Montgomery Bell in 1804. Napier then went into the business on his own. Among his properties was Laurel Furnace in today's Montgomery Bell State Park. Napier lived in this house from 1819 until his death in 1834.

The house was built by Napier's father in 1798 on his thousand-acre Revolutionary War veteran's grant. One reason the house still stands is its sturdy construction; the brick walls are eighteen inches thick.

Old TN 48 intersects TN 48 after 3.4 miles. Turn left (N). It is 2.4 miles to New Dry Hollow Road. Turn left and drive 0.3 mile to the intersection with Cumberland Furnace Road (Old TN 48) in the village of Cumberland Furnace.

Cumberland Furnace is named for the first ironworks on the Western Highland Rim. The ore mined here came from the Great Western Iron Belt, which stretched across Tennessee in a band 15 to 40 miles wide. Dickson County was in the heart of it. And Dickson County had the right combination of resources to make the iron business a success. There was an abundance of high-grade ore, and most of it was near the surface. There was no shortage of timber to make the charcoal used for fuel. Limestone, used as flux to reduce the ore, is abundant in Middle Tennessee. There were also plenty of streams to supply water. And the fruitful valleys provided food for the workers. It is estimated that between 1797 and 1930, iron-ore production in the region was 8,560,000 gross tons. During the same period, pig-iron production was 4,052,500 tons.

The rise and fall of the iron industry on the Western Highland Rim can be traced here at Cumberland Furnace. This is where it began. And this is where it ended. Sometime around 1795, the multitalented James Robertson discovered iron ore and began a furnace here to produce pig iron. But it was not until Montgomery Bell bought out Robertson in 1804 that the industry really began to surge.

In order to devote more energy to his new forge on the Harpeth River and tend to his multitude of other properties, Montgomery Bell sold the Cumberland Furnace to another Pennsylvania iron man, Anthony Vanleer, in 1820. Throughout the next two decades, the iron industry grew and grew, reaching its peak around the time of Bell's death in 1855. Vanleer's holdings eventually grew to over twenty thousand acres.

By the Civil War, the industry was in decline, due in part to the panic of 1857 and the increasing inefficiency of slavery as a means of labor. The war halted the business completely. It rebounded after the war.

Vanleer's fortune passed to his granddaughter, Florence Kirkman of Nashville. During the Civil War, Florence was courted by a young Federal captain, James P. Drouillard. They eventually married. The Drouillards took over the Cumberland Furnace in 1870 and operated it until 1889.

In the meantime, the process for reducing ore was changing. Coke, produced from coal, replaced charcoal as the fuel of choice, and more efficient blast methods were developed. Other places like Birmingham, Alabama, had more of the resources needed.

The declining industry on the Western Highland Rim got a reprieve in the early 1890s, when the Louisville & Nashville Railroad built a branch line from Clarksville into Dickson County—coke could be imported and pig iron exported.

The Warner Iron Company, owned by Nashvillian James C. Warner,

took over the Cumberland Furnace from the Drouillards' company and ran it until decreasing production forced the railroad to abandon the spur to the furnace in 1931. The Cumberland Furnace sputtered on a few more years before finally closing for good in 1936.

Throughout its days as a center for iron production, Cumberland Furnace was the site of a sizable company town. Today, the village holds a remarkable collection of some forty buildings dating from several periods. They range from log slave cabins to stores to warehouses to the Drouillards' massive Italianate country retreat on the hill above town.

Turn left (S) off New Dry Hollow Road onto Cumberland Furnace Road and drive up the hollow through town. Bear right at the fork after 0.2 mile. You will soon reach St. James Episcopal Church, on the right. This church was built by the Drouillards in 1879 down the hill from their grand house. The lovely building, dedicated by noted bishop Charles Todd Quintard in 1882, still houses an active congregation.

The Drouillards built the school next door the same year they built the church. The first minister of the church, the Reverend Charles J.

Hendley, was also the first schoolmaster. The building is now used as a lodge hall.

Return to New Dry Hollow Road and turn left (SW). It is 6.3 miles to TN 49 at the town of Vanleer. The old Cumberland Furnace Railroad Depot is on the left as you leave Cumberland Furnace. New Dry Hollow Road follows the bed of the old spur to Vanleer.

Turn right (N) on TN 49 and follow it for 6.7 miles to the junction with TN 46 on Yellow Creek. Turn left (S) on TN 46. It is 6.2 miles through the prosperous valley of Yellow Creek to Jewel Cave, then another 0.2 mile to Ruskin Cave.

The name of this place, Ruskin, comes from the socialist colony that existed here in the final days of the nineteenth century. The colony was the brainchild of Julius Augustus Wayland, an Indiana socialist who, paradoxically, did well in several capitalist ventures. Among them was his socialist weekly, *The Coming Nation*.

Using profits from his paper, Wayland promoted the establishment of a colony here in Dickson County in 1894. It was first located 5 miles to the south, near Tennessee City, before being moved to this more fertile area on Yellow Creek in 1896. Wayland had been influenced by several socialist writers, including Englishman John Ruskin, for whom he named his colony.

At the colony's zenith around 1897, on its eighteen hundred acres of land, the three hundred members of the Ruskin Cooperative Association operated a highly successful newspaper and printing business, a diversified agricultural operation, a sawmill, a gristmill, a steam laundry, a machine shop, a cafe, a bakery, a school, a commissary, a cannery, and some smaller cottage industries. Several of their products, including the Ruskin Ready Remedy—a medicine "especially recommended and used for years as a certain cure for flesh wounds, cuts, burns, bruises, bites, and an invaluable preparation for throat troubles"—were sold nationwide through mail orders.

In exchange for buying stock in the venture, Ruskinites received housing, food, medical care, and other necessities without charge. Instead of money, they used a scrip known as an "hour," which could be redeemed at the community commissary. It was supposed to represent an hour's work in the association's enterprises. All work was paid at the same rate.

Though the railroad is gone, the L & N Depot still stands at Cumberland Furnace

The colonists valued education. Plans were drawn for a college, the College of the New Economy, but nothing came of them.

Seeds of dissension were sown from the start. The first colonists—the charter members—were an intellectual, somewhat romantic group. But newcomers made up a majority early on, and they tended to be less-educated working people. For the most part, they were just looking for a better life. One of the charter members, commenting on the majority's lack of interest in intellectual pursuits, referred to them as people who chose to sit around at night and "smoke, gossip, and spit tobacco." The colony also attracted its share of deadbeats, anarchists, and free-love advocates. They did not help stabilize the place.

Julius Augustus Wayland lasted only one year at the colony. Dissension among the factions grew and grew. By 1898, they were locked in a series of life-and-death court battles over control of Ruskin. As writer John Egerton points out in *Visions of Utopia*, "The colonists were in court almost as often as they were at work." A judge finally declared the colony hopelessly deadlocked and ordered the corporation dissolved and its assets sold. The colony disbanded in 1899.

The only substantial reminder of the Ruskin colony today is a three-story building, Commonwealth House. This was the printery where *The Coming Nation* was produced and where other for-profit printing jobs were done. The building also housed the communal dining room, lodging for newcomers and visitors, a nursery, a bookstore, a library, and, on the third floor, an auditorium large enough to accommodate seven hundred.

After the colony closed, a college, Ruskin Cave College, operated here from 1904 until 1922. For the next three years, it was a private secondary school. It closed for good in 1925.

As a way to raise money and foster good relations with their neighbors, the Ruskinites held a big Independence Day barbecue each year. People came from miles around and paid a small fee for food and entertainment. That tradition survives. The Ruskin property is now a private recreation area famous for its big Independence Day celebrations.

There are two caves on the property, Jewel and Ruskin. A local girl, twelve-year-old Fanny Rodgers, discovered Jewel Cave while exploring near her home on land her father had purchased when the Ruskin property was

Commonwealth House, the former printery at the Ruskin colony

sold. In the 1920s, new owners outfitted the cave for visitors; when electric lights were installed, the glistening, multicolored stalactite formations reminded cave explorers of jewels. Ruskin Cave, a huge cavern used by the Ruskin colonists as a cannery, does not have such colorful formations.

From the road to Ruskin Cave, it is 3.4 miles on TN 46 to Gillam Hollow Road; turn right. It is then 2.8 miles to U.S. 70 at Tennessee City.

Gillam was the first name for this town, which began as a stopping place for locomotives on the Civil War railroad. The town sits atop the ridge straddling the Tennessee Valley Divide, which separates the watersheds of the Tennessee and Cumberland rivers.

Following the war, a Northern capitalist, W. A. Schoenfeld, purchased a good deal of land in the area with the intention of promoting resettlement of people from the North to this remote part of the South. Schoenfeld had big plans. He platted a town of over twenty thousand lots and petitioned the post office to change Gillam's name to Tennessee City. This new, important-sounding name would attract settlers, he hoped. He was wrong. Tennessee City has remained a quiet country village.

Cross U.S. 70 onto Garner Creek Road and follow it as it eases into the valley of Garner Creek on the Tennessee River side of the divide. Indian attacks were rare in Middle Tennessee after 1805, but one occurred along this creek in 1809. An early settler, William Garner, was killed. His name was later given to this tributary of the Piney River.

At the fork 7.7 miles from U.S. 70, turn left onto Harris Hollow Road, staying on the paved road. You will reach TN 48 after 1.6 miles. Turn right (S). It is 6.6 miles to the crossroads at Pinewood.

The route soon enters Hickman County and drops steeply off the ridge into the pretty, broad valley of the Piney River. Settlement began here shortly after the Third Tellico Treaty in 1805. The county, created in 1807, is named for Edwin Hickman, a surveyor killed by Indians in 1791 near the present county seat.

A courthouse of heavy poplar logs was erected downstream on the Piney River at a place called Vernon, named for George Washington's home. Settlers who came into the southern part of the county following an 1818 Indian treaty wanted a courthouse more centrally located. In 1821, after considerable controversy, a site on the Duck River was selected. The log courthouse at Vernon was dismantled and hauled to the new site by oxcart. It was not difficult to select a name for the new town. It was called Centerville.

Turn left (E) onto Pinewood Road at the Pinewood crossroads and drive 0.3 mile to the brick factory-like building on the left. This structure is one of the few remnants of a remarkable, self-contained agricultural-industrial community that evolved here in the mid-1800s on Samuel Lowry Graham's huge estate.

Orphaned at a young age in North Carolina, Graham and his brother migrated to Tennessee and eventually settled in Columbia in the 1840s. In 1848, Graham bought a mill and five acres here along the Piney River. He soon expanded his operation. Before long, he ran a farm, a gristmill, and a textile mill. Graham did not use slaves, but instead hired wage earners. He provided housing for his workers, with whom he is said to have had a cordial relationship. His holdings eventually grew to eight thousand acres.

Graham was a Union man during the Civil War and won lucrative Federal contracts for products from his textile mill, by then powered by steam. Following the war, the local community grew to about five hundred people and included a farm, a cotton gin, a textile mill, a brick factory, a sawmill, a blacksmith shop, a gristmill, a cannery, a school, a church, a hotel, a general store, and worker housing. The textile mill had forty-four looms and 2,330 spindles.

Frances Helm Graham, Samuel's fist wife, was an active participant in the business operations. She named the place Pinewood after a grove of trees on a bluff overlooking the river. Frances died in 1863.

Graham completed one of the most monumental houses ever built in rural Middle Tennessee in 1868. It had twenty-two rooms, some with sixteen-foot ceilings. The lavish plasterwork was made from molds carved on the place by Italian craftsmen. The original chandeliers were fueled by gas created by burning pine knots. A tub in the bathroom had an overhead shower with sun-heated water from a tank in the attic. A beautiful, winding stairway was hand-carved from Cuban mahogany.

The same year Graham completed the house, he married Thomas Ella Hardeman. He was fifty-six; she was thirty-one. In poor health, Thomas Ella told Graham that if she died, he should marry her former teacher,

Martha Jane Clouston of Franklin. Martha Jane would make a good mother for her children, she said. Thomas Ella did die, just two years after her marriage to Graham. Samuel Graham followed his late wife's instructions and married Martha Jane Clouston in 1872.

Pinewood stayed in the Graham family for a time following Samuel's death in 1892 but was eventually carved up and sold. Tragically, the big house was destroyed by fire in 1975. It stood south of Pinewood Road near the grove of stately white pines visible from the road.

Graham is buried between his first and second wives on the rise between the Piney River and the highway. In honor of his first wife, Frances, he erected the huge granite monument visible today. It was brought by rail to Dickson. From there, it took eighteen mules to pull it to Pinewood.

Return to TN 48 and turn left. Follow TN 48 south as it leaves the Piney River Valley, crosses Mill Creek, goes through Nunnelly, and reaches TN 100 after 7.7 miles.

Mill Creek is named for the first mill in Hickman County, built on the creek in 1806. The mill's capacity was not sufficient to grind all the corn produced in the area. For many years, farmers would travel in caravans to a Dickson County mill on Yellow Creek. The two-way trip usually took about a week.

Nunnelly began in 1882 as a stop on the Nashville & Tuscaloosa Railroad where Lawson H. Nunnelly had a large iron-ore mine. The plan was for a railroad that extended from the Nashville, Chattanooga & St. Louis at Dickson all the way down into Alabama, but the line never made it that far and was never financially successful. The Nashville, Chattanooga & St. Louis took it over as its Centerville Branch in 1883.

Songwriter Beth Slater Whitson was born near Nunnelly in 1879. She published over two hundred songs, including, in 1908, "Let Me Call You Sweetheart."

At TN 100, turn right (SW). It is 5.1 miles to the square in Centerville. Turn onto West End Avenue, which takes off from the square's northwest corner, to see the James Buchanan Walker House, on the left. Completed in 1903, it is an excellent example of the Neoclassical style popular around the turn of the century. Houses of this stature are rare around here.

James Buchanan Walker served as the president of Centerville's First

National Bank from 1913 until his death in 1940. He was elected as the town's first mayor after incorporation in 1905 and oversaw Centerville's transformation from a sleepy country village to a prosperous small town. Walker's sister, Mattie Lou, worked at the bank an incredible seventy years before she retired in 1978. Walker's son, also named James, succeeded him as bank president.

The younger James Walker unwittingly helped launch the career of one of America's best-known entertainers. In the fall of 1940, he asked a young Centerville woman, Sarah Ophelia Colley, to put on a show featuring local children at a bankers' convention to be held in town. Colley was back home after seven years as a traveling theatrical producer for the Sewell Company.

Before the days of radio, television, and movies, when live performances were the norm for entertainment, the Atlanta-based Sewell Company hired talented young women to travel the small towns of the South and produce plays using local talent. As a girl, Sarah Ophelia Colley was infatuated by the Sewell "girls" who came to Centerville, so when she graduated from Nashville's fashionable Ward-Belmont College in 1932, she joined the company.

On her travels, the sophisticated young woman became intrigued by the humor and style of the South. Over time, she developed a character who embodied many of the humorous traits she had observed. While in Aiken, South Carolina, in 1939, Colley was offered twenty-five dollars to play her character at a banquet. On her way to the performance, she made a quick decision to get a costume. She describes her purchase in her autobiography:

> We came upon a store that displayed its merchandise outside on the sidewalk—a table full of shoes and several clothes racks filled with dresses and shirts. . . . I spotted a pale yellow dress made of sleazy organdy. It had a round collar and a cheap-looking grosgrain bow at the neckline that had been attached with a safety pin. The top was sleeveless, and it had a self-belt that rolled the minute you put it on. . . . I found some white cotton stockings . . . and a tacky straw hat, with a brim, that sat flat on the top of my head. I bought some flowers to plop on that and when everything had been totaled up, the entire outfit, from head to toe, cost less than $10.

The hotel ballroom in Aiken had no stage, so she decided to make her entrance from the back of the room and walk through the crowd to the front. "As I passed among the tables in my costume, speaking to people, smiling and saying Howdy, an incredible thing happened to me. I felt myself moving out of Sarah Ophelia Colley into Minnie Pearl."

Her friend James Walker, the Centerville banker, had seen her do Minnie Pearl at the local Lions Club after she left the Sewell Company in 1939. She had even incorporated a local spot, Grinder's Switch, into her routine. Walker explained to Colley that the featured speaker at the bankers' convention was coming from Chicago, and that there might be some dead time between her show with the children and his arrival. Walker asked, "Do you think you could kill some time by doing that character you did at the Lions Club?" Yes, she said, and she did.

A Nashville banker in the audience was so impressed that he spoke to Harry Stone, general manager of WSM radio in Nashville, which produced the Grand Ole Opry. Colley was invited to come to Nashville and audition. She had never cared much for the Opry style of music, but she went, and she landed a part on the show. Neither a singer nor a musician,

Minnie Pearl became one of the best-known characters in the world of country music. And Sarah Ophelia Colley's character became one of the best-known storytellers and comedians in American history.

Horse racing and the gambling that accompanied it were popular forms of entertainment in the earliest days of Middle Tennessee. Centerville had a racetrack in a river bend near town. In their thorough and sometimes amusing *History of Hickman County, Tennessee*, published in 1900, Jerome and David Spence describe what it took to cure some men of the gambling habit.

One day at a race course in the Pluck-'em-in community, a "shabbily dressed" stranger "riding an ugly, slab-sided, bobtailed bay horse, with a mane . . . like a mule," inquired where he might find some men with cattle to sell. Between drinks he took from his flask, he hinted that he had plenty of money to spend. The stranger was directed to a big race near Centerville to be run in a few days. People with cattle to sell would be there, and besides, he could see a good race. He didn't care for horse racing, he said, but he was interested in the men with the cattle.

The stranger was at the race on the appointed day. By the time the contest was to start, whiskey had transformed him into a "swaggering drunkard, who wanted to bet on the race which his appearance showed he could ill afford to lose." He would ride his own old horse in the race.

He had plenty of money to cover his bets, having come to buy cattle. Before long, he was betting against watches, pistols, and overcoats. When the horses lined up for the start, someone noticed the drunk stranger seemed mighty sober all of a sudden. And when the horses were around three-fourths of the track and the stranger and his horse were still well in the lead, it began to dawn on the crowd that no one had seen the man drink.

Shilo True was "the trickiest trickster of them all," and as the Spences point out in their book, "the missionary work that he did that day produced lasting good." That was the last horse-race gambling for many Hickman County residents. Two of the converts, Emmons Church and his father, Abram, made their vow never to gamble again as they rode home—without their overcoats.

After enjoying Centerville, leave town at the southeast corner of the square on Church Street. After 0.1 mile, take Columbia Avenue (Old

TN 50) as it angles off to the right. Bear right at the fork after 2.1 miles and continue another 0.2 mile to TN 50. Turn left (E) and drive 7.9 miles to TN 230 (Littlelot Road). Turn left (N).

TN 230 leads to the pleasant village of Littlelot in the productive valley of the Duck River, where the Western Highland Rim starts to give way to the Central Basin. A major local landowner, Hugh McCabe, donated a quarter of an acre here in 1815 for the construction of a church. As it was being erected, someone remarked that the place did not even have a name. "It's a damn little lot, and we can't give it a big name," Parker Tyler quipped. It has been called Littlelot ever since.

After 4.5 miles on TN 230, turn right onto Turkey Farm Road, a dirt road. Where Turkey Farm Road ends at Hassell Creek Road after 2.3 miles, turn right. Drive 1 mile on Hassell Creek Road—another dirt road—to Primm Springs Road. Turn right on Primm Springs Road and go 1.2 miles to Dog Creek Road. Turn left.

After 0.6 mile, you will come to a confusing intersection just past the bridge over Dog Creek. Two roads take off to the left, an old one-lane dirt road up Puppy Branch Hollow and a new dirt road up the hill. Take the road to the left—the road up the hollow. After 0.2 mile, you will enter the Primm Springs Historic District. Go straight for 0.1 mile to the old hotel.

Think back to the time before air conditioning. Before paved roads. Before screens on windows. Before modern medicine. Now, imagine a place where, in the summer, it is always cooler than the rest of the countryside. A place where there are no flies or mosquitos. Where there is no dust. And where there is a miraculous cure for what ails you. With these images in place, it is easier to understand how Primm Springs once thrived as one of Middle Tennessee's leading mineral springs resorts.

The guest register for July 1920 testifies to the resort's popularity. People came from Asheville, Syracuse, Havana, Shreveport, Tampa, Salt Lake City, Indianapolis, West Palm Beach, Atlanta, Phoenix, Houston, San Francisco, Oklahoma City, Detroit, London, Denver, Washington, Atlantic City, Reno, and Berlin. There were plenty of Middle Tennesseans as well.

They came to this remote part of Hickman County by mule-drawn hack from Columbia. Once here, they usually stayed the summer. Activities included bowling, dancing, swimming, fishing, and just plain relaxing. Visitors would "take the waters," drinking gallons of water from one of the five springs—black sulphur, white sulphur, calomel, arsenic, and lime. At times, four or five hundred people would crowd into the hotel and cottages or just camp on the hillside.

John T. Primm and his wife, Cecilia C. Gannt, natives of Maryland, settled here in 1830. By 1836, the springs were "fitted up for visitors." In their history of Hickman County, the Spences report that one Matilda Stephenson supposedly gained a pound a day here in 1837.

The wife of Maury Countian Daniel Estes, a woman named Bourbon, grew up around here. In the 1860s, when Daniel was ill, she recommended that he come to Primm Springs and "take the cure." He spent a summer here, and he was cured. Estes went back to Maury County, organized a company with twenty-one stockholders, and purchased the springs. It was Daniel Estes who turned Primm Springs into a premier summer resort. His house still stands on the left across from the old store. Estes built three hotels here. The third one, Estes House, still stands in the hollow at the curve in the road.

Hugh Ella Estes, Daniel's granddaughter, eventually took over the man-

Estes House,
the hotel at Primm Springs

agement of the place. When electricity was made available, she declined service—she did not want any trees destroyed to run a line into the resort. After flourishing in the 1920s, Primm Springs went into a decline during the Depression and World War II, and it closed in 1945. Miss Estes and her sister, Fannie, reopened it for Sunday dinners in 1947, still cooking on a wood stove, but the place was finally closed for good in 1965. Hugh Ella Estes lived until 1972.

From time to time, schemes have been advanced to restore Primm Springs and reopen it in some form or other, but as of yet, nothing has come of them.

Continue up the hill on the one-lane dirt road for 0.1 mile to the new dirt road. Turn right and return to the paved road at the bridge over Dog Creek. Backtrack along Dog Creek Road to Primm Springs Road.

Supposedly, a man living on the creek in 1825 was attacked by a "dog wolf" that chased him into his cabin. He retrieved his gun and killed the animal—dog, wolf, or whatever. That is how the creek got its name.

When Edward Mahon bought some land here, he was embarrassed to tell his aristocratic friends back in Maury County that he lived on Hickman County's Dog Creek. So he got a bill passed in the Tennessee legislature changing the name to Cedar Creek. But the name never took. It is still Dog Creek to the people around here.

Turn left on Primm Springs Road and drive 4.3 miles to where it ends at Leatherwood Road, also known as Bratton Road. Turn right. You will cross the Duck River just upstream from a picturesque old iron bridge and reach a fork at 1.3 miles. Stay on Leatherwood Road as it veers left. You will reach TN 50 after 2 miles. Turn left (E). This is the community of Shady Grove. The pleasant, tree-shaded village lies diagonally across TN 50, just south of the highway.

From Shady Grove, it is 2 miles on TN 50 to the Natchez Trace Parkway.

In addition to providing a motor road, the linear park contains the Natchez Trace Scenic Trail, a section of which starts here and extends 25 miles north to Garrison Creek near the town of Leipers Fork. A portion of the hiking and horseback trail travels sections of the original Trace, including a 1.7-mile section that is the longest stretch of the old Trace in Tennessee. (The history of the original Natchez Trace and the creation of

Gordon House

the Natchez Trace Parkway are covered in The Harpeth River Tour, pages 136–38.)

Turn south onto the Natchez Trace Parkway, toward Tupelo. After 0.3 mile, turn into the parking area for the Gordon House.

Travel on the Trace picked up following the government's improvement of the road between 1801 and 1803. About that time, John Gordon, working in partnership with Chickasaw chief George Colbert, began operating a trading post and ferry here on the Duck River.

Gordon had come to the Cumberland settlements from Fredericksburg, Virginia, around 1786 and established himself as an accomplished Indian fighter. He served as Nashville's first postmaster. There is a marker in his honor on the grounds of the Customs House at Eighth and Broad in Nashville.

He moved his wife, Dollie Cross, and their children here to his grant on the Duck River sometime after 1808. Gordon was a valuable lieutenant to Andrew Jackson in his campaigns against the Creeks and Seminoles, spending much of his time working for Jackson as a scout or spy. Gordon died while he was away in 1819.

Dollie Gordon had completed this house the year before. Built in the Georgian-Federal "glorified pioneer" style of the day, it has survived quite well. It was occupied until 1969, when it was acquired for the parkway.

The Western Highland Rim Tour ends at the Gordon House. Columbia is 15 miles ahead on TN 50. Nashville can be reached by traveling north on the Trace.

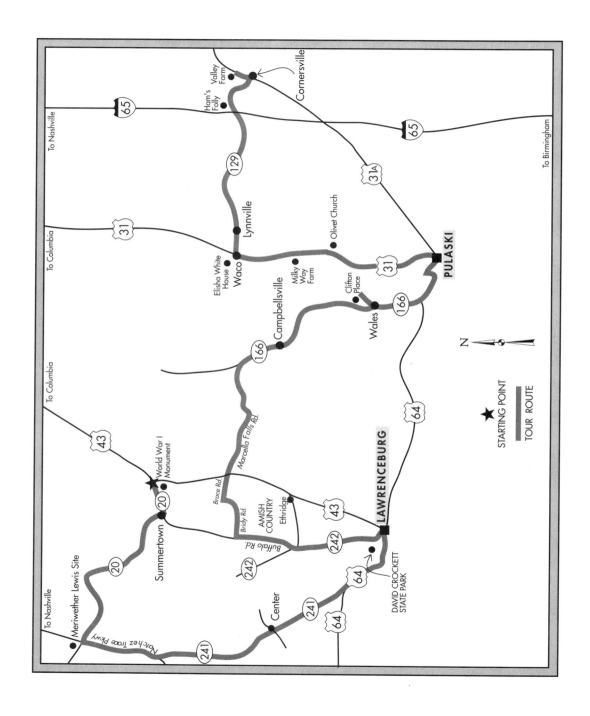

The South Central Tour

This tour visits several areas colonized in organized resettlements—a community of German Catholics who came in the 1870s, one established by the Amish in 1944, and a 1970s commune called The Farm. It travels to the Meriwether Lewis Site on the Natchez Trace Parkway, where the famed explorer mysteriously died in 1809, and visits the site of David Crockett's mill, now in a state park, and the Crockett Monument in Lawrenceburg, where Crockett lived. In Pulaski, it examines the spot where Confederate hero Sam Davis was hanged, the place where the Ku Klux Klan started, and some lovely homes and churches. The tour ends by passing through two of the Middle Tennessee's prettiest small towns, Lynnville and Cornersville.

Total length: approximately 110 miles

This tour starts near Summertown at the junction of U.S. 43 and TN 20. Head west on TN 20.

Where U.S. 43 makes the long climb onto the Highland Rim from the Central Basin south of Columbia, the contrast between the two topographic regions is about as sharp as it is anywhere. Historically, the change in the culture has been as abrupt as the change in the landscape, for since earliest times, there has been something of a rivalry between the uplanders and lowlanders.

The Barrens—that is what the sophisticated planter class called these highlands in antebellum days. And their disdain was not reserved just for the shallow-soil oak forests. They derisively referred to the locals scratching out a living in the high country as "the natives." In 1851, a Mount Pleasant woman sued her husband for divorce, charging that he played around "especially with the loose women of the Barrens." The dislike was mutual. An advertisement in the Columbia paper in 1848 warned Maury County people to keep their stock out of The Barrens.

After 0.7 mile, you will reach the TN 240 junction and a handsome monument in the grassy triangle where the roads meet. Erected in the

World War I monument near Summertown

early 1920s, the monument honors the men from this part of Lawrence County who gave their lives in World War I.

Stay on TN 20. Soon, you will pass a sign announcing that you are entering "Summertown, Unincorporated" and cross the railroad tracks. It is 1.3 miles from the monument through Summertown to the TN 20/TN 240 fork. Bear right, staying on TN 20.

The Central Turnpike, which stretched from Columbia to the Tennessee River, was built through here in the 1840s. Summertown dates to that period. The Highland Rim is just a bit cooler than the low country in the summer, and the place's use as a retreat gave it its name. By the late nineteenth century, Summertown was a fashionable resort, particularly after the railroad came through in 1883. At one time, six hotels operated here.

The hamlet got a big boost following the Civil War when Union veteran Jonathan Hale Marston of Minnesota moved his family here. Marston had been impressed with what he saw of Tennessee during the war, but he was not impressed with the poor quality of the land he found here. He decided to return to Minnesota and had to be talked into staying. He bought one hundred acres and began to promote immigration to the area. In 1882, Joseph J. Crane arrived from Indiana, set up a real-estate business, and began a successful advertising campaign to lure Northern settlers. Summertown as it exists today dates to this post–Civil War period.

News that a railroad was being planned between Columbia and Florence, Alabama, was greeted enthusiastically in Summertown, but the excitement dimmed when it was learned that the line would pass about a mile east of the little resort. It was a disappointment some people in Summertown never got over. A new town, Crestview—named for its location on the Highland Rim's crest—grew up along the railroad, and a rivalry started between Summertown and Crestview in 1883. It lasted until the 1950s. The rivalry is responsible for the sign noting that Summertown is unincorporated.

The two towns joined as Summertown and incorporated in 1907. But things got off to a bad start. Crestview landowners resented paying taxes because the place was named Summertown. Summertown residents refused to pay their taxes because the people of Crestview would receive city services. Elections were a tense time, and the Lawrence County sheriff could always count on being summoned to Summertown.

After four years of turmoil, the town appealed to the Tennessee legislature to revoke its charter. Incorporation ended, but the rivalry did not. Crestview had obtained its own post office. In 1951, the United States postmaster general ordered that one of the post offices close. Another impasse was followed by a compromise—the Crestview facility would remain, but the post office would be called Summertown.

"Don't give up the ship"—that statement is one of America's most famous military commands. Captain David Lawrence spoke the immortal words as he lay dying on the *Chesapeake* during the War of 1812. When a new county on the state's southern border was established in 1817, it was named for Lawrence.

Lawrence County and adjoining Lewis County, created in 1843, have always been popular destinations for colonists, no doubt because of the cheap land. Union veterans came here following the Civil War at about the same time a large colony of German Catholics was established in Lawrence County. Then the Swiss came to Lewis County. In the 1940s, it was the Amish.

In 1971, a large group of hippies settled here. Stephen Gaskin, a charismatic college professor from California, led a school-bus caravan of about three hundred people to Middle Tennessee looking for a place to start a commune. His group settled on 1,750 acres near Summertown. Called The Farm, the commune is still thriving. The population at times has exceeded a thousand. Ida Mae Gaskin runs a midwife center here, and The Farm operates several light industries. It can be reached on Drakes Lane, which turns off TN 20 west of Summertown. Visitors are welcome.

It is 12.8 miles on TN 20 from Summertown to the Natchez Trace Parkway entrance. Turn right (N) and drive 0.3 mile to the log cabin on the left.

Accommodations along the old Natchez Trace consisted of primitive inns called stands, spaced randomly along the route between Natchez and Nashville. Most often, they were run by settlers who were looking to make a little extra money. Robert and Priscilla Grinder ran a stand here, represented now by the reconstructed cabin. It was here that one the great mysteries of American history occurred—the death of Meriwether Lewis.

Robert Grinder was away on October 10, 1809, when a young traveler on the Trace came in for a night's lodging. He was Meriwether Lewis, famed leader of the Lewis and Clark expedition. Priscilla fed Lewis his supper and showed him to his bed in an adjoining cabin. In the early hours of the morning, she heard a pistol shot. As she peered out into the darkness, she saw a man stagger toward her cabin door and try to open it. It was Lewis. He was wounded, he said, but Mrs. Grinder was too afraid to open the door. He stumbled away, vanished into the darkness, then reappeared. He tried to get some water from the well. Then he left her sight again. Too afraid to do anything, Priscilla waited until daylight.

At sunup, Lewis's servants found him in his bed with a massive head wound, part of his skull blown away. He had a wound to his chest, too, as well as slashes on his throat and wrists. He did not live much past dawn.

Lewis's death was called a suicide. He had indeed been disturbed for a while. After Lewis successfully led the expedition all the way to the Pacific Ocean and back, a grateful President Thomas Jefferson, his mentor, had appointed him governor of the Louisiana Territory, with his headquarters at St. Louis. But by the spring of 1809, Lewis was suffering from financial difficulties and was embroiled in a political feud. The secretary of war hinted that Lewis had mismanaged government money, at which Lewis took great offense. There was only one way to confront it, Lewis decided—travel all the way to Washington and clear his name.

Lewis and his party floated from St. Louis down the Mississippi to Memphis, then headed overland to the Natchez Trace. A military officer they encountered along the way became alarmed at Lewis's physical and mental condition. He even heard reports that Lewis had tried to kill himself twice on the trip from St. Louis. Another officer, Major James Neelly, a Chickasaw Indian agent who traveled with Lewis on the Trace toward Nashville, said later that Lewis was ill and deranged. Several times, the party had to stop and rest because Lewis was too ill to continue. But continue it did, at least as far as Grinder's Stand. Neelly wrote President Jefferson that the death was by suicide.

Within a year of Lewis's violent death, one of his friends, renowned ornithologist and artist Alexander Wilson, took it upon himself to investigate the passing of this national hero. Wilson traveled down the Natchez Trace from Nashville to Grinder's Stand and talked to Priscilla Grinder. Lewis was murdered, Wilson concluded, but by whom he did not know.

Replica of Grinder's Stand

From then on, the death of Meriwether Lewis has intrigued historians. It is a controversy that apparently will never die.

In 1848, the state of Tennessee erected a monument near the site of Lewis's death. It stands today in the clearing just beyond the cabin. It is a broken shaft, symbolizing Lewis's premature death. The Meriwether Lewis Memorial Association was formed in 1923 to protect this site. Under the leadership of Nashville historian John Trotwood Moore, money was raised in each of the modern fourteen states Lewis and Clark traveled through on their way to the Pacific. The land was deeded to the federal government and was made a national monument by order of President Calvin Coolidge in 1925. It was later incorporated into the Natchez Trace Parkway. This county—Lewis County—was named for Meriwether Lewis.

Meriwether Lewis Monument along the Natchez Trace

The 300-acre Meriwether Lewis Site at the rugged headwaters of Little Swan Creek is a particularly beautiful place in the spring, when abundant wildflowers bloom on the floor of the oak forest and the dogwoods stand out in the woods like snow. Two hiking trails wind through the park. Visitors may walk on the old Trace as well.

Newburg, near the Meriwether Lewis Site, was the original Lewis County seat, but it was abandoned when Swiss colonists established the town of Hohenwald in 1897. Hohenwald is German for "tall forest."

From the Meriwether Lewis Site, head south on the Natchez Trace Parkway toward Tupelo. At 3 miles, after crossing the Buffalo River, turn right to see Metal Ford, a lovely spot at the foot of some bluffs where the old Natchez Trace crossed the river.

Most Middle Tennesseans would agree that the Buffalo is the region's most beautiful river. Rising near here, it winds for over 120 miles—first west, then north—before it gives its waters to the Duck River. Most of the river is floatable during high water, and the lower half year-round. Outfitters operate out of Flatwoods, a small community on TN 13 west of here.

Buffalo—or bison, to be exact—inhabited Middle Tennessee when the first Europeans arrived. They apparently had not been in the area for too long, though, for excavations of prehistoric sites have not uncovered any buffalo remains. Given what is known about how thoroughly the Indians of the Great Plains used buffalo, if the large animals had been in Middle Tennessee when the prehistoric cultures flourished, there would have been some signs of it. Within just a year or two of the first settlement in 1779, buffalo were gone from Middle Tennessee. They have been reintroduced at TVA's Land Between the Lakes, visited on The Lower Cumberland Tour.

Return to the parkway and continue south. A little less than 1 mile from the Metal Ford turnoff, there is a turnoff to the right for the Napier Mine Site. An exhibit describes the important iron furnace that operated here until the 1920s.

From Napier Mine, it is 1 mile to the exit for TN 241; it is not very well marked, so be alert. Turn right onto TN 241. You will pass Napier Lake, on the left. It is 6.8 miles to the junction with TN 240 in the community of Center.

The Barrens of the Highland Rim's edge recede into the background here, as the land opens up into prosperous dairy-farming country. The route passes the edge of the Laurel Hill Wildlife Management Area, a 14,000-acre preserve highlighted by a 327-acre lake that is popular for fishing and wildlife viewing.

Turn left (NE) at the TN 241/TN 240 junction. After 0.2 mile, turn right (SE), staying on TN 241. It is 5.2 miles to U.S. 64. Turn left (E) on U.S. 64 and drive 4.9 miles to the entrance to David Crockett State Park, on the left.

David Crockett the real person lived here. Davy Crockett the folk hero lives mostly in the minds of fiction writers. But separating fact from fiction is not easy. Indeed, even Crockett himself had difficulty drawing the distinction.

The real Crockett was born not "on a mountaintop in Tennessee," as the song says, but in the Great Valley of East Tennessee, not far from Greeneville, in 1786. In 1811, Crockett moved to Middle Tennessee with his wife, Polly, two sons, and his father-in-law. They lived first in today's Moore County, then in Franklin County southwest of Winchester.

Following David's service in the Creek War under Andrew Jackson and the birth of a daughter, Polly died in 1815. The next year, Crockett married Elizabeth Patton, a widow with two children. In 1817, David, Elizabeth, and the five children moved here along the banks of Shoal Creek. Crockett built a gristmill, a powder mill, and a distillery. Only a short time after his arrival, he was elected justice of the peace, his first political office. He then served as a town commissioner for Lawrenceburg and represented the area in the state legislature in 1821 and 1822.

The Crockett family was devastated in 1821. While David was away at Murfreesboro—then Tennessee's capital—serving in the legislature, a flood washed away the mills on the creek. Crockett was forced into bankruptcy. The following year, the family moved farther west, settling near Rutherford in West Tennessee.

David Crockett first got himself elected to Congress in the mid-1820s. "Obscure as I am, my name is making considerable deal of fuss in the world. I can't tell why it is, nor in what it is to end. Go where I will, everybody seems anxious to get a peep at me." Crockett wrote this in 1834 in his best-selling autobiography, a book written in part to try to separate the legend from the real man. But Crockett was in a dilemma. He wanted to be president, and he knew that the legendary, somewhat comic frontiersman Davy would not be taken seriously as a national leader. Yet it was that very notoriety as a frontiersman that made him famous. Playing his frontiersman role, Crockett made a tour of the Northeast while he was in Congress, an event that some historians say was a major factor in his defeat for reelection in 1835.

Following this defeat, he did what many disillusioned men did in those days. He want to Texas. In 1836, at age forty-nine, he lost his life at the Mission San Antonio de Valero—the Alamo.

The Davy Crockett legend was enhanced considerably by the publication from 1835 to 1856 of the popular *Crockett Almanac*. The Davy depicted there was, to say the least, outlandish. Here was a man who could "run faster,—jump higher,—squat lower,—dive deeper,—stay under longer,—and come out drier, than any man in the whole country." He fought an underwater battle with a twelve-foot catfish, wrung the tail off Halley's Comet, and twisted his pet alligator's tail around his body and rode it up Niagara Falls.

Crockett was later the subject of two plays, one of them called *Davy Crockett; Or, Be Sure You're Right Then Go Ahead*. Starring Frank Mayo, this play was performed over two thousand times between 1872 until 1896 in both America and Europe. The Davy Crockett legend reached its zenith in the mid-1950s, when Walt Disney ran the television series starring

Fess Parker. The song from the show topped the charts, and over $300 million worth of Crockett paraphernalia—shirts, lunchboxes, fake coonskin caps—was sold around the world. It is fair to say now what Crockett himself said—the real man and the legend seem inseparable.

The state park surrounding the site of David Crockett's business along Shoal Creek encompasses a thousand acres and offers a variety of activities, including boating and fishing on Lindsey Lake. The museum features historical and natural programs. It is open only during the summer months.

Leaving the park, turn left (E) on U.S. 64 and drive 1.2 miles to Military Avenue in the heart of Lawrenceburg. Turn right. You will come to the square in the first block of Military Avenue.

Following his success at the Battle of New Orleans in the War of 1812, Andrew Jackson became aware of the need for better overland transportation from Nashville to the lower Mississippi. The Natchez Trace was, after all, mostly an old buffalo trail that had evolved into a road. Jackson convinced the federal government to build a new road, and the Military Road was approved in 1816. It, too, followed old buffalo trails for much of its route, but the Military Road cut 220 miles off the old route from Nashville to New Orleans. The road ran from Columbia through what is now Mount Pleasant, then past today's Lawrenceburg, and on to the Tennessee River, just to the south. It got a big boost in 1824, when it replaced the Natchez Trace as the mail route from Nashville to the old Southwest.

Lawrenceburg was laid out just to the west of the Military Road. In 1821, the road was relocated slightly to go through the new town. Military Avenue follows the old route, as does U.S. 43 in several places between Columbia and Lawrenceburg.

Mexican War monument on Lawrenceburg's square

Standing on Lawrenceburg's square is something unusual—a Mexican War monument. It was erected in 1849 as a memorial to Captain William B. Allen, who was killed in the conflict. The monument was rebuilt in 1895. It honors the response of Tennesseans to the call for volunteers in the Mexican War, which earned Tennessee the nickname Volunteer State.

It is a testament to the power of legend that David Crockett is so revered around Lawrenceburg, for he lived here only about five years. The imposing twenty-foot bronze-and-granite statute of him on the square was erected a hundred years after he left here.

Lawrenceburg's statue of David Crockett

Sacred Heart Catholic Church

A reproduction of the cabin David Crockett used for his office is located on Military Avenue a block south of the square. It now houses a small museum.

When you are ready to leave the square, head north—the way you came in—on Military Avenue. It is 0.3 mile to Burger Street. Turn left. You will soon reach Sacred Heart Catholic Church, on the right.

Sacred Heart is one of four churches that resulted from the immigration of German Catholics into Lawrence County beginning in 1870. It took quite awhile to build this impressive Gothic Revival structure. Construction started with the laying of the cornerstone in 1887, but it was not until 1900 that the bell tower was completed. The bricks were made of native clay and burned on this site, and the lumber and rafters were hand-hewn in nearby forests and brought here for installation. Many of the German homesteaders were gifted craftsmen, and the quality of their work is still evident in both the exterior and interior.

Widespread migration of German Catholics to America occurred about 1860, as Prussia's Otto von Bismarck was forming the unified German nation. The Catholics, many from Alsace-Lorraine, feared persecution by Bismarck's government and conscription into its army. It is ironic that many of the men found themselves in the midst of a war when they arrived in the United States. It was not unusual for some Union units to be made up solely of German-speaking soldiers.

Following the Civil War, economic conditions were grim for many of the German immigrants. A plan was devised to resettle them from the cities, where most of them lived, to farms. Representatives of the Cincinnati German Catholic Homestead Society visited Lawrenceburg during the winter of 1869–70. Land around here was cheap, so the society purchased fifteen thousand acres, much of it still in forest. Resettlement started right away.

The first mass in Lawrenceburg was said by Henry Huesser on October 24, 1870. Father Huesser had immigrated from the German state of Westphalia in 1867. After three months in Lawrenceburg, he moved to the Glenrock community, which changed its name to Loretto, after Saint Loretto. Loretto, Lawrenceburg, and St. Joseph became important Catholic centers.

Before long, the growing German community realized the need for schooling. In 1872, the Sisters of the Precious Blood sent a delegation to Lawrenceburg from Ohio. Instruction began that year. A Catholic school still operates here at Sacred Heart Catholic Church.

Germans and some Poles continued to migrate to Lawrence County, a process that accelerated with the opening of the railroad line from Columbia in 1883. The settlers outgrew their early churches, so they built this one, as well as one at St. Joseph in 1885 and one at Loretto in 1915. Responsibility for staffing the churches shifted from the Ohio-based order that sent Father Huesser to the local diocese.

The distinctly German culture has long since melted into the dominant culture here in Lawrence County, but the churches the immigrants established remain important to the life of the area.

Stay on Burger until it ends at TN 242 (Buffalo Road). Turn right and head north out of Lawrenceburg. After 5.4 miles, Buffalo Road goes straight as TN 242 veers to the left. Stay on Buffalo Road.

About a mile from this fork, you will begin to notice a difference in many of the farmhouses. They are built in a similar, plain style. No electric lines lead to them. Most have windmills. There probably will not be any motor vehicles on the property, but you might see a black buggy in the barn. You are in the middle of Amish country.

TOURING THE MIDDLE TENNESSEE BACKROADS

The history of the Amish goes way back, all the way to Switzerland and the 1525 beginning of the Swiss Anabaptist movement. Around 1695, in a dispute over "shunning"—the practice of avoiding excommunicated members of the Mennonite sect—Jacob Ammann led a breakaway group that wanted to live life more strictly. The Amish, named for Ammann, were persecuted terribly in the German-speaking states for their deviation from the established churches, so when the opportunity to immigrate to the New World came, they took advantage of it.

In 1727, the first Amish sailed for America. They and other German-speaking people continued to arrive until around 1790. Migration started again around 1815 and lasted until the Civil War. The original Amish immigrants settled in southeastern Pennsylvania, then some moved westward into Ohio in 1808, some to Indiana in 1839, and some to Iowa in 1840. Today, the Amish are gone from Europe, but they live in at least twenty American states and one Canadian province. Ohio, Pennsylvania, and Indiana have the largest number of Amish. The Amish population did not grow much in the nineteenth century, but it has doubled every twenty-two years in the twentieth century. The Amish practice no birth control, and the number of live births per family averages seven.

The Amish live only in rural areas, usually interspersed with non-Amish people—or "English," as the Amish call outsiders. They are able to maintain their distinctive way of life by avoiding modern conveniences, living by a strict set of rules, keeping their children out of public schools, and speaking their own language—old Pennsylvania Dutch, or German.

Small, isolated, rural public schools suited the Amish, but when the movement toward school consolidation started in the late 1930s, they began to withdraw their children from school. This led to clashes with civil authorities in several states. It was not until 1972 that the United States Supreme Court held that Amish children could not be forced to attend public secondary schools.

It was just such a row over schools that brought the Amish to Middle Tennessee in 1944. Looking for a place to practice their efficient, diversified farming, they corresponded with the chamber of commerce in Nashville. The Tennessee commissioner of agriculture met with them, and they decided on Lawrence County as a place to relocate. After the initial group came from Ohio in 1944, another group came from Indiana in 1947. There was another migration in 1951. Most of the Amish here are Old Order Amish—the ones who follow the strictest rules—but there are some "reformed" Amish in Lawrence County, too.

In his splendid collection of Amish writings, *Amish Roots: A Treasury of History, Wisdom, and Lore*, John A. Hostetler, himself raised Amish, lists the innovations that Old Order Amish have resisted:

> Buttons on coats and vests, the mustache, men's suspenders in various forms, hats for women, store-bought clothes, detachable collars, modern styles of underwear, patterned dress material, fine shoes, low shoes, women's high-heeled shoes, parted hair, church houses, four-part singing, hymn books with printed musical notes, laypeople's use of Bibles at meetings, Sunday schools, revival meetings, secondary education, central-heating furnaces, carpets, window curtains, storm windows and screens, writing desks, upholstered furniture, brightly painted farm machinery, "falling" top buggies, rubber-tired buggies, buggy steps, whip sockets, dashboards, lawn mowers, bicycles, tractors with tires, tractors for field work, elaborately decorated harnesses, musical instruments, commercial electricity, automobiles, and telephones.

Imagine living in contemporary society without a telephone, electricity, or an automobile. The Amish live this way not because they have any religious convictions against these innovations themselves, but because they believe their unique way of life—which emphasizes humility, simplicity, sharing, and sacrifice—cannot be lived with the distractions of modern life. As Hostetler points out, an Amish man will go to a phone booth and make a call. He just will not have the phone in his house. An Amish will take a ride in a car. He just will not own one.

Here in Lawrence County, the Amish are divided among three congregations. Since they have no churches, their services are held in houses. Social life is limited to church-related events such as weddings and communal work like barn raisings.

One note about visiting Amish country. The Amish are offended by being photographed. Books containing photographs of the Amish can be purchased at the Amish Country Gallery, located on U.S. 43 at Ethridge. The gallery also sells a fine collection of Amish crafts, many of which can also be purchased at individual Amish family farms. The Amish sell their abundant agricultural products, too.

Turn right onto Bridy Road 3.8 miles from the Buffalo Road/TN 242 split. After 2.1 miles, make a sharp left onto Brace Road in the community of Brace. Stay on Brace Road as it makes a sharp right at 0.1 mile, then reaches U.S. 43 after 2.2 miles. Brace is one of the early German Catholic settlements in Lawrence County. The Amish are scattered about here and on the far side of U.S. 43 as well.

Cross U.S. 43 and continue 0.2 mile to Alexander Springs Road. Turn right and drive 0.1 mile to Marcella Falls Road. Turn left. At the fork with Old Military Road at 0.1 mile, stay right on Marcella Falls Road. It is 7.6 miles to TN 166. As you might suspect, Old Military Road follows the route of the road Andrew Jackson's soldiers constructed in the 1820s. The route eases off the Highland Rim into the valley of Factory Creek and enters Giles County.

Marcella Falls, located away from the road on private property, was the site of an important early factory, from which the creek gets its name. In fact, it is hard to find a stream of any size dropping off the Highland Rim that was not the site of a mill of some kind. Falling water was, after all, the only readily available source of energy.

Sometime in the late 1840s, the Marcella Falls Woolen Mill opened here. It was named for Marcella Paine, daughter of a Columbia lawyer. When the railroad came through the area in 1883, commercial activity gravitated toward it, and the Marcella Falls area declined in importance, though a sawmill did operate at the falls well into the twentieth century.

Turn right (S) on TN 166. You will arrive at Campbellsville after 2.4 miles.

A bad relationship with a stepfather is what prompted Hamilton Crockett Campbell and his five brothers and sisters to leave their Hawkins County, Tennessee, home and migrate to midstate. Crockett, as Hamilton Crockett Campbell was called, was one the first settlers in northern Giles County. He is said to have planted the first corn crop in the area in 1809. The settlement that grew up around his property took his name.

A local landmark is the 1856 Campbellsville Cumberland Presbyterian Church, located 0.2 mile up the side road to the left (E) of TN 166.

It is 4.4 miles on TN 166 from Campbellsville to Hannah Road. The historic house on the rise to the left has an unusual appearance. It is really two houses—the original two-story one, built in the Federal style in 1820, and an addition in the rear, built in the Greek Revival style in 1857.

Continue on TN 166 as it crosses a ridge and drops into the fertile valley of meandering Richland Creek. You will reach the community of Wales 3.6 miles from Hannah Road, just past the creek.

Desdemona Phillips was the daughter of early settlers who inherited the land around here. When the railroad came through shortly after her 1852 marriage to William Wales, "Desi," as she was known, and William gave land for a railroad station. That is how this place came to be called Wales.

At the end of the bridge, turn onto the road that angles off sharply to the left. This lovely little lane leads 1.4 miles up Richland Creek's east bank to a magnificent old home, Clifton Place.

It is said that Tyree Rodes constructed Clifton Place in 1812, but the house is in a style that was not built until a decade or two later. Something closer to 1830 is more likely. In any event, Clifton Place, like Gideon Pillow's house of the same name up the road in Maury County, is one of Middle Tennessee grandest.

After the death of Rodes's son Robert in 1887, the 1,025-acre estate was divided into twelve pieces and sold. The buyer of one of the tracts was Phil Rodes. Phil was not part of the family, yet he had lived on the property his whole life—he had been a Rodes family slave. A contemporary news account of the estate sale noted that "everybody expressed the utmost satisfaction that Phil Rodes was able to buy his 108.94 acres. . . . He enjoys the good will of white and black, and consequently everyone was glad his pocket was long enough to purchase a portion of the land he once lived on as a slave."

Return to TN 166 and continue south for 2.7 miles to U.S. 64. Turn left (E) to enter Pulaski. Turn left (E) on Eighth Street 2.4 miles from TN 166. After 0.3 mile, turn right on Madison Street. It is 0.6 mile past Martin Methodist College to the square.

Set among the hills near Tennessee's southern border, Pulaski has lovely, well-preserved neighborhoods that hold some important Tennessee history. The best way to see Pulaski is on foot, and the square is a good place to start. A brochure describing a walking tour of the downtown area can be obtained from the chamber of commerce, located at Madison and Second streets, and at the library, located a few doors down Second.

Selecting the name for this new county, created in 1809, was not easy.

Richland County was the first name suggested. James Robertson—the "Father of Tennessee" and the leader of the Cumberland settlements—gave the name Richland Creek to the Elk River tributary while exploring here in 1783.

Andrew Jackson was on the rise as an important politician in 1809. At his suggestion, the name Giles was given to the new county in a bill that passed the Tennessee House of Representatives. Virginia governor William B. Giles, a friend of Jackson's, had sponsored the Tennessee statehood bill while serving in Congress in 1796.

As a United States senator from Missouri, Thomas Hart Benton proved to be a valuable ally of President Andrew Jackson. But when they both lived on the Tennessee frontier, they were bitter enemies. Benton, serving in the state senate, secured passage of a bill naming the county after Isaac Shelby. Jackson and his allies won. Giles was the name finally selected. (See The Harpeth River Tour, pages 155–56, for more information on Thomas Hart Benton's life in Tennessee.)

Casimir Pulaski was an exiled Polish nobleman who fought with the colonists in the American Revolution. He was killed at Savannah, Georgia, in 1779. Thirty years later, the citizens of newly created Giles County named their county seat for the Polish hero.

The Giles County Courthouse is one of Tennessee's most impressive. Built in 1909, it replaced an 1859 building that burned in 1907.

Sam Davis monument at the Giles County Courthouse

The statue on the south side of the courthouse is of Sam Davis. There is also a Sam Davis shrine on the Pulaski street named for him. One of the handful of statues on the grounds of the Capitol at Nashville is of Sam Davis. The Sam Davis Home at Smyrna is a state historic site. So who was Sam Davis, anyway?

As a young man of nineteen, Sam Davis enlisted in the First Tennessee Infantry at the beginning of the Civil War. The Confederates had the

Federals trapped at Chattanooga in the fall of 1863. Braxton Bragg, the Confederate commander, wanted to keep up with Union troops moving to relieve the siege, so he dispatched a group of scouts to work behind Union lines. Captain H. B. Shaw—known then as "Dr. Coleman," an itinerant physician in the Pulaski area—was the leader. The secret group was called Coleman's Scouts. Sam Davis was one of them.

Grenville Dodge was the man who built the Union Pacific Railroad, the eastern part of the first transcontinental line, completed in 1869. Before that, he was a general in the Union army. In November 1863, he commanded Federal troops in the Pulaski area.

Sam Davis was making his way through the Giles County countryside with some papers. His goal was to get them to General Bragg at Chattanooga. He was stopped by some Jayhawkers, troopers of the Seventy Kansas Cavalry. The papers, it turned out, contained details of Federal plans and activities in Middle Tennessee.

General Dodge was worried. He suspected that the papers had come directly from his own desk. Did he have a traitor in his midst? Dodge had the young Tennessean brought to him.

"I pleaded with him and urged him with all the power I possessed to give me some chance to save his life, for I had discovered he was a most admirable young fellow," Dodge later wrote.

But Davis would not talk. "It is useless to talk to me. I do not intend to do it," Davis replied to the general.

Whether Sam Davis was a spy has been debated ever since the Civil War. He was wearing a Confederate uniform. But his location behind enemy lines and his mission made it seem as if he were a spy. Grenville Dodge treated him as a spy. He decided to have him executed unless Davis revealed the source of the papers. Davis never talked.

"Dear Mother," he wrote. "Oh, how painful it is to write to you! I have got to die tomorrow morning—to be hanged by the Federals. Mother, do not grieve for me. I must bid you good-by forevermore. Mother, I do not fear to die. Give my love to all. Your son, Sam Davis." A chaplain from the Eighty-First Ohio Infantry visited Sam that night. He sang Sam's favorite song, "On Jordan's Stormy Banks I Stand."

The next morning, November 27, Sam Davis rode to the execution site sitting on his coffin. Grenville Dodge tried one last time. "Speak the name of your informant, and go home in safety."

Sam Davis would not budge. "No, I cannot. I had rather die a thousand deaths than betray a friend, or be false to duty."

A Federal officer on the scene wrote years later, "Thus ended a tragedy wherein a smooth-faced boy, without counsel, in the midst of enemies, with courage of highest type, deliberately chose death to life secured by means he thought dishonorable."

In addition to the question of whether Sam Davis was a spy, subject to execution, or simply a soldier who should have been treated as a prisoner of war, there is another mystery surrounding the execution. Who was it that Davis gave his life to protect?

One theory is that Davis got the papers from a man at Campbellsville. The man had sent a boy to Pulaski, and the youngster supposedly stole the papers from the Federals. Another version is that Davis got them from a ranking Union officer. Davis was looking at the man when he was hanged, according to that version. Others say Davis got the papers from his superior, Captain Shaw, alias Dr. Coleman. But the only person who knew for sure was Sam Davis.

From the square, walk one block west on Madison to Third Street to see one of Middle Tennessee's most impressive houses.

It is called the Brown-Daly-Horne House—Brown for Governor John C. Brown, who lived for a time in the original 1855 house; Daly for T. E. Daly, the merchant and banker who rebuilt the house in its grand style in 1900; and Horne for later owners. This house is said to be one of Tennessee's finest examples of the Queen Anne style. It features porticoes, bays, turrets, windows of various shapes and types, a veranda, several porches, and a balcony. The house was carefully restored in 1980 and has been used since then as a bank.

To understand the importance of John C. Brown in Tennessee politics, it is necessary to understand something of Tennessee's unique brand of Reconstruction. Tennessee's state government, unlike that of other Confederate states, was restored before the Civil War ended, so Tennessee escaped Federal martial law. But it did not escape repression. The state government was controlled by militant Unionists called "Radicals,"

Brown-Daly-Horne House

led by William G. Brownlow, who took office as governor in March 1865.

Under Brownlow's leadership, Tennessee enacted harsh laws to punish ex-Confederates, including one that denied them the right to vote. For four years, most Tennesseans suffered under the repressive Brownlow regime. Then, in February 1869, Brownlow resigned to take a seat in the United States Senate. The Unionists controlling Tennessee were deeply divided between the Radicals and the less militant Conservatives. With Brownlow's departure, the influence of the Conservatives grew.

Though DeWitt C. Senter, Brownlow's successor as governor, was a Radical, he favored a more conciliatory approach toward former Confederates and vowed to restore their civil rights. The Conservatives set out to undo much of the Radical program. By 1870, the repression and turbulence of the Brownlow era was ending, and Tennesseans could get on with the task of healing their deep wounds.

As a state, Tennessee essentially started over in 1870. One of the first steps was to write a new constitution. When the Constitutional Convention met in Nashville on January 10, 1870, it wisely selected a moderate, John C. Brown of Pulaski, as its chairman. Though Brown had fought for the Confederacy, rising to the rank of major general, he had vigorously opposed secession before the war.

The convention must approach its task with "wisdom, prudence, and moderation," Brown urged. Under his leadership, the ex-Confederates who dominated the body resisted the temptation to react punitively to the excesses of the Brownlow regime. The document that emerged guaranteed the right to vote and expressly prohibited slavery in Tennessee. This 1870 constitution is the one that still governs Tennessee.

Tennesseans, grateful for Brown's leadership at the Constitutional Convention, elected him the first governor under the new charter. He served two two-year terms, then went into the railroad business in Texas. He later returned to Tennessee to run a rail and coal business, and died while vacationing at Red Boiling Springs in 1889.

John C. Brown was not the first governor from Giles County. Neither was he the first one named Brown. His older brother Neill was the state's chief executive in the 1840s, as was Aaron Brown of Giles County. Aaron was not related to John and Neill. In fact, even though they were both from Giles County, Neill and Aaron Brown were bitter rivals. It was Neill Brown who defeated the incumbent Aaron Brown in 1847.

John C. Brown's imprint here extends beyond the house he once occupied. The large, columned mansion on the opposite side of Madison Street was his home, too. And it was Brown and his wife, Elizabeth, who gave the funds to build the Church of the Messiah, the Episcopal church on the corner. Two of their daughters had died, and they gave the money to build the church in the girls' memory. Designed by George W. Quintard, son of the noted Episcopal bishop, and intended to resemble an English country church, it was completed in 1887. A highlight of the interior is the elaborately carved Gothic reredos.

Pulaski is home to several fine churches in addition to the Church of the Messiah. Walk back to the square and turn left (N) on Second Street to see the massive First United Methodist Church on the square's northwest corner. It was built in 1895.

Walk south on Second Street. One block from the square, you will come

Church of the Messiah

to First Presbyterian Church, a Victorian Gothic structure built in 1882. The congregation that meets here dates to 1828.

From First Presbyterian Church, walk one block south on Second to College Street. The large Italianate house on the corner at 304 South Second, beautifully restored for use as a bank, was home to Thomas Martin.

Martin turned down President James K. Polk's offer of a position as secretary of the treasury. He cared little for politics but was active in just about every other aspect of Pulaski's life before his death in 1870. A banker, he developed the first turnpike here and promoted the railroad that reached Pulaski before the Civil War.

He was also a generous man. In his will, he provided for the establishment of a college, the successor to which is Martin Methodist College. Martin ransomed Pulaski when he paid a $3,000 tribute to keep the town from being torched by Federal troops during the Civil War. He never tried to collect the debt from the city, but after his death, his executor and son-in-law, Judge Spofford, sued and recovered the money for the estate.

Spofford spent the money on a clock for the courthouse cupola. For many years, the bell tolled for one hour on each anniversary of Spofford's 1880

Thomas Martin House, where the Ku Klux Klan started as a social club

death. The clock's bell was used as an alarm as well. In 1907, it rang the alarm that the courthouse itself was on fire. The clock was not saved, but the bell was recast with Judge Spofford's name on it and rehung in the new building.

To the outside world, Pulaski is known as the birthplace of the Ku Klux Klan, formed here at the Martin House. The original Klan had nothing to do with intimidation or terror. It began as a joke in the desperate winter of 1865–66. And it was quite by accident that the Klan discovered the power it could wield over recently freed blacks. The Ku Klux Klan spread rapidly from Pulaski throughout the South, but within five or six years, it was over. Later reincarnations of the Ku Klux Klan were not connected to the original one started here in Pulaski.

Six young, bright, educated Pulaski men, recently home from the war, were bored and restless. Life was bleak that winter in Giles County, as it was throughout the South. There were no jobs. There was no social life. "Why don't we start a club of some kind?" one suggested. An excellent idea, the others responded. At a meeting at a law office on the square, three of the six were assigned the task of coming up with a name for their club. The other three went to work on a set of rules.

The Martins were away on a trip and had asked one of the men to stay in their house. The group's next meeting was held here, and it was here that they selected a name. Someone offered "The Merry Six," but some-one else suggested the word *kuklos*, Greek for "circle." That was their choice, but they changed it to *kuklux*. No one would know what it meant, and that was important. It was to be a secret club. The young men were of Scots-Irish descent, and in recognition of their heritage, they added the word *klan* to their name.

Deciding that they needed costumes, they reached for the first things they could find—the Martins' sheets and pillowcases. They added mean-ingless occult symbols—spangles, stars, and half-moons—cut out of flannel. Cardboard placed in the pillowcases made the hoods stand taller, giving the members a larger-than-life look. The six selected outrageous names, among them the "Grand Cyclops," for their leader. They then went out on the town as clowns. The Ku Klux Klan had no purpose other than fun. As one of the original six later wrote, it "was purely social and for our amusement." The club's function was to "have fun, make mischief, and play pranks on the public."

When other equally bored young men saw the Ku Kluxers, they wanted to join. Most of the Klan's early activity was directed toward farcical initiations of new members, during which the initiates were the butts of practical jokes.

While they met in their "den" in the cellar of an abandoned house, one member stood guard outside on a stump. With his robe extending to the ground and his hood on his head, the guard gave the impression of being about ten feet tall. The sentinel's job was to greet potential members and challenge them with something like "Who are ye that dare to intrude upon our secret precincts?" The initiate was then led into the cellar, where he was generally made a fool of and then initiated into the Klan.

One night, a young black man from a nearby farm happened upon the den. He was startled by the hooded, robed figure. "Who's that?" the young stranger asked. "I'm a ghost," the sentinel responded spontaneously. The man fled in horror.

The sentinel later related his joke to the others in the den. Someone suggested that the fear caused by the outlandish costumes might be put to use. On Third Street, there was a large house occupied by a family of freed slaves, a house that had become "a general rendezvous for the disorderly element of negroes in the community," as Mr. and Mrs. W. B. Romine put it in their book on the Klan. The women of the house "were not merely noisy, but rough, profane and vulgar, [and] took special delight in being offensive and aggressive in their attitude toward white people."

The Klan decided to try an experiment—parade by the house and scare its occupants into more acceptable conduct. They decided that a parade on horseback would be more impressive, so they designed robes for their horses, too. On the appointed night, with both men and horses clad like fools, the Klan paraded to the offending house.

The leader of the Klan politely asked for a drink. An occupant of the house kindly brought out a dipper of water, which the horseman drank. Then he asked for another. He was obliged and thanked his host. The horseman then asked for the whole bucket, and it was brought. He then drank it all, remarking that this was the best water he had drunk since he was killed at Shiloh. Then the Klan rode off.

As it turned out, the leader had a rubber bag hidden under his robe, and the water ran into it. But without any threat or intimidation, the parade had its intended affect. The people in the house on Third Street knew that at Shiloh, the bloody battle fought a few counties to the west in April 1862, many of the men had languished in thirst before they died. These men on horseback must be their ghosts. And Mr. and Mrs. W. B. Romine noted, the "boisterous revelry ceased in that yard quite as suddenly as if there had been a funeral in the family."

As local history writer James Solomon put it, "Soon one man's humor had become another man's horror." Superstitious blacks became the new butts of practical jokes. Before long, the fear caused by the Klan was used to compel what the Klan perceived as acceptable behavior by the freedmen. But it was not just the freed slaves. The Klan struck out against whites as well, particularly carpetbaggers and scalawags.

Students of the Ku Klux Klan differ on what the Klan was really up to. Some say it provided needed stability in a society devoid of law and order. Others contend that it was a racist group intent on depriving freedmen of their newly won civil rights. Whichever the case, news of the Klan spread like wildfire throughout the South. Before long, Klan groups were forming everywhere. By April 1867, with no central authority or discipline, each den became a self-styled "band of regulators." Suppression of blacks and unfriendly whites—not just maintenance of order—became a cause for some of the groups, who achieved success through intimidation, fear, and sometimes violence.

A meeting was held at Nashville's new Maxwell House hotel, at which an official organization was created. Again, whether this was done to bring needed discipline to unruly local dens or to form a racist political force is a subject for debate.

A military-style organization was adopted. The supreme commander of the Ku Klux Klan was the Grand Wizard. Although he never admitted it, former Confederate general Nathan Bedford Forrest became the Grand Wizard.

Forrest was controversial then. He still is. However observers feel about him, it cannot be denied that he was a white supremacist. He traveled throughout the South in 1868 ostensibly on business, but wherever he went, Klan membership grew. So did public outrage over Klan activities.

Even Forrest was becoming concerned about the Klan's excesses by then. In January 1869, he issued "General Order Number One," which called upon Klansmen to curtail their activities and destroy their regalia. This effectively ended the Ku Klux Klan's short life as a cohesive political force. It did not end the Klan altogether, though. Some Klan dens remained active after Forrest's order. In 1871, Congress passed legislation designed to curb some of the abuses.

The end of Reconstruction and the restoration of civil rights to Confederate veterans in the early 1870s placed people who might be in sympathy with the Klan in political power. It was during this post-Reconstruction period that racial segregation was made the law in many states. The Ku Klux Klan, at least the first version of it, faded from existence.

A different Ku Klux Klan emerged in the twentieth century. It has no connection with Pulaski except that, beginning in 1927, the town has been burdened by racist groups drawn to the birthplace of the first Klan. It is interesting to speculate how many twentieth-century Klansmen have a clue that the only reason they wear robes and hoods is because the Martins' sheets and pillowcases were what was readily available to the six young pranksters who started the club.

Leaving the Martin House, walk one block east to First Street. The Ballentine House is the large, two-story, brick Greek Revival house with the recessed porch. Andrew Mitchell Ballentine arrived in Philadelphia from Ireland in 1812. He was penniless. By the 1840s, he and Thomas Martin ranked as the largest taxpayers in Giles County. Ballentine was a merchant and planter, owning lands and slaves in Mississippi as well as Tennessee. He married Mary Goff in 1821, and the two of them gradually acquired the entire square block where their 1840s house now stands.

Return to the square on First Street and turn right (E) on Madison. Walk to the hill east of the square to Sam Davis Avenue. Turn right.

It was here, on a street then known as Farm Lane, that Sam Davis was executed. On the right, a small stone building resembling a Greek tomb marks the spot. The only house along this lovely street that dates from

Davis's time is the 1858 Vaughn-Stacy House, at 111 South Sam Davis Avenue. The rest of the houses in the historic district were built after the Civil War.

Continue down Sam Davis Avenue and cross College Street. You will soon come to Maplewood Cemetery, on the right. Here, an impressive statue of Governor John C. Brown clad in a Confederate uniform stands over his grave. Brown's grave is located near the elaborate mausoleum that keeps the remains of Thomas Martin.

Return up Sam Davis Avenue to Jefferson Street. Turn right on Jefferson, then left on Jones Street. Follow Jones to Washington Street. Turn left (W) to see the Austin Hewitt Home, located on the right at 322 East Washington.

This building, noted for its monumental pedimented portico, has seen many uses. The original part of it dates to the 1830s, when it was used as a female academy. In the 1850s, it was remodeled and the portico added. It was then used as a private residence for many years.

Pulaski businessman Austin Hewitt, who died in 1921, provided in his will that "the whole of my estate be used for founding and maintaining a home for indigent old women of Giles County." The trustees acquired this house, enlarged it, and named it the Austin Hewitt Home. It served the

John C. Brown's grave

Austin Hewitt Home

intended purpose until 1981, at which time it was purchased for conversion into a retirement center.

From the Austin Hewitt Home, return to the square and your car. Drive north from the square on U.S. 31 (First Street). After 2.9 miles, you will reach a beautiful, old one-story house tucked away on the right before the highway crosses Pigeon Roost Creek. It is no wonder that this house is said to be the finest example of the Greek Revival style in Giles County. George W. Tillery, who constructed it around 1840, was a noted builder and carpenter. Tillery did the woodwork on the 1859 Giles County Courthouse.

Continue north on U.S. 31 for 6.1 miles to Milky Way Road. Along the way, the highway crests a ridge and descends into the valley of Richland Creek. James Robertson knew good land when he saw it in 1783. He was right on the mark when he named the creek. This is good farmland.

The lovely Olivet United Methodist Church stands on the right just before a railroad overpass. Built in 1871, this little Victorian building is said to feature some of the best carpentry in Tennessee.

Beyond the railroad, turn left onto Milky Way Road. You will reach the drive leading to the Milky Way Farmhouse after 0.4 mile. It was the richness of the countryside that attracted Frank Mars here in the 1930s.

Mars and his wife, Ethel, started making candy in their Tacoma, Washington, home around 1911. By 1928, they had a company called Mar-O-Bar in Chicago. Their candy bars became enormously popular. They made a fortune.

Mars wanted a safe investment during the dark days of the early 1930s, so he turned to land, horses, and cattle. He bought 3,500 acres here and built one of America's leading farms. Frank Mars provided economic salvation for this area. In the depth of the Depression, as many as 800 men were employed in his massive construction project. When it was over, Mars had some 100 buildings, including 12 cattle barns, 8 horse barns, 2 tack houses, 85 worker cottages, a commissary, and shops. He provided permanent employment to 125 workers, who operated the farm.

The centerpiece was the family home, called the Clubhouse. The two-story Tudor Revival house, made of native stone and logs, was carefully designed to blend into the natural environment.

Milky Way Farm proved to be more than a hobby. Several livestock enterprises were carried on here: the breeding and development of Hereford cattle, the breeding and racing of thoroughbred horses, the operation of a commercial dairy, and the raising of Hampshire sheep.

Frank Mars died prematurely in 1934. His funeral was surely the largest ever held in these parts. A train of twelve Pullman cars brought friends and company employees from Chicago. His body was buried on one of the farm's highest hills. Later, Ethel Mars, who took over the farm and the candy company, had Frank's body moved to Minneapolis for reburial. She sold the farm in 1945 to Albert Noe of Jackson, Tennessee.

Milky Way Farm's clubhouse is sometimes open to the public. If it is not open at the time of your visit, you can still get a view of it by driving another 0.4 mile up the hill on Milky Way Road. A row of abandoned stables flanks the hillside below the house. Some of the farm's massive stone barns can be seen along the road.

Return to U.S. 31 and turn left (N). It is 4.1 miles to Yokley Road at Waco. Turn left. The Elisha White House is on the right after 0.2 mile. Elisha White migrated from Virginia, married Williamson County's Catherine Jane Walker, and moved to Giles County in 1809. Around 1811, the Whites built this sturdy Federal-style house on a hill with a command-ing view of the area. They had nineteen children.

Elisha White House

Backtrack to U.S. 31 and turn left (N). Drive 0.2 mile to the main intersection at Waco; turn right onto TN 129 to reach Lynnville. You will come to the village's business district on the railroad after 1.6 miles.

Lynnville gets its name from Lynn Creek, which in turn is named for the "lynn"—or linden—trees that grew along its banks. The town once stood where Waco is now. Elisha White gave the land for a town at the foot of the hill below his house. Plans were drawn up for a village that would include a public square, a school, a hotel, and other buildings. Two events caused Lynnville to move—it was burned by Federal troops in the Civil War, and the railroad bypassed it.

Today's Lynnville is a quintessential railroad town, with its commercial row facing the tracks. It is as pretty a village as there is in Tennessee, containing a fine collection of Victorian-era houses and lovely churches.

Leaving Lynnville, follow TN 129 east toward Cornersville. You will come to an enormous columned mansion on the left 9 miles from Lynnville.

Ham's Folly

Cornersville United Methodist Church

This home is known as Ham's Folly. James Ham and his wife, the former Tennessee Virginia Woods, hired George Tillery and others to build this distinctive house on the eve of the Civil War. It broke the Hams, and they were sued by carpenters and suppliers who had not been paid. That is how the place got its name.

Continue on TN 129 as it crosses the heights of Elk Ridge—which divides the watersheds of the Elk and Duck rivers—and enters Cornersville. After two right-angle turns, TN 129 reaches Main Street (U.S. 31A).

Cornersville is in Marshall County, but it was here before the county was established in 1836. The town is named for the corners of Bedford, Giles, Lincoln, and Maury counties, which met near here.

Take some time to explore Cornersville, one of Middle Tennessee's most pleasant small towns. Cornersville United Methodist Church—located at the second right-angle turn, next to the park—is practically unaltered from the time it was constructed in 1852. It was built jointly as a church and a Masonic hall, with the church meeting on the first floor and the Masons on the second. This arrangement existed until 1939, when the Masons moved.

Turn right (S) off TN 129 onto Main Street and drive through town. Main Street is lined with beautiful, well-kept two-story white frame houses.

After you have enjoyed Cornersville, turn around and head north on U.S. 31A, continuing past TN 129. On the left 2.6 miles from TN 129 stands a distinctive house called Valley Farm. This home was built in sections over the years, first by James B. Record around 1820 and then by W. L. McClelland after he bought the property. According to tradition, the columned facade was added after McClelland attended Andrew Jackson's funeral at the Hermitage. He came away so inspired that he tried to duplicate the facade here on his own house.

This tour ends near Cornersville. You can continue past Valley Farm to Lewisburg, located a few scenic miles to the north on U.S. 31A. You can reach Interstate 65 from Lewisburg or by backtracking on TN 129.

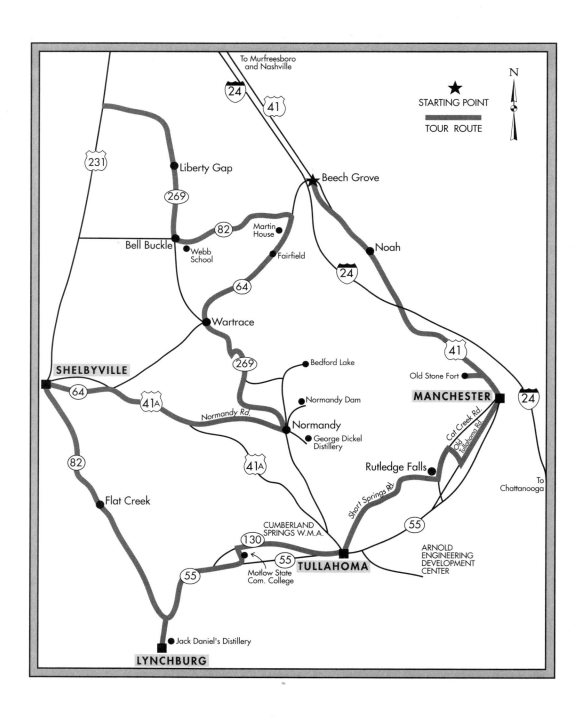

The Duck River Tour

This tour includes the beautiful, rolling valley of the Duck River, an ancient Indian site, and the nation's oldest and best-known distillery. It starts at Beech Grove, where an important but overlooked Civil War battle was fought, then visits Old Stone Fort State Park, the prehistoric site at Manchester. After stopping at Tullahoma, it goes to Lynchburg and the Jack Daniel's Distillery, then on to Shelbyville, with its thriving square and historic residential district. The final stops, in the heart of Tennessee Walking Horse country, are the charming railroad towns of Normandy, Wartrace, and Bell Buckle.

Total length: approximately 106 miles

This tour begins at the junction of TN 64 and Oscar Crowell Road (Old U.S. 41) in the village of Beech Grove, located between Murfreesboro and Manchester. Beech Grove is accessible via Exit 97 off Interstate 24.

Perched on a hill at the northwest corner of this intersection, within earshot of the rush of interstate traffic, a Confederate cemetery stands as a quiet reminder of the important Civil War battle fought in these hills. The fighting that broke out here on June 24, 1863, signaled the beginning of one of the most significant but overlooked phases of the war, the Middle Tennessee Campaign, or Tullahoma Campaign. With a minimum of fighting and a maximum of stealth, it took just eleven days for the Union's Army of the Cumberland to maneuver the Confederacy's Army of Tennessee nearly out of its namesake state and all the way to the Georgia border.

Though overshadowed by concurrent events at Gettysburg in the East and at Vicksburg on the Mississippi, the Middle Tennessee Campaign was a turning point—if not *the* turning point—in the Civil War in the West. It gave the North control of all of Middle Tennessee—then, as now, one of America's most productive agricultural regions. And the nearly blood-less victory led to the Union occupation of the vital rail junction of

Chattanooga, gateway to the Deep South. The campaign also helped liberate Union-sympathizing East Tennessee from Confederate control.

The Middle Tennessee Campaign had its origin in the inconclusive but bloody Battle of Stones River near Murfreesboro. (Stones River National Battlefield is visited in The Cedar Forests Tour, pages 177–79.) Southern fighting men thought they had won a victory on January 2, 1863, but their commander, General Braxton Bragg, retreated anyway. He moved the Confederacy's principal western army south about 30 miles to haphazardly selected positions along the Duck River and its tributaries.

Separating the watersheds of the Stones and Duck rivers—and the larger Cumberland and Tennessee rivers, into which they flow—is the range of rugged hills just north of Beech Grove. For the first six months of 1863, following the violence at Stones River, these hills also separated the Union and Confederate armies.

Despite President Abraham Lincoln's constant prodding, Major General William S. Rosecrans, the Union commander, would not advance on the Confederates until he was satisfied he had enough men and material to overwhelm them. When he finally did move, Rosecrans followed a masterful plan.

The Confederate infantry was camped in clusters beginning near Beech Grove and extending down the Duck River Valley to Shelbyville, a distance of about 20 miles. The most logical route for a Union advance was on the west of the front to Shelbyville, around the steep hills. By choosing the most illogical route—straight through the hills—Rosecrans completely surprised Bragg and his quarrelsome generals.

The Ohio engineer's plan was not complicated. Rosecrans would feint toward Shelbyville with part of his army, then thrust through the rugged hills straight from Murfreesboro to Manchester in the Confederates' rear. The Southerners would have to either turn around and fight or retreat. In either case, Rosecrans hoped to sever their brittle lifeline south, the Nashville & Chattanooga Railroad.

Just north of Beech Grove, the Manchester Turnpike—and the route of today's U.S. 41—passed through the steep hills through narrow Hoovers Gap. Taking Hoovers Gap quickly was the key of Rosecrans's strategy, and for that important task, he selected the mounted infantry brigade of Colonel John T. Wilder. Armed with new Spencer repeating rifles, Wilder's men from Indiana and Illinois took the gap on June 24, 1863, and held it long enough for reinforcements to arrive.

After three days of fighting around Beech Grove and at other points along the Duck River, the Confederates retreated south, first to Tullahoma, then across the Elk River, then to Cowan at the foot of the Cumberland Plateau, and finally over the mountain and out of Middle Tennessee altogether. By July 4, 1863, Middle Tennessee was firmly in Union control. The Federals suffered only 550 casualties out of over 60,000 men engaged. And of those, only 84 were fatalities.

John T. Wilder established quite a name for himself here at Hoovers Gap. Then, just three months later, he became a hero at the Union disaster at Chickamauga, near Chattanooga. At the Chickamauga battlefield, an imposing monument stands in honor of Wilder and his men.

The young, successful iron smelter from Indiana liked what he saw in Tennessee. Shortly after the war, Wilder settled in Chattanooga and rose to prominence in Tennessee industry and politics, serving briefly as Chattanooga's mayor. He later moved to upper East Tennessee, where he built the Cloudland Hotel atop Roan Mountain.

Confederate dead from the fighting around Beech Grove were hastily

Confederate cemetery at Beech Grove

buried where they fell in the pastures and cornfields. When local Confederate veterans returned home from the war, they were disturbed to see some of the remains showing above the ground. In 1866, they decided to rebury the dead Confederates. They selected an old pioneer graveyard atop this small hill, where several of the men had died in a vain attempt to dislodge Wilder's Federals. This is reported to be the first Confederate cemetery in the South.

After visiting the cemetery, head south on Oscar Crowell Road through the village of Beech Grove and past the charming 1888 Beech Grove Cumberland Presbyterian Church. After 1.8 miles, turn right (S) onto U.S. 41. The route passes through the community of Noah and climbs to the Highland Rim before crossing the Duck River and reaching the turnoff for Old Stone Fort State Park after 10.7 miles. Turn right into the park and drive to the visitor center.

Here, on the peninsula where the two forks of the Duck River join and where the Duck begins its turbulent descent off the Highland Rim, an earthen wall encloses a fifty-two-acre plain. If the wall were continuous, it would measure about forty-six hundred feet in length.

Hernando De Soto and his band of Spanish explorers built the fort when they passed through the region in 1540. Or was it Vikings who, on a pre-Columbian trip to Middle Tennessee, built the fort as protection from the Indians? Maybe it was Madoc, a Welsh prince who migrated to North America around 1170. Actually, none of these explanations for the mysterious earthworks is true.

The state of Tennessee purchased four hundred scenic acres here at the forks of the Duck in 1966. That year, a serious archaeological investigation was undertaken. Some of the mysteries were solved. Others will probably never be solved.

Excavation of the walls uncovered limestone rocks about the size one person could carry. Chert and rubble were used as fill around the rocks, and the entire structure was covered with dirt. Radiocarbon dating of charcoal samples found in the wall established that the oldest section was built around 30 A.D. and the newest around 430.

The structure dates from the prehistoric Woodland Period, which lasted from about three thousand years ago to eleven hundred years ago. Just what the place was used for by the Woodland people is not known. It had long been thought that it was a fortification—hence the name Old Stone Fort—but the archaeologists discounted that theory. Higher ground outside the wall would make it easy to attack. There is no evidence of palisaded walls, and the area is much too large to be defended by a relatively small number of people.

It is also noteworthy that, though pottery was used by the people of the Woodland Period, none of it was found in the excavation.

All of this led to the conclusion that the structure was for ceremonial use. The walls were to set apart a special place, a place of some spiritual, social, or political significance.

The state operates a small museum containing exhibits and artifacts from the area. But even without the archaeological site, this would be a splendid place to visit. Two miles of easy paths wind along the bluffs above the cascading forks of the Duck River. There are three major falls, as well as a dam that dates to the time when paper mills operated here.

Except for the obstruction created by the TVA's Normandy Dam—a controversial 1970s project that generates no electricity—and a few small, abandoned mills and pre-TVA hydroelectric dams, the Duck River flows freely from its formation here at Old Stone Fort for 265 miles across Middle Tennessee. It is the longest river completely within the state of Tennessee.

Leaving Old Stone Fort, turn right (S) on U.S. 41 to enter Manchester. Turn left on Fort Street to reach the courthouse square. The beautiful Coffee County Courthouse was built in the Italianate style in 1871 to replace an 1837 courthouse that was destroyed by fire. A local official supposedly "short on his books" was suspected of setting it.

Coffee County Courthouse

General John Coffee, Andrew Jackson's nephew by marriage, was a trusted lieutenant to Jackson in his military days. When a new county was created in 1836, it was named for the War of 1812 hero. Manchester is named for the industrial city in England and reflects the founders' hope that abundant water power from the fall of the forks of the Duck River would make this a major manufacturing center.

Leave the square at its southeast corner on East Main Street. Drive two blocks to Ramsey Street and turn right. It is less than 0.2 mile to U.S. 41. Turn right and go 0.2 mile to Spring Street. Turn left (S) and head out of

Rutledge Falls Baptist Church

Statue overlooking Rutledge Falls

town on the old road to Tullahoma. Soon, the route parallels the railroad.

The McMinnville & Manchester Railroad opened in 1855 to connect with the Nashville & Chattanooga at Tullahoma. The plan was for it to extend all the way into Kentucky, but it never made it that far. It did make it to Sparta and the coal mines on the Cumberland Plateau above it.

Turn right onto Belmont Road 4.1 miles from the square in Manchester; Belmont Road is shown on maps as Wilson Road. Drive 1.2 miles to Cat Creek Road and turn left. It is 1.5 miles to Short Springs Road. Turn right on Short Springs Road at Rutledge Falls Baptist Church.

The Highland Rim in these parts is known as The Barrens. Traveling onto the southern Highland Rim, you may notice that the landscape looks different. Back around Beech Grove, the route passed through fertile valleys created by streams slicing through the rim. On top of the rim, the countryside is dominated by shallow, swampy forests of oak. This accounts for the alternate name—the Oak Barrens. Early settlers considered this part of the state to be wasteland, not good for much of anything but timber and pasture, so they avoided it.

There is an oasis in the Oak Barrens here at Rutledge Falls, where Crumpton Creek has carved out a fertile, little plain. This is one of the most delightful spots in Middle Tennessee.

Lytle D. Hickerson, the first president of the McMinnville & Manchester Railroad, once owned this land. In 1893, his widow, Fannie, had this lovely little Gothic Revival church built in memory of her son, Lytle D. Hickerson, Jr.

Just beyond the church, there is a small parking area on the right in front of an old brick farmhouse. A short path leads from here to Rutledge Falls. On its way off the Highland Rim, Crumpton Creek drops off the ledge into a small gorge dotted on the edges with mountain laurel. An intriguing bronze statue overlooks the impressive falls.

Leave Rutledge Falls on Short Springs Road. It is 1.8 miles to an intersection where Short Springs Road makes a sharp turn to the left; continue following Short Springs Road for 4.5 miles to Hogan Street in Tullahoma. The route passes near the spot for which the road is named. Some 420 acres around Short Springs have been designated a state natural area, known for its profusion of wildflowers.

Turn right on Hogan Street and drive 0.4 mile to Atlantic Street, located just short of the railroad. Turn left. You are now in the Depot Historic District.

It is not difficult to distinguish towns that predate the coming of the railroads from those that grew up around them. At the older towns, the tracks passed on what was then the outskirts, and the depot was often a good distance from the square. In contrast, the business sections of railroad towns usually parallel the tracks. Tullahoma is a quintessential railroad town.

Sitting as it does on an elevation between the Duck River, to the north, and the Elk River, to the south, this was a natural place for the Nashville & Chattanooga Railroad to select as a labor camp when the line came through in 1851. (For details of the construction of the Nashville & Chattanooga, see The Elk River Tour, page 316.) And with the opening of the branch from here to Manchester and McMinnville in 1855, Tullahoma evolved into an important railroad center.

(Above and below)
Houses on Tullahoma's Atlantic Avenue built for Hickerson sisters and Raht brothers

Atlantic Street is actually two streets, one on one side of the tracks and one on the other. A significant residential area grew up across from the business district. Though relatively small, the Depot Historic District holds a fine collection of large homes from the Victorian era. Two of the most interesting are at 308 and 312 North Atlantic. Two brothers, J. D. and F. A. Raht, came from East Tennessee to enter the tobacco business around 1880. They married two sisters, Alma and Minnie Hickerson, daughters of Fannie and Lytle D. Hickerson, president of the branch-line railroad. These houses were built side by side for the Hickersons' daughters and their husbands.

Minnie Raht came to own the family's Rutledge Falls property and was responsible for maintaining it in its pristine condition. Tragedy struck Alma and J. D. Raht in 1912. While staying in a Knoxville hotel, J. D. was killed in a fire and Alma was badly injured; she eventually recovered.

Tullahoma is where Confederate general Braxton Bragg had his headquarters during the six-month lull following the battle at Murfreesboro, and it was to Tullahoma that his army first retreated during the Federals' June 1863 Middle Tennessee Campaign.

Tullahoma's status as an important railroad town guaranteed a swift economic recovery after the destruction of war. Today, this town in The Barrens is one of Middle Tennessee's most prosperous.

This prosperity is due in no small part to the presence of the United States Air Force's Arnold Engineering Development Center (AEDC). During World War II, while the air force was still part of the army, General Henry H. "Hap" Arnold, commander of the Army Air Corps, became concerned about German advances in jet propulsion. He and others proposed the establishment of a center for advanced aerodynamic and propulsion system development. A site at Tullahoma was selected, and in 1951, the center, named in Arnold's honor, was dedicated by President Harry S. Truman.

AEDC, located on a vast 40,000-acre reservation east of town, is the world's largest center for aerospace simulation testing. Over the years, nearly every major aeronautical and space system developed by the United States has been tested here at Tullahoma. Visitors are welcome at the center on weekdays. (Part of AEDC is visited on The Elk River Tour, page 307.)

Part of the land selected for AEDC was once the United States Army's Camp Forrest. Established by the state of Tennessee in 1926 as a National Guard training ground, it was taken over by the federal government during World War II and became a major induction center.

Camp Forrest was one of several places in Tennessee that housed German prisoners of war during World War II. The camp had the capacity for three thousand POWs. Fort Campbell at Clarksville had a POW camp, and one of the largest camps in the nation was at Crossville, where fifteen thousand German and Italian prisoners were kept.

Occasionally, prisoners escaped. Heinz Hoefer, a young veteran of Rommel's Afrika Korps, slipped under the wire at Camp Forrest, walked into Tullahoma, and took the morning train to Nashville. He hoped to get to New York, ship out as a seaman, and make it back home to Germany. But freedom was too much for the young man. He went out for a night on the town in Nashville with an unsuspecting American soldier home on leave. The next day, Hoefer was stopped during a routine check and asked to produce his Selective Service card. He was caught and returned to camp.

An incident even more ludicrous also happened in Middle Tennessee. Werner Schwanbeck was an escaped German paratrooper from Fort Knox, Kentucky. On the morning of February 19, 1945, he boarded a Nashville city bus fully clad in a German uniform, complete with heavy paratrooper boots and the inverted chevron of a private first class. It was the height of the American war effort, but apparently none of the Nashvillians on the bus paid much attention to the strangely dressed young man. Werner rode around Nashville unmolested. Tired, hungry, and frightened, the twenty-three-year-old soldier finally asked the driver in broken English if he could go back to Fort Knox.

When land speculators called this town by the railroad Tullahoma, they selected a unique name. No other place in America has it. Tullahoma is obviously an Indian name. Over the years, a number of theories have evolved about why the town's developers selected it.

One is that it was the name of a horse belonging to Peter Spyker Decherd, an early settler who gave land for the railroad. Decherd named the horse for an Indian chief back in Pennsylvania, the story goes. When he was subsequently given the privilege of naming towns on the railroad, he named one for himself—Decherd—and one for his horse. But when Dorothy Williams Potter thoroughly investigated the source of Tullahoma's name and reported her findings in a local historical journal, she noted that there is no record of any chief in Pennsylvania by that name.

Tullahoma is said to mean "land of yellow flowers" in some Indian language. Potter checked that out, too. Tullahoma does not yield that translation in the language of any tribes that might have passed through this area.

But Potter was able to track the words *tali* and *homa* to the Choctaw language. *Tali* means stone or rock. *Homa* means red. But the Choctaws did not live anywhere near Middle Tennessee, so how did the name get here? There was briefly a Tullahoma in Choctaw country—Tullahoma, Mississippi, that is—started by land speculators in 1833. After only three years by that name, the town became part of the community of Grenada.

Potter's investigation turned up a number of influential Tennesseans who knew about the Mississippi town and could have transplanted the name to the Volunteer State. She connected the Mississippi town to the Tennessee town via noted land speculator John C. McLemore, who was acquainted with one of Tullahoma's developers. Potter concludes that this obscure link is how Tullahoma got its name.

Follow Atlantic Street for two blocks to Lincoln Street. Turn right and cross the railroad to enter downtown Tullahoma. At the intersection with Jackson Street, turn right again. It is 0.5 mile to Wilson Avenue at Oakwood Cemetery. Turn left (W) on Wilson (TN 55/TN 130) and drive 1.1 miles to a fork. Take TN 130, the right fork.

Leaving Tullahoma, the route passes into and out of the 6,079-acre Cumberland Springs Wildlife Management Area. Here, the land has been allowed to return to its natural state, offering a glimpse of what the Oak Barrens must have looked like before being disturbed by man.

You will reach a five-way intersection after 4.1 miles. One of the roads at this intersection is Ledford Mill Road. Though not on the tour, Ledford Mill is located 3 miles down the road to the right. A mill has been on this pleasant site since 1807, but the current version dates to 1880. In recent years, Ledford Mill has housed a museum exhibiting tools from the eighteenth and nineteenth centuries.

Turn left onto Ledford Mill Road. After passing through the campus of Motlow State Community College, you will come to TN 55. Turn right (W). The route now eases off the Highland Rim—notice how the landscape changes—and travels through the beautiful valley of Mulberry Creek before coming to the entrance to the Jack Daniel's Distillery after 7.2 miles. Turn left into the distillery.

Yes, there really was a Jack Daniel, born about 5 miles from here in 1848. At age twelve, he went to work for Dan Call's distillery. Within three years, Daniel became Call's full partner. Call was a pious Lutheran, and shortly after the Civil War, his elders gave him an ultimatum: either quit making whiskey or quit the church. He chose the former and sold out to Daniel.

Cave Spring produces iron-free water at an even fifty-six degrees—water perfect for making whiskey. Daniel bought five hundred acres around the spring and moved what ranks as the nation's oldest registered distillery here in 1866. He brought his nephew Lem Motlow into the business, and Motlow took it over upon Daniel's death in 1911. The business remained in the Motlow family until it was sold to the Brown-Forman Corporation of Louisville.

Tennessee sour mash whiskey—not a bourbon—is still made the way it always has been made right here in the hollow. Visitors can see how it is

Statue of Jack Daniel on the distillery grounds
(Courtesy of Jack Daniel's Distillery)

made, aged, and bottled on the guided tours the distillery conducts. One highlight of the tour is the life-size statue of Jack Daniel carved out of Italian marble in 1941; it stands about a hundred feet from the mouth of Cave Spring.

After enjoying the tour, turn left back onto TN 55. At the stoplight, turn left to reach Lynchburg's square and the 1885 Moore County Courthouse.

Moore is a relatively new county, one of a handful created in Tennessee after the Civil War. It was established in 1871. A popular advertising gimmick for the Jack Daniel's Distillery has been to list itself as being in "Lynchburg, Tennessee (POP. 361)." That boast—"POP. 361"—can no longer be true, at least from a technical standpoint, for Lynchburg and Moore County have done what Nashville and Davidson County did in 1963, formed a consolidated city-county government. But don't look for the Jack Daniel's Distillery to start labeling its bottles "Metropolitan Lynchburg and Moore County (POP. 4,721)" anytime soon.

Ironically, Moore has traditionally been a "dry" county. It was not until

Moore County Courthouse

January 1995 that the distillery was permitted to sell commemorative decanters of Jack Daniel's.

Lynchburg's square is a bustling little commercial area pretty much given over to the tourist trade, though a few local businesses do remain. Take a little time to poke around the shops.

From the square, return to TN 55 and backtrack toward Tullahoma for 2.4 miles to TN 82. Turn left (NW) and head through the strikingly beautiful countryside toward Shelbyville. It is 13.7 miles to downtown Shelbyville.

"The Pencil City" is a Shelbyville nickname. Located on the southern edge of the once-vast cedar forests southeast of Nashville and on the Duck River, which affords abundant water power, Shelbyville was a natural site for the development of cedar slat mills. The Musgrave Pencil Company was founded in 1916 by James Raford Musgrave. After World War I, Musgrave went to Germany and bought machinery for making complete pencils, not just cedar slats. In time, other pencil-manufacturing plants were established in Shelbyville as well.

Over-cutting claimed the big cedars, so the Musgrave Pencil Company took to buying cedar fence rails and logs from houses and barns. In addition to money, farmers could get wire fences in exchange for their cedar fences. Eventually, all the cedar in Middle Tennessee was used up. The several pencil manufacturers in town today use cedar from the Northwest.

Turn left onto Depot Street (TN 64) in Shelbyville. It is two blocks to the impressive square. It contains a well-preserved collection of Victorian-era commercial buildings, especially on the south side, which is made up of fourteen separate buildings.

Bedford County was created in 1807, about the same time as the other old counties in southern Middle Tennessee. It is named for Thomas Bedford, a Revolutionary War veteran who settled in Tennessee. The county seat is named for Isaac Shelby, hero of the Battle of Kings Mountain during the Revolutionary War and the first governor of Kentucky. Shelby explored and surveyed this part of Tennessee.

The Civil War–era courthouse was destroyed by a fire set accidently by Confederate soldiers quartered here during the first six months of 1863. It was replaced by a structure completed in 1873. It, too, was destroyed by fire, but not accidentally. A lynch mob burned it in 1935.

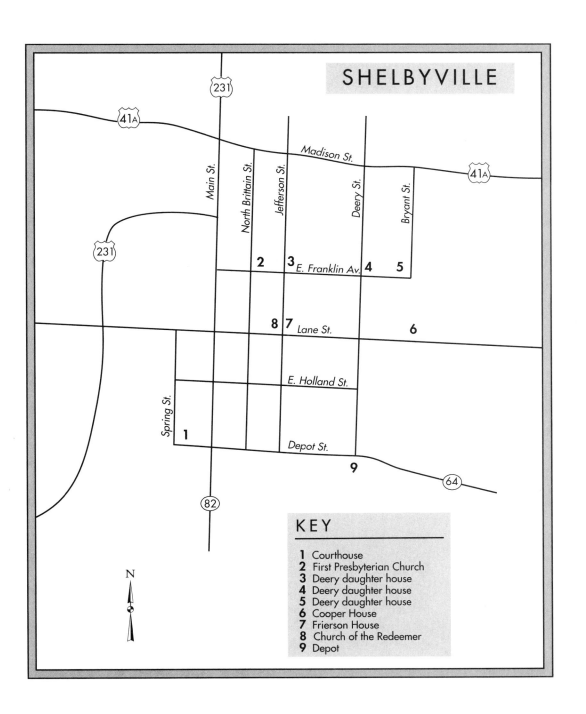

SHELBYVILLE

231
41A
Madison St.
41A
Main St.
North Brittain St.
Jefferson St.
Deery St.
Bryant St.
231
2 3 E. Franklin Av. 4 5
8 7 Lane St. 6
E. Holland St.
Spring St.
1
Depot St.
9
64
82

N

KEY
1 Courthouse
2 First Presbyterian Church
3 Deery daughter house
4 Deery daughter house
5 Deery daughter house
6 Cooper House
7 Frierson House
8 Church of the Redeemer
9 Depot

A young black man accused of assaulting a white schoolgirl was being held for trial, and a crowd gathered intent on lynching him. The governor sent in a hundred National Guardsmen to keep order, but they had little success. The prisoner was moved to a safe place, and someone in the mob took out his frustration by starting a fire in the sheriff's office. The handsome courthouse of today replaced the one destroyed in 1935.

That was not the first lynch mob to gather on the Shelbyville square. A noted lynching happened here in 1892, though it had no racial motive.

The citizenry was outraged by the slashing and beating of a woman by her husband, Bill Bates, who killed his wife over her refusal to give perjured testimony for her father-in-law, Scott Bates, a mule thief. The sheriff turned both the elder and junior Bates over to the mob, and the captives were led from the jail to the courthouse and the so-called heaven tree, which stood nearby. Voices of dissension started to rise over the hanging of Scott Bates—he was just a mule thief, not a cold-blooded killer. "Let the man go!" someone yelled. As both men were being hoisted by the ropes, someone cut Scott loose.

Hundreds witnessed the hanging of Bill Bates, but when it came time to prosecute his killers, not one person could be found to identify them.

Another person who barely escaped the noose at Shelbyville was Union spy Pauline Cushman. An actress, Cushman was banished behind Confederate lines for her alleged Southern sympathies. While entertaining a crowd in Louisville in March 1863, she gave a toast to Jefferson Davis and the Confederacy. She was sent south for "talking secesh." But it was a ruse.

When she got to Union-occupied Nashville, she received her instructions—get behind the Confederates' Duck River line and learn about their defenses. She was cautioned by the provost marshal at Nashville to bring back what she learned in her head, for if she had anything in writing and was caught, that would probably be the end of her.

Cushman eventually found her way to Shelbyville and took a room in a hotel where several Confederate officers resided. Using her charm and good looks, she made it to the room of a young engineer who was drawing plans for defensive fortifications. The temptation was too much for the actress, and when the officer's back was turned, she lifted the plans. She decided to get them to Nashville immediately.

Using stolen clothes, she dressed as a man and rode north looking for a Federal patrol scouting from the Union base at Murfreesboro. But she got caught. She was taken before Braxton Bragg, the Confederate commander, who ordered her court-martialed. She was found guilty and sentenced to death by hanging.

Pauline Cushman cheated the hangman. Becoming seriously ill—either real or feigned—she was kept in jail. Then the Federals' Middle Tennessee Campaign started, and within a few days, Bragg ordered the retreat to Tullahoma. Pauline Cushman was left behind and was set free by Federal troops when they entered Shelbyville.

The Northerners who reached town in June 1863 were greeted as liberators, and not just by Pauline Cushman. Shelbyville was decidedly Union in its sympathies. Many of the town's leading citizens—even some who owned slaves—were against secession and never took up the Confederate cause.

Leave the square by backtracking one block on Depot Street. Turn left on North Brittain Street at the Capri Theater and drive three blocks to East Franklin Street. Park at First Presbyterian Church, located on the corner, for a brief walk through the East Shelbyville Historic District.

Located east of North Brittain and south of Madison Street, the district takes in ten square blocks of the original 1810 town and contains Shelbyville's largest concentration of historic buildings. Most are residences dating from the early 1800s to the early 1900s.

Constructed in 1854, First Presbyterian Church is one of the finest Greek Revival–style churches in Tennessee. It is reminiscent of St. Mary's Catholic Church in Nashville, and the lantern on the top is similar to the one on Tennessee's Capitol. Both Nashville buildings were designed by William Strickland. His influence can be seen in this building, designed by English immigrant William H. Gosling.

From the church, walk east on Franklin Street.

James Deery was an early merchant who gave each of his four daughters lots upon which to build houses. Three of these homes still stand in the East Shelbyville Historic District. You will reach one of them at the corner of Franklin and Jefferson streets; its address is 602 North Jefferson. This is one of the oldest houses in town. The original part of the home

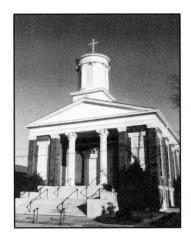

Shelbyville's First Presbyterian Church

(Above and below)
Houses built by James Deery's
daughters

Governor Prentice Cooper House,
featuring James S. Gilliland's
stonework

was built in 1833. The Victorian-era porches are among the several alterations the home has seen over the years.

Continue east on Franklin. Another of Deery's daughter's houses is located at 403 East Franklin, at the corner of Deery Street. This home was built in the 1840s.

Next door at the corner of Bryant Street is the third house, located at 407 East Franklin. Built around 1859, this is one of the most elaborate and pretentious homes in the district.

The fourth daughter's house still stands, too, only in another part of town.

From the corner of Franklin and Bryant streets, return to Deery Street and turn left (S). After one block, turn left (E) on Lane Street to see the enormous Cooper House, located on the left at 413 Lane. This structure is best known as the home of Prentice Cooper, Tennessee's governor from 1939 to 1945. Cooper also served from 1946 until 1948 as the United States ambassador to Peru. This massive house was built by his father in 1904.

The stone wall surrounding the Cooper estate is the work of one of the most intriguing people in Shelbyville's history, craftsman James S. Gilliland. Born a slave in 1858, Gilliland built many stone structures around town in his ninety-one years, including his own unusual house at 803 Lipscomb Street. He was a remarkable man in other respects as well.

He attended Turner Normal Institute, a local school for blacks, where he studied music, among other subjects. In addition to leading a band, he often cut musical scores into his stonework. A tablet he created in 1897 containing part of the score of "Home Sweet Home" was exhibited at the Tennessee Centennial Exposition at Nashville that year.

Gilliland was known for his generosity, often employing men just because they needed work. He was one of the local citizens who organized a relief effort in the 1917 food crisis. A devout Christian, he acquired considerable land— over three hundred acres—and sold it to the poor on terms they could afford. He also maintained an extensive library.

The school Gilliland attended was begun by the African Methodist Episcopal Church in 1885. During the administration of J. H. Turner in 1895, it came to be known as the Turner Normal and Industrial Institute, and bore that name until 1908, when it became Turner Normal College.

It met in several buildings until 1912, when an impressive two-story brick building was constructed. The school housed fifty to sixty boys and a like number of girls and served day students as well. Turner Normal College promoted itself as a place for "the preparation of men and women for usefulness in life through moral, intellectual, and industrial training, with a special emphasis on character building." Financial difficulties forced the school to close in 1927. The building was taken over by the Musgrave Pencil Company for use as a warehouse.

Another remarkable success story from Gilliland's era is that of Wade Gosling, who was also born a slave. In 1878, deciding it was time to go into business for himself, Gosling borrowed twenty-nine dollars from Albert Frierson and started The Great Variety Store. From that point, he went on to become one of Shelbyville's most prosperous businessmen and largest landowners.

But he was not satisfied with just making money. As he notes in his memoirs, he "found it a great help to lay down certain strict rules for myself for reading, study, play, and for my life in every way, and I always tried to follow these, allowing no excuse." Gosling read law under one of the town's most prominent lawyers. After four years, he "stood a verbal examination and was admitted to the bar" as he puts it. He became the area's first black lawyer.

Like Gilliland, he was a voracious reader. His library included "8 volumes of *Chambers' Encyclopedia*, 24 volumes of the *American Encyclopedia*, 10 volumes of *Encyclopedia Britannica*, besides Shakespeare, Dickens, Hugo, *Gaskell's Compendium*, *Peel's Educator*, and other standard works." Gosling studied French and Latin, as well as music. It was his rule to practice "one hundred songs every day and five hundred on Sunday."

From the Cooper House, walk two blocks west on Lane Street to North Jefferson. The impressive Greek Revival house on the corner at 404 North Jefferson is the former home of Erwin James Frierson, a lawyer who came to Shelbyville after having studied in the office of future president James K. Polk in Columbia.

On the opposite corner at 210 East Lane Street is the Church of the Redeemer. This Episcopal church was the original Presbyterian church in town. By the time the Episcopalians took it over in 1934 and added the entryway, it had also served as a Catholic church and a Methodist church. Built in 1825, it is thought to be Shelbyville's oldest building.

Turn right off Lane Street onto North Jefferson Street and walk north to Franklin Street. Turn left to return to your car.

Though not included on the tour, the Tennessee Walking Horse Celebration Grounds are located just east of the East Shelbyville Historic District. The grounds include a museum dedicated to the Tennessee Walking Horse.

The annual Tennessee Walking Horse National Celebration, held for ten days in late summer, draws nearly a quarter-million visitors and thirty-seven hundred entries. Several of the stables offer tours; information about them can be obtained at the museum or at the chamber of commerce, located at 100 North Cannon Boulevard, northwest of the square.

When you are ready to leave the historic district, drive east on Franklin Street to Deery Street. Turn right (S) and go three blocks back to Depot Street. The old Shelbyville Depot, beautifully restored as an adult education center, is on the right at the intersection. For reasons that remain a mystery, the people of Shelbyville did not want the main line of the Nashville & Chattanooga Railroad to come through town, so the depot is located on a branch line completed in 1852, around the same time as the main line.

Turn left (E) on Depot (TN 64) and head out of town. After 3.3 miles, you will come to U.S. 41A. Turn right (SE) and drive 4.8 miles to Normandy Road, crossing the Duck River along the way. Turn left (E) onto Normandy Road.

The house on the right after 0.8 mile has an interesting history. It is said to have been built before 1829, but it is in a style that was not popular until a decade or two later. At any rate, William Oscar Jenkins bought the house in 1941. It was in bad repair, so he had it completely torn down and rebuilt, using the exact same design and most of the yellow poplar lumber, as well as all the doors and windows.

Continue on Normandy Road across a high ridge. After 4.8 miles, you will come to TN 269 at Normandy. Cross the tracks to the row of commercial buildings. The beautiful two-story white frame house to the left of the buildings was built shortly after the Civil War by L. T. Thornberry. At one time, it was used as a boardinghouse.

Normandy is the smallest of three gems strung along the railroad in east Bedford County; Wartrace and Bell Buckle are the others. Normandy grew up where the Nashville & Chattanooga Railroad crossed Norman's Creek. By the 1870s, it was an important market town in this area.

Normandy received a major boost in 1889, when a company was incorporated that developed the residential area east of the railroad. Called the Normandy Immigration, Real Estate, and Labor Association, it sold fifty-seven lots. Not much in the way of business remains in Normandy, but the residential area contains attractive Victorian-era houses and some lovely churches.

There are several interesting sites near Normandy not on the tour. The George Dickel Distillery, located a short distance up Cascade Hollow Road, offers public tours. East of town via Huffman Road are the TVA's Normandy Dam, a new fish hatchery run by the Tennessee Wildlife Resources Agency, and Bedford Lake, owned by the same agency.

Leaving Normandy, recross the railroad tracks to TN 269 and turn right (N). TN 269 is known as Cortner Road, Knob Creek Road, and Albert Dement Highway as it runs through the prosperous, picturesque Duck River countryside between Normandy and Wartrace.

The Sims House is located on the left 7.9 miles from Normandy. Built in 1884 for John Green and Mary Wright Sims, this house stands as the area's best-preserved example of the Queen Anne and Eastlake styles.

Continue on TN 269 to the main part of Wartrace. This railroad town has its share of interesting houses and churches, most of them dating to the 1870 and 1880s. Take time to explore.

Andrew Jackson supposedly gave the town its unusual name. An old Indian war trail came through here. Jackson, who owned land nearby, carved these words into a beech tree by the creek: "This is Wartrail Creek." By the time the railroad was built, the name of the creek had been corrupted to Wartrace, and the railroad gave that name to its depot in 1851.

The most prominent building along the railroad tracks is the Walking Horse Hotel, built in 1917. Jesse Robert Overall and his wife, Nora, operated a hotel called the Overall House at Smyrna in adjoining Rutherford County. The Overalls heard reports from salesmen and other travelers that Wartrace had no hotel, a significant omission in those days, since Wartrace was a busy junction where the branch line to Shelbyville connected to the main line. So they built Hotel Overall.

Floyd's Walking Horse Hotel, formerly Hotel Overall

Floyd and Olive Carothers bought the place around 1930 and changed the name to Floyd's Walking Horse Hotel. It was through the efforts of Carothers and Albert Dement that Wartrace can justifiably boast of being the "Cradle of the Tennessee Walking Horse." Carothers, a renowned horse trainer, bought a plow horse for $350 and patiently trained him into a Tennessee Walking Horse here on the hotel grounds. That horse, Strolling Jim, was selected the first Tennessee Walking Horse World Grand Champion in 1939. Strolling Jim is buried behind the hotel.

The walking horse celebration at Shelbyville got its start at Wartrace. The horse show was the big event at the annual Farmer's Carnival, but by 1935, the show outgrew the limited facilities at Wartrace, so it was moved.

The distinctive features of the Tennessee Walking Horse are its easy gait and easy disposition. It was bred as a riding horse for use on farms, where its running walk provides a gentle, even ride. The breed got its name almost by accident. It had been known as the "Southern plantation saddle horse," the "fox walker," the "all-purpose horse," the "horse of all work," and the "nodding walking horse," among other names. Buyers from outside the region would come to Middle Tennessee looking for "those walking horses," and the name stuck.

The Tennessee Walking Horse has been a special type for some time. But as an organized breed, it dates only to the 1930s. Jim McCord, a newspaperman in Lewisburg—and later Tennessee's governor—met Burt Hunter on the street one day in April 1935, and the two of them agreed that the pedigree of the horses should be registered. The Tennessee Walking Horse Breeders' Association, started that same year, still has its headquarters in Lewisburg. In less than ten years, the popularity of the breed skyrocketed. Since 1935, nearly three hundred thousand horses have been registered.

Bell Buckle is a straight shot up the historic railroad line, now part of the CSX system. Though the quickest way to get there from Wartrace is up TN 269, the tour route goes the long way, meandering through some of Middle Tennessee's most pleasant countryside.

Turn east off TN 269 onto TN 64 leaving Wartrace. After cresting a hill, you will see spread out before you the rich valley of the Duck River's Garrison Fork, where brilliant green pastures sweep up to forested hilltops. This is a transition zone between the Central Basin's rocky cedar forests, to the north, and the Highland Rim's Oak Barrens, to the south.

Even during the chaos of the Civil War, the beauty of this land did not go unnoticed. Lieutenant General William J. Hardee, commander of the right flank of the Confederates' Duck River line, headquartered at Wartrace, wrote in April 1863 that the area was "beautiful and rich in pastures." A visiting British army officer noted in his diary that this is "beautiful country, green, undulating, full of magnificent trees, principally beeches, and the scenery was by far the finest I had seen in America as yet."

It is 4.4 miles from Wartrace to the crossroads at Fairfield.

Just across Garrison Fork, one of the oldest structures in this area stands on the left side of Dr. Jackson Road. The back part of it was once a tavern that offered accommodations to travelers. The structure is reported to have been built in 1790, but that seems a bit early. In 1850, a residence was added to the building by Dr. Robert and Elizabeth Singleton. The Singletons operated a mill here until it was dismantled by advancing Federal troops in June 1863. After the war, the mill was reopened across and up the river in a structure that serves as a residence today.

From the time the first mill was started here in 1812 until the railroad bypassed town in 1851, Fairfield was an important place. It was actually two towns at one time. The west side of Garrison Fork, where the highway now runs, was called Petersburg. Fairfield was on the east side of the river. The two merged into Fairfield in the 1830s.

Continue on TN 64 up the Garrison Fork Valley past some substantial old farmhouses. The Martin House is on the left 2.8 miles from Fairfield.

Barkley and Matthew Martin, two soldiers who fought in the American Revolution, married two sisters, Rachel and Sarah Clay, cousins of Henry Clay, the great senator from Kentucky. The two brothers made an exploratory trip to Middle Tennessee when it was still the frontier. Impressed with this verdant valley, they returned with their families and settled on two thousand acres. This Federal-style house was built in 1809.

The Martins' mother, Elizabeth, was a cousin of John Marshall, chief justice of the United States. Rachel Clay Martin and Grace Martin, wife of another of Elizabeth Marshall Martin's sons, were heroines in their own right during the Revolutionary War. One night while staying with their mother-in-law at the Martins' South Carolina home while their husbands were off at war, they got word that a British courier conveying important dispatches would pass by their house, guarded by two soldiers. They dressed in their husbands' clothes, took pistols, and hid along the road to ambush the British party.

The women so startled the men that they gave up their papers without a fight. Later, the courier and his guards stopped at the Martins' house to spend the night. They explained what had happened at the hands of the two men, never suspecting that the young Martin women were their assailants.

Turn left on TN 82 (Webb Highway) 0.6 mile past the Martin House and continue through this beautiful countryside. After 5.7 miles, the road passes through the middle of Webb School just inside Bell Buckle.

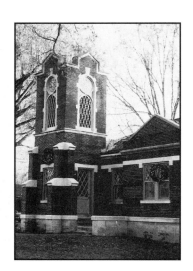

Webb School

Swaney Webb was looking for a place to relocate his school. With his younger brother John, this Civil War veteran and graduate of the University of North Carolina had started a school in the Maury County village of Culleoka, only to grow unhappy about the sale of alcoholic beverages in the town. Bell Buckle was a thriving railroad town in the 1880s, three times its current size. In 1886, the local people offered the Webbs a substantial financial incentive to move the school here. Webb School became a premier Latin boarding school in the South. It counts among its graduates ten Rhodes scholars, the governors of three states, and a host of other prominent people.

Swaney Webb was active in politics as well as education, serving briefly in the United States Senate to fill a vacancy created by an incumbent's death. He lived until 1926. Supervision of the school passed to his son, Will, who ran it until 1952. From then on, it has been run by an independent board of trustees.

The little white frame schoolhouse on the left of the road is the original 1886 building. Called the Junior Room, it was painstakingly restored in 1976 and now houses a small museum.

Continue into Bell Buckle. The old railroad hotel is on the left at the main intersection and a row of shops on the right.

More that its sister towns down the line, Bell Buckle is thriving commercially, having turned itself into a charming little tourist town. Its row facing the railroad is packed with fascinating shops.

Among the several legends regarding the origin of Bell Buckle's intriguing name, there is one that seems the most reliable. At least it is the one most often told. As the story goes, an Indian killed a pioneer settler's cow near a creek and left its bell tied to a tree with a buckle. The creek got the name Bell Buckle. The town took its name from the creek.

Take time to explore Bell Buckle, High and Maple Streets in particular. The town is noted for its charming Victorian-era houses and lovely churches.

Turn north off TN 82 onto TN 269 (Main Street); TN 269 becomes known as Liberty Pike leaving Bell Buckle. The route climbs out of the valley of Wartrace Creek for 4 miles to Liberty Gap, where it crosses the hills that separate the watersheds of the Cumberland and Tennessee rivers.

Liberty Gap played a key role in William S. Rosecrans's successful June 1863 campaign to run the Confederates out of Middle Tennessee. As part of his plan to confuse the Southern forces, he sent a large portion of his army against Liberty Gap. The Union troops had no intention of breaching the gap and marching to Shelbyville. They just wanted to make the Southerners think that is what they were up to. And it worked. The Federals kept a sizable number of Confederates tied up for three days here at Liberty Gap, while the main thrust was 6 miles to the east through Hoovers Gap. As the Southerners retreated to Tullahoma, the Federals here at Liberty Gap backed up, marched to Hoovers Gap, and headed straight for Manchester.

After descending the north face of Liberty Gap, TN 269 levels off in the cedars. At a stop sign 3.5 miles from the gap, stay on TN 269 as it makes a sharp left turn. The road intersects U.S. 231 after passing the edge of the pleasant village of Christiana and crossing the railroad.

The tour ends here. Murfreesboro and Interstate 24 are a few miles to the right (N). Shelbyville is to the left (S).

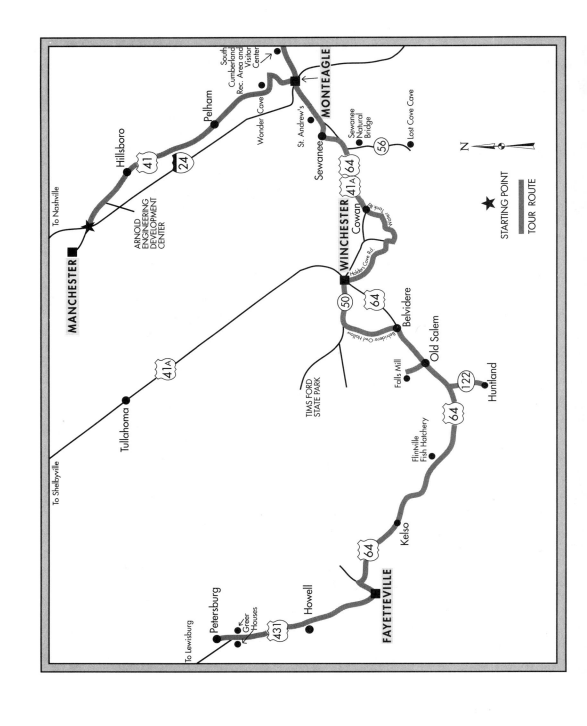

The Elk River Tour

This tour starts near the Elk River's scenic headwaters, circles part of the Cumberland Plateau, then follows the lovely valley of the lower Elk River through some of Middle Tennessee's prettiest towns. On the plateau, it visits Monteagle and Sewanee, home of the University of the South. Off the mountain, it stops at Cowan and its railroad museum and Winchester as well. From the beautiful, green countryside at the foot of the Cumberlands, the tour goes to Fayetteville, with its inviting square and lovely residential neighborhoods. It ends at the well-preserved old town of Petersburg.

Total length: approximately 100 miles

This tour begins just south of Manchester where U.S. 41 crosses Interstate 24 at Exit 114. Travel south on U.S. 41. After 2.8 miles, turn right (W) onto the road leading to the Arnold Engineering Development Center (AEDC). Details about the mission of AEDC are given in The Duck River Tour, page 290.)

At AEDC, the United States Air Force and the Tennessee Wildlife Resources Agency cooperatively manage a 40,000-acre reservation where natural preservation coexists with the world's largest aerospace testing facility. AEDC is considered one of Tennessee's finest wildlife management areas, due primarily to the diversity of habitat, which ranges from a hardwood forest covering about 40 percent of the land to 4,000-acre Woods Reservoir. The property also boasts two registered natural landmarks—Goose Pond, a 158-acre natural marsh, one of the very few undisturbed marshes left on the Highland Rim; and Sinking Pond, a 394-acre area that includes a 149-acre virgin swamp forest.

To say that the deer-herd restoration that began in 1960 with the introduction of sixty-four deer has been successful is an understatement. By the mid-1990s, the deer population reached three thousand. An abundance of other wildlife thrives as well, including wild turkeys, bald eagles, hawks, ospreys, and mink.

After exploring AEDC, return to U.S. 41 and continue south toward Hillsboro. The route emerges from the Oak Barrens and begins traversing the Highland Rim's interior. The fertile fields and green pastures, set against the Cumberland Plateau's escarpment rising on three sides, make this a particularly beautiful drive.

It is 2.8 miles to Hillsboro. The pioneers recognized this as fertile land, so the area around Hillsboro was settled early. Hillsboro was a stop on The Great Stage Road, which once carried travelers between Philadelphia and New Orleans and from Alabama north to Kentucky. The current road between Winchester and McMinnville crosses U.S. 41 at Hillsboro and follows the old stage road.

Incidentally, this is the Hillsboro that caused the village southeast of Nashville to change its name to Leipers Fork.

Stay on U.S. 41 through Hillsboro and enter Grundy County, established in 1844 and named in honor of Felix Grundy, United States congressman and senator and attorney general under President Martin Van Buren.

It is 9.2 miles from Hillsboro to the village of Pelham. Just south of Pelham, U.S. 41 crosses the Elk River, whose waters have tumbled off the mountain to begin a 220-mile trip across the southern part of Middle Tennessee to the Tennessee River in north Alabama.

Turn left off U.S. 41 at the sign for Wonder Cave 3.3 miles from Pelham. You will enter a beautiful mountain cove, make two right-angle turns marked by signs for the cave, and come to the cave itself after 0.6 mile.

Rock City, Ruby Falls—at one time, there seemed to be no limit to the signs hawking mountain attractions to southbound tourists on U.S. 41. Wonder Cave had an advantage—it was the first attraction they came to. And for many Midwesterners, this was their first glimpse of a mountain.

Wonder Cave's proprietors did not want to disappoint visitors, so they decorated the grounds with religious statuary. Cave tours were conducted by lantern, as there were no electric lights in the cave. This added to the excitement. But progress brought the operation to a halt, or almost so. The stretch of Interstate 24 up the mountain was one of the first to be built in Tennessee, and when the traffic left U.S. 41, there was a 90-percent drop in visits to Wonder Cave.

Three Vanderbilt University students exploring here in 1897 discovered

Religious statuary decorating Wonder Cave

the cave. As the twentieth century was getting under way, owner J. J. Raulston started to promote the cave to tourists. He built the impressive log house, which served as a ticket office, gift shop, and residence, and constructed the small stone building at the cave entrance.

The cave is still open in the summer. Visitors can take a guided lantern tour back in the cave for about a mile.

From Wonder Cave, return to U.S. 41, and turn left (S). The road immediately begins a circuitous 3-mile climb to the Cumberland Plateau, gaining a thousand feet in elevation.

Where U.S. 41 intersects U.S. 64 on the top of the mountain, turn left, staying on U.S. 41. You will soon enter the town of Monteagle. Turn left into the Monteagle Sunday School Assembly after 0.2 mile.

Monteagle owes its existence to the Mountain Goat—not an animal, but a railroad affectionately known by that name.

Leslie Kennedy was an Irishman with experience in the Pennsylvania coal fields. He came to this mountain looking for coal in 1850. He found it. Kennedy then interested Nashville lawyer William N. Bilbo in securing investors. Finding little interest in Nashville, Bilbo aroused the interest of New Yorker Samuel F. Tracy.

Tracy and his group of investors were willing to gamble. They formed a company and named it for what was believed to be an Indian word for the mountain—the Sewanee Mining Company. The company engaged engineer A. E. Barney to do what seemed impossible in those days—build a railroad to the top of the mountain. It would connect with the new Nashville & Chattanooga line at Cowan. In 1856, within a year or two of the time the first train made the trip between Nashville and Chattanooga, the Mountain Goat hauled its first load of coal down the mountain.

The Sewanee Mining Company lasted only until 1860. It was taken over by a new company of Tennessee investors and renamed the Tennessee Coal and Railroad Company. The Mountain Goat was eventually absorbed into the Nashville, Chattanooga & St. Louis Railroad. It hauled its last passenger down the mountain in 1971, then was abandoned a few years later.

John Moffat was looking for a new place to live when he came here in 1869. Dissatisfied with the lack of success of his Cincinnati-based Temperance Alliance, the Scottish-born Canadian temperance advocate was riding the Mountain Goat to Tracy City to meet with the Swiss colonists at nearby Gruetli. Right near this spot, the train hit a cow. While the crew was disengaging the cow, Moffat supposedly wandered down a ravine and, impressed by the place's natural beauty, conceived of the idea for a development on the mountain.

Moffat became acquainted with Arthur St. Clair Colyar, the Nashville lawyer and politician who headed the Tennessee Coal and Railroad Company. Colyar shared Moffat's interest in the temperance movement, so when he formed a company to promote settlement on the mountain, he hired Moffat as its manager.

John Moffat brought his family to this narrow strip of the Cumberland Plateau in 1870. In 1881, the former leader of the temperance movement changed the name of his community, Moffat Station, to Mount Eagle, supposedly after a Canadian friend, Lord Mounteagle.

The Monteagle Sunday School Assembly, a thriving summer colony, has nothing to do with Sunday schools today, but it once did. It began as the Moffat Collegiate and Normal Institute—an unsuccessful school promoted by John Moffat—then became a nondenominational Christian assembly, part of the Chautauqua movement begun at Lake Chautauqua, New York, in 1874.

The idea behind a Chautauqua assembly was to combine training for Sunday-school teachers with entertainment and the arts—sort of a combination school session and vacation. The one held in New York State was so popular that others were started around the country. They came to be known simply as Chautauquas.

A Chautauqua was needed in the South, a number of religious leaders concluded, and John Moffat interested them in Monteagle. It was an ideal site, remote enough to give the feeling of a retreat yet easily accessible via the Mountain Goat. The stated purposes of the Monteagle Sunday School Assembly were the "advancement of science, literary attainment, Sunday School interests, and promotion of the broadest public culture in the interest of Christianity without regard to sect or denomination."

The Monteagle Sunday School Assembly's first meeting, held in the summer of 1883, was a huge success, and things took off from there. Eventually, cottages were built. Today, the complex has 162 residences, mostly in the Victorian style. The grounds were planned by William Webster of Rochester, New York, but his elaborate plan was later simplified by F. A. Butler of Nashville.

Adams Edgeworth Inn

The Chautauqua at Monteagle reached its peak in the first two decades of the 1900s and gradually declined thereafter, but it has never ended altogether. It is now more of a summer resort than anything, though there are still cultural programs and arts activities. The Adams Edgeworth Inn is one of two hotels offering lodging to the public. It is open year-round.

After exploring the assembly, return to U.S. 41. Turn left. After 0.5 mile, follow U.S. 41 as it turns left and skirts the boundary of the DuBose Episcopal Conference Center, on the right.

The Fairmount School for Young Ladies was once located here. An unofficial female branch of what was then the all-male University of the South, it operated from 1872 until 1917 on land donated by John Moffat. Among its students was Soong Mei-ling, later Madam Chiang Kai-shek, wife of the president of the Republic of China.

The DuBose Memorial Church Training School started here in 1921 and operated until 1945. Its purpose was to train older men for the Episcopal ministry, with the idea that they would work in rural areas. The school

Claiborne Hall

was named for William Porcher DuBose, the founder and dean of the School of Theology at the University of the South.

Claiborne Hall, the impressive Spanish mission–style building, was built in 1924. It is named for William Sterling Claiborne, one of the school's founders. In recent years, it has served as a conference center.

Continue on U.S. 41. After 2.5 miles, you will reach the South Cumberland Recreation Area Visitors Center, located on the left.

This recreation area is comprised of seven separate natural areas under common management, areas that range in size from 11,400 acres at Savage Gulf State Natural Area to less than an acre at Sewanee Natural Bridge. (For information about Savage Gulf State Natural area, see The Caney Fork Tour, page 383.)

Though not included on this tour, Grundy Forest, one of the natural areas in the South Cumberland Recreation Area, is easily accessible; it can be reached by continuing on U.S. 41 for 3 miles toward Tracy City. At Grundy Forest, an easy trail leads into the beautiful gorge of cascading Big Fiery Gizzard Creek and connects with longer trails leading to the spectacular overlook at Raven Point and to sixty-foot Foster Falls.

No one knows for sure how Fiery Gizzard Creek got its name. In his book, *The Historic Cumberland Plateau: An Explorer's Guide*, Russ Manning relates three theories. One is that a nearby iron-smelting furnace used the creek to test the quality of its coke. Another is that David Crockett burned his tongue on a hot turkey gizzard while camped along the creek. The third is that an Indian chief ripped the gizzard from a turkey and threw it in the fire to get the whites' attention during a treaty negotiation. Whatever the origin, the colorful name adds to the area's intrigue.

From the visitor center, return to Monteagle. At the junction with U.S. 64, head west on U.S. 64/U.S. 41A toward Sewanee. It is 3.6 miles to the entrance to St. Andrew's–Sewanee School, on the right.

In its current form, the school, enrolling about 260 boys and girls, dates to 1981 and the merger of St. Andrew's and Sewanee Academy. Sewanee Academy was the successor to Sewanee Military Academy, which was started in 1909. St. Andrew's began as a school run by Episcopal monks of the Order of the Holy Cross. A notable feature of the 450-acre campus is the Spanish mission–style chapel.

All Saints Chapel

Continue on U.S. 64/U.S. 41A. You will enter a stone gate; veer right off U.S. 64/U.S. 41A into Sewanee and the University of the South. The road into town becomes University Avenue. All Saints Chapel, located on the left after 1.3 miles, is a convenient place to park if you care to enjoy a walk around one of America's most distinctive college campuses; you can pick up a campus map in the admissions office, located across University Avenue from All Saints Chapel.

The heartache Leonidas Polk felt when he passed through this place on July 3, 1863, must have been overwhelming. The Confederate general was leading his infantry corps south, retreating out of Middle Tennessee in a disaster he believed was caused by the incompetence of the Army of Tennessee's commander, Braxton Bragg. But it was more than a military failure that caused Polk's pain. It was the destruction of the school he had helped start just a few years earlier. Leonidas Polk was the driving force behind the beginning of the University of the South.

In his previous life, before he was made a general, Polk was the Episcopal bishop of Louisiana. He conceived the idea of an Episcopal university for the South. In 1856, he met with other Southern bishops to discuss the idea. A site above the "malaria line" was sought, for in those days, the twin plagues of malaria and yellow fever wreaked havoc in the Deep South's lowlands. A mountaintop location would be ideal.

The Sewanee Mining Company, having opened the Mountain Goat line about the same time, was eager to stimulate business along its short route. It donated ten thousand acres of its Sewanee land for the establishment of a university. This "domain" of the University of the South is still intact, allowing the university to boast that it has America's largest campus.

A cornerstone was laid in 1860 and a few small buildings were constructed. Then came the Civil War. Everything stopped. And what little construction had been completed was destroyed. Leonidas Polk never lived to see his dream accomplished. In 1864, a few days short of a year after he led his muddy soldiers over this mountain, a shot from a Union cannon killed the bishop-general near Atlanta. (More information about Polk is given in The Maury County Tour, pages 215–16.)

Charles Todd Quintard, bishop of Tennessee after the Civil War, took up the cause of establishing a university. He, George R. Fairbanks—one of the original trustees—and two priests visited the site in 1866. Quintard and Fairbanks built log houses for their families and took up residence. Quintard's house later burned, but Fairbanks's home, Rebel's Rest, has been restored. It stands on University Avenue diagonally across from All Saints Chapel.

Money was scarce in the post–Civil War South, so Quintard looked to England. There, in 180 days, he preached 200 sermons and received gifts for the school.

Quintard went back to England in 1875 to raise additional funds. During this trip, he met Charlotte Morris Manigault, widow of a Confederate officer, who promptly gave him one hundred pounds. Quintard wrote in his diary, "I shall go back to see Mrs. Manigault." Impressed with his second presentation, she asked the bishop what she should give. He suggested she consider her gift at a service the next day: "There before the God's alter you will decide." After the service, Mrs. Manigault told Quintard, "I will give you your school of theology." And she did.

The centerpiece of the campus is the quadrangle of which All Saints Chapel is a part. Like the other buildings, those in the quadrangle are built of Sewanee sandstone, quarried on the "domain." Most of the buildings were constructed between 1875 and 1915, but All Saints Chapel was not completed until 1957.

The Gothic-style buildings reflect the founders' intent to create a university on the scale of Oxford and Cambridge. Breslin Tower, on the opposite end of the quadrangle from All Saints Chapel, is modeled after Magadalen Tower at Oxford.

Today, the university enrolls eleven hundred undergraduate men and women and seventy-five students at its school of theology.

After enjoying the campus, turn off University Avenue onto Tennessee Avenue and drive to Memorial Cross, located just over 1 mile down Tennessee Avenue. This giant white cross was erected in 1922 as a memorial to "the Sons of Sewanee who answered their Country's Call to Service in the World War 1917–18." The cross was restored in 1982, and memorials were added to Sewanee students and local citizens who served in World War II, Korea, and Vietnam.

Memorial Cross

The cross stands dramatically on the edge of the mountain overlooking the verdant pastures on the Highland Rim a thousand feet below. Several hiking trails wander from the cross along the plateau rim on the university's "domain."

Return to University Avenue and turn right. Turn right (W) on U.S. 64/U.S. 41A in what passes for Sewanee's downtown. Though the name Sewanee is thought to be an Indian name for this mountain, its precise origin is obscure. The mining company used the name first, then the university. To most people, the University of the South is known simply as Sewanee.

TN 56 comes into U.S. 64/U.S. 41A from the left after 0.5 mile. Though they are not included on this tour, two components of the South Cumberland Recreation Area are located down TN 56. Lost Cove Cave—also known as Buggytop Cave—is named for the creek that disappears then reappears flowing out of the cave below a 150-foot bluff; a 2-mile trail leads from the highway to the cave. Sewanee Natural Bridge is a sandstone arch that spans 50 feet at a height of 27 feet; it is just off TN 56 a short distance from U.S. 64/U.S. 41A.

From Sewanee, U.S. 64/U.S. 41A winds down the mountain. There are beautiful views from several pull-offs before the road levels out on the

Cowan Railroad Museum

Highland Rim and enters the pleasant small town of Cowan 6 miles from TN 56. Cross the railroad tracks and turn left into the parking area for the Cowan Railroad Museum.

Cowan made its name as a railroad town. The line through here—the Nashville & Chattanooga, chartered in 1845—was Tennessee's first successful railroad. Construction began in 1848. The first locomotive, the Tennessee, was brought by steamboat to Nashville. It hauled its first train 9 miles to Antioch, now a Nashville suburb, in April 1851. By February 1854, through trains were running between Nashville and Chattanooga.

The Cumberland Plateau was a major obstacle between the two Tennessee towns. It took from 1849 until 1852 to drill a 2,228-foot tunnel through the mountain 1,200 feet above sea level. The steep, winding grades have always required the use of helper engines based at Cowan, so if you see a train coming through, it is likely to have pusher engines on its rear.

The Nashville & Chattanooga Railroad became the nucleus of the Nashville, Chattanooga & St. Louis, formed in 1873, which itself was absorbed into the Louisville & Nashville in 1957. It is now part of the CSX system.

The Cowan Railroad Museum is in the old Cowan Depot, built by the Nashville, Chattanooga & St. Louis in 1904. It is an excellent example of decorative early-twentieth-century railroad architecture. The museum, across the tracks from a pleasant little park, is open May through October.

Cowan was the last stand for the Army of Tennessee during the eleven-day Middle Tennessee Campaign of June and July 1863. General Braxton Bragg, who described himself as "utterly broken down" at Cowan, failed to order the destruction of the tunnel, and the railroad became a vital supply line for the Union army as it moved deeper and deeper into the South.

As Nathan Bedford Forrest's Confederate troopers were bringing up the rear of the retreat through Cowan on July 2, a woman yelled to Forrest, "You great big cowardly rascal, you big cowardly rascal, why don't you turn and fight like a man, instead of running like a cur? I wish old Forrest were here. He'd make you fight!"

After enjoying the museum, turn right (W) on Cowan Street, then right onto Oak Street. Follow Oak to U.S. 64/U.S. 41A. Turn left (W).

Though it is a straight shot of about 6 miles on U.S. 64/U.S. 41A to Winchester, our route meanders on backroads to take in some of Middle

Tennessee's most beautiful scenery. This is good land. The farms are well kept. And the Cumberland Plateau rising in the background adds to the beauty of the place.

After 0.1 mile, turn left onto Water Tank Road. There is a fork at 0.8 mile; bear right. You will reach Goshen Road 2.2 miles from the fork; turn left. Where Goshen turns right at Knight Lane after 0.8 mile, go right, staying on Goshen. You will come to Williams Cove Road after another 0.4 mile; turn right. It is 0.7 mile to Centennial Road; turn left. Drive 1.1 miles to Holders Cove Road and turn right. At the fork after 0.4 mile, stay left on Holders Cove. You will cross the new bypass after another 2.4 miles. Before long, the road becomes Jefferson Street and reaches the square in Winchester.

The 1937 courthouse, a New Deal public-works project, is the seat of government for Franklin County, created in 1807 and named for Benjamin Franklin. General James Winchester of Sumner County was honored by having the town named for him. (Winchester's life is described in The Middle Cumberland Tour, pages 25–27.)

Franklin County was a hotbed of secession before the Civil War, so much so that it tried to secede from Tennessee when the Volunteer State first refused to go along with the Deep South states when they withdrew from the Union.

It was the election of Abraham Lincoln in November 1860 that so inflamed Southern nationalists. Within weeks of the election, South Carolina seceded, followed within two months by six other Deep South states. The Confederate States of America was formed in February 1861. Isham G. Harris, Tennessee's secession-minded governor, promoted a public referendum on secession. However, in a February 9, 1861, election, delegates to a proposed convention who opposed secession outpolled secessionists four to one. Here in Franklin County, the vote was six to one the other way.

A resolution was passed locally and sent to the Tennessee and Alabama legislatures. Franklin County was "out of the Union" and wanted to be out of Tennessee, too, asking to be included in Alabama. The local people raised an infantry regiment for the Confederacy.

Then came Fort Sumter and Lincoln's call for troops to put down the rebellion in the South. Sentiment in Tennessee and the other upper South states changed dramatically. In June 1861, Tennessee became the tenth—and last—of the Southern states to withdraw from the Union.

But Tennessee was too slow for Franklin County residents. That May, before Tennessee seceded, the county's Confederate regiment left for the Deep South to aid the Confederate cause. Peter Turney, an ardent secessionist, led the regiment. He later served as Tennessee's governor from 1893 to 1897.

Incidentally, there is no record of the receipt of Franklin County's secession petition by either the Tennessee or Alabama legislatures. Considering the chaos of the period, that is understandable. Needless to say, Franklin County remains in Tennessee.

Circle around the square to U.S. 64/U.S. 41A. The highways split on the square's northeast corner; turn left (W) on U.S. 64 (First Avenue). The other route—U.S. 41A—is called Dinah Shore Boulevard as it leads away from the square.

Frances Rose Shore was born in Winchester in 1917. When she sang on Nashville's WSM radio during her college days at Vanderbilt University, the theme song of the show was the 1925 hit song "Dinah," a name she eventually took as her own. By the time she died in 1994, Dinah Shore's list of accomplishments was a long one.

She hosted a popular NBC television variety show from 1951 until 1974, a talk show from 1970 to 1984, and finally a show on the Nashville Network from 1989 to 1991. She scored her first number-one recording in 1944 with "I'll Never Walk Alone." Her 1948 hit "Buttons and Bows" spent ten weeks at the top of the charts, a record for a female vocalist that lasted more than thirty years. In all, she had seventy-one hit records.

The versatile singer and actress published three cookbooks, including the best-selling *Someone's in the Kitchen with Dinah*, an interesting blend of Southern and Jewish recipes that reflects her heritage and includes a sampling of recipes from Hollywood celebrities. In Palm Springs, California, where the Dinah Shore Golf Tournament was held for more than twenty years, there is also a street named for her.

After two blocks on U.S. 64, you will reach Trinity Episcopal Church, on the left. This beautiful little Gothic Revival building is virtually unchanged from the time it was built in 1874. The congregation began here in 1859.

Continue past the church to Cedar Street. Turn right.

The house on the left at 309 First Avenue dates to the 1830s. It was used by Union general William S. Rosecrans as his headquarters at the end of the Middle Tennessee Campaign in July 1863.

The house on the northwest corner facing Cedar Street is a Winchester landmark. Smith Morgan Alexander, founder of Winchester's Home Bank and Trust Company, built this Victorian-style house in 1899 and named it Valentine Square after his only daughter, Mary Valentine Alexander.

Follow Cedar through a dogleg for 0.2 mile to a three-way stop. Turn left. You are now on TN 50. Following a turn, TN 50 becomes Lynchburg Road. Stay on it for 4.3 miles to the Owl Hollow community. Turn left (S) onto Belvidere–Owl Hollow Road.

Just ahead on TN 50—but not on the tour—the road to Tims Ford State Park takes off to the right. The park sits on 413 scenic acres overlooking a TVA lake created by a dam built on the Elk River in 1970. The park includes 5 miles of paved bike trails, among other features.

After 3 miles, bear left just past the historic Hillcrest Farmhouse to stay on Belvidere–Owl Hollow Road. It is another 1.4 miles to U.S. 64. Turn right (W). Belvidere stretches along the highway here.

It is not unusual for Middle Tennessee towns to be named for places in North Carolina and Virginia, where the earliest settlers originated, but it *is* unusual for a town to be named for a place in the Midwest. This village is named for Belvidere, Illinois, reflecting the fact that the area was settled by Midwesterners following the Civil War. The name, which means "beautiful view," certainly fits, for the local landscape, within sight of the Cumberland Mountains, is one of Middle Tennessee's most beautiful.

Captain Stephen D. Mather of Illinois, a Union soldier passing through here during the Civil War, realized that the area was prime agricultural land. He bought three hundred acres and relocated here in 1867. Before long, a number of others followed.

A Swiss immigrant and Union veteran named John Kaserman was looking for a place in the South to relocate, too. His doctor warned him that due to a respiratory illness, he would not survive two more Ohio winters. Kaserman and his father, Samuel, traveled through parts of seven Southern states looking for a place to settle before finding themselves southeast

Winchester house used as headquarters by Union general William S. Rosecrans

of Winchester. Impressed with the scenery below the Cumberland escarpment, Samuel said that this was the spot where he wished to spend the rest of his days. It reminded him of his native Switzerland.

John Kaserman promoted widespread settlement of German and Swiss families after he bought his farm in 1868. Most of the settlers did not come directly from Europe, but rather from their homes in several Northern states. Some came from Gruetli, the struggling Swiss colony on the harsh Cumberland Plateau near Tracy City. The settlers started a German Reformed church; through several mergers, that denomination became part of the United Church of Christ. The Belvidere congregation is still active.

Though neither John nor Samuel was a farmer, they took up farming on the worn-out land. Using progressive conservation practices from Switzerland, they restored the area to some of the most productive land in Tennessee.

The drive on U.S. 64 from Belvidere is beautiful. Franklin County's abundant nurseries spread out to the left of the highway, then give way to pastures, which in turn give way to the foothills of the Cumberlands.

You will come to the Old Salem community after 4.8 miles. Turn right (N) onto Salem-Lexie Road. After 1.3 miles, turn left onto Falls Mill Road to reach Falls Mill.

Falls Mill

The impressive three-story brick building was constructed in 1873. But this spot on Factory Creek was used for industry long before that. The first mill opened in 1810. In those days, Franklin County was a leading producer of cotton; by 1815, there were at least twelve cotton gins in the county. The town of Salem grew into an important shipping point, as cotton was carried on flatboats down Beans and Factory creeks to the Elk River and eventually all the way to New Orleans.

The mills gradually shifted their emphasis from ginning to the milling of grain and the production of cotton cloth. Textile mills were called factories, and that is how the creek got its name. Salem started to decline in importance when turnpikes were constructed in the 1840s. Turnpikes provided an alternative to the flatboats, which could travel downstream only when the creeks were flooded. Then the railroad bypassed Salem. Finally, in 1873, the entire town was destroyed by fire.

Two men who were important in local textile milling were Robert N.

Mann and Azariah David. They built the present mill on the site of an earlier mill. Hired to run the mill was a Frenchman, F. J. Rachielles, whose two-story frame residence is nearby.

The brick structure up the creek was built as a gristmill about 1897.

Several different enterprises operated in the Falls Mill building over the years, including a textile mill and a cotton gin. As late as 1935, a cotton gin here produced about a thousand bales per year. The building was also used as a gristmill and a woodworking plant. The large steel waterwheel, the largest of its kind still operating in the United States, was added in 1886.

Robert N. Mann's 1850 house at Falls Mill

Restoration of the structure as a gristmill began in 1968. Milling equipment was purchased from old mills in several states. Today, the mill produces a number of quality grain products. Falls Mill is open to the public year-round. In addition to being the site of a historic mill, this spot on Factory Creek is a pleasant natural area as well.

Retrace your route to U.S. 64 and turn right (W). On the left after 0.2 mile is one of the earliest houses in this area. George Gray, originally from North Carolina, settled here around 1810. Family tradition says that he and his wife, Lucy Benning, finished the house in 1825.

On the left after another 0.2 mile is the Peter Simmons House, built around the same time. Simmons was a major cotton dealer during Salem's cotton-market days.

Stay on U.S. 64 for 0.7 mile to TN 122. Turn left (S) and head for the pleasant small town of Huntland. TN 122 becomes Main Street in Huntland. Stay on Main Street, disregarding TN 122's turn to the right and TN 97's turn to the left. Huntland is a beautiful little railroad town, though the railroad is no longer here. It holds some interesting houses and churches, particularly south of downtown.

You will reach a T intersection near a school 1.8 miles from U.S. 64. Turn around and retrace your route to U.S. 64. Turn left (W). The route now enters Lincoln County. As the Cumberlands continue their southwesterly course into Alabama, the highway swings northwest.

After 8.1 miles, turn right onto Fish Hatchery Road. You will drop through a forested hollow for 0.5 mile to the Flintville Fish Hatchery.

The federal government built this facility here in Warren Hollow, but it is now owned by the Tennessee Wildlife Resources Agency. Rainbow trout are reared here for stocking in fifty or so cool, clear Middle Tennessee streams. The wooded hills surrounding the hatchery comprise a 750-acre wildlife management area. Visitors are welcome at the hatchery.

Warren Hollow takes its name from an industry that used to operate here. It began as the Crosby Spinning Factory in 1837, then became the Warren Woolen Mill in 1839. It was a flour mill from 1890 to 1910.

Return to U.S. 64 and turn right (W). It is 13 miles to the junction with U.S. 231 Bypass (Taylor Thorton Parkway) on the outskirts of Fayetteville.

Along the way, the route descends from the Highland Rim into the valley of the Elk River, passes the village of Kelso, and crosses the Elk River.

There is a little romance attached to the name Kelso. Shortly after the completion of the railroad through here in 1859, a locomotive engineer, a Mr. Allison, asked that a newly built locomotive be named Belle Kelso. He was in love with Belle, one of Lincoln County's fairest and most intelligent young women. She was, in fact, the daughter of Henry Kelso, the little town's leading citizen. Belle was apparently impressed by Allison's gesture. She and the engineer later married.

The stretch of the Elk River from Tims Ford Dam to Fayetteville is a popular float stream and a particular favorite of bass and trout fishermen. Canoe outfitters are available near Kelso.

Turn right at U.S. 231 Bypass and get in the left lane. At the stop sign after 0.3 mile, turn left onto Shelbyville Highway. After 0.1 mile, a road to the right leads to the Elk Cotton Mill. A magnificent house stands on the left.

"Good opportunity for intelligent girls to make a good living at easy work. The Elk Cotton Mill will begin work between the first and tenth of March and want [sic] about 25 women and girls to work in the factory. A sprightly girl of 13 or 14 years of age can learn in a week to make from 50 to 75 cents per day. Widows with large families of girls preferred." So read an advertisement for the mill, which opened here in 1900. It still operates in its classic turn-of-the-century building.

The large house on the left was built in 1858 by John Whitaker for his daughter when she married John Rees. The Rees family started the Elk Cotton Mill.

Rees family home near Elk Cotton Mill

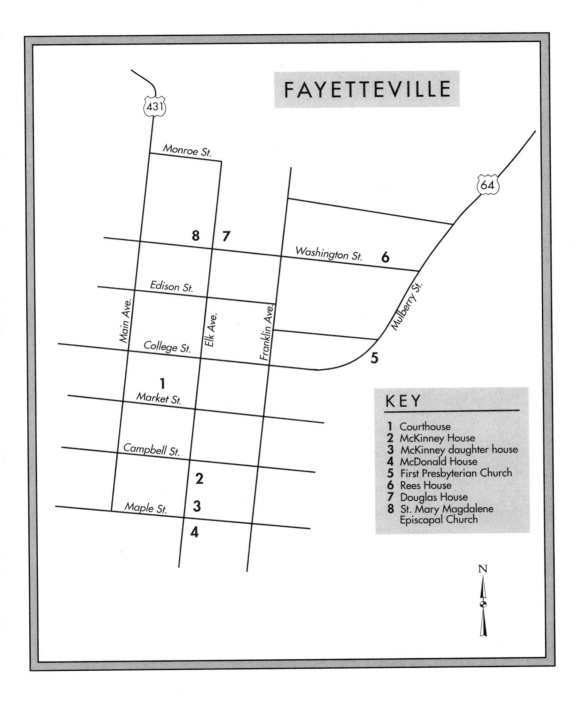

FAYETTEVILLE

431

Monroe St.

64

8 7

Washington St. 6

Edison St.

Main Ave.

Elk Ave.

Franklin Ave.

Mulberry St.

College St.

5

1

Market St.

Campbell St.

2

Maple St. 3

4

KEY

1 Courthouse
2 McKinney House
3 McKinney daughter house
4 McDonald House
5 First Presbyterian Church
6 Rees House
7 Douglas House
8 St. Mary Magdalene
   Episcopal Church

N

Continue past the road to the cotton mill to rejoin U.S. 64; turn right. U.S. 64 follows Mulberry Street and then College Street to Fayetteville's square.

Middle Tennessee has some lovely public squares, but few are as pleasant as this one in the town on the Elk River. Some people say this is due to Fayetteville's proximity to the prosperous high-tech city of Huntsville, Alabama, but whatever the reason, the square is loaded with attractive shops and businesses. Two establishments of note on the south side of the square are Honey's and Bill's, at 109 and 111 East Market Street, respectively. These are genuine old-time pool halls, both known for their "slawburgers."

The beauty of Fayetteville's square is enhanced by the Lincoln County Courthouse. Built in the Georgian Revival style 1972, it looks like it belongs in Colonial Williamsburg.

Another Fayetteville institution, located several blocks south of the square on South Main Avenue, is the old Borden Powdered Milk Plant.

"New South" and "industrialization" became credos of newly established chambers of commerce in the 1920s, during the South's first organized attempt to lure Northern industry. It was this movement that helped spark the Agrarians, a group of writers who advocated retention of the rural lifestyle they believed was the soul of Southern culture. (The story of the Agrarians is told in The Red River Tour, pages 52–53, and The Lower Cumberland Tour, page 80.)

When the Ohio-based Borden Milk Company built its plant in Fayetteville in 1927, it became one of the first industries from the North to respond to this new form of boosterism. Before then, dairy farming had not been widespread in Middle Tennessee, but with a market for their milk, many farmers turned to dairy farming. The plant's presence did much to soften the harshness of the Depression around Lincoln County.

Borden ceased operations here in 1967. Today, the plant serves as a community center and museum.

Fayetteville's most famous structure was a great stone bridge built south of town across the Elk River. Started in 1858 and completed in 1861, it included six elliptical arches spanning 450 feet. There was only one other bridge like it in the United States, and only six in the world.

Union general William Tecumseh Sherman made use of the bridge during the Civil War. When he was moving his troops to Chattanooga to help relieve the Confederate siege in November 1863, he rerouted his troops toward Fayetteville, where, as he put it in a report, the "Elk is spanned by a fine stone bridge." In fact, the bridge enabled Sherman's troops to get to Chattanooga on the timetable ordered by Sherman's superior, Ulysses S. Grant.

The story has often been told around Fayetteville that Sherman ordered the bridge destroyed after his men and wagons got over it. Knowing of Sherman's activities a year later in Georgia, this is not surprising. He supposedly ordered a Major Byrd to blow it up, but the major was so taken by the beauty of the span that he refused. The bridge survived.

It was nature that finally claimed the landmark. The sheriff was sitting in his nearby office on a winter day in 1969 when he heard a loud noise, like thunder. He ran out in time to see the bridge falling into the rain-swollen Elk River.

It does not take much of a history scholar to figure out that Lincoln County is *not* named for the our sixteenth president. It is, of course, in the wrong part of the country, and it was established in 1809, long before the senator from Illinois went to the White House. The county is named instead for General Benjamin Lincoln, a hero of the American Revolution.

The earliest settlers had a fondness for their hometown back in North Carolina, so they named this town after one in the Tar Heel State.

Inadequate transportation inhibited growth in the early days of Lincoln County. Steamboats had been plying the inland waterways for many years before the first one made it to Fayetteville. When the steamboat *Union* came to Fayetteville up the Elk River from the Tennessee River in 1850, something of a "steamboat fever" gripped the town. Funds were raised to build the *Lincoln*, which made its maiden voyage up the Elk in 1851.

Under the best of circumstances, the Elk River was navigable only five months of the year. Even then, overhanging trees, rocks, and sand bars made navigation treacherous. Less than a year after it was built, the *Lincoln* sank, ending Fayetteville's short life as a river port. Modern transportation reached Fayetteville in 1859 with the completion of a railroad line, the Winchester & Alabama, which connected with the Nashville & Chattanooga near Winchester.

Fayetteville's square is not the only well-preserved part of town. Two residential districts listed on the National Register of Historic Places hold collections of houses built during a hundred-year period that began in the early 1800s. Park at the square to enjoy a brief walking tour.

South Elk Avenue runs along the east side of the square. The South Elk Avenue Historic District, located just south of the square, takes in parts of South Elk, East Maple, and East Goodlett streets.

Walk south on South Elk and cross Campbell Street to see the house at 304 South Elk, built by Dr. Charles McKinney around 1825. The house is one of the oldest structures in Fayetteville. Built in the Federal style, it gets its eclectic look from repairs and additions made following storm damage during the Victorian era.

An early settler, Dr. Charles McKinney served as a surgeon in the War of 1812 and the Creek War. It was McKinney who treated Sam Houston for the wounds he received at Horseshoe Bend.

The substantial Greek Revival house next door at 310 South Elk, on the corner of East Maple, was built by Dr. McKinney for his daughter in 1845.

The house across East Maple at 400 South Elk is one of Middle Tennessee's most distinctive homes, an example of Gothic Revival architecture unique in the region. It, too, was built as a gift from a doctor McKinney—Dr. R. R. McKinney, Charles's brother—for his daughter upon her marriage in 1859 to R. A. McDonald.

Diagonally across the street at 311 South Elk stands a fine example of a "Stick Style" Victorian house. Built in 1880, it is noted for its octagonal corner turret and wraparound porch.

After enjoying the South Elk Avenue Historic District, return on South Elk to the square and College Street. Turn right and walk east on College to reach the other historic district, called the Mulberry-Washington-Lincoln District. It takes in the streets of those names, as well as North Franklin Avenue, North Elk Avenue, Bright Avenue, North Main Avenue, and Green Street, all north and northeast of the square.

First Presbyterian Church is located at the corner of College and Mulberry streets. The congregation that meets here dates to Fayetteville's earliest days. The church building built in 1832 was destroyed by a tornado, leading to this entry in the church's records: "February 24, 1851, between

"Stick Style" Victorian house in Fayetteville

Fayetteville's First Presbyterian Church

TOURING THE MIDDLE TENNESSEE BACKROADS

the hours of four and five o'clock this instant, it pleased the Almighty to loose the winds of heaven, and our church was crushed to its foundations. The dismembered fragments reminded us that we have no abiding city here below." The Greek Revival church on the site today was built in 1854.

Leaving the church, bear left on tree-shaded Mulberry Street, one of Middle Tennessee's most beautiful. Take time to enjoy the houses, many of which are marked by the Association for the Preservation of Tennessee Antiquities.

Turn left (W) off Mulberry onto Washington Street. Note the 1870 Italianate house at 408 Washington. Ernest Rees, Jr., a member of the family that started the Elk Cotton Mill, lived here in the mid-twentieth century.

Continue on Washington to the intersection with North Elk Avenue, where two of Fayetteville's most distinctive buildings are located.

You will not find another house in Middle Tennessee like the one on the northeast corner of this intersection. During the steamboat era, it was fashionable to add details to houses that were reminiscent of steamboats. Hence the term "Steamboat Gothic," which applies to the two-tiered, richly

Rare 1894 "Steamboat Gothic" house

St. Mary Magdalene Episcopal Church

ornamented veranda that wraps around this Queen Anne–style house. Homes like this are more often found in steamboat country, particularly along the Ohio and Mississippi rivers.

Hugh Bright Douglas owned a thousand-acre farm outside town. When he decided to build this town house in 1894, he had the lumber cut from his farm, then shipped to Nashville—where it was milled and hand-carved—and then returned to Fayetteville for installation.

St. Mary Magdalene Episcopal Church is located on the northwest corner of the intersection. Like First Presbyterian Church, the original structure on this site—a stone church built in 1883—was destroyed by a tornado, though this one came through in 1952. The new structure was built mainly from the old stone. The church's beautiful alter was unharmed.

Walk south on North Elk Avenue to the square to complete the walking tour.

Drive north out of town on U.S. 431, which takes off from the square on North Main Avenue. Soon, the landscape opens into the beautiful bluegrass valley of Cane Creek.

After 5.7 miles, veer left off U.S. 431 onto the old highway at the community of Howell. The lovely Howell Cumberland Presbyterian Church, on the left, houses a congregation that dates to 1815. The camp meetings held here were so well attended that a school, Rye College, was established. This school for preachers was housed in a small cabin. When the school was not in session, the cabin was used to beat rye and wheat— hence the name. The current church building dates to 1858.

Continue through Howell back to U.S. 431. Turn left.

Joseph Greer settled in this area on the grant awarded for his Revolutionary War service. This son of an Irish immigrant was only twenty years old when he fought in the Battle of Kings Mountain near today's Charlotte, North Carolina. He was chosen to carry the news of the victory to the Continental Congress in faraway Philadelphia. Greer built a cabin here along Cane Creek before building a larger home. He lived until 1831.

Between Howell and Petersburg, the route passes two historic houses, both built around 1858. One, set among the pines on Cane Creek Farm, is located on the right 4.3 miles from Howell; this home was built by Jane Caroline Greer on land she got from her father, Joseph Greer. The other house, built by Alex Greer, is on the left 0.8 mile past Cane Creek Farm.

Take the road to the right 0.8 mile from the Alex Greer House to reach Petersburg's town square.

Petersburg, in its current form, dates to the construction of the Duck River Valley Narrow Gauge Railroad between Columbia and Fayetteville in 1874. After the line was widened to standard gauge and absorbed into the Nashville, Chattanooga & St. Louis a few years later, Petersburg evolved into an important market town on the border of Lincoln and Marshall counties. Like most similar towns, it went into a decline when modern highways decreased the importance of the railroad.

Still, this small town holds an impressive collection of churches and houses along High and Russell streets. Take time to explore.

The tour ends here, at the square in Petersburg. You can return to U.S. 431 and go back to Fayetteville or go north to Lewisburg.

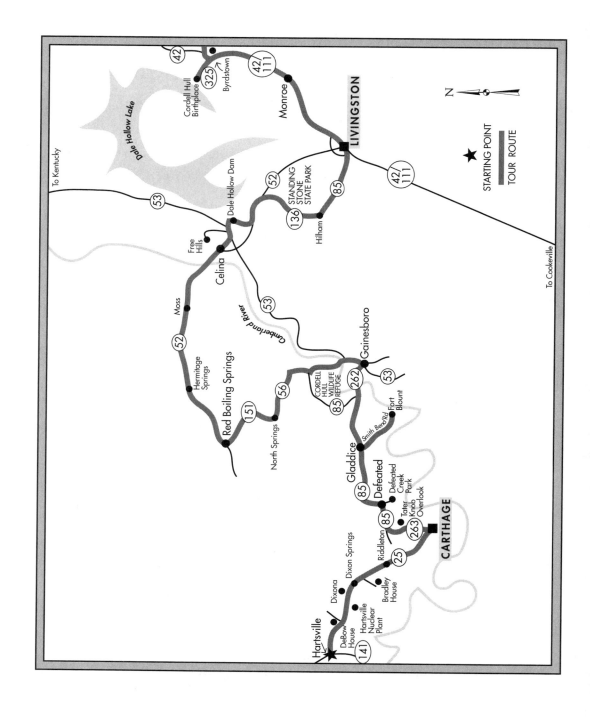

The Upper Cumberland Tour

This tour follows the Upper Cumberland River through its scenic, narrow valley and visits several towns and historic sites and some beautiful natural areas. From its start at Hartsville, it travels to Carthage, then follows the river past Cordell Hull Dam to the site of historic Fort Blount. It visits Red Boiling Springs, grandest of the Middle Tennessee mineral springs resorts, then goes to Celina and Dale Hollow Dam. After traveling through Standing Stone State Park and Livingston, the tour ends at the birthplace of Cordell Hull, winner of the Nobel Peace Prize and father of the United Nations.

Total length:
approximately 156 miles

This tour starts at the courthouse in Hartsville. The town can be reached from Lebanon on TN 141 and from Gallatin on TN 25. The courthouse is located on Main Street.

Defining the part of Tennessee known as the Upper Cumberland is not easy. From the standpoint of the Cumberland River itself, the name Upper Cumberland has been used to describe the river above Nashville, or, at times, the river above Carthage. In broader geographic and cultural terms, however, Upper Cumberland means much more. It refers to a distinct, separate, and some would say unique part of the state.

Folklorist William Lynwood Montell, who has spent a lifetime studying the hills and valleys of the region, describes it this way in his book *Upper Cumberland Country*: "The Upper Cumberland is not *southern* in its folkways, nor is it *Appalachian*. People here never had grits for breakfast until this southern dish was introduced by fast-food chain restaurants. And while residents of the Upper Cumberland may be somewhat more closely aligned to Appalachia than they are to the Deep South, they do not view themselves as part of Southern Appalachia. . . . The Upper Cumberland is a distinctive entity not only in terms of its folk culture but in its geographical location as well."

As used in Tennessee, the name Upper Cumberland usually refers to the Middle Tennessee counties within the Cumberland River watershed upstream from Hartsville. The region extends from the Kentucky border on the north to the McMinnville area on the south and includes practically all of the Eastern Highland Rim, as well as the western part of the Cumberland Plateau. Both this tour and the next one, The Caney Fork Tour, are in the Upper Cumberland.

Trousdale County, of which Hartsville is the county seat, is what local historian Vernon Roddy calls "the runt of the state in size." And it is one of the newest counties, established in 1870. One reason for the establishment of several new, small counties after the Civil War was that the former state constitution—the one enacted in 1834—contained size and distance restrictions for new counties. Freed from those limits by the 1870 constitution, state legislatures created small counties out of existing counties in the 1870s.

Hartsville used to be two towns—Damascus on the east side of Little Goose Creek and Hartsville on the west. The Donoho family settled here around 1797 on a large grant given to Major Thomas Donoho by North Carolina for his Revolutionary War service. The Donohos operated a mill on the east side of the creek, the Damascus side. James and Sarah Hamilton Hart arrived about the same time, settled on Little Goose Creek's west bank, and began operating a ferry. The Harts bought out the Donohos in 1801. Pretty soon, both sides of the creek became known as Hartsville.

Hartsville's character changed in 1892, when the railroad branch was completed. Since then, the town has been known primarily as a tobacco center. The railroad is gone now, but the 1898 depot still stands north of the courthouse on Broadway.

Turney-Hutchins House

From the courthouse, travel east on Main Street past several impressive houses. After 0.5 mile, turn left (N) onto Western Avenue. After passing a factory, look east across the creek bordering the athletic track to see the Turney-Hutchins House. There is not another home in Middle Tennessee like this one. When John Hutchins bought the existing two-story log house on the property in 1857, he wanted to make it over in the Greek Revival style popular with the planter class, so he designed the addition himself. He had no architectural training, and what he came up with was his own hybrid Greek Revival house. The home is surrounded by over two hundred maple trees.

The original log house is one of Middle Tennessee's oldest. Revolutionary War veteran Henry Turney ventured into this area and built a cabin in 1789—a fact established by the discovery that the year had been carved into one of the logs.

Another veteran, William Alexander, bought the property from Turney in 1798. During Alexander's tenure here, Andrew Jackson was a frequent visitor when he came to the noted Hartsville racetrack. Alexander's daughter, Mary Brandon, married William Hall, the man who would succeed Sam Houston as governor when he resigned and left for Texas. (More information about Sam Houston and William Hall can be found in The Middle Cumberland Tour, pages 14–15.)

James R. DeBow House

Continue on Western Avenue to TN 25 (McMurry Boulevard). Turn right (E) on TN 25 to leave Hartsville. After 2.2 miles, you will reach the handsome James R. DeBow House, on the left.

James R. DeBow, of French Huguenot descent, inherited his father's Revolutionary War grant and started building this Italianate house, called Vinewood, as early as 1854. Construction was not finished until 1870. According to local tradition, the meeting to draw the boundary for Trousdale County was held in the front parlor of the James R. DeBow House.

Continue on TN 25. From the crest of the next hill, you will see the lush Cumberland River bottom spread out before you. The huge structure on the horizon is a cooling tower for the TVA's Hartsville nuclear power plant. Or at least is was supposed to be. The plant was never completed.

In case you've ever wondered what $26 billion looks like with all the zeros added, it's $26,000,000,000. That is the debt of the Tennessee Valley Authority, most of it left over from the agency's nearly defunct nuclear power program. The fiscal catastrophe goes back to 1966, when the leadership of the federal corporation decided to embark on the nation's largest commitment to nuclear power. In all, seventeen reactors were planned. Despite warnings that demand for electricity could not support such a massive building program, the TVA plunged ahead.

The Hartsville plant was to have been the world's largest, with four reactors. Over fierce landowner opposition, the TVA took twenty-one hundred acres of prime farmland and went to work building the plant in 1977. Then nuclear power started to go sour, not just in the Southeast, but throughout the world. There were accidents at Three Mile Island in Pennsylvania and Chernobyl in the Ukraine. The public became concerned about safety. Costs escalated rapidly. And the demand for electric power did not approach TVA's inflated estimates.

Conceding that it had overstated demand, the TVA put Hartsville on hold in 1984. Then, in 1994, with nuclear power providing only 13 percent of the TVA's energy but having consumed 44 percent of its budget since 1980, the TVA announced that it was scrapping most of its nuclear power program. The Hartsville cooling tower stands as an expensive monument to a failed policy.

You will enter Smith County and reach Dixona, the house on the left, 3.9 miles from the James R. DeBow House. The earliest part of Dixona, the log structure in the middle, was built by Tilman Dixon in 1789. The columned porch and brick wings are later additions.

Dixona

In 1786, a seemingly insignificant event contributed to the settlement of the Upper Cumberland. Two veterans of the American Revolution, Captains Tilman Dixon and William Walton, who were staying at Mansker's Station in today's Goodlettsville, ascended the Cumberland in a canoe. Their purpose was to locate the lands they would claim for their North Carolina grants. For his 3,840-acre grant, Dixon picked this land. Walton selected his at the mouth of the Caney Fork River at present-day Carthage. These two men, along with Sampson Williams and Moses Fisk, were as responsible as anyone for the settlement of the Upper Cumberland.

Though there were a few brave souls like Henry Turney and Tilman Dixon in this area before the Indian attacks ended in 1795, the eastern limit of the Cumberland settlements was the present-day Castalian Springs area. The pre-1795 trickle quickly turned into a flood. By 1800, there was widespread permanent settlement along the Upper Cumberland and its tributaries. But only up to a point.

The Treaty of Hopewell, entered into with the Cherokees in 1785, was the first Indian treaty negotiated by the new United States government. It drew a line diagonally across eastern Middle Tennessee, then straight west across the southern midstate. Settlers were supposed to stay west and north of the line. When the Third Tellico Treaty of 1805 legalized settlement east and south of the line, settlers spread into the farther reaches of the Upper Cumberland. The eastern part of Middle Tennessee thus has the distinction of being one of the few places in America where people migrated west to east.

Tilman Dixon went back to North Carolina the year he built his log house and married Mary Carlos. They returned and raised a family that included children Americus Vespucius, Don Carlos, Mary Greenway, and Eliza Henry.

Dixona is noted not just for being one of Middle Tennessee's oldest houses, but also as the site of some important events. This is where the first Smith County Court met in 1799.

The Dixons ran an inn here and had some distinguished visitors from time to time. The most famous was Louis Philippe, the duke of Orleans, the future king of France from 1830 to 1848.

Though of royal blood, Louis Philippe was sympathetic to the cause of the French Revolution. Still, he fled France during the terror of 1793. He was in America from 1796 to 1800 and traveled through the West—which included Tennessee in those days—following an itinerary planned by George Washington. Heading east along the old Fort Blount Trail, or Avery Trace, into Middle Tennessee, he took a night's lodging with Captain and Mrs. Dixon in May 1797.

Accommodations here were primitive. The duke had to share a bed with others, something he noted in his diary and complained about to Dixon. "That's the way it is, or, if you prefer, you may sleep out side where the Indians are," Dixon replied. Legend has it that in later years, whenever Louis Philippe encountered anyone from Tennessee, he never failed to inquire whether they still slept four to a bed.

The quaint village of Dixon Springs is located past Dixona. Turn right, then left onto old TN 25, the town's Main Street, which runs parallel to the new highway.

A town started to grow up here on Tilman Dixon's grant around 1803, when John and Robert Allen built a store. (The short marriage of John Allen's daughter Eliza to Sam Houston is described in The Middle Cumberland Tour, pages 14–15.) The Allens' store no longer exists, but a store dating to 1900 still stands on Main Street just east of Rome Road. Another building of interest on Main Street is picturesque Union Church, built in 1878 and used by all denominations.

Union Church

After driving through Dixon Springs on Main Street, you will rejoin TN 25. Continue east. A marker 0.4 mile from the junction notes the location of the Bradley House, which stands down a gravel road called Lovers Lane. Captain James Bradley migrated to the Upper Cumberland before 1800 and eventually came to own two thousand acres of good Cumberland River bottom. His 1805 Federal-style house reflects his prosperity. The house has remained in a remarkably unaltered state for nearly two centuries. It still contains the original mantels, as well as the original chair and picture rails.

Bradley House

Continue on TN 25 toward Carthage. Along the way, the route passes through Riddleton. Haywood Riddle, a politician from nearby Lebanon, made a speech here in 1877, and the people in the crowd were so impressed that they supposedly named the community for him. A school bearing the curious name of Black Gnat Academy was a Riddleton institution for several generations.

After crossing a pair of bluffs above the Cumberland River, TN 25 swings south, where it becomes Main Street in Carthage and enters the downtown area. It is 9.1 miles from the turnoff to the Bradley House to the courthouse in Carthage.

Smith County was created in 1799 but did not have a permanent county seat until 1804. In a contentious vote, a site here on William Walton's grant triumphed over the now-vanished town of Bledsoesborough, which stood near Dixon Springs. Walton moved his family here from Mansker's Station sometime after 1795. He operated a ferry where the Caney Fork River empties into the Cumberland.

The North Carolina native knew how to win an election. The law providing for a vote on where to locate the county seat specified that voting would take place at Walton's Ferry. It was later reported that "Walton furnished unlimited supplies of venison, beef and barbecued bear meat" to the voters, "nor was a full supply of whiskey lacking." The Walton's Ferry advocates, called "the moccasin gang" by the Bledsoesborough faction, defeated the Bledsoesborough advocates, referred to as "the pole cats" by their opposites. The name Carthage was selected for the new town.

Historically, Carthage has been a river town. It was around 1829 when the first steamboat made its way up from Nashville. For the next century, Carthage was an important stop for the Upper Cumberland packets. Steamboat traffic was rather neatly divided between the lower and upper river, and packets from the great inland waterways seldom ventured above Nashville. The Upper Cumberland had its own fleet of smaller packets that roamed the river all the way to Burnside, Kentucky, 325 miles upriver from Nashville. Carthage, Gainesboro, Celina, and smaller places became important stops on the river. And the upper river continued to be the commercial lifeline of its region long after the packets left the river below Nashville.

The Upper Cumberland's rugged terrain substantially delayed construction of railroads into the region. Even after a few were built, they never competed with steamboats as they did in other regions. Then, too, the Upper Cumberland packet trade was not dependent upon cotton and iron, two commodities that vanished from the Lower Cumberland's packets following the Civil War. In was not until the construction of good paved roads in the 1920s that competition from trucks killed the Upper Cumberland steamboat trade.

One of Middle Tennessee's best-known landmarks owes its existence to the Carthage steamboat trade. Nashville's venerable Ryman Auditorium had its origin in the religious conversion of a man who played an important role in the commerce of the Upper Cumberland, Tom Ryman.

Ryman began his river career as a commercial fisherman and made money selling his products to both the Northern and Southern armies during the Civil War. Around 1870, he bought his first steamboat, the *Alpha*, which he brought to Nashville from New Orleans. By 1880, Ryman's fleet consisted of eight boats; before long, Ryman Lines owned over thirty boats. Observing the decline in packet trade on the Lower Cumberland, Ryman turned to the Upper Cumberland. By 1895, he went all out to gain control of the thriving Upper Cumberland packet trade.

In 1881, Ryman was moved by the preaching of noted evangelist Samuel Jones. The steamboat magnate used his considerable wealth to help build what is now Ryman Auditorium for religious meetings, though the structure quickly became an all-purpose facility. Ryman died in 1904 at age sixty-three, much revered by the citizens of Middle Tennessee. At his funeral, more than four thousand people jammed into and around the auditorium, then called the Union Gospel Tabernacle.

From 1943 to 1974, Ryman Auditorium was home to the Grand Ole Opry, earning it the title "Mother Church of Country Music." After several uncertain years following the Opry's move to the suburbs, the auditorium went through a multimillion-dollar restoration and is once again regarded as one of America's premier performance halls.

Getting across the water was of major importance in the Carthage area, situated as it is in rough country crossed by a multitude of waterways. Any history of Carthage is loaded with stories about ferries and bridges. Competition among the ferrymen in the early days was often lively. In an 1836 advertisement, John Cockran announced, "The fine Von-Thromp race horses are being kept at my ferry opposite Carthage, and mares in need of breeding may be brought across the ferry from the north side of the river for free."

The first bridge at Carthage was built between 1906 and 1908 by William E. Myer, a man who later turned to archaeology and explored many of the Middle Cumberland Culture's prehistoric sites. (Myer's archaeological work is described in The Brentwood Tour, pages 101–102, and The Harpeth River Tour, page 139.)

In his book *Tennessee Tales*, Hugh Walker describes an incident at the old toll bridge. A traveling circus, expecting to make a one-day stand in Carthage, brought its animals to the bridge and was met with a demand for five dollars for each elephant that crossed. The circus man pleaded poverty: "For the love of God, Mr. Myer, let them elephants pass." Myer did not budge. So the circus performed south of the river, and the people of Carthage had to pay to cross the Cumberland River to see it. In 1936, the Cordell Hull Bridge replaced the old toll bridge. It has been an important landmark ever since.

Another Carthage landmark is the Smith County Courthouse, an elaborate Second Empire–style structure built in 1875. Smith County was named for surveyor-soldier-politician Daniel Smith, whose house, Rock Castle, starts The Hendersonville-Portland Tour.

Smith County Courthouse

Cullum Mansion

Davis-Hull House

From the courthouse, backtrack on Main Street to Fisher Avenue. The beautiful Carthage United Methodist Church, built in 1889 in the Gothic Revival style, stands on the corner. This church houses a congregation that started in 1808.

Turn right on Fisher. At the end of the street stands one of the few grand Greek Revival houses ever built in the Upper Cumberland. William Cullum constructed this home in 1848. A lawyer who held a number of public offices, Cullum was a member of Congress as a Whig from 1851 to 1855.

Return to Main Street, turn right, and drive to the junction with TN 263. On the left just before the TN 263/TN 25 split stands the Davis-Hull House, an eclectic Victorian-period house completed the same year as Carthage United Methodist Church. Calvin Davis, a successful merchant, built the place. William Hull bought it in 1906. He was the father of Cordell Hull, one of Tennessee's most famous citizens, whose birthplace is visited at the end of this tour.

Take TN 263 as it climbs out of Carthage. After 3.6 miles, you will come to a turnoff on the right for Tater Knob Overlook. Follow the short drive to the parking area, where a paved walk leads up the knob to the

*Cordell Hull Lock and Dam
from Tater Knob Overlook*

overlook. The view of the wide sweep of Horseshoe Bend and Cordell Hull Dam is impressive.

President John F. Kennedy was in Middle Tennessee on May 18, 1963, to deliver a major address at Vanderbilt University. A gold telegraph key had been installed near the podium in the stadium, and by touching the key, Kennedy ignited the first blast at the Cordell Hull construction site. The sound of the explosion, broadcast over the public-address system, echoed through the stands. "You see how easy it is to be president?" Kennedy quipped to the crowd of thirty thousand. "Just push a button."

The dam, constructed by the Corps of Engineers, impounds a 72-mile reservoir. The project created a year-round navigable waterway on the Upper Cumberland. Twenty thousand acres of the reservoir property are protected as a wildlife management area, administered by the Tennessee Wildlife Resources Agency. It is not uncommon to hear the honking of the large resident population of Canada geese.

The popular Bearwaller Gap Trail leads upstream 6 miles from here to Defeated Creek Park. Black bears inhabited Middle Tennessee when the first Europeans came to stay in the late 1700s. It was not uncommon for settlers to come upon cool, shady places where bears liked to "waller." So they called these places "bearwallers." One of the "wallers" was in a small gap along the Cumberland River on the current hiking trail.

Return to TN 263 and turn right. After 1.7 miles, you will reach TN 85. Turn right (E). It is 2.1 miles to the entrance to Defeated Creek Park.

Outsiders have long been intrigued by the names of two nearby communities—Defeated and Difficult. The names have a common origin, an Indian attack on hunters. Food was often scarce in the early Middle Cumberland settlements. Men would travel long distances in search of game. While camped along this creek in the winter of 1786, a hunting party led by John Peyton was attacked by Indians. All but one member of the hunting party was wounded, but the men "defeated" by the attackers made it back to the settlements, though their trip was "difficult."

Tradition has it that years later, John Peyton wrote the Indian leader of the attack, Hanging Maw, and asked for the return of his valuable brass compass. "As for you, John Peyton," Hanging Maw is said to have replied, "I have taken your 'land stealer' and broken it against a tree."

Defeated Creek Park is an exceptionally large Corps of Engineers recreation area offering a variety of activities, including swimming on two sandy beaches. The park has a campground and a marina as well. The Defeated Creek embayment of Cordell Hull Lake has been designated a waterfowl refuge.

It is 2.4 miles on TN 85 from the park to a fork in the road. Stay on TN 85, the right fork. You will cross a ridge and descend into the valley of Salt Lick Creek. This is classic Upper Cumberland country, a rich valley with pastures stretching up to the forested hilltops. You will reach the community of Gladdice after 5.1 miles. Turn right onto beautiful Smith Bend Road. It is 4.7 miles to the river and the site of Fort Blount.

Site of Fort Blount at the "Crossing of the Cumberland"

To understand the significance of Fort Blount, it is helpful to know something of the early roads that led across the Cumberland Plateau into Middle Tennessee. About the time the settlement at present-day Nashville got under way, the pioneers started looking for an alternative to the circuitous route that had brought James Robertson's group to the Middle Cumberland. (See The Middle Cumberland Tour, page 4, for the story of Robertson's trip.)

The first organized effort at a direct route came with North Carolina's authorization of a road in 1787. The following year, a road opened, but it was impassable much of the time. Known by a variety of names, including Fort Blount Trail and Avery's Trace, it ran from near today's Knoxville to this spot—called the "Crossing of the Cumberland"—then continued north of the river to the Cumberland settlements and Fort Nashborough.

In 1797, the Territorial Assembly—this was when Tennessee was the Southwest Territory—authorized the raising of funds to build an alternate road south of the first one. It, too, crossed the Cumberland at this spot.

In 1799, after Tennessee's statehood, the general assembly authorized yet another road. It followed the path of the second road along the stretch from East Tennessee west to near today's Cookeville, where it split from the older road. This new road stayed south of the Cumberland River to the mouth of Caney Fork, thus bypassing the "Crossing of the Cumberland."

Because William Walton was largely responsible for cutting this new road, which stimulated business for his ferry, it came to be called the Walton Road. From its opening in 1801, it evolved into the main Knoxville-Nashville road. To this day, it is the main route of travel over the Cumberland

Plateau. Today's U.S. 70N basically follows the route of the Walton Road from near Carthage to Cookeville, Crossville, and Rockwood at the foot of the plateau's eastern escarpment. Interstate 40 roughly follows the same route.

As early as 1791, Sampson Williams ran a ferry at the "Crossing of the Cumberland." The following year, the territorial government authorized the construction of a fort. Settlers struggling west on the primitive roads needed protection from the Indians, particularly here, where they crossed the river. Fort Blount, named for William Blount, the territorial governor, was occupied by both regular United States Army troops and militia until around 1799. By then, the Indian threat had subsided, and the Walton Road was replacing the earlier route as the main path west.

A town evolved here in this lovely bend in the Cumberland River. It was first called Fort Blount, then Williamsburg, after Sampson Williams, who owned this land. Jackson County was created in 1801. From 1807 to 1819, Williamsburg was the county seat. After the county seat was moved to Gainesboro, Williamsburg gradually declined until it finally ceased to exist. Sampson Williams, the man responsible for its founding, lived until 1841.

Exactly where was Fort Blount? It "was located on the south side of the Cumberland River," one local historian writes. The fort "was on the north side of the general course of the river," writes another. They are both right. That is the conclusion of a thorough study by the Tennessee Division of Archaeology, published in 1989. The first fort was a blockhouse built in 1792 on the Cumberland's south bank. Then, in 1794, it was replaced by a second fort of unknown design in the bend north of the river on Sampson Williams's property.

Retrace your route to TN 85 and turn right (E). It is 5.4 miles to the second junction of TN 85 and TN 262. Along the way, the highway runs parallel to the Cumberland River through the beautiful valley.

Where TN 85 turns left, stay on the main road, now TN 262, as it continues along the river, then crosses it. After 4 miles, you will reach TN 53. Turn left and drive to the Jackson County Courthouse. Note that the state has designated four highways in this part of the Upper Cumberland with confusingly similar numbers—TN 51, TN 52, TN 53, and TN 56. There is a TN 151, too.

The citizens of Jackson County selected the name Gainesborough for their new county in honor of General Edmund Pendleton Gains, who fought with Andrew Jackson in the Seminole War in Florida. Napoleon Bonaparte Young, once the postmaster here, believed in economy, so he got the name shortened to Gainesboro. He could see no reason to waste the ink and spend the effort it took to write the longer spelling.

Historians in this remote Upper Cumberland county are at a disadvantage, for county records were destroyed in two devastating courthouse fires, one in 1872 and the other in 1926. The current courthouse was built in 1927.

From the courthouse, continue on TN 53 for 0.2 mile to the junction with TN 56. Turn left (N) on TN 53/TN 56. Where the two routes split after 1.2 miles, stay on TN 56 as it turns left and crosses the Cumberland River.

Jennings Creek has created a fertile valley through the Highland Rim here. For the next several miles, the route follows the narrowing valley past substantial old farmhouses. Lower Jennings Creek, part of Cordell Hull Lake, is included in the Cordell Hull Wildlife Refuge.

You will reach the community of North Springs 12.9 miles from the Cumberland River crossing near Gainesboro. Turn right on TN 151 and follow it as it passes through a narrow valley and then climbs to the Highland Rim. After 7 miles, you will enter Red Boiling Springs.

Of over thirty mineral springs resorts in Middle Tennessee during the late 1800s and early 1900s, Red Boiling Springs was the grandest. At its peak in the 1920s, guests were accommodated in nine hotels and over twenty boardinghouses. They enjoyed horseback riding, tennis, swimming, boating, fishing, and bowling. At times, orchestras played night and day for dancing.

But it was the sulphur water that first drew people here. A man named Shepherd Kirby is credited with discovering the healing powers of the water. Kirby was cutting wood when a splinter hit him in the eye. An infection developed. He discovered that the mineral water from one of the numerous springs soothed his eye, and before long, the infection healed. He credited the water. This was in 1840.

There is another story, too, though not as well known. It involves Sooky

Goad, who lent her name to a compound called "Aunt Sooky's Salve," made, of course, with a "secret formula." She suffered from dropsy, but her health was completely restored after drinking the sulphur water. Word of her cure spread, and before long, people were camping in tents around the springs to take the curative water. Aunt Sooky Goad, incidentally, was Shepherd Kirby's sister. In this version of the discovery of the springs' healing power, Kirby got the idea to use the water to treat his eye from his sister.

A New York investor, James F. O. Shaughnessey, acquired two hundred acres here along Salt Lick Creek. By 1895, he was advertising a new hotel. His promotion included a long list of ailments that could be cured by the water. Guests drank three types of water—red, black, and white—each with its own distinctive properties and taste, and each promoted as a cure for different diseases. Water from a fourth spring was too strong to drink but was used by masseurs in the bathhouse. It was called "double and twist" water, for that is the reaction of those who dared to drink it—they doubled over and twisted on the ground.

It is no accident that the mineral springs resorts were located on the edge of the Highland Rim. Beds of shale along the rim's margin impede the vertical flow of water, and water moving along the shale bubbles to the surface. The mineral content of a spring is determined by the length of time its water is in contact with iron sulfide in the shale. Some springs, such as Bennett Spring here at Red Boiling Springs, give pure limestone water free of sulphur and minerals, the type of water that is good for making whiskey and other beverages. In the 1920s, Coca-Cola had a bottling plant here to take advantage of this pure water.

Pump for red water at Red Boiling Springs and Donoho Hotel

Why did the spa at Red Boiling Springs decline? Modern medicine played a part. As research uncovered the cause of diseases, it became obvious that the water here did not have miraculous curing power, as was previously believed. The Great Depression did not help either. But it was paved roads and automobiles that really did in Red Boiling Springs. People became mobile, and there was a big world to see and explore. This spa no longer held the excitement it once did, and the place gradually faded.

Then, in 1969, the town of Red Boiling Springs was devastated by a flood that claimed several lives and did millions of dollars in damage. Ironically, the flood stimulated something of a rebirth. Government-funded redevelopment resulted in several improvements, including the park along the creek.

Three of the old hotels remain open to the public and are noted for serving some of the best food in Middle Tennessee. The Thomas House, located on the right as you enter town, was built as the Cloyd Hotel in 1932. It was the third hotel on this spot. The Donoho Hotel, just past it, with its wide, inviting porch, was built in 1914. On the left past it is Armour's Red Boiling Springs Inn, built in 1924 as the Counts Hotel.

The town has a welcome center in the park. In season, visitors can stop there to pick up a brochure describing a twenty-two-stop walking tour of Red Boiling Springs. They can also get information about the annual Folk Medicine Festival, held in July.

TN 151 ends at TN 52 in downtown Red Boiling Springs. Turn right (E) and head toward the Clay County seat of Celina.

The Hermitage Springs community, on the way to Celina, was a mineral springs resort, too, though not on the scale of Red Boiling Springs. The two hotels built here around 1900 did not last much beyond 1920.

After the highway passes through the community of Moss and drops back into the valley, it crosses the Cumberland River and enters Celina some 24 miles from Red Boiling Springs. The courthouse is on the right.

From the bridge, glance to the left to see the Obey River flowing from the right into the larger Cumberland. The Obey is a major tributary that is now impounded for much of its length by Dale Hollow Dam. Here at Celina, the tour leaves the Cumberland just below where it flows out of Kentucky and begins following the general course of the Obey.

Like Trousdale County, where the tour started, this small county was established in 1870. This is the original courthouse, built in 1872. The courtroom is furnished with its original handmade pews.

Celina grew up around a ferry that started here in the early 1800s. It was a thriving town by the time the Civil War came, but was destroyed during the war and had to be rebuilt.

When they hear it said that people around Celina once made their living "rafting," outsiders usually have to ask what this means. Rafting is how the Upper Cumberland's vast timber resources were shipped downstream on the Cumberland when timber dominated the region's economy from

Clay County's original 1872 courthouse

TOURING THE MIDDLE TENNESSEE BACKROADS

1870 until about 1930. One rafter put it this way: "Well, that's all there was to do around here. There wasn't no factories; there wasn't nothing to do and that's the only way anybody had of getting any money. There was logging, rafting, and running the river. And that was the only sale we had for timber at that time."

Money changed hands when farmers and other landowners sold their logs to timber buyers. It changed hands again when the logs were delivered at processing towns such as Celina. Then the logs were sold again at a market, usually in Nashville. It is estimated that as early as 1874, some 22,500,000 board feet of logs were rafted down the Cumberland to Nashville. In 1884, lumber cut at Nashville's 20-plus mills totaled 86,165,000 feet, and as many as 1,400 rafts tied up there. It was not an uncommon sight to see rafts lining the river for 25 miles above Tennessee's capital city.

The log rafts were usually around 250 to 300 feet in length. Some were only a single tier of logs wide, but the larger ones had as many as three tiers. A crew of five plus a pilot manned the rafts. The pilot had to know every foot of the river, and his orders had to be instantaneously obeyed by the men manning the oars. Some pilots were legendary for their ability to steer their rafts down the narrow river—among them were Bill Bybee, Bob Riley, and Cal Hamilton, who seemed to have a sixth sense when it came to the river. Cordell Hull once worked as a pilot, too.

One of the crew members doubled as a cook. The men would gather for their meals in the little shack that passed for a pilothouse. Since food was not always abundant, they had to be resourceful. A number of tales are told about Bob Riley's ability to forage his way down the Cumberland— like the time he conned a woman into believing the turkey he was caught stealing was really a loose turkey he had brought on the raft from Celina. And there was the time he killed a calf on the riverbank. By the time the owner came to investigate, Riley had put rubber boots on the animal's hind legs and a rain slicker over the rest of it. Uncle Bob, as Riley was called, sobbed as he told the farmer it was his brother, who had just died with small-pox. The farmer fled. He did not want to be contaminated with the disease.

Some men earned a living by "drifting." Logs would invariably get loose, and "drifters" would intercept them as they came floating down the Cumberland. The logs were branded, so a drifter knew which timber buyers they belonged to. He would hold the logs for the owner, who paid a fee for recovered logs.

Log piracy was not unknown on the river. Some men would saw off the ends of logs to remove the brand, then sell the logs.

The vast timber resources of the Upper Cumberland were not limitless. Starting about 1915, rafting started to decline. By the time the Great Depression hit, the trade was just about over. It was completely gone by 1940.

Timber is still big business in the Upper Cumberland, however, as evidenced by the forest products industries between Red Boiling Springs and Celina. Though Nashville remains a major hardwood milling center, the Upper Cumberland has abundant energy to run the mills and good roads to get lumber out of the region, making it the prime location for milling operations. Secondary industries like the making of furniture, prefabricated housing, and flooring are important in the region, too.

In Celina, circle around the courthouse. Where TN 52 turns right just past the courthouse, go straight (E) on Lake Avenue. It is 1.3 miles to TN 53. Turn left (N). You will cross the Obey River and pass the road to the Free Hills community.

Free Hills is one of the most unusual settlements in the Upper Cumberland, or in the entire state of Tennessee, for that matter. Virginia Hill was a slave owner from North Carolina who wanted to free her slaves, so she purchased two thousand acres in this remote country, moved her slaves here, and set them free—thus the name Free Hills. Some people in this hilltop village are direct descendants of Rubin Hill, a freed slave who, at age thirty-one, married a sixteen-year-old slave girl named Sarah and received a land grant of four hundred acres. Not all of the Free Hills residents are descended from Virginia Hill's slaves, for following emancipation, other blacks in the region migrated to Free Hills. Cal Hamilton, the famed raft pilot, came from Free Hills.

After 1.4 miles on TN 53, turn right toward Dale Hollow Dam. The road passes the Dale Hollow National Fish Hatchery. Operated by the United States Fish and Wildlife Service, the hatchery produces almost two million trout annually for stocking in waters in Tennessee, Kentucky, and Alabama. It is open to visitors.

Take the right fork 0.5 mile from TN 53 and cross the dam.

Dale Hollow Dam, completed by the Corps of Engineers in 1943, gets its name from the hollow named for the Dales, a pioneer family. The lake is unusually clear, making it popular for scuba diving, as well as boating, swimming, and fishing. The world-record smallmouth bass came out of Dale Hollow in the 1950s. The lake is also one of the best places to observe wintering bald eagles and the ospreys that visit in the spring. The Corps of Engineers sponsors eagle-viewing tours each January.

From the end of the dam, the road climbs steeply away from the lake through rugged hills. After 2.2 miles, it reaches TN 52. Turn left (E). It is 4.9 miles to Timothy and TN 136. Turn right (S) at the sign for Standing Stone State Park and follow TN 136 as it enters the park and reaches the park headquarters after 1.7 miles.

Standing Stone is another of Tennessee's parks developed as a Depression-era public-works project. The 1,000-acre park is surrounded by a 10,000-acre multiple-use state forest.

The "standing stone" was a large rock on the Walton Road near today's Monterey. It was said to resemble a big, gray dog and was supposedly a marker that separated lands claimed by different Indian groups. The stone eventually broke, and a remnant of it has been mounted on a monument in a Monterey park. No one seems to know how this park came to be named for the stone, for this area had nothing to do with it.

Visitors to the park enjoy one of Tennessee's best displays of wildflowers in the spring. The park also offers 10 miles of trails and boating and fishing on the park lake. But Standing Stone State Park is best known for its marbles. Each year, it hosts the National Rolley Hole Marbles Championship.

The traditional pastime of shooting marbles has all but vanished, except for here on the Highland Rim in Clay County, Tennessee, and adjoining Monroe County, Kentucky, where it is serious business. At one time, there was even a "marble yard" at the Clay County Courthouse in Celina. A marble yard is a rectangle of compacted, level soil twenty-five feet by forty feet, often rimmed by a plank for spectators. The game, played by teams of two, has a rather complex set of rules, but the object is to get a marble in a hole. The marbles are shot with tremendous speed, often from distances as great as ten feet. Ordinary glass marbles cannot withstand the impact,

WPA dam at Standing Stone State Park

so a cottage industry has grown up in these hills making "rolley hole" marbles. You can pay as much as fifty dollars for a good one made of flint.

The rolley hole tournament here at Standing Stone has attracted a fair amount of national attention. The first one in 1983 was covered by NBC television news. Since then, the ESPN sports network has covered the tournament, held in August.

Continue down the steep hill past the park headquarters and cross the beautiful stone dam that creates the park lake.

On the left just past the dam is the reconstructed 1808 home of Moses Fisk, a man who played many prominent roles in the development of this part of Tennessee. Born in Massachusetts in 1759, Fisk was educated at Dartmouth College. Dartmouth has its origins as a school for Indians, and in 1796, the college's president persuaded Fisk to come to Tennessee to study the feasibility of establishing a mission among the Cherokees. Fisk returned to Dartmouth to report on the prospects, then came to the Upper Cumberland frontier, where he worked as a surveyor.

It is said that Moses Fisk was offered the presidency of the University of

North Carolina, but the gifted New Englander preferred to remain on the frontier. His talent in mathematics was recognized in 1801, when he was chosen to be one of the men who set the boundary between Tennessee and Virginia. He did some surveying again in 1817 to settle a border dispute with Kentucky.

Fisk was instrumental in the formation of Smith, Jackson, and Overton counties. In 1799, he served as the first clerk of the Smith County Court. He laid out the town of Hilham in 1805 and had visions of the place becoming a major town, even going so far as to plan a network of turnpikes leading to it.

Moses Fisk's first love was education. In 1806, he and Sampson Williams started Fisk Female Academy at Hilham, one of the first schools of its kind in America. It lasted only a year but was followed by a school for boys, where several of Tennessee's most distinguished men were educated.

A major landowner, Fisk is said to have owned over thirty thousand acres across the Upper Cumberland at the time of his death in 1843. Celina is named for his oldest daughter.

Home of Moses Fisk

It is 5.2 miles from the stone dam to Hilham. Turn left (E) on TN 85 and drive 7.8 miles to the junction with TN 42/TN 111 on the edge of Livingston. Turn left. Where TN 42/TN 111 Bypass turns left after 0.3 mile, go straight into Livingston on TN 85 (Main Street) to the town's charming square.

After the 1805 treaty with the Cherokees authorized settlement of this area, Overton County was created out of Jackson County. It is named for John Overton, the Nashville lawyer-planter who with friends Andrew Jackson and James Winchester founded Memphis.

The town's lovely little courthouse was built in 1869 to replace one burned by guerrillas during the Civil War. The Upper Cumberland does not readily come to mind when the Civil War is mentioned. Massive armies did not sweep back and forth across the countryside, as in the Middle Tennessee heartland. No major battles were fought here. Nevertheless, the region was devastated by the war, brought to its knees by the treachery of guerrillas operating under the guise of loyalty to the Union or Confederate causes. Citizens of this hill country were deeply divided. Here as in nearby Kentucky, it really was "brother against brother."

Overton County Courthouse

The most notorious of all the guerrillas was Champ Ferguson. He came from just over the border in Kentucky but moved into Tennessee when the war started. Several tales explain why Ferguson became such a vicious Confederate sympathizer. One is that some Union guerrillas made his wife and daughter strip and paraded them naked along a road. Ferguson supposedly tracked one of these men all the way to a hospital near Bristol, where, in late 1864, he killed the man in his bed. Champ Ferguson's gang was particularly active against the Kentucky Home Guards, the pro-Union militia. It was not uncommon for the guards to be tortured to death if caught by Ferguson's men. Ferguson was tried in a military court at the end of the war and hanged in Nashville in October 1865.

Just as ruthless on the Union side was Tinker Dave Beaty of neighboring Fentress County. He headed a group called Beaty's Independent Scouts. Like Ferguson's gang, Beaty's men took advantage of the complete breakdown of civil authority during the war. Under the guise of aiding the Union cause, they raped, pillaged, and killed all across the Upper Cumberland. Their favorite targets were the families of men who were away fighting for the Confederacy.

One of Livingston's favorite sons was A. H. Roberts, a respected lawyer and educator who was elected Tennessee's governor in 1918. He only served one two-year term, but much happened during his short tenure. Significant tax and fiscal reforms were enacted, schools were greatly upgraded, and the first workmen's compensation law was passed. But it was Roberts's involvement with the suffrage movement that is his greatest legacy. And it contributed to his defeat in the next election.

By the time Roberts won the Democratic primary in 1920, the Nineteenth Amendment—which guaranteed women the right to vote—had been ratified by thirty-five states, one short of the number needed for approval. Suffrage proponents saw Tennessee as one of three states where chances for passage were good. Right after the August primary, Roberts called a special session of the legislature to consider the proposal.

The eyes of the nation were on the Capitol in Nashville. Women's rights advocates such as Carrie Chapman Catt came to lend their support. In a spirited session, the measure easily passed the senate but passed the house by only one vote. The house speaker, a suffrage opponent, called for a reconsideration, then did not call up the reconsideration bill when he perceived that the tide was turning against him. Suddenly needing to stop a reconsideration vote from occurring, representatives who opposed suffrage boarded a train for Athens, Alabama, to prevent a quorum. The entire reconsideration ploy was held to be void. On August 24, 1920, Governor Roberts signed the certification that put the Nineteenth Amendment over the top.

Roberts's Republican opponent, Alfred A. Taylor, won the November election. A. H. Roberts spent the remainder of his years in Nashville, where he died in 1946.

TN 52 comes in from the left at the square. Continue on Main Street, now TN 52, past the square. Where TN 52 splits from TN 294 after 1.1 miles, take TN 294 to reconnect with TN 42/TN 111. Bear right on TN 42/TN 111 and head toward Byrdstown.

On the way to Byrdstown, you will pass through Monroe. This was the first Overton County seat, established at a crossroads in 1810. After it had served three decades as the county seat, agitation started to move the seat to Livingston, located nearer to the center of the county. The 1833 vote for the move was close—so close, in fact, that one man's trickery may have made the difference.

Jesse "Ranter" Eldridge was taking some of his neighbors to Monroe from a remote area of the county to cast their votes. After spending the night with friends along the way, the group awoke to discover that someone had stolen their horses. Ranter's neighbors quickly forgot the vote and turned their attention to catching a horse thief. They never made it to Monroe.

They didn't have to look too far to find the man responsible for the missing horses. It was Ranter Eldridge, who had turned the horses loose during the night. All the people there that night were Monroe backers—except for Ranter. He was for Livingston.

It is 16.5 miles on TN 42/TN 111 to the junction with TN 325 (Star Point Road). Turn left (NW) and drive 1.6 miles to Cordell Hull's birthplace, a state historic site.

Stand for a moment and contemplate two scenes. One is the log cabin in front of you. The other is the United Nations complex in New York. It is almost beyond comprehension that the man who was responsible for the United Nations began his life in this humble one-room cabin in the remote Tennessee hills. For his effort toward world peace, Cordell Hull was awarded the Nobel Peace Prize in 1945.

It is difficult to go anywhere in this part of Tennessee without coming across something named for Cordell Hull. It seems that just about every county seat claims that Hull practiced law in an office there. He did, in fact, live several places in the Upper Cumberland, and he held a number of offices, too —state legislator, judge, congressman, and senator. He is best known, though, for his service as secretary of state under President Franklin D. Roosevelt from 1933 to 1944.

During his twenty-one years in Congress, Hull followed a populist agenda, fighting successfully for an income-tax law that was favorable to the average American and for antitrust and antimonopoly legislation. He was a strong advocate of free trade and international cooperation, especially with his "Good Neighbor Policy" toward Latin America.

The Hull family was living in a rented cabin on this spot when Cordell was born in 1871. Before long, his father, William—or Billy, as he was known—got into the timber business. The family prospered. Moving to more comfortable surroundings, the Hulls lived for a time in the large Davis-Hull House on Main Street in Carthage.

Of his son, Billy Hull once said, "Cord wasn't set enough to be a school teacher, wasn't rough enough to be a lumberman, wasn't sociable enough

Birthplace of Cordell Hull

TOURING THE MIDDLE TENNESSEE BACKROADS

to be a doctor and couldn't holler loud enough to be a preacher. But Cord was a right thorough thinker."

"A thorough Tennessee tongue-lashing" is how some have described Secretary of State Hull's parting words to the Japanese diplomats who were in his office on December 7, 1941—the "Day of Infamy." At the very moment they were meeting, Japanese planes were attacking the United States Pacific Fleet. Following Pearl Harbor, Hull guided American diplomacy during World War II and paved the way for the United Nations before ill health forced him to retire in 1944.

Cordell Hull never lost the modesty he learned growing up in the Upper Cumberland. Once, Congressman Joe L. Evins visited Hull and asked his forerunner in Congress which of his many honors and achievements he valued most. "I know I should say that raising the morality of international relations was perhaps my greatest achievement. But, to be honest, I must say that being elected chairman of the Democratic Party in Clay County at the age of 18 was my greatest thrill," Hull responded.

Cordell Hull died in 1953 and is interred at the National Cathedral in Washington.

Return to TN 42/TN 111 and turn left (NE). After 0.6 mile, turn right onto TN 325 to reach Byrdstown and the Pickett County Courthouse.

Pickett is Tennessee's youngest county, created in 1879. It is also Tennessee's smallest county in population. It was not, as is sometimes asserted, named for Confederate general George E. Pickett, the leader of Pickett's Charge during the Battle of Gettysburg. Instead, it was named in honor of Howell E. Pickett, a state representative who sponsored the legislation establishing the county.

The tour ends at Byrdstown. Cookeville is 40 miles southwest on TN 42/TN 111. To see more of the Upper Cumberland, stay on TN 325. It leads to U.S. 127 and Sergeant Alvin York Historic Site, then on to Big South Fork National River and Recreation Area.

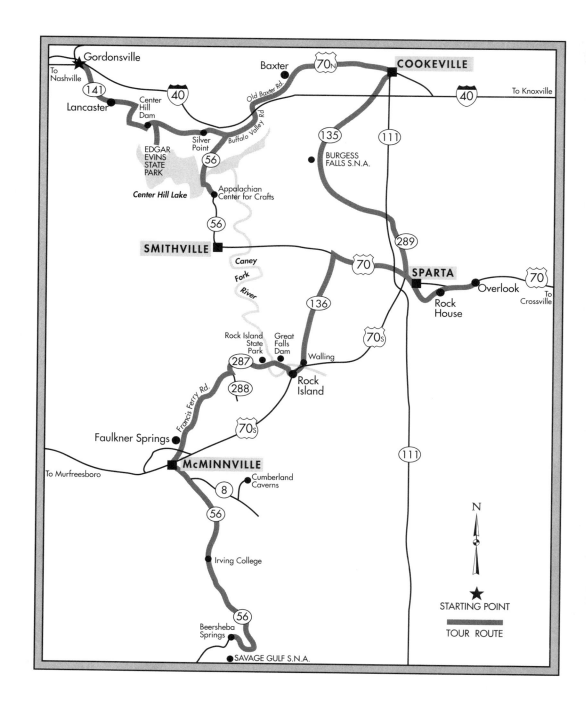

The Caney Fork Tour

This tour in the Upper Cumberland region follows two of the state's most scenic rivers, the Caney Fork and the Collins, and goes to one of its most beautiful lakes, Center Hill. In addition to stopping at the towns of Cookeville, Sparta, and McMinnville, it visits Burgess Falls and Great Falls at Rock Island State Park. The tour ends on the edge of the Cumberland Plateau at the old resort of Beersheba Springs and Savage Gulf State Natural Area.

Total length: approximately 146 miles

This tour begins on the edge of Gordonsville at the junction of TN 141 and TN 53, located 0.4 mile south of Exit 258 off Interstate 40 near Carthage. Travel east on TN 141 into Gordonsville.

Gordonsville has always been a prosperous, lovely little town, the principal trade center of the part of Smith County called "South Side." The Caney Fork and Cumberland rivers divide the county into three parts of about equal size. Until fairly recently, there were only two or three bridges over the rivers. So each of the county's three parts—the other two are "North Side" and "Forks of the River"—maintained rather separate identities.

This small town has traditionally been thought of as having two parts, the upper and the lower towns, each with its own set of businesses and residences. Most of the businesses today are in the upper town, for a fire on Christmas Eve 1924 wiped out much of the lower town.

As with most places in the remote Upper Cumberland, developments in transportation figure prominently in the history of Gordonsville. TN 141 follows the route of the old turnpike that ran east from Lebanon and connected with the Walton Road coming from the mouth of Caney Fork at Carthage. (For the story of the Walton Road, see The Upper Cumberland Tour, pages 342–43.) When the turnpike via Lebanon opened around 1830, the main route of travel from Nashville to Knoxville shifted south of the Cumberland River, and the route north of the river through Carthage and Gallatin lost its importance. Today's Interstate 40 parallels the old turnpike to Lebanon.

At the eastern edge of Gordonsville, you will come to the junction with TN 264. Go straight (E) on TN 141 for the long run through Lancaster to Center Hill Dam.

The road to the left, TN 264, leads to the old Stonewall Bridge over Caney Fork and on to the quaint villages of Stonewall and Elmwood. Built in 1906, the bridge was for several generations the only link between South Side and the Forks of the River. The one-lane, wooden-floored structure is something of a landmark in these parts, a picturesque old bridge of questionable safety. It was finally replaced in 1972.

Smith County's best-known residents live on the river downstream from the Stonewall Bridge, the Albert Gore, Sr., family on Caney Fork's west bank and the Albert Gore, Jr., family on the east bank.

The senior Gore grew up around here. After working his way through college as a truckdriver, farmer, teacher, and feed-mill operator, he finished at Middle Tennessee State in 1933. He was interested in politics from the time he was elected Smith County school superintendent. He was appointed Tennessee's commissioner of labor in 1937 and was elected to the United States House of Representatives in 1938 and the United States Senate in 1952. He served eighteen years in the Senate.

The younger Gore, born in 1948, was only twenty-eight when he was elected to the House from the same district in 1976. He was elected to the Senate six years later before becoming vice president of the United States in 1993.

Father and son are not shy about giving credit for their political success to another family member. Pauline Gore is a woman of some prominence in her own right. Born in rural West Tennessee in 1912, she moved with her family to Jackson, where she attended high school. After finishing Union University, she became the second woman ever to enroll at the school of law at Vanderbilt University. While at Vanderbilt, she lived at the YWCA to save money and worked as a waitress in the coffee shop at Nashville's Andrew Jackson Hotel from five-thirty to ten o'clock each night.

The Smith County school superintendent commuted to Nashville three nights a week to attend night law school and often stopped for coffee before his return drive to Carthage. The handsome young man caught the attention of the Vanderbilt law student, and before long, they were dating. Pauline LaFon finished Vanderbilt, then left for Arkansas to practice law. But she returned to Tennessee, and in 1937, the year Albert, Sr., finished law school and became Tennessee's labor commissioner, they were married.

Past the junction with TN 264, TN 141 swings away from the Caney Fork River, crosses a ridge, passes through the village of Lancaster, and then parallels the river for several miles.

An interesting aspect of the Caney Fork Valley is the number of houses in the Gothic Revival style. This is rare in Tennessee—rare in the whole South, for that matter—for the style popular in rural America in the late 1800s never caught on in this part of the country. The houses were characterized by front gables— often three of them—and decorative vergeboards that evolved into the familiar gingerbread.

The Gothic Revival cottage was popularized by two pattern books by landscape designer Andrew Jackson Downing, published in 1842 and 1850 and widely circulated and used later in the nineteenth century. The wood ornamentation visible today on many houses along Caney Fork was not available locally, and it was probably not until the railroad came through that Gothic Revival detailing was added to existing houses. However it happened, these unusual houses add a beautiful touch to an already beautiful part of Middle Tennessee.

Pearling. Read any account of life along Caney Fork and you will find that some people made their living collecting pearls from the shells of the mussels that once thrived in the rivers of the Upper Cumberland.

In *Tennessee Tales*, Hugh Walker describes how it all started. Two Murfreesboro boys fishing along Caney Fork in 1881 pulled up some mussels to use as bait. When one of the boys opened a shell, a pearl rolled out. They took it to a druggist, who in turn sent it to Tiffany's in New York. A few days later, the boys received a check in the mail for eighty-three dollars. From then on, searching for pearls around here was a major activity. One newspaper reported in 1913 that a Lancaster man found a forty-gram pearl estimated to be worth six hundred to eight hundred dollars.

The mussel shells had value, too. Collectors sold them for use in making buttons.

The mussels that yielded the pearls thrived in shallow, swift-running water. With the construction of locks and dams along the Cumberland and Caney Fork rivers, the practice of pearling died out. By World War I, it was over.

Past Lancaster, TN 141 enters DeKalb County. Created in 1837 out of existing counties, it is named for Baron Johann DeKalb, a German officer who served as a major general in the Continental Army during the American Revolution.

When the first white explorers came into the Cumberland country, they found vast stands of cane along the river bottoms, a sure sign that the land was rich. The stands along this river must have been impressive, for they started calling it the Cumberland's "caney fork." The Caney Fork River is the largest Cumberland River tributary, flowing 140 miles from its headwaters on the Cumberland Plateau across the Eastern Highland Rim to its mouth at Carthage.

In 1832, the *Harry Hill* chugged all the way up the Caney Fork to Sligo Landing, starting the steamboat trade on the river. That landing, off today's U.S. 70 between Sparta and Smithville, evolved into the largest one on the Caney Fork. As late as 1887, when the "tide" was right, seven packets made regular trips to and from Sligo.

This stretch of river is particularly scenic as it sweeps around broad bends and beneath towering cedar-covered bluffs. It is popular for canoeing and fishing, especially trout fishing. The cold waters discharged from the bottom of Center Hill Lake create ideal conditions for cool-water species. Bird-watching is popular here, too. Occasionally, wintering eagles can be spotted in the large trees along the river.

It is 10.6 miles from the junction of TN 141 and TN 264 outside Gordonsville to Center Hill Dam, built by the Corps of Engineers in 1948; a road to the left at the campground leads 0.2 mile to the base of the dam and the powerhouse. Continue on TN 141 as it climbs to the top of the dam and joins TN 96. Turn left and cross the dam. A Corps of Engineers visitor center is on the left 1.2 miles from the junction. It is another 2 miles to the entrance to Edgar Evins State Park, on the right. Turn into the park and drive to the park visitor center.

The tower at Edgar Evins State Park overlooks Center Hill Lake.

This park takes in six thousand acres of the rugged knobs surrounding Center Hill Lake. These pieces of the Highland Rim, broken off by the Caney Fork River and its many tributaries, give the place a mountainous appearance. The beautiful lake is the focus of the park, which features a marina where boats can be rented.

When you are ready to leave the park, return to TN 141 (Wolf Creek Road) and turn right (E). The route makes a long climb to the Highland Rim. As you enter the Silver Point community, perched on the fingers of the rim, you will reach the West End Church of Christ after 5.9 miles.

This building has a unique history. It was not built as a church, but as a school for blacks—Silver Point Christian College. Fisk University graduate G. P. Bowser ran a tiny Church of Christ school in Nashville that was struggling financially. In 1909, he moved it to this remote part of Putnam County. He thought that in a rural setting, students could raise their own food, sell the surplus, and thereby cut school costs. A well-known black evangelist named Marshall Keeble and other Church of Christ leaders assisted in the effort. The school moved into an abandoned public school, and the local authorities appointed Bowser a public-school teacher.

By 1915, enrollment at the school had grown to fifty-nine students, seven of whom were boarding students, and the faculty and students published a monthly religious magazine, the *Christian Echo*. For day students, tuition ranged from fifty cents to a dollar per month. Boarding students paid an additional six dollars per month. An ex-slave and former Union soldier, Henry Clay, helped the students build and sell farm wagons.

But the school's financial troubles continued, so Annie C. Tugwell, one of the teachers, went to Nashville to request help from noted evangelist David Lipscomb, founder of Nashville Bible College, now David Lipscomb University. "Young Lady, I don't have any money, but I have friends who do. And I am going to see that you can have a school where the Bible can be taught daily," Lipscomb told her. He solicited the help of one of his patrons, wealthy Nashvillian A. M. Burton.

Burton visited Silver Point, where he found eight acres of poor land and two dilapidated buildings. He bought new grounds for the school, set up a board of trustees that included himself, Clay, and Keeble, the evangelist. Burton had the materials shipped in to build the brick building that stands today.

West End Church of Christ

But sustaining a school here was probably not practicable to begin with, and it closed a few years later. A marker in front of the brick church honors the old school.

Continue through Silver Point for another 1 mile to TN 56; Interstate 40 is just to the left. Turn right (S) on TN 56 and follow it along a ridge that juts out into Center Hill Lake. After 5.4 miles, the road crosses the lake and the Caney Fork River on the Hurricane Bridge. Turn left at the end of the bridge and drive 1.3 miles to the Appalachian Center for the Crafts.

The Appalachian Regional Commission was created by Congress in the 1960s to coordinate and fund economic development in America's most impoverished region. To satisfy several powerful members of Congress, the commission's jurisdiction was extended well beyond Appalachia. It even takes in part of Mississippi. The chairman of the Senate Appropriations Committee was from Mississippi.

Joe L. Evins was a member of Congress whose support was needed. He saw to it that all the Upper Cumberland—not just the part in the Appalachian Mountains—was included in the area to receive federal funds. Evins, from nearby Smithville, served in the United States House of Representatives from 1946 to 1976. When a decision was made to use federal funds to help build a center to promote Appalachian crafts, Evins—chairman of the House Appropriations Subcommittee on Public Works—got the crafts center built near Smithville on 180 acres of Corps of Engineers land overlooking Center Hill Lake.

The center struggled for a few years after it opened in 1979, but it is now thriving as part of Cookeville's Tennessee Technological University. Upperclassmen live in housing at the center while they earn their bachelor of fine arts degrees. Nondegree programs are offered as well. The center boasts a permanent faculty of nationally recognized artists in clay, metals, glass, fibers, and wood. The facility is open year-round and includes exhibits and sales galleries.

The Upper Cumberland is a good place for a regional crafts center. Due to its remoteness, people here have traditionally gotten by with what they made themselves. The region has exported its crafts, too. The citizens of this area around Caney Fork have a long history of making products for resale.

Andrew Lafevre, born in 1774, migrated to Tennessee from Virginia by way of Kentucky. By 1824, he and his family lived in the Caney Fork Valley. Five of Lafevre's six sons were potters, and the industry they started lasted a century. The clay in the area is suitable for a wide range of products—churns, pitchers, jugs, bowls—all of which were shipped down the river. The census of 1850 listed seventy-seven potters in Tennessee. Twenty-six of them lived here along Caney Fork.

Return to TN 56 and retrace your route toward the Interstate 40 junction. Just short of the interstate, turn right on Buffalo Valley Road, marked Putnam County 15. It is 7.5 miles to the town of Baxter; where the road crosses Interstate 40 at another exit, it becomes Old Baxter Road.

Mine Lick is what this area was called at first. John Allison came from North Carolina in 1807 to claim his Revolutionary War grant, and with him was his son, Joseph, nicknamed "Mine Lick." "Uncle Mine Lick," as he was called in later years, was a noted storyteller. His identity became inseparable from the community's.

The town itself sprang up after the railroad came through. In 1902 the people named it after the railroad's president, Jere Baxter.

In the void after the Civil War, the Methodist Church established a number of schools throughout the South. One of them, Baxter Seminary, was located here. Its stated purpose was to offer "a Christian education to the boys and girls of the Cumberland Plateau who need to work their way in order to secure an education. It trains them in Christian citizenship for a life of usefulness." Under contract with the Putnam County School Board, it provided secondary education for this part of the county. But the school was in poor condition for much of its early existence.

In 1923, the Methodists appointed Dr. Harry L. Upperman of Pennsylvania—an excellent fund-raiser—as president of the school. Under his leadership, the school grew and improved. To pay their expenses, students worked in a variety of jobs around the campus. Agricultural students raised grain, vegetables, cattle, and poultry to supply the dining hall. By 1940, Baxter Seminary enrolled 325 day and boarding students from twenty Upper Cumberland counties and was a respected secondary school. Upperman retired in 1957, and Baxter Seminary became a regular county high school. Henry Upperman is still revered in these parts. The local high school is called Upperman in his honor.

Tennessee Central Depot at Cookeville

Continue 0.6 mile past Baxter to a fork; bear left. After 0.8 mile, you will come to TN 56. Turn left (N), then right (E) onto U.S. 70N. Head for Cookeville, traveling parallel to the route of the old Walton Road, the one authorized by the legislature in 1799 that brought thousands of settlers into Middle Tennessee.

After 6.6 miles on U.S. 70N, which becomes West Broad Street entering Cookeville, you will come to a major intersection. Bear left at this fork, staying on West Broad. It is 0.6 mile on West Broad to the old Tennessee Central Railroad Depot.

The "Hub City of the Upper Cumberland," Cookeville likes to call itself. It is, in fact, the region's major trade center and its largest town. That has not always been the case, for by Middle Tennessee standards, Cookeville is relatively new. Its current status dates to about 1900, after the coming of the railroad.

Most of Tennessee's early railroad development consisted of north-south routes. It was not until well after the Civil War that an effort was made to build a line across the width of the midstate. The railroad to Cookeville owes its existence to Alexander Crawford, a man who came from Pennsylvania and acquired mineral and timber rights to thousands of acres east of Cookeville on the Cumberland Plateau, then promoted the Nashville & Knoxville Railroad to exploit his resources. Under his leadership, a line was completed from the end of the Nashville, Chattanooga & St. Louis's Lebanon branch to Cookeville in 1890—"a glorious event indeed for Cookeville and Putnam County and for the Cumberland region," reported the local paper. The N & K was soon extended east to Monterey on the Cumberland Plateau.

Next, a man known as the "silver-tongued promoter" entered the picture. He was Jere Baxter. The wealthy Nashvillian dreamed of a line from the Tennessee River on the western edge of Middle Tennessee to Harriman in East Tennessee. He acquired the N & K from Crawford interests in 1893 and renamed it the Tennessee Central. Using leased prison laborers who were often inhumanely exploited, Baxter pushed the line east to a connection with the Southern Railroad's Cincinnati-Chattanooga line near Harriman.

The Nashville, Chattanooga & St. Louis and its parent Louisville &

Nashville wanted to keep their monopoly on traffic into and out of Nashville, so they opposed Baxter's efforts. When the Nashville, Chattanooga & St. Louis refused to allow the continued interchange of traffic at Lebanon, Baxter just built his own line from Lebanon to Nashville. That explains why two railroads connected the Wilson County seat with Tennessee's capital city at one time. Then Baxter built the TC beyond Nashville to Clarksville and on to Hopkinsville, Kentucky, and a connection with the Illinois Central.

The result of Baxter's efforts was a Tennessee Central Railroad that connected with major rail lines on both the east and the west and gave this remote area access to markets nationwide. Residents who had been subsistence farmers were able to switch to staples for export, and cars loaded with corn, tobacco, mules, hogs, chickens, and eggs left Cookeville on the TC for distant markets. And the railroad brought goods into the region as well.

Passengers were hauled on the TC, too. The line had a depot in Nashville at the site of today's Riverfront Park. The TC never had dining cars, but passengers could buy lunch on the train. A crew member would take orders, then wire them to a station down the line. Local housewives would prepare lunches and sell them on the train when it arrived. Passenger service was discontinued in the 1950s, but excursion trains still run on the old TC from Nashville east to Watertown.

News that the railroad would build a depot west of Cookeville's square created quite a sensation. Land values in what came to be known as "West Side" skyrocketed. Within a year of the opening of the line, over fifty residences had been built, and by 1900, there were five hotels. Cookeville, which until then had been a quiet village of fewer than five hundred people centered around the courthouse square, was transformed into a trade center. And the coming of the railroad is why Cookeville has two downtowns—the one here by the depot and another 0.5 mile east at the square.

The TC built this beautiful depot in 1909. It remains the best-preserved and most unusual-looking railroad station in Middle Tennessee. The city of Cookeville owns it and uses it for a museum.

Never profitable, the Tennessee Central went into receivership from time

Putnam County Courthouse

to time. Traffic declined when U.S. 70N was built in the 1930s, then declined even more after the completion of Interstate 40. The railroad went bankrupt in 1968 and was sold off in three pieces to major lines. The Nashville-to-Cookeville line is owned by a local rail authority today.

At the depot, Broad Street follows a dogleg right, then left. Stay on Broad for 0.4 mile to the Putnam County Courthouse.

Land-hungry settlers struggling through this area on the Walton Road were bound for the fertile Middle Tennessee heartland and had little interest in these uplands. But some did stay, mostly in the rich bottoms along the rivers and creeks. Those who lived here in the first half of the nineteenth century were dissatisfied with the trouble it took to get to the courthouses in Sparta, Gainesboro, and Livingston, so they decided to create a new county. It proved to be a difficult task.

The Tennessee General Assembly created Putnam County in 1842, at a time when the state constitution contained strict size and distance limitations for new counties. The people of Jackson and Overton counties, out of which much of the new county was formed, brought suit, claiming the

TOURING THE MIDDLE TENNESSEE BACKROADS

establishment of Putnam County violated the constitution. A court issued an injunction, and the county was never formed.

In a similar dispute in East Tennessee, the Tennessee Supreme Court ruled in 1848 that courts did not have the authority to stop the creation of new counties. This decision, coupled with the election of Richard F. Cooke to the state senate, prompted a new move to create Putnam County. In his first term, 1851–53, Cooke was successful in getting a bill through the senate, but it died in the house. The next session, he persuaded his colleagues that a survey made since the last session showed that the constitutional requirements had been met, and the bill creating Putnam County passed in 1854.

Cooke's legislation provided that the county seat be named for him. After the customary squabble over where to locate it, Cookeville was laid out on this hill above two springs. No one seems to know why or who suggested it, but the new county was named for Israel Putnam, a native of Massachusetts and hero of the American Revolution. The current courthouse was built in 1900.

Circle the courthouse and backtrack on Broad Street for two blocks to Dixie Avenue. Turn right. It is 0.8 mile along this lovely, shaded street of substantial homes to the main entrance to Tennessee Technological University, on the left.

To some people, Jere Whitson was an impractical dreamer. But he had a vision for a college in the Upper Cumberland and set out to build one. Dixie College was chartered in 1909 and held its first full term in 1912 on a campus donated by Whitson. Like so many "colleges" in those days, Dixie was not a full-fledged institution of higher learning, but more of a secondary school. The school was not financially successful. In 1914, it merged with Putnam County High School.

The push to start Dixie College stalled momentarily in 1909 when the Tennessee legislature passed an act calling for the creation of a teachers college in each of the state's three grand divisions. The people of Cookeville promoted their town as the site for the Middle Tennessee school, but Murfreesboro was selected instead. The interest of the local people in having a state college did not die, however, and in 1916, the state established Tennessee Polytechnic Institute here on the campus of Dixie College.

The eagle atop Derryberry Hall

TPI remained primarily a technical high school until 1924, when the state authorized it to start a four-year college program. The high school was phased out, and in 1933, TPI granted its first baccalaureate degree. It was in engineering, reflecting the school's technical emphasis. TPI's enrollment grew and its curriculum expanded. In 1965, it was elevated to a university comprised of other colleges in addition to engineering. Tennessee Technological University is today a comprehensive state university. Still located on the old Dixie College campus, it is laid out in roughly the same manner as Dixie was planned.

In fact, the main administrative building, Derryberry Hall, was built as part of Dixie College. It was completely remodeled in 1960 and given a new front. Tennessee Tech's sports teams are known as the Eagles. Mounted above Derryberry Hall is a large metal eagle weighing seventy pounds, with a wingspan of four and a half feet. It got there as a result of a prank.

The president of the school, Dr. Everett Derryberry, had seen the eagle decorating a hotel at Monteagle and had unsuccessfully tried to buy it. The hotel later burned, and three Tech students went to Monteagle, sawed off the eagle, and brought it to Cookeville in a pickup truck. The eagle's owner, John Harton—a former state treasurer—protested. Governor Frank Clement intervened in the dispute, promising to pardon the students if they were charged and convicted of theft. The governor's involvement apparently pacified Harton, for he ended up donating the eagle to the university in 1958. It was mounted atop Derryberry Hall in 1961.

Henderson Hall, located behind Derryberry Hall, is the original 1931 engineering building, though in recent years it has been part of the arts and science college. This distinguished example of Georgian Revival design has not been altered since it was built.

Retrace your route on Dixie Avenue, only go past Broad Street one short block to U.S. 70N (Spring Street). Turn right and drive 0.6 mile to TN 135 (Willow Street). Turn left. Head south on TN 135, which becomes Burgess Falls Road where it crosses Interstate 40. You will arrive at the entrance to Burgess Falls State Natural Area after 10.7 miles. Turn right into the parking area.

When Tom Burgess came here to claim his Revolutionary War grant, it was easy for him to name this river Falling Water. It rushes off the nearby

Cumberland Plateau, then plunges dramatically into the valley of the Caney Fork over what is arguably Middle Tennessee's most beautiful waterfall. The little river was an obvious source of energy, so the Burgess family built a gristmill, where the early settlers came to grind their corn. The swift Falling Water River later provided the power for a sawmill that gave residents their first access to milled lumber.

The city of Cookeville recognized the advantages of rushing water. In 1924, it built a steel-and-earthen dam for an electric-generating station. Water was diverted from the lake through a wooden flume cut through the ridge to a powerhouse below the falls.

A massive flood in 1928 destroyed the dam and powerhouse. When they were rebuilt, the dam was constructed of concrete, rather than earth. The coming of TVA power rendered the old facility obsolete, and it produced its last electricity in 1944.

The citizens of Cookeville had the wisdom to preserve this area for its scenic beauty and outdoor recreation potential. In 1950, they began a co-operative management program with the state of Tennessee. The ultimate result was the establishment of Burgess Falls State Natural Area in 1971. Time has healed many of the wounds from previous uses, and today this is

Old hydroelectric dam at Burgess Falls

one of Tennessee's most beautiful natural areas. A short trail meanders along the river below the dam past several smaller falls to Burgess Falls itself, where the river drops 130 feet straight into the gorge.

After enjoying Burgess Falls, return to TN 135 and turn right (S) to enjoy a pretty drive across an undulating countryside of well-kept farms with the Cumberland Plateau as a backdrop. TN 135 follows several roads before reaching TN 289 on the edge of Sparta after 5.9 miles. An old drive-in theater stands on the left just before the junction. Built as the Park-Away Drive-in 1948, it was the first drive-in theater in the Upper Cumberland. Before then, anyone wanting to go to a drive-in movie had to travel all the way to Nashville.

Turn left on TN 289. It is 2.5 miles to Brackman Way (U.S. 70) in Sparta. Turn left (E) and drive 0.7 mile to Church Street, just short of the courthouse. Turn left (N) onto Church for a swing through the old section of Sparta. Its streets, shaded by large trees, are lined with interesting houses and pretty churches. Stay on Church Street to Everett. Turn right and drive to North Main. Turn right again and return to Brackman Way at the square. Cross Brackman diagonally to the right and go around the courthouse.

White County Courthouse

This lovely stone building may look old, but it isn't. It was completed in 1975. White County is an old county, though, established in 1806. The act creating the county did not specify for whom it was named. Though there is some question, it is believed it is named for John White, an adventurer, Revolutionary War veteran, and "squatter" who settled near here in 1789, before the 1805 treaty with the Cherokees made it legal. No one knows how the name Sparta was selected either, but the best guess is that it just appealed to someone who had a fondness for ancient names.

The county seat was first located on the Caney Fork River at Rock Island but was moved here in 1810. Some people wanted to locate the courthouse west of the Calfkiller River, while others wanted it on the east. The east faction won out when the owner of the land offered it for free.

The name Calfkiller is of obscure origin, too. There were scattered settlements of Cherokees around here when the first white settlers came, and one of their leaders was called Calf Killer—so the story goes. There is another story that the river got its name when an early settler drove his cattle in the river, only to see them swept away and drowned.

One of the more intriguing characters in the history of Sparta was Sam Turney, a lawyer from the same family as Henry Turney, whose remodeled 1789 log house is on The Upper Cumberland Tour, and Peter Turney, the secession zealot and later governor who led the attempt to withdraw Franklin County from Tennessee when Tennessee did not secede with the first wave of Southern states. (See The Elk River Tour, pages 317–18, for a description of the secession crisis in Franklin County.)

Sam Turney had the peculiar habit of sitting in a Sparta hotel cutting his own hair. When someone asked him how he could do it, he replied, "I guess I know the shape of my own head."

Some of lawyer Turney's trial tactics would hardly meet modern ethical standards. In the days before copies of documents were made, he was known to eat warrants and indictments that charged his clients, thus freeing them. In a case where he represented a man charged with counterfeiting, he ate the suspect bill and replaced it with a real one. "Take the bill to the bank and let them determine if it is counterfeit," Turney insisted. It was real, all right, the banker said. Turney's client was set free.

Leave the square at its southeast corner by traveling east on Maple Street; after 0.2 mile, the road becomes Gaines Street. You will reach a Y intersection after another 0.1 mile. Bear right, staying on Gaines through a pleasant neighborhood of old homes. Gaines becomes Country Club Road and intersects Lester Flatt Road 1.3 miles from the Y intersection.

If Bill Monroe is rightly honored as "the father of bluegrass music," then Lester Flatt is one of the princes. Flatt grew up in a musical family near Sparta. He joined Monroe in 1944, at about the same time as a young banjo player from the North Carolina mountains named Earl Scruggs. From that point, bluegrass music as it is heard today took form. Flat and Scruggs left Monroe's band in 1948 and started their own band, the Foggy Mountain Boys, featuring Lester's vocals and rhythm guitar and Earl's lightning-fast, distinctive banjo style.

Flatt and Scruggs contributed to the popularity of bluegrass music as much as anyone. Under the sponsorship of Nashville's Martha White Flour, they toured the Southeast, played regular radio shows, appeared on the Grand

Ole Opry, and had their own syndicated television show. But the popularity of bluegrass was still limited pretty much to the South, particularly the Southern mountains, until the late 1950s, when the Kingston Trio scored a big hit with "Tom Dooley." A form of popular music called "folk" burst on the scene and carried bluegrass with it.

Interest in bluegrass music spread way beyond its traditional base. Lester Flatt and Earl Scruggs achieved nationwide recognition when their music was the theme for the popular 1960s television show *Beverly Hillbillies* and when their "Foggy Mountain Breakdown" was part of the 1967 Academy Award–winning film *Bonnie and Clyde*. Flatt and Scruggs split in 1969, but both continued their careers as giants in bluegrass music. Lester Flatt is buried here in Sparta.

Continue past Lester Flatt Road as the route follows the old Nashville-Knoxville highway up its long ascent of the western escarpment of the Cumberland Plateau. The Rock House is on the right after 2.4 miles, just before the intersection with U.S. 70.

No one knows when the Rock House was built, but it seems to have been between 1835 and 1845. Tradition has it that Barlow Fisk, cousin of Moses Fisk, the noted Upper Cumberland educator, hired a man named Sam Denton to build it as a stagecoach stop.

The Rock House

A few years after the Walton Road opened as the main route into Middle Tennessee from the east, an alternate road came into use. It left the Walton Road near today's Crossville, reached Sparta, then went on to Nashville by way of McMinnville and Murfreesboro; U.S. 70S roughly follows the same route today. This new road became the official Knoxville-Nashville mail route in the 1820s, and a thriving stage business developed. The crude stands that provided accommodations on the Walton Road gave way to more substantial inns on the new road, and the Rock House was apparently one of them. The new road was a toll road; tolls were collected at the Rock House.

Turn right (E) onto U.S. 70 and continue up the mountain. After 1.4 miles, turn left into the overlook.

This overlook—part of the old highway—offers a splendid view across the Eastern Highland Rim and the ridges that are outliers of the Cumberland Plateau.

Overlook on the edge of the Cumberland Plateau

This westernmost range of the Appalachians extends from eastern Kentucky down into Alabama across the width of the Volunteer State and constitutes one of Tennessee's principal topographic regions. Though overshadowed in the public's mind by the Great Smokies on Tennessee's eastern border, "Tennessee's other mountains" possess a wealth of scenic beauty and offer a bounty of outdoor recreation opportunities. The best-known preserves on the plateau are Fall Creek Falls State Park and Big South Fork National River and Recreation Area, but there are others just as scenic.

One of them located near here is Virgin Falls Pocket Wilderness, one of several areas set aside by the Bowater Southern Paper Corporation on its vast Cumberland Plateau timber holdings. The small wilderness area includes four impressive waterfalls on the plateau's edge above the Caney Fork River, including 110-foot Virgin Falls itself, which flows out of a cave and disappears into a sink. The hike to the falls and back takes all day. Virgin Falls Pocket Wilderness is not on this tour, but the trailhead can be reached by continuing east on U.S. 70 for 4.3 miles to DeRossett; the parking area is 7.9 miles down the road to the right.

When you are ready to leave the overlook, descend the mountain on U.S. 70. It is 6.5 miles back through Sparta to the junction with TN 111 west of town. Continue west on U.S. 70 for 5.1 miles to the junction with TN 136 (Old Kentucky Road). Turn left (S). It is 11 miles to Walling and U.S. 70S.

Old Kentucky Road is just what it says—an old road to Kentucky. This free road extending from Kentucky to Alabama was in use as early as 1813 as a drovers' road, thus giving it its alternate name—Kentucky Stock Road. Farmers would drive their stock out of the region for resale. It was not uncommon to see the road clogged with cattle, sheep, hogs, and turkeys.

There is a spring near the Shady Grove community called Darkey Spring. Old Kentucky Road was a favorite route for slave traders, who would buy slaves in Kentucky and take them to the emerging cotton plantations in the Deep South. The use of the spring as an overnight stop for the caravans of human cargo gave it its name.

Indians used to travel several well-worn trails through the uninhabited hunting grounds between the Ohio and Tennessee rivers, an area that includes today's Middle Tennessee. This stretch of Old Kentucky Road follows the Chickamauga Path, which ran from the Tennessee River into what is now Kentucky.

A house that was believed to be haunted once stood on Old Kentucky Road near Walling. Pleasant Carter Templeton, a Confederate soldier from Walling, died in a Federal hospital in Nashville in 1864, and his body was returned here to White County in a copper-lined, sawdust-packed coffin. His mother was in poor health and did not expect to live long, so she had the coffin put upstairs, to be buried with her.

She made a recovery, though, and lived until 1892. But she left the coffin and body in the house. It is said that she wore ruts in the floor beside the coffin by sitting in her rocking chair knitting, sewing, and singing songs. Some people say she looked at her son's body daily, while others say she kept blankets around Pleasant to keep him warm. After they were buried together in 1892, stories of ghosts persisted until 1967, when the house caught fire and burned to the ground.

Turn right (W) on U.S. 70S. The highway travels along a bluff above the Caney Fork River and Great Falls Lake before crossing them. After 1.5 miles, turn right onto TN 287 (Great Falls Road) and drive through the gate into Rock Island.

The area around Rock Island has played many important roles over the years. It was here that the Chickamauga Path crossed the Caney Fork River, and it was here in 1793 that one of the last of Middle Tennessee's Indian fights occurred. Rock Island has been an important industrial site and in more recent times a popular spot for outdoor recreation.

The physical setting is remarkable. Three rivers come together here—the Caney Fork, Collins, and Rocky. After receiving the waters of the other two, the Caney Fork crashes through a deep gorge where, in the space of 2 miles, it drops nearly a hundred feet. The Great Falls of the Caney Fork, this is called. The island for which the area is named sits in the Caney Fork near the mouth of the Rocky River.

It was near the island that the first settlement in this area started in the late 1790s, about the same time that a ferry began to operate across the Caney Fork. For a time after White County was created, Rock Island was the county seat. It is said that several early sessions of the Tennessee Supreme Court were held here.

Things changed dramatically in 1881 with the completion of a railroad line through here. The town migrated from its original site at the island to the railroad. The interesting little Rock Island depot still stands just inside the village gate.

Rock Island Depot

As early as 1830, McMinnville's Asa Faulkner began taking advantage of the area's abundant water power. By the late 1800s, he was the area's leading industrialist. In pursuit of his dream to build a factory at the Great Falls of the Caney Fork, he designed a large, three-story brick building to be constructed right next to the river. He died in 1886, and the task passed to Clay Faulkner, one of his sixteen children. Clay Faulkner and H. L. and Jesse Walling completed the Great Falls Cotton Mill in 1892. A whole company town—called Fall City—was built around the mill.

The flood of 1902, the worst in memory on the Caney Fork, washed away the mill's waterwheel and housing. The mill was not reopened, and the company town faded from existence.

Rock Island's next life came in 1917 with the completion of Great Falls Dam by the Tennessee Electric Power Company. The dam created a lake that backs up on the Caney Fork and the other rivers. Starting in the 1920s, wealthy Nashvillians began using Rock Island as a summer retreat,

The cotton factory at Great Falls

a practice that continues to this day. Their rustic cabins sit along the Collins River part of the lake just upstream from the dam. When the Tennessee Valley Authority took over the production of electricity in Tennessee, it also took over Great Falls Dam.

The latest chapter in Rock Island's life came in the late 1960s with the establishment of Rock Island State Park. The park takes in 883 acres downstream from the dam and offers a variety of recreation options.

Stay on TN 287 as it swings right at a fork. You will reach Great Falls Dam 1 mile from U.S. 70S. The lane to the summer colony takes off to the left just before the bridge; continue on TN 287. The old cotton factory is 0.3 mile past the dam. A parking area and a picnic area are just past it.

The view here is impressive. Great Falls is in the gorge below, and the powerhouse is visible downstream. Water backed up in the Collins River is diverted through a flume to generate electricity. When the water level is high, water flows through underground passages in the narrow ridge between the Collins and the Caney Fork, then drops in several spectacular waterfalls to the Caney Fork below.

Just across the road from the factory, set in a pretty little mossy cove, is a fascinating structure called Witch's Castle, or Spring Castle. No one knows for sure what its purpose was, but the charming little house was apparently built by the power company around the time the dam was constructed.

Witch's Castle at Great Falls

Continue west on TN 287 as it crests the narrow ridge between the two rivers. After 0.9 mile, turn into the main entrance to Rock Island State Park. The road forks past the visitor center. The right fork leads to a picnic area and an overlook above the Blue Hole, a huge eddy on the Caney Fork River; a hiking path descends steeply into the gorge and follows the river downstream. The left fork drops into the gorge to a natural sandy beach at Badger Flat. Here, the river ends its tumultuous path through the gorge and empties into the slack headwaters of Center Hill Lake.

From the park, continue west on TN 287 for 4.2 miles to the Berea community. Turn left (S) on TN 288. After 0.8 mile, where TN 288 turns left, go straight on Francis Ferry Road. It is 7.4 miles to the crossroads at Faulkner Springs. After crossing a bridge, turn left onto Faulkner Springs Road.

Clay Faulkner was a talented and resourceful entrepreneur. The cotton mill he and the Walling brothers built at Great Falls was only one of his

ventures. Another was Mountain City Woolen Mills, located along Charles Creek. As at Great Falls, an entire company town sprang up here. Gorilla Pants were among the products produced at Mountain City Woolen Mills— pants so strong that even a gorilla could not destroy them.

Faulkner tired of traveling to and from McMinnville each day. In 1896, he told his wife, Mary, that if she would move near the mill, he would build the finest house in Warren County. And he did. It is the splendid Queen Anne–style house on the corner. The meticulous construction took about a year, and Clay Faulkner supervised every detail. The interior and exterior walls rest on a foundation set on solid bedrock. The gingerbread ornamentation on the wraparound porch is some of the finest anywhere.

Clay Faulkner died in 1916. Mary sold Falcon Rest, as they called it, three years later. The house served as a hospital and nursing home until 1968. George and Charlien McGlothin bought it in 1989, carefully restored it over a period of five years, and opened an attractive bed-and-breakfast called Falcon Manor.

Follow Faulkner Springs Road into McMinnville; you will cross U.S. 70S

Bypass. As the road enters town, it becomes Spring Street. You will reach Morford Street (U.S. 70S) 2.7 miles from Faulkner Springs. Turn right (W). After three blocks, turn left (S) on High Street, then make a left (E) onto Main Street.

The Black House, located at the corner of High and Main, is McMinnville's oldest home. The original part of it was built in 1825 on a thirteen-acre tract on what was then the edge of town. Built in the Federal style, it has been altered in the Greek Revival tradition. The house is named for Dr. Thomas Black, who bought it in 1874. Black was a well-respected physician who served as McMinnville's mayor in the 1880s.

Two of Middle Tennessee's loveliest churches stand diagonally across from each other on Main Street past the Black House. First Presbyterian Church was completed in 1871 and First United Methodist Church in 1888. Clay Faulkner was a member of the Methodist church. When he made the bricks for Falcon Rest, he made enough for this church, too.

Continue east on Main. The people of McMinnville are justly proud of their library, located at the corner of Main and Chancery streets.

William Harrison Magness had the good judgment—or good luck—to have sold his considerable securities holdings before the great crash of 1929. With his cash, he was able to get good buys during the Great Depression. Magness was a generous man, a bachelor who saw the need for education and the value of a good library. In 1931, when hardly anyone had money to do much of anything, Magness built this magnificent library resembling a Greek Temple. Included in the 12,000-square-foot building was an apartment he built for himself, but he never occupied it. In his will, probated in 1936, Magness also made a generous contribution for the maintenance of the library.

The 1897 Warren County Courthouse is past the library on Main Street. Just as White County was created out of Smith County in 1806, Warren County was created out of White County in 1809. It is named for Joseph Warren, the Boston physician-patriot who participated in the Boston Tea Party in 1773, dispatched Paul Revere on his famous ride in 1775, and was killed at the Battle of Bunker Hill that same year.

The monument at the southwest corner of the courthouse testifies to the awful carnage of the Civil War. John H. Savage, commanding officer of the Sixteenth Tennessee Infantry, erected this monument in 1904 in honor of the men of the regiment who lost their lives in the conflict. There are enough names to cover all four sides of the obelisk.

Though it no longer exists, another prominent McMinnville institution was the Southern School of Photography, which operated from 1904 until 1929. W. L. Lively, the school's proprietor, was a leading photography pioneer, and it was here in McMinnville that he built the world's largest camera, measuring eleven feet by six feet by five feet. The prints made with it—measuring thirty inches by sixty inches—are still considered masterpieces. Some are displayed by Eastman Kodak in Rochester, New York, and some at the Smithsonian in Washington.

Leave the courthouse on Main Street (TN 56). Follow TN 56 southeast from town across the Barren Fork River for 1.6 miles to where TN 8 takes off to the left. If you care to take a brief side trip, head down TN 8 for a few miles to visit Cumberland Caverns—a major attraction in this area, a registered national landmark, and Tennessee's largest cave.

In 1807, Aaron Higgenbotham became the first owner of the property where the cave is located. He is credited with discovering the massive cave. According to tradition, while walking along the old Chickamauga Path surveying his lands, he felt a rush of cool air from a hole in the ground. With the aid of a lighted torch, he crawled in to investigate. Amazed at what he found, he decided to venture deeper into the cave, but as he carefully made his way along, he slipped. The torch fell far below, and Higgenbotham found himself in utter darkness and silence.

He had no choice but to stay put and hope that he would be found. He had left his knapsack and surveying instruments on the trail—perhaps someone would find them and figure out where he was. Toward the end of the third day, a search party did find his gear near the narrow entrance. Using candles, they entered the cave and found Higgenbotham. After that day in 1810, the cave was known as Higgenbotham's Cave.

Now called Cumberland Caverns, the cave is open to the public from May through October.

Continue south on TN 56.

It should be obvious by now that you are in the heart of nursery country. The first nursery was established in this area in 1874, but it was the entry of Jonathan H. H. Boyd into the business a few years later that began the McMinnville area's transformation into "the nursery capital of the South." The family of this pioneer grower is still in the business here.

Nurseries are big business around here. In fact, nursery production ranks fourth among Tennessee's cash crops—behind tobacco, cotton, and soybeans. Of the state's 44,000 nursery acres, 33,000 are within the six-county McMinnville area, which produces $78 million in gross sales annually. Of that amount, 64 percent comes from Warren County growers.

Why has this area become one of America's leading nursery areas? Habitat diversity is the main reason. The elevation ranges from nearly 900 feet at McMinnville to 1,900 feet on the Cumberland Plateau. A 1,000-foot rise in elevation is comparable to the climatic difference 300 miles north, and this diversity enables a wide range of species to be grown here. Many Northern plants reach their southern terminus here, and many Southern plants reach their northern limits. Soil types are diverse here, too, ranging from the moist bottoms of mountain coves to rocky ridges with shallow soil.

It is 7 miles on TN 56 from the TN 8 junction to Irving College.

This crossroads takes its name from a proprietary school started here in 1835. After its building burned in 1844, it reopened in 1845 as a strict Latin school. By 1850, students were enrolled from most Southern states. Fifty-seven students lived in dormitories and many more in nearby private homes. The school reopened after the Civil War and remained in operation until the advent of universal public education in Tennessee around 1900. The school's buildings were then converted to a public school.

Stay on TN 56 past Irving College as the route enters Grundy County, crosses the Collins River, and continues up the river's narrow valley on one of Middle Tennessee's prettiest drives. The road crosses the Collins for the last time 9.5 miles from Irving College. Here, the river is dry most of the year. It goes underground upstream from this bridge and reappears near a church down the road.

From the bridge, the highway climbs through several switchbacks up the escarpment of the Cumberland Plateau. After 3.4 miles, just as TN 56 crests the mountain, a road to the right leads into the Beersheba Springs community, while a road to the left leads to Savage Gulf State Natural Area. Follow the little lane to the right for less than 0.2 mile into Beersheba

Springs; turn right at the crossroads to reach the old hotel, perched on a bluff overlooking the Collins River Valley.

The status of Beersheba Springs as a premier summer resort dates to 1854, when John Armfield bought the property. If ever there was a study in contrasts, it was Armfield. He was born into an old North Carolina Quaker family, yet he made his fortune dealing in slaves. Slave traders were not favored in polite society, yet Armfield enjoyed the friendship of the elite of his day. Armfield lived among the wealthiest of planters but was content to live here on this isolated mountain late in life.

His connection with Tennessee seems to have come from a chance encounter with Isaac Franklin, the Sumner County native whose home, Fairvue, is on The Hendersonville-Portland Tour. Young Armfield was driving a stage in Virginia. Impressed with his perseverance, Franklin brought him to Tennessee and made him a partner in his slave-trading business. Armfield married Franklin's niece and managed the partnership's business in Alexandria, Virginia, from which point slaves were transported to the growing market in Mississippi and Louisiana. Franklin and Armfield got out of the slave business in 1836. They returned to Sumner County, though they both maintained interests in Louisiana, where they traveled frequently. Beersheba Springs was already a summer resort when Armfield first visited in the early 1850s.

In the course of looking after his varied business interests, John Cain, a successful McMinnville merchant and landowner, often traveled in the company of his wife, Beersheba. While on a trip to the head of the Collins River in 1833, Beersheba wandered up the mountain on a faint, old trail—the Chickamauga Path—and discovered the mineral spring that came to be named for her; the spring is marked today by a small stone arch on the right just before the first little lane into the community. Realizing the area's potential as a resort, Cain and some other McMinnville men bought the land around the spring. By 1839, they had constructed cabins and begun a rather primitive resort.

It was John Armfield who made Beersheba Springs a premier resort for the elite. He bought the property in 1853 and built twenty summer "cottages"—each one different, and each one strikingly beautiful—between 1856 and 1858. Armfield constructed a hotel in front of the 1839 log cabins,

The hotel at Beersheba Springs

too; those cabins still stand behind the hotel. Armfield ran the resort for a few years before he sold it to a group of investors.

The Armfields made Beersheba Springs their year-round home. During the Civil War, it was a refuge for prominent Confederate-sympathizing civilians. Following the Southern army's flight from Middle Tennessee in the summer of 1863, Beersheba Springs was the target of endless attacks by bushwhackers—outlaws who were mostly deserters from both armies taking advantage of the breakdown of civil authority. It is a wonder the hotel and cottages survived.

Armfield continued as the dominant person at Beersheba Springs until his death in 1871. He is buried in the Armfield Cemetery, located two cottages past the hotel.

Nashvillians had always been a part of Beersheba Springs, and the trend continued after Armfield's death; today, the community is mostly a retreat for Nashvillians. The hotel changed hands many times after Armfield owned it. Since the 1940s, it has served as a conference center for the United Methodist Church.

Two of the most impressive cottages in Beersheba Springs are just past the hotel. The handsome brick cottage with the circular pavilion was built

Turner Cottage, one of the many originals at Beersheba Springs

TOURING THE MIDDLE TENNESSEE BACKROADS

by John Armfield for Dr. Thomas J. Harding in 1857. The cottage past it was built around the same time for John Meredith Bass—a banker, mayor of Nashville in the 1830s, and a longtime personal friend of Armfield's.

After enjoying Beersheba Springs, head back to TN 56 and take the road to Savage Gulf State Natural Area, the largest unit of South Cumberland State Recreation Area.

Savage Gulf State Natural Area is named for one of the three gorges, or "gulfs," that branch out from the headwaters of the Collins River. Savage Gulf itself—named for the pioneer Savage family—holds a 500-acre old-growth forest of massive hardwoods, one of the few remaining in the eastern United States.

Established in 1973, the natural area takes in over 11,400 acres and offers 50 miles of hiking on trails ranging from the easy walk in from the visitor center to strenuous routes over boulder-strewn creek beds. From the visitor center, a paved walkway leads to the Great Stone Door, a narrow, 150-foot-long crevice in the bluff line that permits passage to the gorge below. Rappelling is also a popular activity here. Other highlights include several waterfalls, as well as views of the Cumberland wilderness from 1,000-foot bluffs.

The tour ends here, at the river's remote headwaters. From TN 56 at Beersheba Springs, you can return to McMinnville or continue to Altamont and Tracy City, then follow U.S. 41 to Monteagle and Interstate 24.

Appendix

Parks and Recreation Areas

Bledsoe Creek State Park
400 Ziegler's Fort Road
Gallatin, TN 37066
615-452-3706

Burgess Falls State Natural Area
Route 6
Sparta, TN 38583
615-761-3338

Cedars of Lebanon State Park
328 Cedar Forest Road
Lebanon, TN 37087
615-443-2769

Cross Creek National
   Wildlife Refuge
Route 1, Box 556
Dover, TN 37058
615-232-7477

Cumberland Caverns
Route 9
McMinnville, TN 37110
615-668-4396

David Crockett State Park
1440 West Gaines
Lawrenceburg, TN 38464
615-762-9408

Dunbar Cave State Natural Area
401 Old Dunbar Cave Road
Clarksville, TN 37043
615-648-5526

Edgar Evins State Park
Silver Point, TN 38582
615-858-2446

Harpeth State Scenic River
Kingston Springs, TN 37082
615-797-9052

Henry Horton State Park
Chapel Hill, TN 37034
615-364-7724

Land Between the Lakes
Golden Pond, KY 42211
502-934-5602

Long Hunter State Park
2910 Hobson Pike
Hermitage, TN 37076
615-885-2422

Montgomery Bell State Park
Box 39
Burns, TN 37029
615-797-3101

Natchez Trace Parkway
Route 1
Tupelo, MS 38801
601-842-1572

Paris Landing State Park
Route 1
Buchanan, TN 38222
901-642-4311

Radnor Lake State Natural Area
1160 Otter Creek Road
Nashville, TN 37220
615-373-3467

Rock Island State Park
Route 2
Rock Island, TN 38581
615-686-2471

Ruskin Cave/Jewel Cave
2803 Yellow Creek Road
Dickson, TN 37055
615-763-2810

South Cumberland State
   Recreation Area
Route 1
Monteagle, TN 37356
615-924-2980

Standing Stone State Park
1674 Standing Stone Park Highway
Hilham, TN 38568
615-823-6347

Tennessee National
   Wildlife Refuge
810 E. Wood Street
Paris, TN 38242
901-642-2091

Tims Ford State Park
570 Tims Ford Drive
Winchester, TN 37938
615-967-4457

Warner Parks
50 Vaughn Road
Nashville, TN 37221
615-370-8050

Historic Sites and Areas

The Athenaeum
808 Athenaeum Street
Columbia, TN 38402
615-381-4822

Bowen-Campbell House
Box 781
Goodlettsville, TN 37072
615-859-2239

Bradford-Berry House
   (Hazel Patch)
252 E. Main Street
Hendersonville, TN 37075
615-822-0789

Carnton
1345 Carnton Lane
Franklin, TN 37064
615-794-0903

Carter House
1140 Columbia Avenue
Franklin, TN 37064
615-791-1861

Cordell Hull Birthplace
Route 1
Byrdstown, TN 38549
615-864-3247

Cowan Railroad Museum
Cowan, TN 37318
615-967-7365

Cragfont
Route 1
Castalian Springs, TN 37031
615-452-7070

Falls Mill
134 Falls Mill Road
Belvidere, TN 37306
615-469-7161

Fort Donelson National Battlefield
101 Petty Street
Dover, TN 37058
615-232-5706

Jack Daniel's Distillery
Box 199
Lynchburg, TN 37352
615-759-6180

James K. Polk Home
301 W. Seventh Street
Columbia, TN 38401
615-388-2354

Mansker's Station Frontier
   Life Center
Caldwell Lane
Goodlettsville, TN 37070
615-859-FORT

Narrows of the Harpeth State
   Historic Area
Kingston Springs, TN 37082
615-797-9052

Newsom Mill State Historic Site
Kingston Springs, TN 37082
615-797-9052

Old Stone Fort State
   Archaeological Park
Route 7
Manchester, TN 37355
615-723-5073

Port Royal State Historic Area
3300 Old Clarksville Highway
Adams, TN 37010
615-358-9696

Rock Castle
Rock Castle Lane
Hendersonville, TN 37075
615-824-0502

Stones River National Battlefield
3501 Old Nashville Highway
Murfreesboro, TN 37129
615-893-9501

Trousdale Place
183 W. Main Street
Gallatin, TN 37066
615-452-5648

University of the South
Sewanee, TN 37375-1000
615-598-1286

Wonder Cave
Pelham, TN 37366
615-467-3060

Wynnewood
Castalian Springs, TN 37031
615-452-5463

Chambers of Commerce

Brentwood Chamber of Commerce
5211 Maryland Way
Suite 1080
Brentwood, TN 37027-5011
Phone: 615-373-1595
FAX: 615-373-8810

Byrdstown–Pickett County
    Chamber of Commerce
P.O. Box 447
Byrdstown, TN 38549
Phone: 615-864-7195

Cheatham County
    Chamber of Commerce
108 S. Main Street
Ashland City, TN 37015
Phone: 615-792-6722
FAX: 615-792-6722

Clarksville Area
    Chamber of Commerce
312 Madison Street
P.O. Box 883
Clarksville, TN 37401-0883
Phone: 615-647-2331
FAX: 615-645-1574

Cookeville–Putnam
    County Chamber of Commerce
302 S. Jefferson Avenue
Cookeville, TN 38501
Phone: 615-526-2211
FAX: 615-526-4023

Dale Hollow–Clay County
    Chamber of Commerce
P.O. Box 69
Highway 52
Celina, TN 38551
Phone: 615-243-3338

Dickson County
    Chamber of Commerce
P.O. Box 339
119 Highway 70 East
Dickson, TN 37055
Phone: 615-446-0919
FAX: 615-441-3112

Franklin County
    Chamber of Commerce
P.O. Box 280
Winchester, TN 37398
Phone: 615-967-6788
FAX: 615-967-9418

Gainesboro–Jackson
    County Chamber of Commerce
P.O. Box 827
Gainesboro, TN 38562
Phone: 615-268-0971

Gallatin Chamber of Commerce
P.O. Box 26
118 W. Main Street
Gallatin, TN 37066
Phone: 615-452-4000
FAX: 615-452-4021

Giles County
   Chamber of Commerce
100 S. Second Street
Pulaski, TN 38478
Phone: 615-363-3789
FAX: 615-363-3789

Goodlettsville
   Chamber of Commerce
100 S. Main Street
Suite D
Goodlettsville, TN 37072
Phone: 615-859-7979
FAX: 615-859-1480

Grundy County
   Chamber of Commerce
HCR 76, Box 578
Gruelti-Laager, TN 37339
Phone: 615-779-3462

Hartsville–Trousdale
   County Chamber of Commerce
200 E. Main Street
P.O. Box 34
Hartsville, TN 37074
Phone: 615-374-9243
FAX: 615-244-8846

Hickman County
   Chamber of Commerce
P.O. Box 126
Centerville, TN 37033
Phone: 615-729-5774

Houston County Area
   Chamber of Commerce
P.O. Box 270
Municipal Building
Erin, TN 37061
Phone: 615-289-4108
FAX: 615-289-5436

Humphreys County
   Chamber of Commerce
124 E. Main Street
P.O. Box 733
Waverly, TN 37185
Phone: 615-296-4865
FAX: 615-296-2135

Lafayette–Macon
   County Chamber of Commerce
208 Church Street
Lafayette, TN 37083
Phone: 615-666-5885
FAX: 615-666-6969

Lawrence County
   Chamber of Commerce
P.O. Box 86
Lawrenceburg, TN 38464
Phone: 615-762-4911
FAX: 615-762-3153

Lebanon–Wilson
   County Chamber of Commerce
149 Public Square
Lebanon, TN 37087
Phone: 615-444-5503
FAX: 615-443-0596

Lewis County
   Chamber of Commerce
12 E. Main Street
P.O. Box 182
Hohenwald, TN 38462
Phone: 615-796-4084
FAX: 615-796-3794

Lincoln County–Fayetteville
   Chamber of Commerce
P.O. Box 515
Fayetteville, TN 37334
Phone: 615-433-1234
FAX: 615-433-9087

Lynchburg–Moore
   County Chamber of Commerce
East Side of Square
P.O. Box 421
Lynchburg, TN 37352
Phone: 615-759-4111

Manchester
   Chamber of Commerce
110 E. Main Street
Manchester, TN 37355
Phone: 615-728-7635
FAX: 615-723-0736

Marshall County
   Chamber of Commerce
227 Second Avenue North
Lewisburg, TN 37091
Phone: 615-359-3863
FAX: 615-359-3863

Maury County
   Chamber of Commerce
308 W. Seventh Street
P.O. Box 1076
Columbia, TN 38402-1076
Phone: 615-388-2155
FAX: 615-380-0335

McMinnville–Warren County
   Chamber of Commerce
P.O. Box 574
110 S. Court Square
McMinnville, TN 37110
Phone: 615-473-6611
FAX: 615-473-4741

Nashville Area
   Chamber of Commerce
161 Fourth Avenue North
Nashville, TN 37219
Phone: 615-259-4755
FAX: 615-256-3074

Overton County
   Chamber of Commerce
310 McHenry Circle
P.O. Box 354
Livingston, TN 38570
Phone: 615-823-6421

Perry County
   Chamber of Commerce
P.O. Box 908
Linden, TN 37096
Phone: 615-589-2455

Rutherford County
   Chamber of Commerce
P.O. Box 864
302 S. Front Street
Murfreesboro, TN 37133-0864
Phone: 615-893-6565
FAX: 615-890-7600

Shelbyville–Bedford County
   Chamber of Commerce
100 N. Cannon Boulevard
Shelbyville, TN 37160
Phone: 615-684-3482
FAX: 615-684-3483

Smith County
   Chamber of Commerce
P.O. Box 70
130 W. Third Avenue
Carthage, TN 37030
Phone: 615-735-2093
FAX: 615-735-2093

Smithville–DeKalb
   County Chamber of Commerce
P.O. Box 64
Courthouse Square
Smithville, TN 37166
Phone: 615-597-4163

Sparta–White County
   Chamber of Commerce
16 W. Brockman Way
Sparta, TN 38583
Phone: 615-836-3552
FAX: 615-836-2216

Springfield Chamber of Commerce
100 W. Fifth Avenue
Springfield, TN 37172
Phone: 615-384-3800
FAX: 615-384-1260

Stewart County
   Chamber of Commerce
Spring Street, Watson Building
P.O. Box 147
Dover, TN 37058
Phone: 615-232-8290
FAX: 615-232-4973

Wayne County
   Chamber of Commerce
Courthouse Room 303
P.O. Box 675
Waynesboro, TN 38485
Phone: 615-722-3631

Williamson County
   Chamber of Commerce
109 Second Avenue South
Suite 107
P.O. Box 156
Franklin, TN 37065-0156
Phone: 615-794-1225
FAX: 615-794-5759

Bibliography

Recreation Guides

Brandt, Robert S., ed. *Tennessee Hiking Guide*. 2d ed. Knoxville: University of Tennessee Press, 1988.

Chappell, Susan. *Day Trips from Nashville*. Kansas City, Mo.: Two Lane Press, 1994.

Hamel, Paul. *Tennessee Wildlife Viewing Guide*. Helena, Mont.: Falcon Press, 1993.

Hemmerly, Thomas E. *Wildflowers of the Central South*. Nashville, Tenn.: Vanderbilt University Press, 1990.

Kiser, Maude Gold. *The Treasure Hunters Guide to Historic Middle Tennessee and Southern Kentucky: Antiques, Flea Markets, Junk Stores, and More*. Nashville, Tenn.: Gold-Kiser Company, 1994.

Manning, Russ. *The Historic Cumberland Plateau: An Explorer's Guide*. Knoxville: University of Tennessee Press, 1993.

Richards, Ann, and Glen Wanner. *Bicycling Middle Tennessee: A Guide to Scenic Bicycle Rides in Nashville's Countryside*. Nashville, Tenn.: Pennywell Press, 1993.

Robinson, Rob, and Chris Watford. *The Deep South Climbers Companion*. Chattanooga, Tenn.: Elysian Fields Press, 1993.

Sehlinger, Bob, and Bob Lantz. *A Canoeing and Kayaking Guide to the Streams of Tennessee*. Ann Arbor, Mich.: Thomas Press, 1979.

Summerlin, Vernon. *Two Dozen Fishin' Holes: A Guide to Middle Tennessee*. Nashville, Tenn.: Rutledge Hill Press, 1992.

Other Books

Alderson, William T., and Robert M. McBride, eds. *Landmarks of Tennessee History*. Nashville: Tennessee Historical Society and Tennessee Historical Commission, 1965.

Allen, O. Tom. *Trousdale Country, Tennessee History*. Dallas, Tex.: Curtis Media Corporation, 1991.

Arbuckle, J. W., and Alan C. Shook. *The Mountain Goat*. Johnson City, Tenn.: Overmountain Press, 1992.

Arnow, Harriette Simpson. *Seedtime on the Cumberland*. New York: Macmillan, 1960.

———. *Flowering of the Cumberland*. New York: Macmillan, 1963.

Ash, Stephen V. *Middle Tennessee Society Transformed, 1860–1870: War and Peace in the Upper South*. Baton Rouge: Louisiana State University Press, 1987.

Bandy, Anna Grace, ed. *It Happened in White County*. Sparta, Tenn.: White County Retired Teachers Association, 1986.

Beach, Ursula S., and Eleanor Williams. *Nineteenth Century Heritage: Clarksville, Tennessee*. Oxford, Miss.: Guild Bindery Press, 1989.

Bedford County Historical Society. *Doors to the Past: Homes of Shelbyville and Bedford County*. Shelbyville: Bedford County Historical Society, 1969.

Bowman, Virginia McDaniel. *Historic Williamson County: Old Homes and Sites*. Nashville, Tenn.: Blue and Gray Press, 1971.

Brandau, Roberta Seawell, ed. *History of Homes and Gardens of Tennessee*. Nashville, Tenn.: Parthenon Press, 1936.

Brehm, H. C. *Port Royal: An Early Tennessee Town*. Nashville, Tenn.: Mini-Histories, 1982.

Burns, Frank. *Wilson County*. Memphis, Tenn.: Memphis State University Press, 1983.

Butler, Margaret. *Legacy: Early Families of Giles County*. Pulaski, Tenn.: Sain Publications, 1991.

Cannon, Sarah Ophelia Colley. *Minnie Pearl: An Autobiography*. New York: Simon and Schuster, 1980.

Carter, Cullen T., ed. *History of Methodist Churches and Institutions in Middle Tennessee, 1787–1956*. Nashville, Tenn.: Parthenon Press, 1956.

Cisco, Jay Guy. *Historic Sumner County, Tennessee*. 1909. Reprint, Nashville, Tenn.: Charles Elder—Bookseller, 1971.

Clements, Paul. *A Past Remembered: A Collection of Antebellum Houses in Davidson County*. Nashville, Tenn.: Clearview Press, 1987.

Cohen, Nelle Roller. *Pulaski History: 1809–1950*. Pulaski, Tenn.: 1951.

Connelly, Thomas Lawrence. *Army of the Heartland: The Army of Tennessee, 1861–1862*. Baton Rouge: Louisiana State University Press, 1967.

———. *Autumn of Glory: The Army of Tennessee, 1862–1865*. Baton Rouge: Louisiana State University Press, 1971.

Cooling, Benjamin Franklin. *Forts Henry and Donelson: The Key to the Confederate Heartland*. Knoxville: University of Tennessee Press, 1987.

Coppinger, Margaret Brown, et al. *Beersheba Springs, 150 Years, 1833–1983: A History and Celebration*. Beersheba Springs, Tenn.: Beersheba Springs Historical Society, 1983.

Corlew, Robert Ewing. *A History of Dickson County, Tennessee*. Nashville: Tennessee Historical Commission and Dickson County Historical Society, 1956.

Cornwell, Ilene J. *Footsteps along the Harpeth*. Nashville: 1976.

Crane, Sophie, and Paul Crane. *Tennessee Taproots*. Old Hickory, Tenn.: Earle-Shields Publishers, 1976.

Crawford, Reuben. *Lincoln County*. Fayetteville, Tenn.: 1991.

Crutchfield, James A. *The Harpeth River: A Biography*. Nashville, Tenn.: Blue and Gray Press, 1972.

———. *Early Times in the Cumberland Valley*. Nashville, Tenn.: First American National Bank, 1976.

———. *Williamson County: A Pictorial History*. Virginia Beach, Va.: Donning Company, 1980.

———. *A Heritage of Grandeur*. Franklin, Tenn.: Carnton Association, 1981.

———. *The Natchez Trace Parkway: A Pictorial History*. Nashville, Tenn.: Rutledge Hill Press, 1985.

Curtis, Sandy. *A Look at the Past*. Lawrenceburg, Tenn.: Basham's Print Shop, 1976.

Davis, Louise Littleton. *Frontier Tales of Tennessee*. Gretna, La.: Pelican Publishing Company, 1976.

———. *More Frontier Tales of Tennessee*. Gretna, La.: Pelican Publishing Company, 1978.

DeLozier, Mary Jane. *Putnam County, 1850–1970*. Cookeville, Tenn.: Putnam County, Tennessee, 1979.

Dickinson, Calvin, ed. *Lend an Ear: Heritage of the Tennessee Upper Cumberland*. Lanham, Md.: University Press of America, 1983.

Douglas, Byrd. *Steamboatin' on the Cumberland*. Nashville: Tennessee Book Company, 1961.

Durham, Walter T. *The Great Leap Westward: A History of Sumner County, Tennessee, from Its Beginnings to 1805*. Gallatin, Tenn.: Sumner County Library Board, 1969.

———. *Old Sumner: A History of Sumner County from 1805 to 1861*. Gallatin, Tenn.: Sumner County Library Board, 1972.

———. *Rebellion Revisited: A History of Sumner County, Tennessee, from 1861 to 1870*. Gallatin, Tenn.: Sumner County Museum Association, 1982.

Durham, Walter T., and James W. Thomas. *A Pictorial History of Sumner County*. Gallatin, Tenn.: Sumner County Historical Society, 1986.

Egerton, John. *Visions of Utopia*. Knoxville: University of Tennessee Press, 1977.

———. *Nashville: The Faces of Two Centuries, 1780–1980*. Nashville, Tenn.: PlusMedia Inc., 1979.

Eldridge, Robert L. *Bicentennial Echoes of the History of Overton County, Tennessee*. Livingston, Tenn.: Enterprise Printing Company, 1976.

Ellis, Willie McGhee. *Historic Rock Castle: A History of Hendersonville and the Surrounding Area*. Nashville, Tenn.: Parthenon Press, 1973.

Ewell, Leighton. *History of Coffee County, Tennessee*. Manchester, Tenn.: Doak Printing Company, 1936.

Faulkner, Charles H. *The Old Stone Fort: Exploring an Archaeological Mystery*. Knoxville: University of Tennessee Press, 1968.

Ferguson, Robert B., et al. *The Middle Cumberland Culture*. Nashville, Tenn.: Vanderbilt University Press, 1972.

Garrett, Jill K. *A Guide to Points of Interest in Maury County*. Columbia, Tenn.: Maury County Chapter, Association for the Preservation of Tennessee Antiquities, 1967.

———. *Maury County, Tennessee, Historical Sketches*. Columbia, Tenn.: 1967.

———. *"Hither and Yon": The Best of the Writings of Jill K. Garrett*. Columbia, Tenn.: Maury County Homecoming Committee, 1986.

Hall, William. *Early History of the South-West*. 1852. Reprint, Gallatin, Tenn.: Edward Ward Carmack Sumner County Public Library, 1968.

Henderson, C. C. *The Story of Murfreesboro*. Murfreesboro, Tenn.: *News-Banner* Publishing Company, 1929.

Henderson, Deborah Kelley. *Robertson County's Heritage of Homes*. Springfield, Tenn.: Robertson County Antiquities Foundation, 1979.

———. *"It Is a Goodly Land": A History of the Mansker's Station and Goodlettsville Area*. Goodlettsville, Tenn.: John Claude Garrett, Sr., 1982.

Horn, Stanley F. *The Army of Tennessee*. 1941. Reprint, Norman: University of Oklahoma Press, 1952.

Hostetler, John A. *Amish Roots: A Treasury of History, Wisdom, and Lore*. Baltimore, Md.: Johns Hopkins University Press, 1989.

Howell, Isabel. *John Armfield of Beersheba Springs*. Beersheba Springs, Tenn.: Beersheba Springs Historical Society, 1983.

Hughes, Mary B. *Hearthstones: The Story of Historic Rutherford County Homes*. Murfreesboro, Tenn.: Mid-South Publishing Company, 1942.

Kelly, Sarah Foster. *West Nashville: Its People and Environs*. Nashville, Tenn.: 1987.

Klein, Maury. *History of the Louisville and Nashville Railroad*. New York: Macmillan, 1972.

Kluger, Richard. *Simple Justice*. New York: Vintage Books, 1977.

Krammer, Arnold. *Nazi Prisoners of War in America*. Briarcliff, N.Y.: Stein and Day, 1979.

Lindquist, Patricia E. A. *The Pictorial History of Fayetteville and Lincoln County, Tennessee*. Virginia Beach, Va.: Donning Company, 1994.

Little, Vance. *Historic Brentwood*. Brentwood, Tenn.: JM Publications, 1985.

———. *Granny White and Her Pumpkins*. Brentwood, Tenn.: 1993.

Logsdon, David R., ed. *Eyewitnesses at the Battle of Franklin*. Nashville, Tenn.: Kettle Mills Press, 1991.

Maggart, Sue W., and Nina Sutton, eds. *The History of Smith County, Tennessee*. Dallas, Tex.: Curtis Media Corporation, 1987.

Malone, Bill C., and Judith McCulloh, eds. *Stars of Country Music*. Urbana: University of Illinois Press, 1975.

Matthews, Larry E. *Cumberland Caverns*. Huntsville, Ala.: National Speleological Society, 1989.

Matthews, Ruth Robinson. *A Light on the Cumberland Plateau: The Story of Baxter Seminary*. Nashville: Commission on Archives and History, Tennessee Annual Conference, United Methodist Church, 1975.

McAlester, Virginia, and Lee McAlester. *A Field Guide to American Houses*. New York: Alfred A. Knopf, 1984.

Merritt, Dixon, ed. *The History of Wilson County*. Lebanon, Tenn.: County Court of Wilson County et al, 1961.

Montell, William Lynwood. *Don't Go up Kettle Creek*. Knoxville: University of Tennessee Press, 1983.

———. *Upper Cumberland Country*. Jackson: University Press of Mississippi, 1993.

Moore, Lewis E., ed. *Glimpses of Lawrence County*. Columbia, Tenn.: Columbia State Community College, 1970.

Norton, Herman Albert. *Religion in Tennessee, 1777–1945*. Knoxville: University of Tennessee Press, 1981.

Pittard, Mabel. *Rutherford County*. Memphis, Tenn.: Memphis State University Press, 1984.

Prince, Richard E. *The Nashville, Chattanooga & St. Louis Railway: History and Steam Locomotives*. Green River, Wyo.: 1967.

Putnam, A. W. *History of Middle Tennessee*. 1859. Reprint, Knoxville: University of Tennessee Press, 1971.

Robbins, D. P. *Century Review of Maury County, Tennessee: 1807–1907*. Columbia, Tenn.: Board of Mayor and Aldermen of Columbia, 1905.

Roddy, Vernon. *The Lost Town of Bledsoesborough, Tennessee*. Hartsville, Tenn.: Upper Country People Probe, 1984.

———. *Thousands to Cure: On the Early Story of Red Boiling Springs*. Hartsville, Tenn.: Upper Country People Probe, 1991.

Rogers, E. G. *Memorable Historical Accounts of the White County Area*. Collegedale, Tenn.: College Press, 1972.

Romine, Mr. and Mrs. W. B. *A Story of the Original Ku Klux Klan*. Pulaski, Tenn.: *Pulaski Citizen*, 1924.

Seals, Monroe. *History of White County, Tennessee*. 1935. Reprint, Spartanburg, S.C.: Reprint Company, 1982.

Shelbyville Times-Gazette. Shelbyville Times-Gazette *Sesquicentennial Historical Edition, 1819–1969: Turn Back the Clock 150 Years*. Shelbyville: *Shelbyville Times-Gazette*, 1969.

Sims, Carlton C., ed. *A History of Rutherford County*. Murfreesboro, Tenn.: 1947.

Smith, Reid. *Majestic Middle Tennessee*. Prattville, Ala.: Paddle Wheel Publications, 1975.

Smith, Samuel D., and Stephen T. Rogers. *Historical Information Concerning the Fort Blount–Williamsburg Site, Jackson County, Tennessee.* Nashville: Tennessee Department of Conservation, Division of Archaeology, 1989.

Solomon, James. *Times from Giles County.* Pulaski, Tenn.: 1976.

Spence, Jerome D., and David L. Spence. *A History of Hickman County, Tennessee.* Nashville, Tenn.: Gospel Advocate Publishing Company, 1900.

Sullivan, Lyn. *Back Home in Williamson County.* Franklin: 1986.

Sulzer, Elmer G. *Ghost Railroads of Tennessee.* Indianapolis, Ind.: Vane A. Jones Company, 1975.

Sword, Wiley. *The Confederacy's Last Hurrah: Spring Hill, Franklin, and Nashville.* Lawrence: University of Kansas Press, 1992.

Tayse, Moldon Jenkins. *Jackson County, Tennessee.* Gainesboro, Tenn.: 1989.

Warden, Margaret Lindsley. *The Saga of Fairvue: 1832–1977.* Nashville, Tenn.: 1977.

Watkins, Sam R. *"Co. Aytch": A Side Show of the Big Show.* New York: Macmillan, 1962.

Williams, Eleanor. *Cabins to Castles: Clarksville, Tennessee.* Jackson, Miss.: Guild Bindery Press, 1992.

Womack, Walter. *McMinnville at a Milestone, 1810–1960.* McMinnville, Tenn.: Standard Publishing Company, 1960.

Young, Thomas Daniel. *Tennessee Writers.* Knoxville: University of Tennessee Press, 1981.

Articles

Bailey, Clay. "Looking Backward at the Ruskin Cooperative Association." *Tennessee Historical Quarterly* 53 (1994): 100–129.

Beeler, Dorothy. "Race Riot in Columbia, Tennessee: February 25–27, 1946." *Tennessee Historical Quarterly* 39 (1980): 49–61.

Betterly, Richard D. "St. John's Episcopal Churchyard: Material Culture and Antebellum Class Distinction." *Tennessee Historical Quarterly* 53 (1994): 88–99.

Bigger, Jeanne Ridgway. "Jack Daniel Distillery and Lynchburg: A Visit to Moore County, Tennessee." *Tennessee Historical Quarterly* 31 (1972): 3–21.

Braden, Kenneth S. "The Wizard of Overton: Governor A. H. Roberts." *Tennessee Historical Quarterly* 43 (1984): 273–94.

Chitty, Arthur Ben. "Sewanee: Then and Now." *Tennessee Historical Quarterly* 38 (1979): 383–400.

Cooling, Benjamin Franklin. "Forts Henry and Donelson: Union Victory on the Twin Rivers." *Blue and Gray* 9 (February 1992): 10–20, 45–53.

Corlew, Robert E., III. "Frank Goad Clement and the Keynote Address of 1956." *Tennessee Historical Quarterly* 36 (1977): 95–107.

Cummings, Charles M. "Robert Hopkins Hatton: Reluctant Rebel." *Tennessee Historical Quarterly* 23 (1964): 169–82.

Durham, Walter T. "Kasper Mansker: Cumberland Frontiersman." *Tennessee Historical Quarterly* 30 (1971): 154–77.

———. "Thomas Sharp Spencer, Man or Legend." *Tennessee Historical Quarterly* 31 (1972): 240–55.

———. "Tennessee Countess." *Tennessee Historical Quarterly* 39 (1980): 323–40.

Eisenhower, John S. D. "The Election of James K. Polk, 1844." *Tennessee Historical Quarterly* 53 (1994): 74–87.

Evins, Joe L. "The Cordell Hull Birthplace and Memorial." *Tennessee Historical Quarterly* 31 (1972): 111–28.

Garrett, Jill K. "St. John's Church, Ashwood." *Tennessee Historical Quarterly* 29 (1970): 3–23.

Gregory, Rick. "Robertson County and the Black Patch War, 1904–1909." *Tennessee Historical Quarterly* 39 (1980): 341–58.

Hall, Howard. "Franklin County in the Secession Crisis." *Tennessee Historical Quarterly* 17 (1958): 37–44.

Highsaw, Mary Wagner. "A History of Zion Community in Maury County, 1806–1860." *Tennessee Historical Quarterly* 5 (1946): 3–34, 111–40, 222–33.

Holliman, Glenn N. "The Webb School Junior Room, the Symbol of a School." *Tennessee Historical Quarterly* 36 (1977): 287–304.

Lanier, Robert A. "The Carmack Murder Case." *Tennessee Historical Quarterly* 40 (1981): 272–85.

Lawlor, Richard D. "The Iron Horse Comes to Lebanon." *Tennessee Historical Quarterly* 31 (1972): 360–71.

Lofaro, Michael A. "The Legendary Davy Crockett." *Tennessee Conservationist* 52 (1986): 2–5.

Loyd, A. Dennis. "The Legend of Granny White." *Tennessee Historical Quarterly* 27 (1968): 257–61.

McBride, Robert M. "The 'Confederate Sins' of Major Cheairs." *Tennessee Historical Quarterly* 23 (1964): 121–35.

McDade, Arthur. "The Strange Case of Meriwether Lewis." *Tennessee Conservationist* 56 (1990): 2–4.

Morrow, Sara Sprott. "St. Paul's Church, Franklin." *Tennessee Historical Quarterly* 34 (1975): 3–18.

Roth, David E. "The Mysteries of Spring Hill, Tennessee." *Blue and Gray* 2 (October-November 1984): 12–38.

Stankard-Green, Linda. "The Good Times Roll: Rolley Hole." *Tennessee Conservationist* 56 (1990): 8–10.

Sword, Wiley. "The Battle of Nashville." *Blue and Gray* 11 (December 1993): 12–50.

Thorne, Charles B. "The Watering Spas of Middle Tennessee." *Tennessee Historical Quarterly* 29 (1970): 321–59.

Tretter, Evelyn Kerr. "Rock Island State Park." *Tennessee Conservationist* 53 (1987): 9–11.

Warden, Margaret Lindsley. "The Fine Horse Industry in Tennessee." *Tennessee Historical Quarterly* 6 (1947): 134–47.

Weiler, Patsy. "The CCC: Roosevelt's Tree Army." *Tennessee Conservationist* 56 (1990): 2–5.

Wills, Ridley, II. "The Monteagle Sunday School Assembly: A Brief Account of Its Origin and History." *Tennessee Historical Quarterly* 44 (1985): 3–26.

———. "The Eclipse of the Thoroughbred Horse Industry in Tennessee." *Tennessee Historical Quarterly* 46 (1987): 157–71.

Index